ENERGY TRADING & INVESTING

ENERGY TRADING & INVESTING

Trading, Risk Management, and Structuring Deals in the Energy Markets

Davis W. Edwards

New York   Chicago   San Francisco   Lisbon   London   Madrid
Mexico City   Milan   New Delhi   San Juan   Seoul   Singapore
Sydney   Toronto

ISBN   978-0-07-162906-5
MHID   0-07-162906-8

McGraw-Hill books are available at special quantity discounts to use as premiums and sales promotions, or for use in corporate training programs. To contact a representative please e-mail us at bulksales@mcgraw-hill.com.

This book is printed on acid-free paper.

CONTENTS

PREFACE

The inspiration for this book came early in my energy trading career. Previously, I had traded a variety of other products. However, after the boom years in the stock markets in the 1990s and the real-estate boom in the early 2000s, energy became the hot new area around 2005. A wave of financial professionals, including me, left our previous trading desks to join the "new" energy market. Of course, it wasn't really a new market, but with the fall of Enron and market deregulation, trading opportunities were wide-open and expanding.

From the start, there was a huge culture clash between long-term energy traders and Wall Street traders. On Wall Street, the old intuitive traders had lost out to disciplined traders with technical backgrounds. Called *quants*, these math-savvy traders with degrees in physics, science, or engineering had taken over traditional trading desks by being more disciplined and organized. And, now, those same quants had set their eyes on invading the old-boy network of the energy markets. The U.S. government also wants to change the energy markets and make them more efficient at allocating money to energy projects.

More disciplined trading and a government desire to project consumers from "predatory" speculation is in the midst of transforming the energy market from a "wild west" of short-term trading into a set of businesses with a long-term focus. It is a market in flux, and *Energy Trading & Investing* is written for every smart person who looked at a problem and said, "I could do it better than those guys," but didn't quite know where to get started. This is the book that I wished I'd had when I started trading energy. It grew out of the notes that I made then and later used to train new analysts. This book explains the energy market, how financial professionals trade energy products, and how they manage their business. It is written at the introductory level, without the use of jargon or complicated mathematics.

My philosophy on trading is that *there is no substitute for understanding what is actually going on*. Details are important. While writing this book, I had to fight back the temptation to eat up a lot of pages on interesting mathematical details to keep the discussions at a reasonable length.

My major goal here is to provide a comprehensive introduction of energy trading from the first principles of exploration all the way to deal structuring. Even in a book of this size, that's a lot of material to cover.

I decided to tackle this material using the divide and conquer method. *Energy Trading & Investing* is organized to introduce energy trading in several steps. The first part—the executive summary—is a microcosm of the entire book. It's the abbreviated version for people who want a nontechnical overview of the energy market without a lot of details. It's a good starting point that hits most of the key points in the book. I expand on the summary in later chapters.

The detailed sections start with a discussion of each energy product. These are products like electricity, natural gas, and oil. Next, I go into a cross-disciplinary discussion. I show how chemistry, physics, and option pricing all affect energy trading. I then move on to a discussion of specialized energy topics like alternative energy investments, energy storage, and transmission. I finish up with a discussion of how traders actually manage their trading through risk management techniques.

To make things easier, I begin each chapter with a summary that lets you know what to expect from the chapter. Not every chapter is important to every job, and right at the start I try to indicate why each chapter is important. Stylistically, I break up discussions every couple of paragraphs and separate beneficial, but off-topic, details into sidebars.

In a number of examples, I use financial options to model nonfinancial assets like power plants, storage facilities, and undeveloped oil wells. In the industry, this is called a *real options* approach. Because of their simplicity and relatively few parameters, I have found that options are a useful way for me to think about real-life issues. I also think it is a good way to make people comfortable with options mathematics. That doesn't imply that options are universally superior to other approaches to solving these problems. For example, Monte Carlo simulations are commonly used to solve the same problems. However, statistical sampling techniques, like Monte Carlo simulations, make for less intuitive descriptions of how to solve a problem.

I also include several discussions on global climate change and pollution. These issues are closely linked to the power industry and are shaping its future. Any solution to the world's energy problems will probably require consumers to use less power. However, this isn't a book about conservation. It is about meeting 100 percent of consumer demands for power in a cost affordable and ecologically sensible manner.

I owe a debt of gratitude to my wife, Angela, for her help on
Without her editing and assistance, this book would never have
the ground. My brother, Colin, was also instrumental with his
editing. I would also like to thank my editor at McGraw-Hill, Lean Spiro,
and my agent, John Willig, for their enthusiastic support of this project. Finally, I would like to thank my longtime boss at Bear Stearns, Eli Wachtel.
He took a chance to put a young guy in charge of a lot of money and a team
of traders, and I am grateful for having been offered that opportunity.

Davis W. Edwards
New York, 2009

1.1

AN OVERVIEW OF THE ENERGY MARKETS

 **30-Second
Summary**

Purpose

This chapter summarizes the most important points in the book. It provides an introduction to the energy market and an overview of energy trading. The chapter is structured the same as the entire book, and is a summary of the major topics that will be discussed in detail.

Summary

The energy market is a collection of interrelated businesses focused on delivering electricity and heating fuel to consumers. One set of businesses finds and develops new sources of power—drilling for new fuel reserves or developing better solar panels. Another group transports these sources of power closer to end consumers using pipelines or cargo ships. Other businesses generate power: power plants, wind farms, and solar installations. Additional businesses, like public utilities, are responsible for actually distributing power and natural gas to consumers. The energy sector affects almost every facet of the U.S. economy.

The fragmented nature of the energy market means that most people only see a small portion of the whole market. The energy market is shaped by the details of its subindustries. Ultimately, the market revolves around drilling for fuel reserves, building power plants, and running power lines. Each of these subindustries has unique aspects that need to be understood by decision makers. However, it is also important to understand how the entire market fits together.

The major commodities in the energy market are natural gas and electricity. Coal, carbon emissions (greenhouse gases), nuclear power, solar power, and wind energy are also all part of this dynamic market. Oil is also an energy product. However, oil is more influential as a source of energy for cars than as a source of electricity and heat. Energy has always been a major industry, but with deregulation allowing more active trading, it has also become a major financial market. It now stands alongside stocks, bonds, and other commodity markets as an equal. With the influx of Wall Street and financial interests, a large body of people are now involved in energy trading.

Many complex aspects of energy trading are due to the physical characteristics of energy commodities. Energy is hard to transport and store. Like other commodity markets, a large portion of energy trades are settled by the physical delivery of a commodity. When delivery or receipt is required as part of a trade, it is called a *physical trade*. When a trade involves only the transfer of cash—without a physical delivery—it is called a *financial trade*. Physical trading is both more complex and financially rewarding than financial trading.

Several major energy products (electricity and heat) can't be easily stored—they must be generated as they are needed. They are also expensive to transmit over long distances. Because of this, power and heat are typically generated close to the consumers who need those products. As a result, the energy market is further divided into another two pieces: a collection of small local markets concerned with today's activity (*spot markets*) and a separate market concerned with national expectations of the future (*the forward market*). Unlike the stock or bond market, the energy spot and forward markets aren't closely linked. This is because it is impossible to buy electricity at one point in time, store it, and deliver it at a later point in time.

Common Terms

Physical Contracts. Contracts settled by a physical transfer of a commodity from one owner to another.

Financial Contracts. Contracts settled by a transfer of cash. Financial contracts are used by investors who don't wish to take delivery of a commodity like crude oil but still want an exposure to prices.

Spot Market. A spot transaction involves a transfer of goods *on the spot*. A synonym for *spot* is *cash*, as in *cash market* or *cash transaction*.

Forward Market. A forward transaction involves a transfer of goods at some point in the future. For example, an agreement to have natural gas delivered six months in the future.

Arbitrage. To make a risk-free profit by simultaneously buying one security and selling another. A common assumption in option pricing is that arbitrage opportunities do not exist. Or, if they do exist, they do not last for long.

Liquid Asset. An asset that is easy to buy or sell on short notice. A U.S. government bond is an example of a liquid asset.

Illiquid Asset. An asset that is hard to buy or sell on short notice. A nuclear power plant is an illiquid asset. It may be worth a lot, but it might be hard to resell a power plant for a fair price.

From a trading perspective, the spot markets are complicated. They are full of local regulations and subject to a laundry list of physical constraints. The most liquid markets are the forward financial markets. It is tempting to ignore the physical markets in favor of the easier to understand financial markets—however, this is a mistake. The financial markets contain hundreds of features that are inexplicable unless the physical markets are understood. The complexity of the physical spot markets defines energy trading. Individually, none of these issues are difficult to understand—but there are a lot of distinct issues to keep track of.

The energy market is composed of many separate products concerned with the production and delivery of electricity and heat. Of these, the two most important are natural gas and electricity. Coal, carbon emissions, and alternative energy are examples of some secondary commodities in the energy market. Oil is also an energy product, but it is more influential as a source of energy for cars than as a source of electricity and heat. However, the economic impact of oil is so large that it plays a major role in every aspect of energy trading.

Major Players

To produce electricity and heat, you have to locate some fuel, get the fuel to where it needs go, and turn the fuel into something useful. The start of the process—finding fuel—is usually performed by exploration companies. The fuel has to be extracted and prepared for transport by a drilling company. In specialized parts of the market like solar power, manufacturing solar panels replaces exploration and mining. Likewise, hydroelectricity requires a civil engineering firm to construct a dam.

Next, the fuel needs to be transported somewhere useful. Natural gas can be transported as a gas in a pressurized pipeline or it can be turned into a liquid and transported by cargo ship. If liquefied, the natural gas needs to be returned to gaseous form after transportation. Coal is transported on trucks and railroads. Oil is transported by tanker ship and liquid pipelines. Of course, not all portions of the market require transportation—the sun handles delivery of solar energy by itself.

Finally, useful products must be produced and distributed to end users. Public utilities and merchant power operators generate electricity at power plants. Then they transmit their power to customers over a power grid maintained by a *Transmission System Operator* (TSO). Natural gas is moved out of transcontinental pipelines and into the systems of local gas utilities. Local gas utilities distribute natural gas to consumers through their own pipeline networks. Petroleum products need to be refined and transported to local residences and gas stations via truck.

Common Terms

Regulated Market. A market where a legislature votes on decisions concerning how to run an industry.

Deregulated Market. A market where legislative involvement has been removed to allow for a more efficient marketplace. Usually a substantial amount of government oversight remains in place.

In the electrical power industry, transmission systems (power grids) are often run by local governments. When a TSO is unaffiliated with the local government, it is called an *Independent System Operator* (ISO). An ISO that crosses state boundaries is also commonly referred to as a *Regional Transmission Operator* (RTO). Most electricity trading occurs on power grids run by RTO/ISOs operating in deregulated markets; that is, markets that allow free trading of electricity. Local rules vary between power grids. However, most *deregulated* power markets are still highly regulated. In this book, TSO is used to describe any power grid operator, and RTO/ISO is used to describe the operator of a power grid in a deregulated market.

Allowing anyone to trade electricity is a relatively new concept. Prior to deregulation, only power plants owned by utilities could sell power into a power grid. After deregulation, anyone could build a power plant, produce power, and offer that power for sale. In deregulated markets, utilities have shifted away from running power plants to concentrating on operating transmission grids. There are power plants now owned by power traders and operated by specialized service companies. These changes revolutionized the power industry—they created a market for electrical power.

The last groups of market participants are the traders, investors, and marketers. Financial trading has grown up around the physical trading business. Funding exploration or building new manufacturing plants isn't cheap—it requires raising capital from investors. Local utilities need to use financial contracts to guarantee a steady supply of fuel and electricity for their customers. Power plants need to buy fuel and sell their electricity. Major industrial facilities might want to guarantee future supplies of affordable power. Financial firms might wish to speculate on the price of power. To do this, any of these parties can enter into transactions. These transactions can be done *over the counter*—directly between two parties—or by using an intermediary organization (often an *exchange*). Energy products are commonly traded on the *New York Mercantile Exchange* (NYMEX) and the *Intercontinental Exchange* (ICE).

Common Terms

Power Marketer. A company specializing in the buying and reselling power.

Long an Asset. A trader is long an asset if he benefits when the price appreciates.

Short an Asset. A trader is short an asset if he benefits when the price declines.

The ramification of buying an asset in the future is often confusing. For example, a trader who agrees to buy an asset at a fixed future price benefits if the future price goes up; he has already locked in a price. However, a trader who agrees to buy an asset in the future without fixing the price benefits if that price declines; he can then buy more cheaply. To clarify the financial implications of owning an asset in the future, traders will use the terms "long" and "short" instead of "buy" or "sell" to describe their financial exposures.

Natural Gas

Natural gas is a fossil fuel used for heating and producing electricity. It is a combination of colorless, odorless gases composed primarily of methane (CH_4). It often contains substantial amounts of other hydrocarbons, like ethane (C_2H_6), propane (C_3H_8), and butane (C_4H_{10}). The composition of natural gas varies from location to location. It is often found mixed with nitrogen, carbon dioxide, and other trace gases. Natural gas is considered "dry" when it is almost pure methane, and "wet" when it has substantial quantities of the other hydrocarbons. Its central role in the energy industry is due to its characteristic as a clean, comparatively inexpensive fuel—almost all the electrical power generators that have been built in the United States for the past 20 years use natural gas as a fuel.

Natural gas is extracted from underground wells and transported to customers through pipelines. End users of natural gas are often called the *burner tip* because gas appliances were once fitted with special dispersing heads to make natural gas suitable for lighting, cooking, and heating. Modern appliances no longer use burner tips, but the nickname has stuck.

Natural gas pipelines are located throughout the country and are capable of providing a constant supply of gas to consuming regions.

Natural gas hubs are located at the interconnection between major pipe-lines. The most important—Henry Hub—is located on the Gulf Coast, about halfway between New Orleans and Houston. Henry Hub is the delivery location for the NYMEX natural gas futures contract and is used as the benchmark for all natural gas sold throughout the United States.

Like many other energy products, the forward and spot markets for natural gas are distinct from one another. There is an extremely well-defined seasonal component to forward prices. Prices in the forward market tend to mirror consumer demand—both are high in the winter and fall dramatically in the spring of every year. Spot prices don't show the same kind of seasonality. However, despite the different behaviors, arbitrage between the two markets is impossible without a physical storage facility. It is possible to make a profit buying gas on the spot market, storing it, and selling it for future delivery. However, this requires an ability to make physical trades—to take delivery and store large quantities of a gas—which many market participants lack.

Common Units

Because the composition of natural gas can vary substantially, it is commonly described in terms of its heat energy rather than as a volume- or weight-based measurement. *Heat energy* is the amount of energy that can be obtained from burning a substance.

Btu (British Thermal Unit). A Btu is a measurement of heat energy used in the United States. Heat energy is commonly traded in millions of Btus (MMBtu).

Bcf (Billion cubic feet). A common measurement of natural gas storage facilities. There are approximately 1 million MMBtus (million Btus) in 1 Bcf (billion cubic feet) of natural gas.

J (Joule). A measurement of heat energy in most of the world. Commonly, energy is traded in thousands of joules (kilojoules, kJ) or millions of joules (megajoules, or MJ). One Btu is equal to 1054.35 Joules.

Electricity

Generating electricity is one of the major purposes of the energy market. Electricity is used to power a large variety of modern devices and is so common that it is hard to imagine life without it. Unfortunately, electricity can't be stored and it's very expensive to transmit over long distances. Consequently, there is no national electricity market—it's a collection of small regional markets with unique characteristics and regulations. In each of these markets, supply and demand must constantly be matched, which results in a highly volatile spot market.

The most important physical markets are the daily power auctions held in each region. These auctions allow power producers to sell their electricity to consumers on their local power grid. Typically, they allow the sale of power by hourly increments on a day-ahead basis or in five-minute increments during the day that power is to be delivered. These auctions are the mechanism for setting the price of power in a region. Most speculative power trading goes on in forward markets that are separate from the daily power auctions. The forward markets are typically based on the price of delivering power at a major hub. Time horizons for forward trades range from the rest of the current month to approximately five years out.

As a general rule, on the day of delivery, the price for electricity is the same for all the participants in a local market. All producers receive the same price per megawatt and all consumers pay the same price per megawatt. This is called the *clearing price* for power. In deregulated markets, the clearing price is based upon bids submitted by power producers. These bids contain a price schedule matching volumes of power to prices. Power plants are activated in lowest to highest cost order until the consumer demand is met. The clearing price of power is set by the cost of the most recently activated power plant. The cost of bringing the last unit of electricity into the market is called the *marginal price* of power, and the most recently activated plant is the *marginal* power plant. In general, the clearing price is set by the marginal price of power.

Electrical demand changes constantly. Every time a light is turned on or a computer is turned off, the load on the power grid changes. Since electricity can't be stored, this changing demand must constantly be matched against supply. There is a huge infrastructure built to manage the real time balancing of electricity supply and demand. Being able to estimate average demand is a critical part of both the physical and financial energy markets.

Power usage is cyclical. The demand for power varies by the season, day of week, and time of day. Daytime power is a different product from nighttime power. August power is a different product than January power. This has a big effect on the trading of power. There isn't a single electricity product. Instead there are hundreds of separate electricity products that differ based on location, month or season, and time of day.

Daytime hours (usually 7 A.M. until 11 P.M.) are called *peak* hours. Nighttime hours are called *off-peak* hours. Every region of the country uses slightly different definitions for their power products. As a result, power products are commonly described in shorthand. This abbreviation is always weekdays by hours. For example, 7×24 refers to power 7 days a week, 24 hours a day. Peak power is 5×16 or 7×16 (depending on whether weekends are included). If weekends aren't included, there will be a separate 2×16 product. Off-peak hours are typically 7×8.

It is also important to understand that electrical supply and demand are regional phenomena. Each area of the country has an electrical market with unique features. These differences can make trading electricity between adjacent power grids profitable. Transporting power is called *wheeling*. For example, the Pacific Northwest contains abundant hydro plants that produce extremely cheap electricity when there is sufficient water flow on local rivers. Sometimes after a major snow melt in the spring months, the price of electricity can fall to zero or negative since the dams can't be closed and every other power plant needs to be penalized for continuing to produce power. Because this power is inexpensive, transporting it into Northern California can be profitable even though a lot of the power is lost in transport.

Common Units

Electricity is commonly described in units of *power* and *energy*. In physics, power is the rate at which work can be done. This is similar to a speed of a car (for instance, a car is traveling at 60 miles per hour). Energy is an amount of work. This is similar to the distance that a car travels (a car traveled 60 miles per hour for four hours, to go 240 miles).

MW (Megawatt). A unit of power used to measure the electrical energy that can be produced by a power plant or carried by a transmission line.

MWh (Megawatt hour). A measure of energy. It is the product of power (measured in megawatts) multiplied by some period of time (hours).

Electrical Generation

Although there are many ways to produce electrical power, most power plants use a similar technology—generators driven by superheated steam. Fossil fuel plants burn oil, natural gas, or coal to produce this steam. All of these fossil fuels produce greenhouse gases like carbon dioxide (CO_2) when they are burned. Compared to the other fuels, coal-fired generation produces two to three times the pollution of the other fuels at a fifth of their cost. Nuclear generators use nuclear fission to turn water into steam. Nuclear fuel provides a lot of electricity per weight—a pound of highly enriched uranium is approximately equal to a million gallons of gasoline. But enriched uranium is subject to severe shortages and is difficult to store safely once it is discarded.

A lot of modern research is exploring alternative energy sources. Geothermal power plants tap into steam released from the Earth as part of a standard steam turbine. Geothermal power is efficient, but it is limited to specific geographic areas. Wind power plants use the wind to directly spin the copper wires inside a generator to create an electric current. Hydroelectric dams use falling (or flowing) water to spin the generator. Solar power facilities turn the sunlight directly into electricity.

In many power plants, superheated steam is a by-product of producing electricity. A recent trend in power plants is to reuse this steam instead of releasing it into the atmosphere. This is called *cogeneration*. If a power plant can sell steam in addition to its power output, it becomes much cheaper to operate. As a result, the final products of a cogeneration plant are often described as both heat and electricity. Topping cycle plants produce electricity first, and then use the exhausted steam for heating. In contrast, bottoming cycle plants first produce heat for an industrial process and then use the leftover heat to power a steam generator.

The efficiency at which a plant converts fuel into electricity is called its *heat rate*. It is typically expressed as a ratio of heat input to work output (for example, Btu/kWh or MMBtu/MWh). A lower heat rate implies a more efficient power plant.

Electrical Transmission and Distribution

Once power is generated, it needs to be brought to the customer. *Transmission* refers to the bulk transfer of power from the power plant to a substation via high voltage lines. *Distribution* refers to the transfer of power from a substation to various consumers using much lower voltages.

Power plants, transmission lines, and substations form the power grid—a set of interconnecting power lines that provide multiple ways to route power between any two locations. The redundancy of a power grid is crucial for reliability—it prevents any single line from overloading. This helps to prevent blackouts due to a single point of failure.

Most power lines are overhead lines—they are attached to tall poles suspended safely above ground level. In urban areas, electrical power lines are sometimes buried. However, burying lines makes them much less reliable and harder to maintain. Buried lines are uncommon in suburban and rural areas.

The choice of voltage and location for power lines is a trade-off between safety, reliability, and efficiency. As part of the transmission process, power is wasted—it's converted into heat that must be dissipated on the power line. This waste can be reduced by using higher voltages. However, higher voltage lines are more dangerous than lower voltage ones. As part of the delivery process, power plants use transformers to increase voltage for long distance transmission, and then decrease voltage for local distribution.

AC and DC Power

Most power is transmitted using alternating current (AC) power lines rather than direct current (DC) lines. With AC power, the voltage and current on the power line alternate directions making an oscillating wave. The terminals have no fixed positive or negative voltage. The primary advantage of AC power is that it's simpler to build an AC transmission system since the voltage can be easily scaled up or down to match a specific voltage.

Both types of currents are created by placing a conductive wire into an electromagnetic field. When this happens, the electrons are pushed away from the negative part of the field and toward the positive side of the field. If the magnetic field stays constant, all the electrons will move in the same direction.

Placing a negative charge at one end of the wire will start to accelerate the electrons close to that point away from it. The electrons closest to the magnetic field will be accelerated faster than electrons farther away. Because it is moving fastest, the last electron in line will slam into the electrons ahead of it. This creates a chain reaction as each subsequent electron is pushed into the next electron in line. This is similar to a multiple collision on a highway where a shockwave moves between cars although the individual cars don't move very far. Creating a shockwave from the other end of the wire will return all the electrons back to their initial state.

There are two ways of getting power through a power line. The first way to pass power through an electrical line is through the movement of electrons. This is called *direct current (DC)* power. Another way is through the "shockwave" caused by the collision of electrons. This wave, properly called an *electromagnetic wave*, propagates down the wire much faster than any of the individual electrons can move. This is called *alternating current (AC)* power. It is possible to transfer energy through a power line using electromagnetic waves rather than the motion of individual electrons.

On a DC power line, whenever the line is used to provide power to some point, the voltage on the line will decline after that point. For a power grid serving variable consumer demand, this means that it will be very hard to predict the voltage on certain parts of the power grid. However, when they produce DC electricity, power plants do not need to worry about synchronizing themselves with other power plants.

The challenge with AC power is different. Although it is easy to change the voltage on the power line, it is necessary that every power generator oscillates their voltage at precisely the same time. Otherwise, the shockwaves from different power generators will collide and cancel out. AC power creates a synchronization problem that gets progressively more complicated when a large number of power generators are involved.

Congestion

Given sufficient transmission capability, the price of power throughout a grid will be the same cost everywhere. It will be equal to the cost of the most recently activated generator. However, in periods of peak demand, the power lines connecting low cost generation plants to consumers may become overloaded. To relieve that overloading, power plants closer to the actual demand will need to be activated out of the usual order of cheapest to most expensive. Rather than spreading that higher cost between all members of the power grid, only those customers in the congested area will pay higher prices. Because this price only occurs for a single location, this is known as the *Locational Marginal Price* (LMP). Most of the United States is moving toward this model of allocating costs to consumers.

To help customers manage the price risk of having purchased power at a major node and then paying a higher price for power due to congestion, a financial instrument—Financial Transmission Rights (FTR)—can be traded. FTRs are contracts between two parties that take opposite sides of an obligation to pay or receive the difference in price between two nodes. If there is no congestion, the price at the two nodes will be the same. However, if there is congestion, one party has to pay the other. This payment can go either way—either party can end up paying or receiving cash. Sometimes that isn't what is desired, so these contracts can be structured as options. FTR options allow one party to pay an up-front fee (a premium) to avoid paying congestion costs at a later point. Essentially, buying an FTR option is like buying insurance against bad prices due to congestion.

Mechanics of the Physical Electricity Market

In the United States, the physical energy markets are run as daily auctions by *Independent System Operators* (ISOs). Usually, there are two auctions: a day-ahead auction and a real-time auction. The day-ahead auction is an hourly auction for the following day. The real-time auction occurs throughout the day whenever extra generation is required. Generators participate in the auction by submitting offer curves (their generation levels associated with prices) and their technical constraints (start-up costs, minimum up time, and so on). After collecting offers from generators, the ISO selects the winning generators in a manner that minimizes the cost to the market.

The two auctions are distinct from one another. When creating a bid, a generator needs to decide whether to attempt to sell all of their power in the day-ahead market or to reserve some capacity to sell into the real-time market. There are potentially greater profits in the real-time market, but the risk of being inactive is also higher. In most cases, the bidding strategy used by a power plant will be dictated by its physical characteristics—how quickly it is able to come online, and its efficiency at converting fuel into electricity. If a generator is not selected to operate in the day-ahead market, it is still eligible to participate in the real-time market.

However, since these are physical markets, the generators participating in the real-time auction need the ability to deliver power. Because of this, usually only generators that can start up quickly or that have excess capacity participate in the real-time auction. Primarily for this reason, most of the generation capacity is allocated in the day-ahead market—the real-time market is used for balancing short-term fluctuations and unexpected demand.

Oil

Oil, or petroleum, is a liquid fossil fuel formed when decaying plant life becomes trapped in a layer of porous rock. After millions of years, heat and pressure convert decaying plant life into hydrocarbons. Some of these hydrocarbons are gases, others are solids, and still others are liquids. Petroleum is the generic name for any hydrocarbon that is liquid under normal temperature and pressure conditions. Like other fossil fuels, the mixture of hydrocarbons in petroleum can vary widely. When petroleum is first extracted from the ground, it is called *crude oil*. After crude oil is distilled, there are specific names for each liquid (gasoline, heating oil, and so on). The term "petroleum" refers to crude oil and all of the products refined from it.

The liquid properties and high energy density of petroleum make it a popular fuel for vehicles. Compared to hydrocarbon gases like methane or propane, petroleum contains a lot of energy per unit of volume. For example, a tank of a hydrocarbon gas, like propane, will only fuel a backyard grill for a couple of hours. However, the same volume of gasoline will be sufficient to drive a car for several hundred miles. Additionally, compared to solid hydrocarbons like coal, liquids are much easier to move around inside an engine.

Crude Oil Markets

The trading of crude oil is dominated by the relationship between suppliers and consumers. The major consumers of crude oil are the industrialized nations in North America, Europe, and the Asian-Pacific region. The major exporting regions are less developed countries in the Middle East and South America.

From a trading perspective, crude oil is the most important petroleum product. Historically, major oil refiners have considered it less risky to be located near consuming areas in industrialized countries rather than near the producing areas. As a result, there is an active global trade in transportation of crude oil. The refiners trade for and transport crude oil over long distances, to be refined near the consuming region. As a result, there is not a global market for refined petroleum products. Typically, the prices for these refined petroleum products are regional in nature—they are determined by local supply and demand.

There are many varieties of crude oil. The two most common crude oil benchmarks are *WTI* and *Brent* contracts. *WTI crude* is a common benchmark for crude oil produced in the United States. *Brent crude* is a common European benchmark for crude oil produced in the North Sea. There are no similarly liquid trading contracts for Persian Gulf crude oil, although spot prices from Oman and Dubai are commonly available.

Common Units

Barrel (bbl). In the United States, petroleum of all types is traded by volume. A barrel contains 42 U.S. gallons (in the United States), or approximately 159 liters (metric units).

Tonnes (t). In Europe, oil is typically traded by weight. A tonne (or metric ton) is a unit of mass equal to 1,000 kilograms, or approximately 2,204.6 U.S. pounds.

Conversion Between Barrel and Tonne. A rough approximation is that there are 7.5 barrels in one tonne of crude oil. However, because the composition of crude oil can vary substantially, each type of crude oil will have its own conversion ratio. These can range from approximately 7.2 barrels per tonne (for Persian Gulf crude) to about 7.5 barrels per tonne (for premium light crude like WTI or Brent).

Crude oils are typically described by their *density* and *sulfur content*. Low density (*light*) crude oils have a higher proportion of light hydrocarbons that can easily be converted into high value products like gasoline. In contrast, *heavy* crude oils contain a larger portion of low value products that require additional downstream processing to be valuable. The density of crude oil is apparent by visual inspection—light crude oil will flow freely, while heavier crude oil will be more viscous.

High sulfur content is highly undesirable for crude oil. Sulfur is a major pollutant and can only be removed through expensive processing. *Sweet* crude oil has low sulfur content, while *sour* crude oil contains a much higher amount.

The most valuable types of crude oil are light, sweet crudes. Both WTI and Brent crude fall into this category. These are commonly called premium crude oils.

Distillation and Crack Spreads

Refined petroleum products are created by separating crude oil into various pure liquids. Crude oil contains a variety of different liquid hydrocarbons mixed together; everything from gasoline to heavy oil. To create useful products, it is necessary to separate these liquids from one another. This is done through distillation. Since each type of liquid hydrocarbon turns into a gas at a different temperature, the most common way to separate mixed liquids is to place them into a large container and heat them. As the temperature rises, the liquids will turn into a gas one at a time. This gas can be suctioned off and then returned to liquid form in a separate container by cooling. It is often necessary to go through this process several times before a sufficiently pure product is created.

A single barrel of crude oil is turned into a large number of separate refined products. Of these, the most valuable products are gasoline, diesel fuel, and heavy fuel oils. It is impossible to produce just one distilled product without producing the others. The process of converting crude oil into gasoline involves creating every refined petroleum product at the same time. If a refiner wants to produce more gasoline, it is also necessary to produce more of other distillates like diesel fuel, home heating oil, and asphalt.

The process of distillation links the prices of refined petroleum products to crude oil prices. If the price of crude oil rises, all of the refined products will become more expensive. However, there is a different type of link between the prices of the refined products. If a gasoline shortage forces refiners to increase their gasoline production, the market will become flooded with a glut of the other petroleum products. As a result, there is often a negative correlation between the prices of the refined products. The relationship between crude oil and distilled products is known as the *crack spread*.

Coal

Coal is a solid hydrocarbon fuel that is readily available throughout the world. It is easy to store and relatively inexpensive to produce relative to the amount of electrical power it can generate. In many ways it is the perfect fuel. Unfortunately, it is a major source of carbon (CO_2) and sulfur (SO_2) emissions. The pollution that results from burning coal has made it unpopular among consumers.

Coal is the least expensive way to generate electricity. However, again, it has the drawback of being the most polluting fossil fuel. The competing desires for cheap electricity and less pollution are at odds with one another. Global efforts to reduce carbon emissions have typically deadlocked on the issue of coal powered generation. Most countries want to use coal-fired power plants for cost reasons, and would like other countries to stop using them because of pollution concerns. Coal is approximately one-fifth the cost of other fuels. As bad as pollution is, having electrical bills five or 10 times higher is not a viable option for the economic health of most countries.

Because the price of coal is generally low, transportation makes up a much higher percentage of the delivered cost than of other fossil fuels. As a result, most coal is used within a couple hundred miles of where it is mined. By far the biggest application for coal is electrical generation. Electrical power plants and coal mining companies are often located close together. As a result, there are relatively few people buying or selling coal on the open market. Coal is important to electrical generation, but not a heavily traded financial product by itself.

Emissions Markets

Motivated by signs of global climate change, countries have begun taking steps to reduce global levels of carbon dioxide, sulfur dioxide, and nitrogen dioxide emissions. The two most popular ways to limit pollution are through taxes and through cap-and-trade systems. Of the two, only the cap-and-trade system is a trading market.

Cap and trade sets a limit on the amount of a substance that can be produced. Everyone producing that substance is required to have a license for their production. This has the advantage of ensuring a cap on pollution levels. When licenses are freely tradable, anyone with an ability to shift to a less polluting technology can do so and make a profit by selling their licenses. By reducing the amount of licenses over time, a free market encourages the most economical changes to be made first. The two main problems facing cap-and-trade systems are how to distribute licenses and how to enforce compliance.

Because emissions markets create a valuable good from nothing, there is an intense debate over how licenses should be initially distributed. There are drawbacks to every approach, whether they are public auctions, assigning rights based on historical usage, or assigning rights based on population.

Tracking carbon dioxide emissions is also complicated. Lots of activities—everything from breathing to burning fossil fuel—produces carbon dioxide. Many activities remove carbon dioxide from the air as well—everything from planting a garden to injecting carbon dioxide into an underground storage facility. It is impossible for governments to monitor, require licenses, or provide carbon credits for all of those activities. This makes enforcement of carbon markets problematic.

The emissions markets are also closely linked to the use of coal to generate electricity. Although it produces more pollution, coal can produce electricity for a fraction of the cost of any alternative fuel. To a large extent, the goal of the emissions market is to make it possible to continue to use coal as a major source of electricity and reduce carbon emissions through other means.

TECHNICAL PRIMER

The technical primer is a brief introduction to some of the more complicated parts of energy trading. The goal of this section is to give the reader a more intuitive understanding of these topics.

Pollution

The combustion of fossil fuels produces a substantial amount of greenhouse gas emissions and other pollution. There are a number of different types of pollution. The first general category of pollution is caused when impurities or small particles trapped in the fuel are released into the air when the fuel is burned. The second type of pollution is an intrinsic part of combustion—the creation of greenhouse gases. Greenhouse gases don't present a health hazard and are generally safe. However, when large quantities of greenhouse gases are released into the atmosphere, they have the potential to change the world's climate.

Carbon dioxide is an odorless, nontoxic gas formed by the combustion of organically derived fuels. Organic fuels are composed of long chains of carbon molecules that can be broken down by combining them with oxygen. A spark is required to kick off combustion, but afterward it is a self-sustaining process that produces more heat than is required to start the fire. The process of combining carbon with oxygen produces carbon dioxide. It is impossible to burn carbon-based fuels (which encompass nearly all fuels) without producing carbon dioxide. Large amounts of CO_2 can strengthen the greenhouse effect.

The Greenhouse Effect

The Earth's atmosphere allows visible light to pass through and absorbs infrared light, as depicted in Figure 1.1.1. Sunlight can pass through easily, warms the Earth, and converts into infrared light. This light is radiated away from the Earth, but much of it is absorbed by the atmosphere. This traps heat near the surface of the Earth. The Greenhouse Effect is vital for the survival of plants and animals, but too much carbon dioxide causes the atmosphere to absorb too much infrared energy and raises global temperatures.

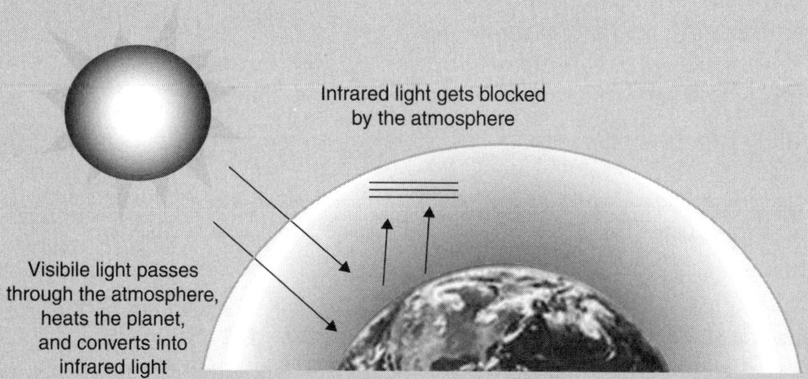

Infrared light gets blocked by the atmosphere

Visibile light passes through the atmosphere, heats the planet, and converts into infrared light

Figure 1.1.1. Graphic depiction of the Greenhouse Effect

Nitrogen and sulfur oxides are also produced during combustion. Nitrogen is present in the atmosphere, and trace amounts of sulfur are commonly trapped in fossil fuels. When these oxides combine with water, they form acid rain. Acid rain is a regional problem that can kill vegetation and wildlife. Although most rain is slightly acidic, when large amounts of acid build up in a small area, it is poisonous.

Heavy metals like mercury, lead, and plutonium are often trapped in fossil fuels and released in the combustion process. When these metals build up in the body, they don't decay. A large enough accumulation of these substances is toxic to humans and wildlife.

Fly ash and soot are general terms for inert particulate matter trapped in fossil fuels. Commonly, these are supersmall grains of sand or coal that were not completely burned. When suspended in the air, it is easy for these particles to get caught inside someone's lungs. This will create breathing problems, and can lead to lung damage and diseases like silicosis.

as, Liquids, and Solids

All substances have two major types of properties: *chemical properties* and *physical properties.* The chemical properties of a substance determine how it combines with other substances. For example, combustion is a chemical reaction between a fuel and oxygen. Physical properties involve changes in substances that don't represent a chemical change. Water turning into steam when heated is an example of a physical phase shift. These shifts are generally reversible.

Another important physical property of materials is that if you compress a gas, it gets hot. If you want to compress it enough to make it into a liquid, you need to cool it substantially. If you don't keep it cool, it will start to expand again. The ability to shift substances between liquid and gas forms and compress gas is the key to air-conditioning and refrigeration systems.

Physical phase shifts are the reason distillation works. Gases and liquids will separate at certain temperatures. This is helpful for distillation but problematic for other processes. For example, the temperature in pipelines isn't constant. As a result, liquids often condense inside a pipeline when natural gas cools down. This causes a problem because these pipelines are airtight, so the liquids can't evaporate.

Electrical Circuits

Electricity is a term used throughout this book to mean power obtained through the movement of charged particles—most commonly electrons—through some type of conductive material like a metal wire. A more precise term for this quantity is *electrical current.* Electricity is actually a general term that can refer to a number of different types of electromagnetic forces.

Electromagnetism is one of a couple fundamental forces that hold the universe together. For the purpose of energy trading, the most important property of electromagnetism is that magnetic fields can create electric currents in metals, and vice versa. By using this relationship, it is possible to move charged particles, like electrons, by manipulating magnetic fields. The combination of motivating force (a spinning magnet), along with a supply of electrons (found in conductive metal wires), and a closed path for them to move around (a circuit), is the basis for the electrical power industry.

One way to think about electricity is like water moving through a river. The amount of water that moves through the river determines how much work can be done. Unless it evaporates along the journey, the amount will be the same throughout the river's length—even though the pressure and width of the river might change in places.

In some places the river might be wide and slow, and at others narrow and fast. In a power line, voltage and current work much the same way. The voltage of an electrical line is similar to water pressure, and electrical current is similar to the size of the channel. For a fixed amount of power, voltage and current are inversely proportional. Just as water pressure will increase if the nozzle of a hose is narrowed, voltage will increase if electrical current is reduced.

Like evaporation reduces the water in a river, friction can cause wasted energy on a transmission line. More water is lost when a river is wide and slow than when it is narrow and fast. Electricity works the same way. The amount of power lost during transmission is proportional to the length of the power line and the speed of the electrical current—high voltage/low current lines lose less power than the other way around. As a result, power grids typically convert electricity to high voltages for long distance transmission and then lower the voltage just before it is delivered to consumers.

Another concept is that electrical power needs to flow in a loop. It needs to flow in and out of every location—it can't stop anywhere. Continuing the pipe example, water flowing through a channel can only produce work when it is flowing (like a river powering a sawmill). If the flow of electricity is ever stopped, an electromagnetic field will build up, resulting in a potentially dangerous shock when it is reconnected. A related problem is a short circuit. Short circuits are like poking a hole in a straw and then trying to use the straw to drink.

Most power is transmitted using alternating current (AC) power lines rather than direct current (DC) lines. With AC power, the voltage and current on the power line alternate directions, making an oscillating wave. The terminals have no fixed positive or negative voltage. The primary advantage of AC power is that it's simpler to build an AC transmission system—the voltage can be easily scaled up or down using transformers.

Statistics

Statistics is the branch of mathematics focused on organizing, analyzing, and summarizing data. A substantial amount of trading vocabulary comes from the mathematical discipline of statistics. Two of the most important terms are *volatility* and *correlation*.

Volatility is used by traders to describe the risk of holding an asset. It measures the likely dispersion of prices between two periods of time. Mathematically, it is defined as the standard deviation of continuously compounded returns. A highly volatile asset is one that commonly experiences large price changes. The term "volatility" does not describe the investment merit of a trade.

Correlation is used by traders to describe how closely two things are related. When two assets are highly correlated, their prices tend to move together. There may or may not be a causal relationship between the two assets. Correlation can result from either random chance or a shared cause for behavior.

Financial Options

An option is a contract between two people. It gives the buyer of the contract the right, but not the obligation, to buy or sell property at some future date at a fixed price. The right to buy is called a *call option*. The right to sell is called a *put option*. Options have an up-front cost, called a *premium*, which is paid when the buyer purchases the option. For the option buyer, options have limited downside risk. These traders will either lose their premium or will make a profit.

Options are an all-or-nothing type of instrument. It is possible to buy a million dollars worth of options and lose the entire investment if the options expire worthless. Buying an option contract is similar to buying insurance. Most often, the purchaser will pay a premium and have the option expire worthless. Occasionally, the option will pay off big. Even though the size of the downside is small (losing the premium) compared to the potential upside (a big profit), the odds of making a profit are stacked against the option buyer. The option seller is taking on a risk from the buyer, and needs to be compensated for taking that risk.

Two common applications for options are risk management and modeling energy investments. In the energy market there are a lot of physical decisions that need to be made on a daily basis. Do I turn the power plant on and convert my fuel into electricity? Do I lock in a fuel supply for the winter now or should wait a little longer? Should I invest in building a new power line between Oregon and Northern California? Option theory provides a way to quantify those decisions.

From a transaction standpoint, option trading requires both a buyer and a seller. The seller takes on the possibility of a big loss in exchange for money up front. The buyer pays a *premium* to the seller for that service. If the option pays off, the seller will need to find the cash to pay the buyer. With options, money is not magically created, it is simply transferred between the two parties. The option buyer is described as being *long the option* or being *long volatility* (since rare events will mean a big profit). The option seller is described as being *short the option* or being *short volatility* (since rare events will mean a big loss).

The amount of money that needs to be transferred between the buyer and seller is determined by the *payoff* of the option. Every option is assigned an *exercise* or *strike price*. This is the fixed price at which trading can occur in the future. For example, a call option involves the right to buy an asset at a fixed price. The owner of a call option benefits when an asset price rises above the strike price. This allows the owner to buy at a lower price than is otherwise available. The owner can also make an immediate profit by reselling the asset at the current price.

Call Payoff = Asset Price − Strike Price

if the Asset Price > Strike Price at expiration.

A put option works similarly. A put option gives the owner of the option the right to sell an asset at a fixed price. If the asset price is greater than the fixed price, a put option is worthless. No one will willingly sell at a lower price than necessary. However, if the fixed price is higher than the asset price, the put buyer makes a profit by selling at a higher price.

Put Payoff = Strike Price − Asset Price

if the Strike Price > Asset Price at expiration.

Option Valuation

Options theory has simultaneously revolutionized the financial markets and caused a huge number of financial collapses. The mathematics behind option pricing can be very complicated. However, the basic principles are straightforward. Options prices are calculated by approximating their actual behavior.

Using models to value options isn't a perfect process. Real life is more complicated than any model. As a result, option models are not a substitute for understanding what is actually going on. Very complex models usually mean that few people actually understand the situation. As a result, simple models, even when they have flaws, are usually preferred over complex models. The more people understand a model, the less chance it has of failing disastrously. It is often easier to address weaknesses in option models by making observation easier than to create more complicated models.

Option models are based on assumptions about asset prices. There is a standard set of assumptions that defines commonly traded, *vanilla*, options. When the standard assumptions work reasonably well to describe the behavior of the underlying prices, option valuation is easy. It is possible to plug numbers into a well-known option pricing formula. In other cases, the standard assumptions don't work so well.

In those cases, it is necessary to use a more complicated approach to calculating option prices.

Options that use nonstandard assumptions about prices are commonly called *exotic options*. Knowing when to use an exotic option model requires understanding what is going on in real life. Option formulas basically say that "I can be used if x, y, and z are true." It is up to the user of an option to determine if x, y, and z are true in their specific case. If not, some other formula needs to be found. There is a substantial amount of academic literature describing nonstandard option models.

While it is possible for model assumptions to change over time, option models seldom experience a catastrophic failure overnight. Usually, problems in an option model start showing up years before there is an economic impact. It is up to the people using the model to identify when things aren't working and make sure problems are fixed quickly.

Modern option trading sprung out of research by Fischer Black, Myron Scholes, and Robert Merton in the late 1960s and early 1970s. Their research combined earlier ideas of dynamic hedging, price diffusion, and put/call parity into a continuous time framework. This allowed the creation of an easy to use option pricing formula. This Black Scholes formula opened up option trading to the masses. It and related work on continuous time finance revolutionized the financial markets and won a Nobel Prize.[1]

The concept behind option pricing is counterintuitive to many. Options are priced by replicating their payout by continuously trading the underlying product. By and large, the approach that was first developed by the 1970s, *dynamic hedging*, still works well today. The general concept of dynamic hedging is that it is possible to duplicate the payoff of a stock option by constantly trading the stock and a risk-free investment (usually a government bond). This concept has been carried into the energy market.

Options are closely associated with volatility. Since there is an asymmetric payout for holding an option, a large price move that has a 50/50 chance of going up or down helps the buyer of the option more than the seller. The potential losses of the buyer are limited, but the potential profit is not. An option buyer benefits from large price moves, and an option seller benefits from price stability.

---

[1] Myron Scholes and Robert Merton won the Nobel Prize in 1997. Fischer Black had died in 1995, but the Swedish Academy strongly indicated that he would have been a co-winner had he still been alive. While these gentlemen were not the only contributors to option pricing theory, their work opened up the options markets to general investors.

Spread Options

The *spread option* is especially common in the energy market. They are used to price a large variety of physical energy deals. With spread options, the owner of the option benefits when the difference between two prices is above a certain level. This is like a normal option except with a two asset prices. Alternately, this is like an option with a variable strike price. A spread option can be constructed to look like a standard option payout in a couple of ways. One way is to set the "price" of the option equal to the spread between the two assets:

Call Payoff = (Asset Price 1 – Asset Price 2) – Strike Price

Another way is to lump the second asset price into the "strike price":

Call Payoff – Asset Price – (Asset Price 2 + Strike Price)

The prevalence of spread options in energy deals is a result of the way the energy market operates: there is focus on moving energy from one location to another, storing it for sale at a later point, and converting it from one form to another. The profitability of doing these actions depends upon the spread between two prices compared to the cost of doing the conversion—the price here versus the price there compared to transportation costs, the price now versus the price later compared to storage costs, and the price of fuel versus the price of electricity compared to conversion costs.

Valuing spread options is substantially more complicated than valuing options on single assets. In the two asset case, the correlation between the two assets is very important. The spread between the prices of two highly correlated assets will behave differently than the spread between two uncorrelated assets. In fact, the correlation between the two assets becomes the single most important factor in the option valuation. There often isn't a good way to estimate this correlation either—historical data may be misleading, and there isn't usually a liquid enough market to determine the correlations being used by other people in the market.

Because of correlation's effect on the price of spread options, and the difficulty in estimating it, correlation requires a lot of scrutiny. Managing the risk of an options portfolio requires building an infrastructure to examine correlations between products. Incorrectly estimating correlation is the single easiest way to mess up an option valuation. This estimate isn't just important when a spread option trade is initiated—it needs to be monitored over the entire life of the trade.

ELECTRICITY MODELS

Various aspects of the electricity market are complicated enough that they merit individual discussions.

This section starts by examining the supply and demand of electricity. These topics are covered in reverse order starting with an examination of consumer demand. In most regions there is a relatively stable baseline demand for electricity. Most of the variability in demand is a result of the weather. Over very long time frames—a decade, for example—economic growth and residential trends also become important.

The next chapter examines the electrical supply—specifically, how independent system operators (ISOs) pick which power plants will operate each day. Power plants must submit quotes to the ISO. Power plants are continually activated and deactivated depending on the demand for electricity. The plants willing to offer power at the lowest cost are selected before the higher cost units. However, all power plants get paid the same price for their power. Every operating plant gets the price submitted by the *marginal* plant—either the last one activated or the next one to be turned off (depending on whether demand is increasing or falling).

After that, several important electricity trading topics will be examined in detail—models of power plants, long distance transmission lines, and various electrical generation technologies.

Demand for Electricity: Spatial Load Forecasting

Spatial load forecasting is the study of *where* and *when* power will be required. Since power can't be stored and must be generated on demand, it is necessary to anticipate changes in demand. In the context of this book, *load* is synonymous with *demand for electrical power*. "Load" is an electrical engineering term referring to the power consumed by a circuit or drawn from a power line. In the short term, load forecasts are used to schedule power plants for operation and maintenance. In the long run, load forecasting is used to construct new power lines, build new power plants, and build infrastructure projects.

One of the most important characteristics of a region is the minimum amount of power that has to be supplied at any given time to a power grid. This minimum level is called *base-load power*. It sets a threshold on the number of power plants that will be operating full-time the entire year. On the other end of the extreme is predicting the maximum amount of energy that will be required at any given time (the *peak demand*). Power grids use estimates of peak demand for capacity planning to ensure sufficient power to meet any demand in a region. However, traders can use the same information to predict how often power prices will spike and when those spikes will occur.

Forecasting the Supply of Electricity: The Generation Stack

Power prices are set by nondiscriminatory auctions—every power producer is allowed to submit bids, the lowest bidders become the winners, and all winners receive the same price for their power. Usually there are two auctions: TSOs lock in the majority of the required supply in day-ahead auctions, and then use real-time auctions to fill in unexpected shortfalls.

Because of the nature of the auctions, certain power plants tend to be very influential in setting the price of power. The most influential are the ones on the *margin*—either the last plants selected for operation or those that just missed being selected. As the bidding strategy for power generators is often largely determined by the physical characteristics of the power plant, it is possible to group plants into general categories. *Base-load* generation plants produce power cheaply, are expensive to shut down, and want to run continuously even when demand is at its lowest level. *Peaking* generation plants provide short bursts of power in periods of maximum demand—they are cheap to keep inactive, start up quickly, and don't need to be very efficient. *Mid-merit* generation fills the gap between the two extremes. Demand for power will determine which of these general categories is *on the margin*.

Base-load generation plants are defined by being relatively inexpensive to operate and expensive to start up or shut down. Hydro, nuclear, and coal plants all fall into this category. Hydro plants don't have any fuel costs and may not be able to shut down without flooding nearby communities. Nuclear plants require the use of control rods to slow down the nuclear reaction—without cooling, the nuclear reaction keeps on going at maximum capacity. The effect is that nuclear plants need to burn fuel (control rods) in order to slow down. Coal plants are easier to shut down, but can be expensive to restart if allowed to cool down completely. Most of these plants run full-time—they are rarely on the margin, and offer power at low costs in order to avoid going offline.

The other extreme, peaking generation, provides short-term electricity during periods of peak demand (typically summer afternoons). The primary consideration is that these plants need to start up quickly and be cheap to maintain. They don't need to be cheap to operate—conserving fuel is an afterthought. Many of these power plants are essentially jet engines. Fuel is pumped in and ignited; there is a minimum of moving parts and a lot of wasted heat energy. Many of these plants only operate a couple hundred hours a year. In order to recover costs, these plants will charge very high prices for electricity.

Mid-merit plants are somewhere between the two extremes. In many cases these plants are older, less efficient base-load plants that are no longer cost effective enough to run full-time. In other cases these are highly efficient natural gas plants that are easier to cycle than the base-load generators. These generators are commonly on the margin, and show a lot of variability in their bidding strategies. Base-load generators are always going to bid low: they need to operate full-time. Peaking generators are always going to bid high: they are extremely expensive to operate. Most of the time, mid-merit plants are going to control how power is priced in a region.

There is a fair amount of gamesmanship in setting these prices. On one hand, power plants want to get the highest price possible for their product. But on the other hand, since there is a single price for power in a region, it isn't important to be the top bidder. As long as a power plant is operating, it is getting the same price as the highest bidder. There is no downside to bidding a zero price if someone else sets the price at a higher level. The marginal power plants—the ones actually setting the price—have the most complicated task. The most common strategy among mid-merit power plants is to bid some capacity at or slightly below cost and then offer progressively more capacity at higher prices.

Tolling Agreements

A *tolling agreement* is an arrangement where a power marketer (someone who trades electricity) rents a power plant. These agreements can be for any length of time (often 20 or 30 years) and divide the job of running a power plant between two parties. One party maintains the power plant for a preestablished fee, while the other party—the trader—makes all of the economic decisions. The trader (the power marketer in a tolling agreement) is responsible for supplying fuel to the plant and selling the resulting electricity into a competitive market. The trader takes on all of the economic risks and earns most of the profits (everything above the fixed maintenance fee).

A common approach to modeling power plants is to price them as a series of spread options. The power plant operator can produce electricity by burning fuel. The payoff is the difference between the two prices and the operating cost of the plant. In general, when the price of power is above the generator's cost of production, the generator can run profitably. Otherwise, it can shut down and receive nothing. To differentiate electrical generation models from the broader category of spread models, they are often called *spark spread models*.

There are dangers to using options to approximate physical behavior—a spread option model can ignore important physical aspects of generation like the time it takes to turn on (*ramp up* or *cycle*) and variable costs (like start-up and cooling that vary based on the ambient temperature). A generator might take longer to start in the winter than during the summer. Options assume power plant decisions can be made instantaneously. No matter how quickly a power plant can be cycled, it is going to be slower than instantaneous decisions implied by a spark spread model. Other real life issues—like the effect of local regulations regarding grid reliability—can also be difficult to quantify.

Because spark spread option models are less constrained than actual generators, they run the risk of overestimating profitability. This overestimation can be as high as 20 percent to 30 percent. This can result in large errors in profit estimates and value-at-risk calculations. Since the magnitude of this error depends on local characteristics, there isn't a rule of thumb that can be used as a "correction factor"

Another criticism of spark spread option models is that they are "reactive"—in essence, they assume that a generator simply turns on or off in response to the current price. In reality, the optimal schedule for a generator must anticipate price changes, perhaps incurring a loss in some periods in order to position the generator to capture higher expected profits later on. Again, there is no one size fits all rule for this. The relative importance of this problem is different for each generator.

Finally, it is far easier to price a power plant if each decision to produce power is independent of earlier decisions. In some cases power plants are *path dependent*—whether the power plant was operating yesterday will factor into the decision on whether it operates today. This means that the simpler models may not be appropriate. More complicated models are harder to verify, take longer to run, and are more likely to be invalidated over time. Under most circumstances, using simpler models is preferable to using complicated models. However, because simple models are not always appropriate, it is necessary to test them regularly.

Wheeling Power

The cost of electrical power depends on both generation and transmission costs. Minimizing the total cost for power involves balancing these two requirements. Transmission costs are lowest if electricity is produced where it is used, while generation is much more efficient at larger power plants. There has always been a trade-off between large centralized power plants and less efficient local plants. *Wheeling* refers to the long distance transmission of power; *wheeling models* analyze the trade-off between generation and transmission costs.

The purpose of wheeling is to get low cost power into an area of high prices. If allowed as a free market activity, it can help lower the cost of power for consumers. As a result, wheeling is one of the primary reasons why the electrical markets were deregulated. There are a number of practical applications of wheeling models. They can be used to examine construction of new high-efficiency power plants or long distance transmission lines.

High-efficiency power plants and alternative energy plants often have specific locations where they need to be located. Their lower cost of power needs to offset the cost of transmitting power from that location. For example, a cogeneration plant needs to be located adjacent to a large user of their steam output. A hydroelectric plant needs to be located on a river at a dam, and solar facilities need to be located in sunny areas.

Another application for wheeling models is analyzing transmission of power between two power grids. There are three major interconnected groups of power grids in the United States: the Eastern Interconnect (east of the Rocky Mountains), the Western Interconnect (west of the Rocky Mountains), and ERCOT (Texas). Within each of these groups, it is possible to transmit power between the constituent power grids. For example, it is possible to purchase power in the Midwest and transmit it to the Gulf Coast. Since the Midwest tends to have coal power plants on the margin, and the Gulf Coast has natural gas plants on the margin, this provides a way to profit from any divergence in the price of coal and natural gas. This behavior also looks like an option: a fixed cost is paid to rent capacity, and there is a payoff if the prices diverge.

Financially, wheeling deals are interesting because they allow traders to buy an option based on the construction costs of the equipment rather than on the financial value of the option. This is a key aspect of trading physical products—option premiums can be extremely expensive. If the construction costs are affordable, physical investments provide an alternate way to get the financial exposures at a lower cost. Of course, the trader can *lock in* a profit by selling off the financial option and pocketing the difference in costs as a profit.

Solar Power

Solar power is one of the most promising sources of renewable energy. There are two main types of solar power, *photovoltaic solar* power and *thermal solar* power.

Photovoltaic (PV) power, produced by solar panels exposed to sunlight, converts solar power into electricity. The type of equipment and the intensity of the sunlight directly affect the amount of power produced by a solar panel. Correctly estimating the amount of power that will be produced by a solar installation is critical to its successful adoption. If estimates are too conservative, solar power will be deemed uneconomical and bypassed for other technologies. If estimates are too high, there will be a power shortfall and the economic goals of an installation won't be met.

Thermal solar power uses sunlight to produce heat. In many cases this heat can be used to produce electricity by powering steam turbines or to replace electricity that would have been used to produce heat. There are many types of thermal solar installations. They can be anything from small-scale systems to heat outdoor pools to electrical generation facilities. A big advantage of solar power is that heat is relatively easy to store, and this allows these facilities to operate around the clock. Although they can only store heat during the day, they can use the stored heat anytime.

Solar radiation varies throughout the year—it is affected by weather, the changing location of the sun, and the amount of daylight. The angle of the solar panel, its efficiency of handling direct and diffuse light, and the surrounding environment all effect how much power is collected. To analyze solar installations, historical averages of solar radiation are used. These averages are collected by the regional or national governments and provided for the purpose of estimating solar installations.

Wind Power

The wind is another source of renewable energy. It has been used for thousands of years as a pollution-free way to power windmills and sailboats. Since the 1970s, specialized windmills, called *wind turbines*, have been built to harness the wind as a source of electrical power. These windmills are typically grouped into *wind farms* and located in areas exposed to sustained high winds.

Wind is inherently unpredictable. Not only does it blow irregularly, but the amount of energy in wind is proportional to the cube of the wind speed. Fast gusts contain far more energy than slow steady breezes. As a result, the wind supplies irregular bursts of power. Occasionally, wind energy will provide a lot of energy. But most of the time, it will not provide much energy at all. Since efficient power plants usually need to run continuously, meeting the shortfall due to irregular wind energy often means that a power grid is forced to rely on highly inefficient peaking generation that can cycle on and off quickly. The environmental benefit of wind power can be a mirage if it requires even infrequent use of standby generation.

Wind turbines can be expensive to install and maintain due to the constant stress that the wind places on their moving parts. When exposed to high winds for prolonged periods, a substantial amount of torque is placed on the frame of the turbine. This can cause the superstructure to break down and deform over time. This is especially a problem when there are a number of wind turbines in close proximity. When a wind turbine is alone, the air flow around its fan blades is fairly predictable. However, when there are a large number of wind turbines together, the turbulence from the blades of the upwind units can cause chaotic air flow over the downwind units. This puts unpredictable stresses on the superstructure of the turbines and can lead to sudden equipment failure.

The two most common reasons for consumer opposition to wind farms are the danger they present to migratory birds and aesthetic considerations. Wind turbines are often placed on major migration corridors due to the steady sustained winds in those areas. As birds fly past, they can be hit by the spinning blades and killed. Environmental groups are concerned that if wind power becomes common, the wild bird population will be decimated. People who consider wind farms ugly and who don't want them destroying the scenic beauty of nature are also against them.

Nuclear Power

Although it is not a renewable fuel, nuclear power is an alternative to fossil fuel–based electricity generation. Nuclear power plants, like coal-fired power plants, operate by producing superheated steam to drive electrical turbines. Both coal and nuclear plants benefit by operating at extremely high temperatures. The higher the temperature that these plants can operate at, the more efficient they become. A low temperature plant might return 25 percent of its heat energy as electricity. A larger, hotter plant might return 50 percent to 60 percent of its heat energy as electricity.

The primary difference between nuclear and coal plants is the way they generate heat. Nuclear power plants generate heat through nuclear fission, which breaks protons and neutrons free from the nucleus of the nuclear fuel. This isn't a combustion process, so no carbon dioxide is produced. However, nuclear power produces a different type of pollution: radioactive waste.

When concentrated, uranium—the fuel used in most nuclear reactors—is highly toxic. The fuel can also be very difficult to obtain. Although there is a lot of uranium in the earth's crust, it is seldom found in large deposits. There are a limited number of areas where sufficient quantities can be found to make its extraction economically feasible. Another worry is that the refining process is often identical to the process needed to make fuel for nuclear weapons. As a result, concerns of nuclear weapon proliferation are closely linked to the construction of nuclear reactors.

Energy Storage

Because storing electricity is not economical on a large scale, it is generally described as not being possible. While this is a sufficient description for the general market dynamics about the relationship of the spot and forward market, it does obscure technologies that people have developed for electricity storage.

Electricity can be stored by converting it into another form of energy, like kinetic energy or heat, and then using that energy to generate electricity. Even though the efficiency of these conversions is usually low, there are cases where it becomes economically worthwhile. For example, whenever electricity can be obtained for very low cost, even inefficient storage systems are economical if they were inexpensive to build. There are a large number of ways to store energy. Some of the examples used in this section discuss pressurized gas, kinetic energy, and gravity. It's equally possible to use chemical energy to store energy in a battery or to use a capacitor to store voltage directly.

NATURAL GAS

This section introduces transportation and storage models of the natural gas market. The key to understanding these models lies in understanding the physical nature of gases. Since it is a gas, transporting and storing natural gas requires different technologies than those used for solids (like coal) or liquids (like oil).

Gas isn't very dense—it contains substantially less energy per volume than either solids or liquids. Natural gas (methane) is one of the least energy dense hydrocarbon gases—it has much less energy per volume than a gas like propane. As a result, it isn't practical to use tanks to transfer natural gas for heating or industrial use. Because natural gas needs to be kept at super-cold temperatures (−260° F) to remain a liquid, it is also impractical to distribute natural gas to consumers in that form.

Because of these constraints, natural gas is typically moved through the country via gas pipelines. This is a very efficient way to transport gas, but pipelines do have some limitations. Gas needs to be continually injected into the pipeline from a well or storage facility and removed at the *burner tip*—the locale of the natural gas consumer. Since gas moves from areas of high pressure to areas of lower pressure, it is important that the pipeline maintain the proper ratio of pressure throughout its length. If the pressure at the burner tip were to be higher than the pressure at the well head, gas would flow back into the well.

In practical terms, this means that if a pipeline is operational, neither the injections nor removal of gas can be allowed to stop. If gas isn't added continuously at the injection point (to create a high pressure zone) and removed at the burner tip (to create a low pressure zone), gas won't flow in the proper direction, and the pipeline won't operate. This is a very important concept: for a pipeline to operate, neither injections nor removals can stop just because they are uneconomical. Gas pipelines provide a public service—sometimes they can't be turned off. If no consumer is using the gas at the burner tip, and there isn't any storage available, it might be necessary to burn off the excess gas or make otherwise uneconomical decisions.

To prevent wasting gas, a popular solution is to store it in a storage facility. Unused oil wells, salt mines, and aquifers have all been modified for storing natural gas. Typically, these have to be kept at a higher pressure than the pipeline—to allow gas to eventually flow out of the storage facility and back into the pipeline.

Transportation

Compressor stations are the key to transporting natural gas through pipelines. These stations create suction on one side (the intake side) and high pressure on the other side (the discharge side). Gas flows by expanding—it moves from the high pressure discharge point of one station to the low pressure suction point of the next station. Choosing the right number of compression stations to ensure reliable service is a key aspect of the pipeline business.

When arranging transportation on a pipeline, there are two major levels of service: *firm* service and *interruptible* service. Firm service is offered with a guaranteed availability except when prevented by acts of *force majeure*.[2] Firm service is highly reliable but also highly expensive compared to *interruptible* service, which is offered on a "best

---

[2] Force majeure, derived from French, means "greater force." This is a common clause in contracts that frees both parties from liability in cases of wars, natural disasters, and other extraordinary events. Typically, these events are outside the control of either party, which would prevent one or both from fulfilling their obligations under the terms of the contract.

efforts" basis and is relatively cheap. However, it can be interrupted for any reason and may not be available at all. There are a number of valid reasons why interruptible service might be disrupted. The most common reason is to balance the flow of gas on a pipeline. Because of the nature of gas, its movement can never be precisely controlled. Optimizing even a relatively simple pipeline can get very complicated. Although "firm" and "interruptible" are commonly used general descriptions of service levels, each pipeline company will have a slightly different definition for the types of services offered.

Pipelines get paid substantially more for guaranteed levels of service than for service that is likely to be interrupted. The economics of a pipeline are based on balancing the need for redundancy in the system (allowing the sale of higher margin guaranteed service) against the cost of additional compression stations and pipes.

Storage

After gas is transported, it may not be necessary to use it right away. Fortunately, it is possible to store natural gas for extremely long periods of time. Most natural gas is already millions of years old. Pipelines need to keep operating around the clock, but demand is more cyclical, and natural gas must either be stored or burned off. Storage facilities help to smooth out these periods of short-term supply and demand. These facilities are located on both ends of pipelines.

Demand for natural gas is highly seasonal—the highest demand comes during the winter (for heating) and during the summer (to provide electricity for air-conditioning). Storage facilities allow stockpiling of gas during periods of low demand for use in higher demand periods. This storage also provides a crucial margin of safety for short-term regional changes in demand. Storage facilities differ by the quantity of gas that can be stored and how quickly it can be removed.

All storage facilities work in a similar fashion—a large volume suitable for storing natural gas is found and connected to a gas pipeline. Unless it is nearly empty, the pressure in the storage facility will be higher than the pressure of a pipeline. Gas will need to be compressed to get it into the pipeline. This compression is done by applying suction to a pipeline (similar to attaching a vacuum cleaner to it). As long as the suction is stronger than the pressure in the storage area, the gas will flow into the storage area and not back into the pipeline. When the suction is turned off, the connection between the storage facility and pipeline has to be closed.

The speed at which gas can be extracted will depend on the pressure of the storage facility. As a result, the extractable gas is generally divided into two pieces: *base gas* (or cushion gas) and *working gas*. The base gas is used to create sufficient pressure to get the working gas out of the storage facility in a reasonable amount of time. Base gas is usually never removed during normal operation. Operators of a storage facility have to trade off having a large volume of working gas that can only be removed slowly or a smaller volume of working gas that can be removed quickly. During periods of peak demand, some of the base gas can be removed from the facility and delivered as working gas. However, over the long run, since removing the gas cushion slows down the speed at which gas can be removed (because removing gas lowers the pressure of the storage facility), keeping a fixed cushion of gas is required to meet ongoing operational requirements.

The need for maximum pressure is a major physical constraint on a storage facility. Higher pressure means that you can store more gas in a given volume and get the gas out more quickly. However, it can also cause structural problems—more stress on the facility—and a greater possibility of gas escaping into the environment. Since there are a fairly limited number of locations suitable for the storage of natural gas, the pressure constraint is usually a function of what can be found, rather than what is desired.

For a particular area, there is a limited inventory of possible locations suitable for storing natural gas. The cheapest and most reliable storage is depleted gas reservoirs. The highest performance facilities are converted salt caverns. In areas where neither of those two is available, aquifers can be used. Aquifers are permeable layers of underground rock often containing groundwater. From a performance perspective, salt caverns are far superior to the other options—they can stand up to significantly higher pressures.

Liquefied Natural Gas

Another major trend in the natural gas market is to import it from other countries. It isn't feasible to build pipelines across the ocean, so instead natural gas is transported as a liquid. It turns into a liquid at −260°F and becomes 600 times denser than its gaseous form. Specially insulated tanker ships can be used to transport the natural gas across long distances. When a liquid natural gas (LNG) tanker reaches a port, the LNG can be turned back into a gas by heating it. At that point it can be placed into a pipeline for delivery to consumers.

From an environmental perspective, transporting natural gas is fairly safe. Other than being freezing cold, it is nontoxic and noncorrosive. When it is left exposed to the atmosphere, perhaps by a spill, liquid natural gas will rapidly evaporate without leaving a residue. Because of the speed at which it evaporates, natural gas also does not pose a large explosion risk. Natural gas is only explosive in concentrations between 5 percent and 15 percent of air. This can occur when gas is trapped in an enclosed space like a house or a storage facility. But in any other concentrations, it will not ignite. Anytime a large amount of flammable substance is in one place, there is some fire risk. However, there is much less risk with natural gas than with either oil or coal storage facilities.

There are no LNG contracts currently being traded. However, being able to transport LNG around the globe makes the natural gas market a global market rather than a set of regional ones. For example, without LNG, the natural gas markets in Europe and the United States are completely separate. However, with the ability to transfer supply from one region to another, prices will start to converge toward a single global price.

RISK MANAGEMENT

Modern financial risk management is usually a combination of two practices: *mark-to-market accounting* and an *analysis of earnings volatility*. Typically, the risk of a portfolio is synonymous with its earnings volatility—often summarized by a measure called its *value at risk* or VAR.[3] The VAR is highly dependent on the choice of accounting methodology. While risk management practices vary widely, almost all risk management is at least partially based around a VAR methodology. In this context, the term *earnings* and the term *profit and loss* (P&L) are interchangeable.

VAR summarizes the risk of a portfolio by predicting the size of P&L movement that will occur with some frequency. For example, it is possible to calculate an estimate of the largest P&L move that will occur approximately once a month. VAR simplifies a large distribution of possible earnings into a single point. Not everyone uses the same frequency for VAR—some people prefer points that are more likely to be accurate and can be checked commonly, while others prefer numbers more representative of a worst case scenario. There are three main steps to calculating a VAR number:

1. Construct a distribution of possible P&L moves (usually by examining what types of moves have happened in the past).
2. Turn all the moves into positive numbers and sort the P&L into a new distribution.
3. Find the value in the nth percentile of the distribution (the 95th and 99th percentiles are popular choices for VAR).

---

[3] VAR is pronounced "var" and rhymes with "car" and "far."

Figure 1.1.2 depicts the three steps.

By picking a single point, VAR produces a simpler estimate of risk than having to use the entire distribution of predicted results. VAR gives up accuracy for simplicity. In many cases different assets can have the same VAR, as seen in Figure 1.1.3.

The methodology for calculating the percentile also can vary between firms. Some risk managers prefer to examine only losses, others prefer to look at the volatility of both profits and losses. If only losses are examined, the VAR is called a *one-sided VAR*. If both profits and losses are examined, it is called a *two-sided VAR* (Figure 1.1.4). A two-sided VAR will force an asset to have the single VAR regardless

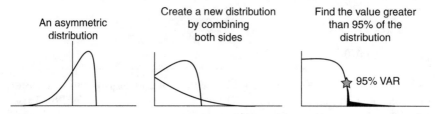

Figure 1.1.2.   Graphic depiction of a two-sided VAR calculation

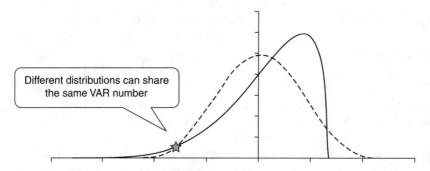

Figure 1.1.3.   VAR simplifies a distribution of expected P&L by a single value

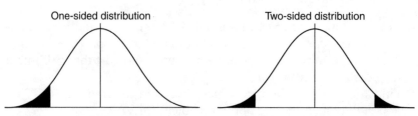

Figure 1.1.4.   In a one-sided distribution, all of the samples come from one side (usually losses). In a two-sided distribution, outlier events are examined from both profits and losses.

of whether it is long or short; a one-sided VAR will have different VARs depending on whether an asset is bought or sold. Having a single VAR per asset is useful when combining portfolios—buying and selling the same asset should show zero VAR.

Weaknesses of VAR

Because VAR is a single number, it has some limitations: it abstracts away the fundamental behavior of a portfolio. Typically, P&L is not normally distributed—there isn't an equal chance of making and losing money. Many energy assets, particularly the ones that can be modeled by options, have asymmetrical payoffs.

For example, a peaking power plant is going to lay idle for most of the year—it will lose money regularly whenever it is inactive. In all but the summer months, small operational charges will accumulate daily. A couple times a year—usually hot summer afternoons—the power plant will have the opportunity to make large windfall profits as it is pressed into duty. Figure 1.1.5 is a payoff diagram of a portfolio that benefits from volatility.

VAR poorly describes portfolios that don't have symmetric risks. This example shows the P&L distribution for a portfolio that is "long volatility"—a portfolio that benefits from large P&L movements and increasing volatility.

With this kind of seasonal effect, it might be possible to have season-specific VAR distributions, but that isn't a general solution to the problem. A gas pipeline that is selling firm delivery will make steady profits until a problem is encountered, then the pipeline will hemorrhage money. There might be some seasonality to equipment failures—but the P&L is not going to show nearly the seasonality as a

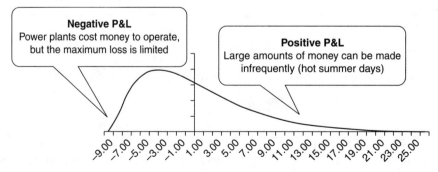

Figure 1.1.5. A skewed distribution has limits losses on one side and has windfall gains on the other

peaking power plant where the price of power is determined almost exclusively by a seasonal factor: temperature.

Ultimately, VAR is an approximation—being simple means that it gets implemented and examined regularly. However, it is not going to handle all types of portfolios well. Sometimes additional analysis will be required. There are so many possible special cases that no general model will be able to address them all. This doesn't make VAR worthless, just limited. It is useful precisely because it is a simple measure.

Combining VAR Estimates

Combining VAR numbers for a lot of assets can be complicated. The correlation between the portfolios will determine if the risks add or subtract. There are some rules of thumb that can be used as a guideline. First, VAR is always a positive number—risk (volatility) can be zero, but can never be less than zero. Next, unless two assets are perfectly correlated, their combined VAR will be less risky than the sum of their individual VARs. Finally, a combined VAR will usually never be less than the difference between the individual VARs.

For example, if a portfolio with a $500 VAR is combined with one combined with a $100 VAR, the combined VAR will be somewhere between $400 and $600. If the risks offset each other, the VAR will decrease. This will lead to a VAR less than $500. If the risks do not offset, the VAR will be greater than $500.

If one-sided estimates are used, it is possible different VARs will be assigned to the same position depending on whether it is long or short. This is particularly common in options books since they have asymmetric long/short payoffs. This causes a problem when one-sided VAR estimates are used—when long and short option positions are combined, the sum of the VAR won't equal zero. Sometimes there are good reasons to use one-sided distributions. However, operationally it makes consolidating risk calculations less reliable. Keeping VAR as a volatility measure avoids a lot of problems.

Deltas, Gammas, and Other Greeks

Often it is necessary to describe a portfolio with more information than a VAR analysis provides. VAR provides an estimate of P&L volatility, but doesn't address questions like, "Do I expect to make or lose money if the price of oil continues to rise?" or, "How much money do I expect to make or lose if an unlikely event becomes more likely?" These types of questions can be answered by additional pieces of information— usually called *Greeks* because they are commonly represented by symbols for the Greek alphabet.

The two most important Greeks are *delta* and *gamma*. These terms are developed from mathematical descriptions of velocity and acceleration. They always relate one asset to another asset—a *Greek* is meaningless without understanding which two assets are being compared. The first asset is typically called the *primary asset* (or just *asset* for short), and the second asset is called the *underlying asset* (often just called the *underlying*). The first Greek, delta (symbol Δ) indicates the amount of money that the first asset will make or lose when the underlying asset moves up or down. The second Greek, gamma (symbol Γ) indicates how much the delta will change when the underlying asset moves up or down in price.

An asset can have a nearly infinite number of deltas and gammas—one for every other asset in the world. A lot of those comparisons won't actually be useful—many will be downright misleading. Ultimately, the purpose of a Greek is to predict behavior: it's no good if there isn't a strong cause/effect relationship between the assets. Neither delta nor gamma is a stand-alone piece of information like a price—a Greek is always a comparison between two assets. In many cases Greeks are treated like stand-alone pieces of information; the underlying assets are assumed to be common knowledge.

Delta is important primarily because it can relate an entire portfolio to the movement of a couple of key numbers. For example, a portfolio of stocks might be related to the movement of the S&P 500 index. Alternately, it can be used to compare a derivative to its underlying asset—the value of a call option on IBM to the IBM stock price. In the energy world, deltas get more complicated. Power can't be stored—the spot and forward markets are disconnected. In most markets, options typically use the spot asset as an underling asset. In the energy markets, the spot price can't be used. Instead, a power asset will need to be compared to a time series of underlying assets (the forward price curve).

The second Greek, gamma, is often more important than delta. Gamma is the Greek most closely scrutinized by risk managers. It isn't as directly informative as delta. However, it indicates a more crucial piece of information: what will happen to a portfolio when the market goes crazy. Gamma indicates the exposure of a portfolio to volatility—whether a portfolio will benefit or lose money when the market really starts to move.

Mark-to-Market Accounting

Mark-to-market accounting is the process of using the current *market price* to value assets. The market price is the price that an asset could fetch if it were to be sold into the market that day. In practice, this usually means that prices are based on recently published exchange quotes. In some cases, where published prices aren't available, the portfolio may be marked to a theoretical price called a *mark-to-model* price. Mark-to-market accounting is common in trading organizations because it eliminates many ways to misrepresent the state of a portfolio. It is often forced onto energy portfolios when mark-to-market accounting is used in other parts of the firm. However, in energy trading, mark-to-market accounting has some disadvantages that are important to understand in a risk management context.

Before discussing the disadvantages, there is a big advantage to using mark-to-market accounting—it is fairly intuitive. If an asset is purchased for $100 and rises to $120, under mark-to-market accounting it will show a $20 profit even if the asset hasn't be sold yet. The alternative, *accrual accounting*, keeps assets marked to their purchase price until they are actually sold. Accrual accounting can be misleading when it comes to long-dated assets because the value of those assets isn't regularly updated. For an investment portfolio that is actively traded in a liquid market, mark-to-market accounting accurately and clearly represents the economics of the investments.

On the downside, mark-to-market accounting assumes there is a liquid, fair market for price discovery. It tends to fail catastrophically when markets can be manipulated or are illiquid. Most of the models discussed in this book—power plants, storage facilities, and almost everything modeled as an option—do not have liquid markets. Many of these assets are priced off models incredibly sensitive to a couple of rates that can't be observed—a perfect example of an unobservable rate is the correlation between the two sides of a spread option.

Also, it is fairly common for there to be unintended consequences of choosing mark-to-market accounting. For example, many funds force a mandatory liquidation when VAR limits are exceeded. In an illiquid market, it may not be possible to sell an expensive asset immediately. Under mark-to-market accounting, this would be priced as worthless. If other traders hold the same type of asset, and anyone actually sells for zero, this can wreak havoc in the marketplace. Mark-to-market accounting can badly exacerbate illiquid market conditions.

Mixing mark-to-market instruments with *accrued* instruments also creates problems. An extreme example might be a power plant that has completely locked in fuel supplies and sold its power for the next 20 years using OTC forwards. The power plant is hedged—there should be limited market risk or cash flows prior to the date of electricity delivery. However, if the plant receives accrual accounting and the hedges are mark-to-market, large "phantom" profits and losses will make the book look substantially riskier than it is in reality.

Managing Model Risk

The possibility that either the methodology or assumptions used to value assets becomes invalid is called *model risk*. Poor assumptions and incorrectly designed models cause risk management problems in every financial market. But the complexity of energy models and their extended lifetimes make these problems especially common in the energy markets.

The energy market is full of nonstandard instruments and models of physical assets. Many energy companies will use models to value assets with lifetimes of 20 years or longer—things like power plants, pipelines, and natural gas wells. Even if the model was sufficient when first developed, it can still fail before its lifetime is up. Assumptions made 15 years earlier are often invalidated due to regulatory changes, population shifts, and technological changes. Exacerbating this problem is the problem of employee turnover—commonly, the original developers of the models have moved to other jobs when problems develop. After a number of years, organizations need to take steps to ensure that someone still understands every model that is in production.

Another issue common across many energy products is that many physical trading points aren't very liquid. These trading points often need to be approximated by prices at a nearby hub. The implicit assumption is that the actual price will experience the same changes as the local hub. Sometimes this is a good assumption. At other times the expected relationship between the two points breaks down after a couple of years.

Another assumption that can cause problems is the correlation between two assets. The importance of spread options in energy was discussed earlier. The value of these deals is incredibly sensitive to the correlation between the two underlying assets. In these cases, the correlation can't be readily determined from an independent source—it must be estimated and reviewed regularly.

Counterparty and Credit Risk

Finally, the energy market is full of agreements made directly between two counterparties. Assessing the ability of counterparties to meet their contractual obligations is crucial to the energy business. There are two parts to examining credit risk: establishing the magnitude of the risk (credit exposure) and the likelihood of the risk (credit quality). Getting this information correct is important—firms will have hard limits on how much exposure they can have to a single counterparty. If estimates of loss are too high, business will be hurt—it won't be possible to make trades. If the estimates are too low, there is risk of a catastrophic counterparty collapse.

Credit exposure identifies how much money could be lost in event of a default. At its simplest, calculating credit exposure can assume a complete loss on every contract. This does place an upper bound on the potential loss, but also tends to overestimate its severity. A more accurate estimate must include the probability of recovering assets through a bankruptcy proceeding. Certain debts (preferred debt) have priority over other debts. It is important to understand where the contracts in question fall in the recovery order.

Credit quality is the other aspect of modeling credit risk. It attempts to describe how likely a firm is to default on its payments. This is a forward-looking measure—many energy contracts last several years. There are a number of ratings agencies that provide credit ratings. These ratings can be augmented by in-house research focusing on a couple of key counterparties. There can be several layers to this analysis: a counterparty's credit risk will depend on the credit quality of its own clients. Finally, a company is less likely to default if its large trades have moved in its favor, and more likely to default if trades have moved against it.

As a summary, credit risk can't be eliminated—but it can be mitigated through the use of collateral and managed through supervision. If controls are too strict, it will be impossible to conduct an ongoing business. The possibility of missing trading opportunities and damaging relationships because of counterparty exposure limits needs to be balanced against the need to protect against a huge loss. Neither extreme is good—a happy medium needs to be found.

1.2

TRADING MARKETS

 30-Second Summary

Purpose

This chapter introduces several financial concepts related to trading and investing. It starts off as a review of concepts mentioned in the previous chapter and then goes into a lot more detail.

Summary

The energy market is a type of commodity market that specializes in electricity, heat, and fuel products. Difficulties in storing and transporting energy products distinguish energy trading from other commodity markets. In most financial markets, future prices are linked to current prices by the ability to buy a product today and store it for future delivery. However, buying and holding is difficult in the energy market. Many types of energy are impossible to store. In other cases, a steady supply of new product is constantly reaching the market. As a result, current prices and future prices are rarely linked. Instead, energy markets tend to experience cyclical variations in prices.

Key Topics

- Energy trading markets are a type of commodity market that consists of both physical exchanges of cash for energy and forward markets where exchanges are arranged ahead of time. Most energy trading occurs in the forward markets.
- It is impossible to substitute energy products that are not at the same time and location. For example, electricity in New York is different than electricity in California.
- Many concepts developed for other financial markets—like dynamic hedging and risk management—have to be modified to take into account the inability to aggregate risks among energy products at different locations and delivery dates.

Trading means buying, selling, and exchanging commodities. Not all energy markets are *trading* markets. Sometimes it is possible to buy a commodity, like gasoline at a service station, and not be able to resell it. The difference between a cash market and a trading market is that it is possible to buy and sell in a trading market.

The most important commodities in the energy market are natural gas and electricity. Additional energy commodities are oil, gasoline, alternative fuels, pollution, weather derivatives, and carbon emissions. All of these products are related to the generation of either heat or electricity. Electricity and heat cannot be easily stored or transported. In most cases, arrangements to store or transport energy have to be made in advance. Because of this, it is difficult to trade most physical energy commodities on short notice. As a result, *energy trading* primarily consists of buying and selling agreements to deliver power at some point in the future. The *time* and *location* where the energy needs to be delivered is a key component in these agreements.

In most financial markets, the price for future delivery is closely related to the price for immediate delivery. It is possible to buy the product today, hold the traded product for a while, and be able to resell the product in the future. Because of this relationship, one can react to expectations of future prices by trading for immediate delivery.

Energy, and thus the energy market, is different. If physical electricity is purchased the current day, it is necessary to use it immediately.

By itself, energy isn't intrinsically valuable. Heat to warm a house is only valuable in the right place and time. For example, in the summer, home heating isn't valuable at all. Quite the opposite. In hot weather, people pay money to remove heat from their homes. Likewise, if an extremely cold winter in Chicago causes natural gas prices to skyrocket upward, owning undeliverable gas somewhere else isn't very valuable. Only the natural gas that can actually be delivered to customers will be worth the high prices. The spot prices in Chicago don't reflect expectations of future prices. Customers need heating immediately and can't put off their purchase until prices are cheaper in six months. Nor can all of Chicago relocate overnight to an area with more supply or warmer weather.

Spot and Forward Markets

In the *spot market*, commodities are delivered on the day of the transaction. Spot transactions are usually consumers purchasing small quantities of a commodity for immediate use. The *forward market* is a financial market where delivery is scheduled at some agreed upon point in the future.

Spot Market

The spot market, also called the *cash market*, is the market for instantaneous delivery of a commodity. The spot market gets its name because the transaction is done "on the spot." This is the market with which

Supply and Demand

Traders commonly think of asset prices as being set by supply and demand. This is often a good description of commodity markets where consumers bid on a limited supply of goods. A fundamental economic concept in a free market is that prices will gravitate to a level where the supply and demand are equal.

Law of Demand. Higher prices reduce demand.
Law of Supply. Higher prices increase production.

Theoretically, the intersection of supply and demand determines the fair price for an asset. However, in practice, supply and demand don't always respond to price changes. The degree that they do is called *elasticity*. In many cases, supply and demand are constant regardless of how much the price changes. When this happens, there is a disruption in prices. Prices skyrocket when demand exceeds supply. Prices crash when supply exceeds demand. Both events occur fairly commonly in the energy market.

There is a substantial lag between high prices and increased supply in the energy market. Increasing energy supplies usually involves making long-term capital investments like the construction of a new well, refinery, or power plant. These investments are not typically made in response to short-term changes in price. These assets will only be built if a permanent change in prices is expected, and even then might take a substantial amount of time to construct.

Another problem is caused by consumers being unable to substitute one type of energy demand for another. They cannot relocate where they live, modify their car to run on an alternate fuel, or do without heating in the winter. To a large extent, energy consumers are a captive audience.

ordinary people are most familiar. Trades in the spot market involve the physical transfer of an agreed upon quantity of a standardized product for a specific price. Buying a meal at a fast food restaurant is an example of a spot market transaction—the buyer gets immediate delivery of a standardized product for a set price. Another example of a spot transaction occurs when a light switch is turned on. The owner of the light switch buys electricity and immediately takes delivery of the product. Trading in the energy spot market is restricted to people who can either deliver or use power immediately.

The spot market for energy is complicated by the fact that producers don't know what the actual energy demand will be ahead of time. Consumers can turn on electrical devices and set the thermostats whenever they want. It is left to the local electric utility to cope with meeting that demand. When someone turns on a light switch, power needs to be immediately provided. It isn't possible to substitute another type of power—when a homeowner in New York turns on a light, the power company has to provide power in New York. Providing power somewhere nearby, like New Jersey or Connecticut, won't meet the New York demand.

Because of the inability to transfer energy products without preparation, there are a large number of local spot markets. Each can have its own rules and regulations. The prices in each are determined by local supply and demand. As a result, since supply has to be arranged ahead of time, spot prices can be extremely volatile. It is easy for an unexpected change in demand to lead to either a shortage or a glut in local supplies.

For related reasons, high spot prices in one area don't necessarily mean that nearby prices will also be high. It is very possible that one region can have a surplus of power and another a shortage when real-time transfers between the two markets are impossible. For example, if a power plant in California unexpectedly needs to go offline, prices there will spike upward as inefficient and expensive backup generators are turned on. A nearby power market, like Oregon, might not see any price change—that market might still have a sufficient supply of power to meet local demand.

The high price volatility in the local spot markets and the lack of correlation between adjoining regions tends to disappear in the forward market. While there is still time to arrange transfers of power or line up fuel supplies, prices tend to be based on macroeconomics. For example, if a power plant outage is expected in six months, there is probably time to arrange cost effective backup generation rather than relying on units that can be brought up to speed immediately.

Local regulation is another feature of the spot markets. Every municipality can have specific rules governing the physical delivery of power within its boundaries. Some markets might have prices set by government legislation, while other markets might be open to competitive prices. Spot markets subject to heavy government regulation are called *regulated markets,* while markets with competitive pricing systems are called *deregulated markets.*

Forward Markets

Forward trading markets allow buyers and sellers to agree on transactions ahead of time. For physical contracts, this gives both sides sufficient time to prepare for delivery or receipt of a physical commodity. For example, a trader might agree to deliver 500 MMBtus of natural gas at Henry Hub three months in future at a price of $8.12 per MMBtu.

Trades in the forward market are generally specified by several factors:

- **Underlying Instrument.** The commodity being traded, usually with a description of minimum quality standards that must be met. Often, this is just called the *underlying*.
- **Quantity.** The amount of the commodity that must be delivered.
- **Delivery Price.** The price per unit due at delivery
- **Delivery Date.** The date at which the underlying instrument will be delivered.
- **Delivery Location.** The location at which the underlying instrument will be delivered.

From an economic perspective, allowing buyers and sellers to negotiate trades ahead of time reduces the volatility of energy prices. Energy is hard to store and transport. Giving large producers and consumers the opportunity to line up trading partners ahead of time reduces the uncertainty caused by short-term imbalances between supply and demand.

Trading—meaning the buying and reselling of assets—occurs almost exclusively in the forward market. The exceptions to this are cases where a trader has the ability to immediately deliver the physical asset or where he can buy a physical asset and relocate or store it.

The Spot Market Has Higher Volatility

Nearby futures contracts are more volatile than contracts with several months to expiration. This is because distant forward prices are primarily influenced by seasonal expectations, while spot prices are determined by much more volatile short-term variations in supply and demand (Figure 1.2.1).

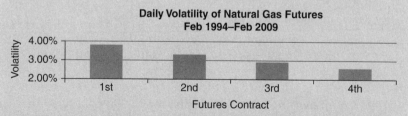

Figure 1.2.1. Diagram showing how volatility decreases with time. Ordinal numbers indicate months to expiration. The first contract is one month from expiration, the second is two months away, etc.

Physical and Financial Settlement

Not everyone has the desire or capability to take physical delivery. Historically, less that 1 percent of futures contracts go to physical delivery. The remainder are settled in cash or liquidated prior to being exercised.

For example, if a trucking company wants to reduce its exposure to diesel fuel prices, it might buy crude oil contracts since the price of diesel fuel is correlated to the price of crude oil. That way, if the oil/diesel relationship continues to hold and the price of diesel fuel rises, the trucking company will offset its increased fuel costs with a profit on its investment. Of course, if the price of fuel falls, the savings to the trucking company would be largely eaten up by losses in the forward contracts. Essentially, the trucking company is attempting to lock in fuel costs. However, regardless of what happens to prices, the trucking company doesn't want to take receipt of a lot of crude oil. It only wants the financial exposure.

When energy contracts are closed out in cash prior to delivery, this is called a *financial settlement*. When the trade is closed out by physically transferring a commodity, it is called a *physical delivery*. When a contract is *closed out*, the two counterparties to the trade essentially enter into a new trade that offsets the original trade.

TRADES AND POSITIONS

After a trader executes a trade, he has a position in the commodity. A *trade* is a transaction; a *position* is the net exposure that results from one or more trades. If a trader makes three transactions to buy crude oil, the combination of all of those trades is known as a position. Positions are often described by the terms "long" and "short." When the trader benefits from a rise in the price of the commodity, he is said to have a *long position*. If the trader will benefit from a fall in the price of a commodity, he is said to have a *short position*.

A long position benefits from an increase in prices. For example, if a gasoline/crude oil spread is defined as the price of gasoline minus the price of oil, a long spread will benefit from a rise in gasoline prices or a fall in oil prices. In other words, the trader is long when he benefits from the spread growing larger. Long positions are commonly associated with owning an asset or agreeing to buy at a fixed price in the future.

Trading Tip: A short position will benefit from a decrease in prices. For example, a trader will be short crude oil if he has agreed to sell it to someone at a fixed price. The selling price is set, and the cheaper that the trader can obtain a supply, the greater the profit. As a result, the trader benefits from a fall in the price of crude oil. A short position is commonly associated with agreeing to sell a commodity at a fixed price in the future.

A trader can *close out* or *liquidate* a transaction by entering into an *offsetting* trade. Closing out a contract means to have no further risk or responsibility for a trade. Quite commonly, it is impossible to close out a contract. For example, if the trade was a direct contractual agreement between two parties, both parties need to agree to dissolve the agreement. If a trader negotiated contracts to buy natural gas directly from one party, for instance, and sold it to another, the trader is not necessarily free of his contractual obligations. The trader would still need to arrange receipt of the commodity from the first party and delivery to the second.

Long and Short Rather Than Buy and Sell

Traders tend to use the terms "long" and "short" to describe their positions rather than relying on the terms "buy" and "sell." The latter terms get confusing when they are applied to transactions in the future.

For example, when a trader agrees to buy oil at the market price a year from now, he is "short" oil. The trader benefits when the price of oil falls because then he can buy more cheaply. However, if the trader agrees to buy oil at a specific price a year from now, he is "long" oil. The more expensive that oil becomes, the more money he saves from buying at a fixed price.

It gets even more confusing when simultaneous purchase and sale of things is in the future, as when a trader agrees to purchase oil at the market price and sell it at a fixed price. Purchasing oil at the market price is a short position. The trader benefits from the drop in prices. Agreeing to sell at a fixed price is also a short position. The trader benefits from the ability to sell at a high price when prices fall. Overall, the trader benefits if oil prices fall and is at substantial risk if prices rise.

The danger is that someone skimming the trades will see a buy and a sell trade and think that the position is closed out. However, the trader has an open—and very active—position.

- A *long position* always benefits from a rise in prices. Long positions are always indicated by a positive sign.
- A *short position* always benefits from a fall in prices. Short positions are always indicated by a negative sign.

Always convert trades into long and short positions. Don't rely on being able to mentally sort out buy and sell terminology as an indication of trading exposures.

OTC AND EXCHANGES

There are two ways for energy products to be traded. It is possible for trades to be made directly between two parties or through an intermediary called an *exchange*. When trades are made directly between two counterparties, they are called *over the counter* (OTC) transactions. When trades are made through an exchange, they are called *exchange traded* transactions.

Over the Counter

OTC trades are direct contractual agreements between two parties. These trades involve signing a contract each and every time a trade is made. Like any other contract, both parties assume liability for the creditworthiness and reliability of the other party. If one party goes bankrupt, there usually is no immediate recourse except to attend bankruptcy proceedings. It can also be difficult to get out of a contractual agreement since both sides need to agree to modifications to the contract.

To simplify trading and contract negotiations, most OTC agreements are based on a standard agreement produced by the *International Swaps and Derivatives Association*. The most important feature of ISDA agreements is that all agreements between two parties form a single contract. This is important in bankruptcy cases because the credit risk under ISDA contracts is limited to the net amount of all contracts.

For example, SolidGoldPower Inc. might have an agreement with Unreliable Corp. to receive 10 million MMBtus of natural gas and deliver 1 million MW/hours of power. If Unreliable Corporation went bankrupt and the trades were not combined into a single contract, Unreliable Corp.'s liabilities (its delivery of natural gas to SolidGoldPower Inc.) would be frozen by the bankruptcy court, but SolidGoldPower Inc. would still be required to deliver power to Unreliable Corp. This would be disastrous to SolidGoldPower Inc. It would need to find another supplier of natural gas, pay the costs to arrange last minute delivery, and then give all of its electrical output to Unreliable Corporation. With ISDA clauses in the contracts, Unreliable Corporation is required to deliver the natural gas if it wants to receive the electricity because it can't selectively freeze line items in a contract.

Companies with weaker credit scores will often need to insure their credit quality in order to convince others to trade with them. *Credit default swaps* (CDS) provide insurance against contractual defaults. A credit default swap allows a party with poor credit quality to buy insurance from someone with better credit quality. Essentially, this swaps a high risk counterparty for a low risk counterparty. It is important to note that CDS trades do not completely eliminate credit risk. There is still the possibility that neither the CDS buyer nor the issuer of the CDS will be able to meet their obligations.

Some of the major downsides of OTC agreements are the credit risk, contractual paperwork, and difficulty in initiating and liquidating trades.

Exchanges

Because of the difficulties associated with direct contracts, the number of people that can enter into OTC trades is often very limited. To make the markets more accessible to a wider audience, trading is often done on an exchange. Exchanges act as an intermediary where both sides of a trade agree to a transaction, but instead of transacting with one another, they enter into agreements with the exchange. This eliminates the counterparty risk associated with directly trading with a counterparty and makes it easier to buy and sell contracts.

For example, if a small hedge fund, GetRichNow Partners, wants to purchase financial electricity contracts in the OTC market, it would need to sign an ISDA agreement with all of its potential trading partners before entering into any trades. It would be an overwhelming job to sign agreements with every other small hedge fund on the speculation that someday a trade might occur. This would make it very difficult for the hedge fund to carry on its business of quick trading.

With an exchange, much of that paperwork can be eliminated. Everyone who wants to trade can sign a single agreement with the exchange. This also allows traders to monitor the credit risk of a single counterparty—the exchange—for potential risk exposures. Even better, since exchanges are required to have solid financial backing for their commitments and can protect themselves by requiring that every trader submits a good faith deposit, they are generally a very safe counterparty.

Exchanges make it much easier to enter and exit trades and allow anonymous trading. Entering and exiting a trade doesn't leave any residual credit risk to other people. Additionally, since all trades are made with the exchange, it isn't necessary to know the financial details of other traders or have them know your details. It is even possible to transact anonymously using a broker. The trades will be reported with the broker's ID rather than the trader. Only the broker will know who initiated the trade.

The primary limitation on exchanges is that they can't offer a lot of choices for contracts. To appeal to a large audience, contracts have to be standardized. Typically, there will only be a couple contracts on each commodity. For example, all NYMEX natural gas contracts specify delivery at the Henry Hub just south of Lafayette, Louisiana. This means that while there is a large liquid market for the Henry Hub contract, arranging for delivery in New York City isn't so easy.

In practice, traders tend to use exchange-traded contracts as much as possible. For things they can't do on an exchange, they will then try to arrange OTC trades.

Finally, it is important to note that while the exchange is the counterparty for every transaction, it is just matching up buyers and sellers. The exchange is only taking on the credit risk of each trade and not acting as a principal. The exchange protects itself by requiring traders to deposit good faith deposits called *margin*. As a result, there will always be an equal number of buyers and sellers for each exchange-traded contract. Margin is described later in the chapter.

FINANCIAL CONTRACTS

Cash Trades, Futures, Forwards

The three most common types of energy trades are *cash trades, futures,* and *forwards*. Cash trades are an exchange of a physical commodity for cash in the spot market. Both futures and forwards are contracts to buy an asset at a future date at a prearranged price. Futures are traded on an exchange; forwards are traded in the OTC marketplace. Futures and forwards have different names because of the substantial differences between OTC and exchange-traded markets.

Futures are highly standardized contracts traded on an exchange. They have a limited number of product grades, delivery locations, and delivery times. The commodity must be delivered at the time specified by the exchange, in the location specified by the exchange, and at the quality level (grade) specified by the exchange. The possible permutations of these factors are very limited. Additionally, when futures settle, the counterparty for the delivery will be chosen by a *clearinghouse*. Exchange rules will determine how the buyers and sellers are matched up.

Because every futures transaction is made with the same counterparty (the exchange), futures are freely transferable. It is possible to trade in and out of a position without revising the contract. In comparison, forwards are agreements made directly between two parties. They can be highly customized. However, any modifications to the contract, including closing out the trade, require a revision to the contract. This typically means lawyers negotiate modifications to the original agreement.

Margin

The most important difference between futures and forwards is that futures are margined. *Margin* is a good faith deposit required by the exchange to ensure that traders meet their obligations. Usually, trades will require an initial margin of between 5 percent and 10 percent of the contract's value. The initial margin will usually be large enough to cover any one-day movement in the price of a commodity.

Then there will be daily adjustments to good faith deposit based on the daily change in price of a commodity. Essentially, the daily adjustment will transfer money between traders. Every day, traders on the unprofitable trade will need to deposit more money into their margin accounts. That money will be paid into the accounts of the traders on the profitable side of the trade. Those traders can then remove the money and spend it. The exchange's clearinghouse is responsible for handling all the debits or credits applied to each account.

For example, when a trader buys a futures contract for a 10,000 MMBtus of natural gas for December delivery priced at $6.35, the total value of the contract is $63,500 with an initial margin set by the exchange of $6,750. The trader will have to deposit that initial margin into a *margin account*. When the trader closes his position, he will get that deposit back. The next day, the price of oil falls by $0.15, giving the trader a loss of $1,500. That means the trader will have to deposit an additional $1,500 ($0.15 loss × 10,000 units) into his account. That $1,500 will be transferred into the margin account of some trader holding the other side of the position. The trader will not get the daily margin back when the account is closed. If instead of falling, the market rose $0.25, the trader would have received $2,500.

Every day, futures are assigned a price, called a mark-to-market price, that determines whether the commodity moved up or down. This price is the same for both buyers and sellers and determines whether they need to pay or receive money. Every time the official closing price of an asset changes, there must be a transfer of money. Essentially, the trades are closed and reopened every day.

Because of daily margining, a future contract is characterized by a series of small payments throughout the life of the contract. Every day a little bit of money is transferred between the buyers and sellers of the contract. In contrast, OTC forwards typically don't require money to change hands until the day of delivery. At that point, if the trade is financially settled, forwards will involve a single large transfer of money. If the forward trade is physically settled, it will involve an exchange of money for a physical product.

From the standpoint of an exchange, daily margining limits the exchange's exposure to counterparty risk. Since the mark-to-market price should give a fair indication of where trading occurs, the exchange only needs to cover the risk of holding an asset for a single day. For example, if a trader fails to make a daily margin call, the exchange can take ownership of that futures contract and the initial margin supporting that contract. It will then liquidate the contract and keep the initial margin. As long as the initial margin covers the one day of losses that the exchange is taking on the deal, the exchange will make a profit from the liquidation.

Since the risk taken on by the exchange is proportional to the daily price moves, initial margins will be higher on more volatile commodities. Generally, the initial margin will be slightly larger than the biggest one-day move expected in a commodity. It can also be based on the perceived creditworthiness of traders. Small traders, or those without strong credit, might be asked to submit a larger good faith deposit than large traders, or those with strong credit.

Swaps

Another general category of financial agreements, a *swap*, is any agreement between two parties that obligates them to exchange something in the future. It is a vague term that can be used to describe many different types of financial transactions including futures and forwards.

The most common type of swap is a fixed/float swap. These are often future or forward trades (by a different name) that settle in cash rather than by the more typical delivery of a fixed commodity. In this type of swap one trader agrees to supply a commodity in the future for a price fixed on the day of the trade. The actual value of the commodity won't be known until the day of delivery. For example, a borrower wants to lock in his ability to take out a 20-year mortgage in one year. The borrower and the lender agree that 6 percent is a fair price for the *fixed rate*. Since the actual interest rate for next year isn't known right away, both the borrower and lender are taking on a risk that rates will change. Next year's rate is called the *floating rate*.

When the "price" of a swap is displayed on an exchange, it is the fixed rate that is being described. The fixed rate changes constantly based on where people are making trades. Usually the prices are publicly disseminated so everyone in the market knows the going rate for locking in a future price. A swap is usually a balanced trade when it is entered; both sides of the trade considered it equally good. There is only an exchange of money when the swap expires.

Options

An option is a contract between two people. It gives the buyer of the contract the right, but not the obligation, to buy or sell property at some future date at a fixed price. The right to buy is called a *call option*. The right to sell is called a *put option*. Options have an up-front cost, called a *premium*, which is paid when the buyer purchases the option. For the buyer, options have limited downside risk. Buyers will either lose their premium or they will make a profit.

Options are similar to futures where one party has the right to freely cancel the trade. Options provide a way to ensure a worst-case price of an asset in exchange for an up-front premium. This premium can be very expensive. As a rule of thumb, buying options frequently loses money but occasionally makes a big profit. Selling options gives the opposite payout—a steady stream of small profits interrupted by occasional large losses.

Options are a complex enough topic that we will deal with them at length separately in Chapter 3.4, "Financial Options."

TIME VALUE OF MONEY

Money on hand is almost always worth more than a promise of money in the future. After winning the lottery, given the option of receiving payment of $10 million today or receiving the money 10 years in the future, most people would rather get paid today. Even if both payments were absolutely guaranteed, the ability to invest the money received today makes it a better alternative.

It would be a much tougher decision to choose between taking $10 million today and $25 million in 10 years. The trader would have to compare the size of the later payment against the expected investment return from investing the $10 million. The lottery winner's expected return from his investments is called his *individual rate of return* (IRR).The consensus of every market participant's IRRs is called an *interest rate*.

Interest rates are a measure of the time value of money and quantify the relationship between the *present value* of money (the value of cash received today) and the *future value* of money (the value of cash received sometime in the future). For example, a 10 percent annual interest rate implies that the market consensus is that $100 in cash to-day is equivalent to $110 a year from now. Alternately, at the same interest rate, the present value of $100 a year from now is approximately $91 today.

A separate complication to interest rates is the likelihood of getting paid. As a result, there is a large number of interest rates available. The primary difference between interest rates is who is responsible for paying the money in the future. The more likely the debtor is to meet his obligations, the lower the interest rate. An example of a very low risk investment might be U.S. Treasury bonds. These interest rates determine what the U.S. government pays to borrow money (Fed Funds rate). Another popular benchmark for interest rates is the London Interbank Offered Rate (LIBOR), the rate at which major banks borrow unsecured money from one another.

Regardless of which interest rates are used, they all have several features in common. The first is that the rate varies depending on when the cash is expected. In general, the further off the expected payment, the less valuable it is in today's dollars. This isn't usually a linear process either. For example, the interest rate for receiving payment two years from now is usually not twice the interest rate received for a one year delay. An example of the U.S. Treasury interest rate curve is shown in Figure 1.2.2.

Interest rates, the shape of the interest rate curve, and the relative importance of credit quality, all change over time. A sharply sloping interest rate curve will typically occur when investors want their money immediately. If current investment opportunities are considered especially promising, having money today would allow investors to benefit from those opportunities. As a result, a very steep yield curve generally indicates a very positive outlook for the economy.

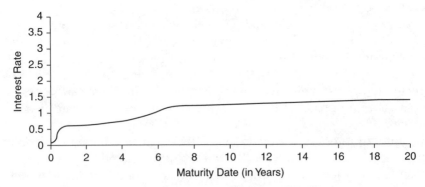

Figure 1.2.2. Example of a relatively normal interest rate curve based on U.S. Treasury bonds

In contrast, a flat yield curve generally indicates a negative outlook on the economy—investors are more willing to wait for their money if they don't have any good investing opportunities.

Normal Yield Curve	Flat Yield Curve
When current investment opportunities look good, yield curves usually have a well-defined upward slope (Figure 1.2.3).	A flat yield curve might indicate a recession or lack of current investment opportunities (Figure 1.2.4).

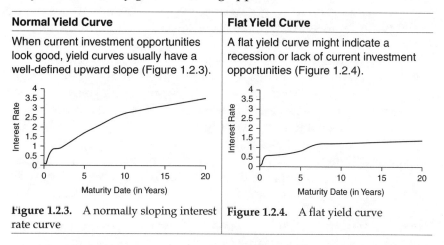

Figure 1.2.3.   A normally sloping interest rate curve

Figure 1.2.4.   A flat yield curve

Likewise, it is possible for every interest rate to move up or down together. When all interest rates move together, it is called a *parallel shift* (Figure 1.2.5). These can occur because of concerns about credit quality or because a government is trying to inject money into or remove money from the economy. This generally indicates a shift in economic conditions.

Because they change over time, interest rates affect the value of cash flows that will be received in the future. For example, at a 10 percent annual interest rate, the present value of $1,000 received in five years is $621. Through the bond markets, it is possible to sell that $1,000 in exchange for cash. However, if interest rates drop to 5 percent, the present

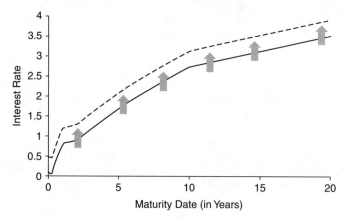

Figure 1.2.5.   Parallel shift in interest rates

value of the $1,000 payment rises to $784.[1] For a trading company that routinely swaps its forward cash flows for money today, or vice versa, a change in interest rates represents an actual gain or loss in cash.

This is important to energy trading since most energy trades occur in the future. Interest rates have a big impact on the profitability of future cash flows. Going back to the previous section, which discussed differences between futures and forwards, consider when these two instruments receive payments. A forward agreement has a single large cash flow that will occur at the end of the contract. In comparison, a futures trade will have small cash flows every day until maturity. The single large payment a long time in the future will be much more affected by interest rates than smaller payments occurring soon.

For small amounts of money, this effect might be small enough to ignore. For larger amounts, this can become a major source of risk. For example, a power company enters into a long-term contract to sell 500 megawatts of power an hour to an industrial facility between the hours of 7 A.M. and 11 P.M., five days a week, for 20 years. This is the output from just one fairly large power plant. If the price for a megawatt of power averages $75, that is a $3.1 billion exposure.

UNIQUE FEATURES OF THE ENERGY MARKET

Negative Prices

The established dogma in most trading markets is that prices can never be zero or negative. This isn't the case in the energy market. While zero or negative prices aren't especially common, they do occur. This can wreak havoc on many financial calculations. For example, in the stock market, a trader might remark that "the market is up 3 percent today." However, for an asset with a negative price, dividing by the previous price will give an undefined or misleading result if prices are zero or negative.[2]

---

[1] A future payment is essentially a bond. Bonds are more valuable when interest rates are low than when interest rates are high. Bond prices and interest rates move in opposite directions. The financial market that trades interest rates is called the Bond Market or the Fixed Income market.

[2] Negative prices break risk management systems. Finding the problems can take a long time and be extremely confusing if no one understands what happens with negative prices. Most people have a hard time grasping that a trading portfolio can be up 10 percent, lose a million dollars, and that the computer program calculating those numbers can be working as intended. In short, negative prices cause problems.

For example, if too much voltage is placed over a power line without any electricity being used, the power lines will melt. To incentivize power producers to decrease their power production, power grid operators sometimes make prices negative. Because of the costs associated with restarting power plants, many power plant operators would rather give power away for free than shut down their operations. Unfortunately, that preference can't be allowed to destroy a transmission grid, which means that sometimes power producers need an extra motivation. The common way to incentivize producers to shut down is to charge them for every megawatt of power they produce. In periods of negative prices, consumers can actually get paid for turning on all their lights.

Cyclical Markets

As mentioned earlier, in markets where commodities are rarely created, are storable, and never get destroyed, forward prices are based on the cost of buying the commodity in the spot market and holding onto it. Particularly if the commodity produces a benefit from being stored, like stocks produce dividends, forward prices will always be higher than spot prices.

In contrast, energy prices are based on an intersection of supply and demand. Storing energy costs money, and the value of storing it decreases the more easily energy can be produced in the future. Combined with the fact that energy is destroyed when it is used, the fundamental relationship between spot and forward prices in the energy market is vastly different than financial markets when a "buy and hold" strategy is viable.

Energy prices tend to be dominated by short-term supply and demand issues. For example, a natural gas refiner might not be able to cost effectively shut down his plant for the weekend and restart on Monday. If the industrial steel plant that uses the natural gas doesn't operate on the weekend, there will be a surplus of gas on the weekends. Unless someone else can use it, or there is enough storage available, the price of natural gas on the weekend will be very low. The refiner will take whatever he can get paid rather than destroy the gas that is being produced. It doesn't matter whether the world will run low on natural gas in 20 years. Today's price is set by today's supply and demand considerations.

As a result, because prices are related to supply and demand, the future prices of many energy products tend to look cyclical.

Buy and Hold Markets	Cyclical Markets
In markets where a buy and hold arbitrage is possible, futures prices tend to slope upward from the spot price, and the spot price incorporates expectations of future price moves (Figure 1.2.6).	In many energy markets, it is not possible to store commodities easily. As a result, forward prices tend to be cyclical. In the natural gas graph, prices are high in the winter and low in the spring, summer, and fall of each year (Figure 1.2.7).
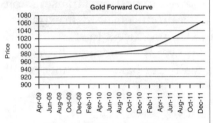	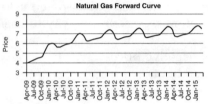
Figure 1.2.6. Steadily ascending forward prices is typical of a buy and hold market	**Figure 1.2.7.** A cyclical, bumpy forward price curve is typical of energy commodities

Illiquidity

In *liquid* markets it is easy for buyers and sellers to meet one another. It is also relatively easy to convert a financial instrument or commodity into cash. As a general rule, it is a mistake to assume that energy markets will be liquid. One reason for illiquidity is the high percentage of contracts that are negotiated directly between two parties. While any exchange-traded contract is usually fairly liquid, directly negotiated OTC contracts are not. As a general rule, any contract that requires a team of lawyers to negotiate a modification to any of the terms can't be considered liquid.

Another reason is the importance of time and location to energy products. If an owner of an industrial facility in Alaska wants to lock in power prices, there are a limited number of parties that can actually deliver power to that location. There are no exchange-traded contracts that settle nearby, so it will be necessary to find someone willing to make an OTC trade. For example, an electrical marketer might trade with the industrial facility for a large enough expected profit. However, if that marketer wanted out of the position, there wouldn't be anyone left to transact with. Other marketers are going to be afraid of making trades with the first marketer—if the trade is so good, why would he want out of it? And it will probably be impossible to unwind the trade with the industrial facility, which is probably happy about being able to lock in their power prices.

Finally, an issue related to liquidity is that energy market participants tend to react as a group. It is not unusual for all of the petroleum refiners or all power plant owners to come to approximately the same conclusions about the direction of the market at the same time. This creates a problem for trading since a liquid trading market requires both buyers and sellers, preferably in equal numbers. If everyone makes the same decision at the same time, there isn't any trading.

Price Transparency

Compounding the problem of illiquid markets is the problem that accurate pricing information commonly does not exist. Unless trades are made on an exchange, energy trades are private contracts between two parties. Neither party is under an obligation to make those prices public. Quite often, energy traders consider pricing information to be competitively sensitive and actively discourage price dissemination.

A number of companies provide estimates of OTC pricing. These estimates are not actual prices, but rather, indicative prices about where trades might be made. The data for these estimates comes from surveys. Historically, traders were often caught providing misleading data on prices in an attempt to influence trading. The Federal Energy Regulatory Commission (FERC), the government agency that regulates energy trading, has since cracked down on the practice. However, if trading hasn't occurred in a region recently, estimating the likely cost of executing a trade can still be extremely difficult. If the trade is initiated by a motivated buyer, the price may be a lot higher than expected. Similarly, if a seller is highly motivated to complete a transaction in a particular region, prices may be a lot lower than previously estimated.

Outright and Spread Trades

An *outright* position in a commodity is a bet that it will go up or down in price. For example, an outright long position in electricity is a bet that electricity prices are going to rise in the future. However, because many energy prices are cyclical, directional bets on energy prices don't generally provide a good opportunity for speculation.

Spread trades are an alternative way of making energy trades. They involve a simultaneous purchase and sale of related products as with buying natural gas and selling electrical power, or agreeing to buy natural gas in Louisiana and sell it in New York. In the first case, buying gas and selling power allows the trader to benefit if the price of electricity rises faster than the price of fuel used for power generation. In the second case, the trader will benefit if the regional price of natural gas in New York—a major consuming region—rises relative to the price of natural gas in a producing region. In both cases the trader is relatively insulated from the actual direction of power prices. This allows the trader to concentrate on the relationship between the two prices rather than the price of energy as a whole.

Compared to other markets, a very high proportion of energy trades are spread trades. The combined volatility of a simultaneous purchase and sale of related commodities is typically much lower than the volatility of an outright position. Since margin costs are proportional to the risk of holding a position, spread trades (trading two instruments simultaneously) can actually be cheaper than owning an outright position. Offsetting trades in one financial instrument with trades in a related financial instrument is called *hedging*. Because of the popularity of spread trading, the most common spreads have specific names, as can be seen in the listing that follows:

Spark spreads are the difference between the price of electricity and the price of natural gas. They approximate the profit that natural-gas-fired power plants make by burning natural gas to produce electricity. Natural gas plants determine the price of electricity in many regions.

Dark spreads are the difference between the price of electricity and the price of coal without considering emissions costs. Coal-based power plants set the price of power in some regions, and dark spreads are commonly used in conjunction with the trading of carbon dioxide emissions. Dark spreads approximate the profit from operating a coal-fired power plant.

Crack spreads are the difference between the price of refined petroleum products (usually gasoline and heating oil) less the price of crude oil. Most commonly, crack spreads are a three-commodity spread. Crack spreads approximate the profitability of a crude oil refinery.

Frac spreads are the difference between the prices of propane and natural gas. Natural gas is the primary raw material used in the production of propane. This spread approximates the profit from converting natural gas into propane.

Basis

Because spread trades are so common in the energy market, terminology related to spread trading has a different meaning than in other financial markets. In any financial market, the term "basis" refers to a spread between two prices. However, in most financial markets, basis refers to the difference in price between the cash price of a commodity (the spot price) and some forward price.

Hedging

Hedging is a financial term that means to reduce risk by taking a position that offsets the risk of an existing position. Hedging is often done when liquidating the original position is impossible or not desired. For example, if a trader has a long position through an OTC transaction, it is difficult to get out of that contract. He might hedge that position by taking the opposite position in an exchange-traded instrument.

In most cases hedging is used to lock in profits or eliminate risk on an untradable position. For example, a natural gas trader might agree to supply natural gas to a power plant in Florida for the next 10 years at a fixed price. Given the length of the contract, the natural gas marketer faces a huge risk from a rise in natural gas prices. The marketer is selling the gas at a fixed price, but still must obtain the gas. If gas prices rise, the marketer could quickly find himself selling natural gas at loss. The marketer doesn't want to get rid of the position, but neither does he want to be exposed to large price moves until he can line up a firm supply of gas. To reduce the risk of rising commodity costs, the trader might decide to hedge that risk with natural gas futures. Since the futures don't deliver the gas to the right place, he can't use them to actually supply the gas. However, since most natural gas delivery locations are highly correlated in the futures market, he can use the futures to protect himself against a rise in natural gas prices.

But since the energy market doesn't have stable relationships between forward prices and spot prices, *basis* does not refer to a time effect. For example, in the energy market, the expected difference between the three-month forward price and the spot price will vary by season. Energy tends to be expensive in the summer and winter. It is inexpensive in the spring and fall. As a result, no one watches the rolling spot/forward relationship closely—it is just as cyclical as the prices.

Common Term

Basis. In the natural gas market, the term "basis" refers to the difference in price between two physical trading locations. There is only one liquid trading location for natural gas in the United States—the Henry Hub (the NYMEX settlement location). Basis swaps allow users to use NYMEX futures and then exchange the Henry Hub price for the price at a different physical location.

Instead, in the energy market, the location of power is important. As a result, in the energy markets, particularly natural gas trading, basis refers to the difference between two locations. Since there is only a single delivery point for futures, the most common use for basis is to describe the difference in price of a specific location from the price at the futures delivery location.

Common Terms

Actual.   A term that refers to a physical commodity. This term differentiates the actual commodity from financial contracts on that commodity. Since most energy trading occurs in the forward market, it is usually necessary to specify when the physical commodity is being traded. For example, "I bought 10,000 barrels of oil actuals; they are sitting on a tanker ship offshore Houston, Texas."

Cash Market.   A market where cash is exchanged for the immediate delivery of a commodity. The terms "physical market," "cash market," and "spot market" are generally synonymous.

Counterparty Credit Risk.   The financial risk due to uncertainty about a trading partner's ability to meet their financial obligations. Credit risk varies with the profitability of trades. As a trade becomes more profitable, the harder it becomes for the other party to meet that obligation. Similarly, there is very little credit risk with an unprofitable contract (you will always have to pay someone, even if your counterparty goes bankrupt).

Credit Default Swap.   A CDS allows a party with poor credit quality to buy "credit insurance." CDS trades swap the credit quality of the credit risk for someone with better credit. CDS trades do not eliminate credit risk—there is still the possibility that the issuer of the CDS will not be able to meet their obligations.

Deregulated Market.   This term refers to elimination of a government-created monopoly in order to introduce competition into a spot market. It most commonly refers to the breakup of government power generation monopolies in order to introduce competitive power markets.

Energy Information Agency.   The EIA is a branch of the U.S. government that produces official energy statistics.

Exchange.   Any organization that maintains a marketplace where securities or commodities are traded. Securities traded on exchanges tend to be highly standardized. Exchanges act as the counterparty for all traders. They require that traders post margin as a good faith deposit.

Federal Energy Regulatory Commission. The FERC is the branch of the U.S. federal government responsible for regulating the interstate trading of energy products.

Financial Market. A market trading for financial products like futures or forwards. Financial markets are different from markets where a physical commodity is exchanged for cash.

Forwards. These are OTC-traded contracts for the delivery of a product at a future date. These contracts are typically not margined and involve no cash flows prior to the delivery date. Most commonly they are direct agreements between two parties and governed by the ISDA master agreement.

Forward Market. A market where the exchange of goods or services is arranged for a later date. Most energy trading is done in the forward market.

Fungible. A common financial term meaning a good or commodity that can be freely substituted for another unit of the *same* commodity. For example, a share of IBM stock is a fungible contract—any share of common stock can be exchanged for any other share of IBM common stock. A megawatt of power is not a fungible quantity—it is impossible to substitute a megawatt of power in New York for a megawatt of power in Los Angeles. However, a megawatt of power in New York Zone A delivered at 11 A.M. on Friday, December 5, 2008, is a fungible commodity.

Futures. Exchange-traded contracts for the delivery of a product at a future date. Typically, these contracts are freely tradable and require that mark-to-market profits and losses be settled every day through margin payments.

Hedge. Offsetting positions that reduce the risk of the combined portfolio. Hedging is the act of making trades that offset the risk of current positions.

ISDA. The International Swap and Derivatives Association is an international trade association consisting of most major institutions that participate in privately negotiated derivatives contracts.

ISDA Agreement. A standard set of clauses included in almost all OTC contracts. Every contract using ISDA clauses refers to the ISDA master agreement maintained by the International Swaps and Derivatives Association. The most important clause in the master agreement is the "netting of positions" provision. This substantially reduces the counterparty risk of privately negotiated derivatives deals.

Liquidity. A financial instrument is liquid if it can be easily exchanged for money or other financial product. A product is illiquid if it cannot be easily exchanged for cash or other financial products.

(Continued)

Long. A trading position where the trader benefits from an increase in the price of the position. Commonly, a long position involves owning an obligation.

Margin. In the energy markets, the *initial margin* on a contract is a good faith deposit of money that needs to be put down to enter into a deal. It is returned after the trade settles. *Daily margin* is a daily cash settlement of the change in price of the contract. The initial margin to enter a trade can vary depending on the trader, but everyone will pay (or receive) the same daily margin settlement depending on what side of the trade they are on.

Mark-to-Market (MTM). The process of assigning a price to a financial instrument or contract based on recent trades in similar instruments or contracts.

Natural Hedge. Positions that have not been taken on for the purpose of reducing risk but still have that effect. For example, a transportation contract to move natural gas from one location to another is naturally hedged against natural gas prices. The owner of the transportation contract is short natural gas at the source (he benefits from buying cheaply) and long natural gas at the destination (he benefits from selling at a high price). The combination of those two positions is a natural hedge against a change in natural gas prices since both the source and destination are likely to move up and down together.

Notional Value. The face value of a contract. The notional value of an agreement to sell 1,000 barrels of oil at $80 is $80,000. The notional value of a contract does not generally change over the life of the contract, and may or may not have any relationship to either the trading profits or risk of a contract.

OTC. The over the counter market is for privately negotiated deals without the use of an exchange as an intermediary. OTC trades involve a high degree of credit risk but can be highly customized to meet specific trading requirements.

Physical Market. A market where cash is exchanged for the immediate delivery of a commodity. Physical market, cash market, and spot market are generally synonymous.

Position. The net amount of goods or services owned by an investor. Positions are described as long when the owner benefits from a rise in prices, and short when the owner benefits from a drop in prices.

Regulated Market.   A term that describes a physical spot market dominated by a government monopoly. Regulated markets are still fairly common in local electrical markets.

Security.   A fungible contract representing some financial value. This is a catchall term describing almost any type of tradable contract, like a future, exchange-traded option. In contrast, OTC contracts are usually not considered securities because they can't be sold or exchanged without modifying the original agreement.

Short.   A trading position is described as short when the trader benefits from a decline in the price of the position. Commonly, a short position involves owing someone an obligation.

Spot Market.   A market where cash is exchanged for the immediate delivery of a commodity. Physical market, cash market, and spot market are generally synonymous.

Trade.   A trade is an exchange of goods or services.

2.1

NATURAL GAS

 30-Second Summary

Purpose

This chapter introduces natural gas trading.

Summary

The natural gas market is one of the largest, most established energy markets. Natural gas is an important fuel for home heating and electricity generation. It is an abundant, clean-burning fuel that exists as a gas at room temperature. Natural gas is a mixture of hydrocarbon gases, the most abundant of which is methane. Because it is a gas, it has to be contained in pressurized storage and distributed through pipelines. Once those pipelines are constructed, the transportation costs of natural gas are small compared to other fuels.

Key Topics

- As a gas, natural gas is difficult to transport and store.
- There is a large infrastructure of pipelines built to transport gas around the North America and European markets. The installed base of consumers linked to these pipelines is a largely captive audience because of the cost to replace this system with other fuels.
- Natural gas prices are often quoted as a spread relative to an index. In North America, that spread is relative to the price at Henry Hub, a major pipeline interconnection on the Gulf Coast.
- Natural gas spot prices are heavily influenced by weather.
- Natural gas futures prices are cyclical.
- Natural gas futures prices are not linked to spot prices and carrying costs in the same way that the future prices for stocks, bonds, and gold are linked to their spot prices.

Natural gas plays a central role in the energy industry. It is cleaner burning than coal and less expensive than petroleum. In the late twentieth century, the low cost of natural gas made it a very popular fuel for household heating. As a result of the infrastructure built during that time, natural gas has cemented its role as a primary residential fuel. In addition, the limited carbon emissions, operational flexibility, and efficiency provided by natural gas make it a popular fuel for power generation. Almost all of the fossil-fuel–based power plants built in the United States since 1990 can burn natural gas. Consequently, there is a strong link between electricity prices and natural gas prices.

Natural gas was once thought of as an extremely cheap alternative fuel, but this is no longer the case. Long gone are the days when natural gas was burned off as an unwanted waste product of oil drilling. Historically, a prolonged period of low natural gas prices in the 1970s and 1980s led to a construction boom in natural gas infrastructure. Increased consumer demand eventually caused an increase in prices, but the infrastructure still remains. For most municipalities, it would be prohibitively expensive to replace this infrastructure to support another fuel. This makes North America highly dependent upon natural gas for both heating and electricity.

From a physical perspective, natural gas is a nonrenewable fossil fuel used to provide heat and generate electricity. It is a combination of colorless, odorless gases found underground. Natural gas is primarily composed of methane (CH_4) but often contains substantial amounts of other hydrocarbons, like ethane (C_2H_6), propane (C_3H_8), and butane (C_4H_{10}). Natural gas is considered "dry" when it is almost pure methane, and "wet" when it contains substantial quantities of the other hydrocarbons. It is also common to find it mixed with other nonhydrocarbon gases like nitrogen and carbon dioxide. Because the composition of natural gas varies so widely, it is commonly traded in units of heat energy like British Thermal Units (Btus) or Joules, rather than in units of volume (like cubic feet). It is important to know the relationship between energy content and volume for dry gas.

- There are approximately 1,000 Btus per cubic foot of dry natural gas.
- There are approximately 1 million MMBtus (million Btus) in 1 Bcf (billion cubic feet) of natural gas.
- For consumers, natural gas is typically sold in *therms*. A therm is 100,000 Btus, or one-tenth of an MMBtu.

Natural gas is most commonly transported through pipelines. Some of these pipelines are transcontinental in length, while others span a single town. Transcontinental pipelines move natural gas from producing regions to consuming regions. Local pipelines deliver gas to consumers in a limited geographical area. Pipelines are used because the primary component of natural gas, methane, contains a relatively low amount of energy per volume. Longer chain hydrocarbons like propane or butane contain enough heat energy to make it practical to transport them in pressurized metal containers. However, since methane requires a much larger storage container to hold the same amount of heat energy, and since it is impractical to use very large pressurized containers, natural gas is instead transported by pipeline.

Natural gas can also be transported in liquid form. To turn natural gas into a liquid, it must be supercooled to −260°F. This process is called *liquefaction*. However, since most consumers lack the specialized equipment to handle supercold liquid gas, natural gas is almost always returned to gaseous form before it is delivered to customers through the local distribution pipelines. The biggest advantage of liquefaction is that liquids are much denser than gases. Because of this, they will contain substantially more heat energy per unit of volume. Transporting natural gas as a liquid avoids the logistical problem of keeping the gas stored in an extremely large high-pressure container for an extended period. Liquefied natural gas is used primarily for long-distance transportation of natural gas over oceans, where building a pipeline is impractical. Sometimes it is also used for storage. (Liquefied natural gas is discussed more detail in Chapter 5.3.)

Comparing Gasoline to Natural Gas

One gallon of gasoline contains 124,000 Btu, and takes up about 0.13 cubic feet of space. For the same amount of energy, 100 cubic feet of storage would be required to store natural gas at the atmospheric pressure. It is possible to compress natural gas to higher pressures. For example, a typical air tank used for scuba diving stores air at 200 to 300 times atmospheric pressure. However, at 250 times atmospheric pressure, natural gas requires three times the storage space of gasoline, as well as a very heavy pressurized cylinder. As supercooled liquid, natural gas contains about two-thirds the energy stored in the same volume of gasoline.

Major Market Participants

There are a wide range of businesses associated with extracting natural gas from the ground and delivering it to customers. Exploration companies search for natural gas reserves underground. Drilling companies extract the natural gas from the ground and transport it to a processing facility. At the processing plant, impurities are removed from the raw natural gas as it is separated into its component hydrocarbon gases. Then the dry natural gas (methane) needs to be transported to customers. Natural gas is transported by interstate pipelines or tanker ship. After it arrives in the consuming region, it must be stored until a consumer is ready to take delivery. Finally, when customers turn on their gas, it needs to be delivered by a natural gas distribution pipeline.

Most of the companies on the physical side of the natural gas business specialize in one or two of these areas. Each area of natural gas production is relatively complicated, and it is hard to be equally good at every job. Moreover, the skills necessary for running physical businesses are very different than the skills used for speculating on financial commodities. The job of trading natural gas is left to natural gas marketers.

Marketers who buy and sell natural gas are speculators and investors who want exposure to the trading markets. Often these are Wall Street firms or spin-offs from integrated energy companies. Occasionally they are branches of a service company. Trading does not show the steadily increasing, safe profits desired by the stockholders of a service-based organization. Because of this, many natural gas service companies no longer maintain large trading desks. They don't want to run the risk that an otherwise strong company will be destroyed by a couple of bad trades.

There are no hard rules preventing the physical businesses from being gas marketers. Many marketers started out associated with a physical company, and most physical companies still maintain a trading desk after they leave the marketing business. For example, physical companies often need to execute trades to eliminate the price risk of holding raw materials. Even the most conservative firms will occasionally make some speculative trades. Because of their expertise in a specific area, a specialist company can often recognize investment opportunities before other market participants. However, as a general rule the goal of most physical natural gas companies is to make their profits in a hard-to-enter market niche and leave the speculation to other people.

A lot of specialized knowledge is required to be a gas marketer. Marketers handle much of the paperwork that ties the various parts of the energy industry together. In the natural gas world, they do this by arranging for storage and transportation of natural gas. They have to handle the relationships, legal agreements, and processing necessary for trading with a variety of different businesses in multiple markets. Typically, this requires extensive operations and legal teams. Marketers also need to have contractual agreements with everyone they trade with and to continually monitor their creditworthiness. Because having a large number of industry contacts is a business necessity for marketers, they tend to have a wider focus than the physical companies— they typically trade a wide variety of commodities like electricity, coal, oil, and emissions credits.

The Physical Natural Gas Business

- **Exploration.** Companies actively involved in the search for new sources of natural gas.
- **Drilling.** Companies focused on extracting natural gas from underground reservoirs and moving the gas to processing plants.
- **Processing.** Companies focused on converting raw natural gas into a standardized commodity—nearly pure methane gas is called "dry natural gas."
- **Interstate Pipeline Transportation.** Companies focused on maintaining interstate pipelines connecting producing areas (or LNG shipping terminals) to consuming regions.
- **LNG Transportation.** Companies focused on transporting natural gas across oceans in tanker ships. Usually, the natural gas is cooled to −260°F and turned into a liquid. LNG is an abbreviation for *liquefied natural gas*.
- **Storage.** Companies focused on maintaining large underground facilities to store natural gas.
- **Distribution.** Companies focused on taking natural gas from a transportation company or storage facility and delivering it to consumers.

Exploration and Extraction

Natural gas is commonly found dissolved in oil fields, coal beds, and underground rock formations. It is produced from decaying organic materials located in areas where the gases can't disperse. In nature, this commonly happens when organic material is caught between layers of impermeable rock. In nature, natural gas deposits can be millions of years old. However, natural gas can also be created by decomposing organic materials like the plants and animal wastes found in modern garbage dumps.

In nature, when organic material decomposes, methane is a common by-product. Most of the time this methane disperses into the atmosphere. However, when an impermeable material prevents the gas from dispersing, it can become trapped underground and later extracted. Most commonly, when gas is trapped underground it is not located in a large open cave. Instead, gas is forced into small holes in the rock, and disperses in the rock layer surrounding the decaying material (Figure 2.1.1).

If the rock layer trapping the methane has the right physical properties, it is possible to remove the gas by drilling through the impermeable layer of rock. Typically, exploration companies look for a permeable layer of rock located underneath an impermeable layer of rock (Figure 2.1.2).

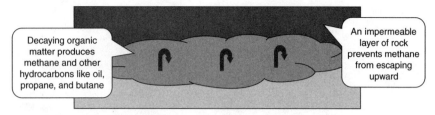

Figure 2.1.1. Decaying material is sometimes covered by an impermeable layer of rock, which prevents the methane from escaping upward and dispersing

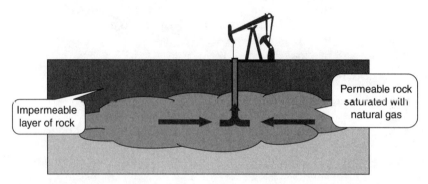

Figure 2.1.2. To extract natural gas from where it is trapped, the methane has to be able to flow toward the well

Porous, permeable rock is the best type of rock for storing natural gas. It has lots of small, connected holes that allow a substantial amount of gas to be removed. The pores are the small holes in the rock. Rock formations must contain enough storage space to have an economically significant amount of gas in one area. Also, the pores in the rock must be connected to each other. Otherwise, the gas can't flow between the holes, and only the gas near the exit pipe will be removed. The physical characteristics of the rock forming a gas reservoir have a direct impact on the speed with which natural gas can be recovered from the ground.

In addition, the performance of natural gas wells is determined by the pressure of the gas in the well. Gases move from areas of high pressure to areas of low pressure. In conjunction with the natural tendency of a gas to rise, placing a vacuum at the mouth of a reservoir will pull the gas upward. The speed of this upward movement depends on the pressure of the gas in the reservoir. When it is first removed, the gas is at its highest pressure and will move quickly up. As gas exits the reservoir, the pressure will decrease, and it will exit more slowly. Eventually, there will no longer be an economically significant amount of gas leaving the reservoir and the well will be closed. This process can be sped up by injecting water into the well. Since methane doesn't dissolve in water, this will increase the pressure on any remaining gas.

Porosity and Permeability

In the energy industry, rock is typically defined by its porosity and its permeability. The performance of natural gas wells and storage facilities is closely related to their geology (Figure 2.1.3).

Porosity

In layman's terms, porosity refers to the number of holes in a rock. Usually, this is given as a ratio of empty space in a rock as a percentage of its total volume. Most rock will have some holes, but the size, variety, and type can vary widely between different types of rock.

Permeability

Permeability refers to the amount of interconnection between pores. Usually, this is measured by how easily a liquid can pass through a porous structure. It is possible for a porous material to be impermeable. For example, foam coffee cups have a high porosity (making them good insulators since the air trapped in the pores is a poor conductor of heat) and low permeability (which prevents liquids from leaking through).

A permeable rock   A porous, permeable rock   A porous, impermeable rock

Figure 2.1.3.   Graphics illustrating the different types of rock formations

Processing

Because natural gas is not pure methane when it comes out of the ground, it is necessary to bring it up to a consistent quality standard. All of the particulate matter and liquid water in the gas have to be removed to prevent damage to pipelines and consumer equipment. Trace pollutants like hydrogen sulfide and mercury have to be removed. The gas needs to meet a standard for energy per unit volume. For example, in North America the heat energy of natural gas sold to consumers needs to be in the range of 1,035 Btu ± 5 percent per cubic foot at standard temperature and pressure.

Larger hydrocarbons, like propane and butane, turn into liquids at a warmer temperature than smaller hydrocarbons, like methane. As a result, they need to be removed from the natural gas to prevent liquid from building up in a pipeline. Engineers utilize the different dew points of hydrocarbons to separate combined gases. The primary way of separating a combined gas into individual gases is to progressively cool the combined gas until it reaches a temperature where the larger-chain molecules turn into liquids. At that temperature, the smaller molecules remain a gas, and the liquids can be siphoned off to leave only the simpler hydrocarbon gases. This process can be repeated a number of times to remove multiple hydrocarbons.

Pipeline Transportation

Natural gas is most commonly transported through pipelines. As mentioned before, the main problem with transporting natural gas is its low energy density. Methane is the simplest hydrocarbon gas and contains less energy per volume than more complex hydrocarbon gases like propane or butane. Pipelines avoid this problem by providing a continuous feed of gas to customers and operating at moderate pressures.

Interstate pipelines make a profit transporting natural gas for customers. These companies straddle the line between public utilities and for-profit businesses. Pipeline services range from guaranteed delivery of gas—the most expensive option—to various degrees of nonguaranteed service. Customers pay different rates depending on their desired level of service. Because pipelines serve an important role as a public utility, the interstate pipeline business is highly regulated and overseen by the *Federal Energy Regulatory Commission* (FERC). Some of the regulations include limits on new construction, limits on the rates that can be charged, and rules to ensure nondiscriminatory access.

Pipelines are often connected to one another. A natural gas *hub* is the location where two or more pipelines connect. A *citygate* is a special type of hub where interstate pipelines connect to local distribution networks. Most natural gas trading occurs at either hubs or citygates. The most important natural gas hub in North America, Henry Hub, is located on the U.S. Gulf Coast about halfway between New Orleans and Houston (Figure 2.1.4). Henry Hub is the delivery location for the NYMEX natural gas futures contract and is used as the benchmark for natural gas sold throughout the United States. The Henry Hub price plays a major role in the energy market—similar to the role played by

U.S. Natural Gas Pipeline Network, 2008

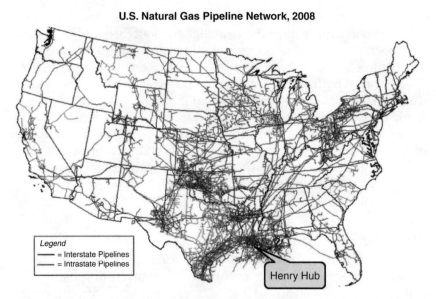

Legend
—— = Interstate Pipelines
—— = Intrastate Pipelines

Henry Hub

Figure 2.1.4.   In addition to connecting 13 major natural gas pipelines, the Henry Hub is the trading location for NYMEX natural gas futures
(*Source:* Energy Information Agency [October 2008])

the S&P 500 index for U.S. stocks. But unlike those other indexes, the benchmark for natural gas is not an average—it is actually the price of gas at a single location.

Henry Hub Futures Contract

The natural gas futures contract traded on the NYMEX (New York Mercantile Exchange) is the most important natural gas contract in North America. The underlying commodity for this contract is natural gas delivered at the Henry Hub, which is located near the Louisiana Gulf Coast at the interconnection of 13 pipelines. Most natural gas forward prices—and most electricity ones too—are heavily based on this contract.

Basis Prices

The terminology for natural gas trading is different than other financial markets. When natural gas prices are quoted by a trader, the quote is usually in relation to the Henry Hub price. This is called a *basis price*.

For example, if the price at Henry Hub is $8.52 and the price for physical gas at Waha Hub (a trading location in West Texas) is $8.70, the basis price for Waha Gas would be $0.18. The term "price" can refer to either the basis price or the actual price, depending on the context. If you asked for the price of gas from a natural gas trader, they would probably assume that you mean the basis price, and quote $0.18. If you asked a utility operator the price of gas, they would assume that you mean the actual price of $8.70. Regardless of the way the price is quoted, the cost to the consumer is the same.

This pricing terminology is a result of how natural gas is traded. Most commonly, natural gas is traded using futures that are priced at the Henry Hub price. The basis price quoted by traders is similar to a transportation price to get gas from the Henry Hub to another area. The *index price* of natural gas is the price at the Henry Hub. The actual price of natural gas, the *all-in price,* is the combination of the index price and the basis price.

Common Terms

Actual.   An adjective that refers to the actual physical commodity that is delivered at the completion of a contract. It can also be used as a noun, for example, "I traded natural gas actuals at Chicago City Gate."

All-in Price.   The price of physical natural gas at a specific location.

Basis Price.   The spread between the actual price and the index price at a specific location.

Index Price.   In the United States, the price at the Henry Hub is the primary index for natural gas prices.

Basis Positions

An *actual position* means being exposed to the outright price of gas in some location. For example, a trader who owns the gas physically located somewhere is exposed to the actual price. Sometimes, this is called an *all-in position.*

A *basis position* means an exposure to a basis price rather than an outright price. Since the basis price is a spread, a basis position is an exposure to two locations—the basis location and the index location. For example, the Waha basis price is the difference between the actual price at Waha Hub minus the index price. Similarly, a long basis position at Waha Hub is similar to being long gas physically located at Waha Hub and short gas physically located at the Henry Hub (the index location).

Basis Trading

To trade natural gas, traders usually enter into two trades: a futures trade at the Henry Hub and a basis swap that exchanges the Henry Hub exposure for an exposure at some other location. The market is structured this way to help traders find trading partners. Natural gas futures (the Henry Hub contracts) are standardized contracts available over an exchange. These contracts eliminate concerns with counterparty credit risk and allow trades to be netted together. Traders get the bulk of their trading done quickly at the Henry Hub, and finish off trading when a suitable counterparty is found at a specific location. Trading at the Henry Hub is very liquid—large volumes can be executed quickly with minimal transaction costs. In general, it is much harder to find counterparties to trade at other locations.

How a Pipeline Operates

It is very expensive to build new pipelines, and the infrastructure required to keep a pipeline operating is extremely elaborate. Predicting how gas will disperse through an extended system of pipes is a complicated job. Some important concepts of pipelines are introduced in this section and discussed in greater detail in Chapter 5.1, "Natural Gas Transportation."

Storage

The operational requirements of pipelines make storing natural gas necessary. Pipelines can't stop operating. For a pipeline to operate, gas has to be continuously added to one end and removed from the other. Interstate pipelines can be thousands of miles long, and if stopped, might take several days to resume operating at full capacity. As a result, it is impossible for most pipelines to shut down completely. Consumer demand is less constant—consumers don't need a steady supply of natural gas around the clock. Thus, it is often necessary to store natural gas at both ends of a pipeline. This provides a cushion to balance the required continuous flow of the pipeline with refinery outputs and variable consumer demand. Natural gas is stored at the start of a pipeline to prevent interruptions at gas refineries from disrupting the pipeline. Gas is stored at the end of a pipeline to help match up the continually flowing pipeline to consumer demand.

Simple Pipeline	More Complicated Pipeline
In general, gases flow from areas of high pressure to areas of low pressure until the pressure in the two areas equalize. A simple pipeline is very similar to a straw connecting two areas. The gas in the high pressure area flows straight through to the low pressure area (Figure 2.1.5).	It is much more difficult to keep a branching pipeline working predictably. For example, in a branching pipeline, the gas flow will depend on the relative pressure between each of the four ends. Unless all four end points are kept precisely balanced, the pipeline could easily route gas to the wrong location (Figure 2.1.6).

Figure 2.1.5.   Gas moves from high to low pressure

As the gas moves from high to low pressure, the high pressure will fall, and the low pressure will rise. To keep a pipeline operating, it is necessary to continually add gas to the high pressure area and continually remove gas at the low pressure area. Otherwise, the pressure in the pipeline will equalize and the gas will stop moving.

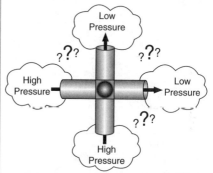

Figure 2.1.6.   When a pipeline has multiple connections, it is much harder to predict where the gas will move

As mentioned earlier, in gaseous form natural gas isn't very energy dense—it takes a large reservoir to store a significant quantity of heating energy. In general it isn't practical to build a large enough storage container aboveground. As a result, in gaseous form, natural gas is typically stored in underground reservoirs. If it is stored aboveground, it is usually liquefied and stored in an insulated container rather than as a pressurized gas.

There are a limited number of sites around North America that can be used to store natural gas (Figure 2.1.7). Natural gas storage requires large reservoirs located in the right area. Storage reservoirs are most commonly located close to refineries, at hubs that connect major pipelines, or close to where the gas will ultimately be used. Another consideration is that the size of the reservoir needs to be large enough to make it cost effective to hook it up to a pipeline. Pipelines get harder to coordinate when they have lots of connections. Additionally, much of the cost of storing natural gas is a consequence of the necessary equipment to pump gas into the storage facility. This same equipment is required for both large and small facilities, and small

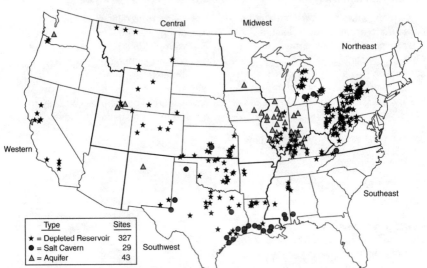

Figure 2.1.7. Map showing the locations of underground natural gas storage facilities (*Source:* Energy Information Agency [October 2008])

facilities lack the volume for a reasonable economy of scale. This is the reason why there are only about 400 natural gas storage facilities around the country.

Distribution

Most customers don't receive gas directly from the interstate pipelines. Typically, gas is delivered to consumers by a local distribution company. These companies maintain an extensive network of small pipes throughout each regional distribution area. Such local delivery networks are substantially different from the interstate pipelines. Local distribution networks have to maintain connections to every home and business regardless of the economic profitability of each connection.

As a result, local distribution networks are very expensive to maintain. Local delivery charges account for a large portion of the retail price of natural gas. On utility bills, the cost that most customers pay for their natural gas will be a combination of the citygate price (the price of the gas delivered to the local utility from an interstate pipeline) and a local delivery charge. Commonly, local delivery charges make up about half the total retail cost of natural gas.

Trading and Marketing

There are several common types of natural gas trades. The simplest possible type is a directional bet on the entire natural gas market. For example, that the market is going to go up or down in price. However, since natural gas prices are cyclical, it is more common for traders to try to speculate on one aspect of the natural gas market by entering into spread trades.

A *spread trade* is any trade where a trader benefits from the price difference between two securities by buying one security and selling another. These trades are popular because they eliminate a trader's exposure to the entire market moving up and down. What follow are some examples.

- **Location Spreads.** These speculate on the price difference between two locations. Depending on demand, natural gas prices can be substantially different between two different locations. Natural gas transportation is not instantaneous, and storage is often limited. In periods of peak demand, some areas will have a greater demand for gas than can be supplied through the pipeline or storage facilities. The price of gas in those regions will rise until more supply can be brought in. In other cases, a period of moderate weather might decrease demand, creating a supply glut and causing prices to plummet. An example of a location spread trade can be found in Chapter 5.1, "Natural Gas Transportation."

- **Heat Rates.** These trades speculate on the relationship between natural gas prices and electricity prices. In general, the price of electricity closely mirrors natural gas prices. Using a power plant, it is possible to turn natural gas into electricity. This keeps natural gas and electrical prices linked together most of the time. However, since two very different mechanisms are used to determine the prices of power and natural gas, they don't move together all of the time and it is possible for a trader to benefit from that volatility. These trades are described in more detail in Chapter 4.3, "Tolling Agreements."

- **Time Spreads.** These speculate on the price difference between periods of high and low demand. For example, it might be possible to speculate on a colder than normal winter by betting that gas prices will be high. The trader might buy winter gas and sell spring gas to eliminate directional exposure to the entire market. Examples of calendar spreads can be found in Chapter 5.2, "Natural Gas Storage."

- **Swing Trades.** These spread trades rely on the physical ability of the trader to store natural gas over short periods. Pipelines must operate around the clock. However, demand for gas varies considerably even over short time periods like a week. For example, a lot of gas is used on Monday mornings to restart industrial facilities and reheat offices after the weekend. Comparatively less gas is used late at night on Saturday because there is no industrial demand and houses are less heated after people are asleep. As a result, it is often possible to pick up inexpensive natural gas when demand is low and resell it when demand is high. This requires the ability to store the natural gas. These trades are discussed in Chapter 5.2, "Natural Gas Storage."

Spot and Forward Markets

Like many other energy products, the forward and spot markets for natural gas are distinct from one another. Spot markets involve buying gas for immediate delivery. Forward markets involve buying gas for delivery sometime in the future. These markets are separate because gas production, transportation, and storage have to be arranged ahead of time.

If there is a shortage in natural gas expected in a couple of weeks, it is usually possible to increase production and bring in more supply. However, if there were a shortage today, there is no real way to get more supply immediately. It is difficult to move a large quantity of gas into or out of storage quickly or transfer in supplies from nearby areas on short notice. In the forward markets, prices are determined by macroeconomic issues—the expected average relationship of supply and demand in the future. In the spot market, prices are based on the supply that is on hand *right now* and consumer demand *right now*. As a result, the spot markets are substantially more volatile than the forward markets.

In markets where spot and forward commodity markets are linked, usually there is a constant amount of the commodity, and it isn't consumed when it is used. The spot and forward markets for those products are linked by the ability to buy the commodity in the spot market and store it for future delivery. Since the commodity is never used up (like a gold bar or a stock certificate), those assets aren't affected by short-term fluctuations in supply. Natural gas does not work the same way. A continuous supply of new natural gas is constantly required, consumer demand changes constantly, and it is difficult to store and transport.

Long-term buy-and-hold strategies are of limited use in natural gas trading. Gas has no intrinsic value by itself—it is the products created by burning natural gas that are valuable (heat or electricity). Moreover, gas in storage is no easier to deliver than gas newly extracted from the ground, unless the storage is located near a consuming area. In fact, the most common storage facilities are actually previously emptied gas wells. As a result, buy-and-hold strategies are essentially the purchase of undeveloped gas reserves. Traders use storage facilities to balance supply and demand for periods less than a year. For example, traders might buy gas in the summer to sell during the next winter, but they aren't going to buy gas and hold it for several years as a long-term investment.

That doesn't mean there isn't a spot/forward relationship in forward natural gas prices. However, this relationship is more complicated and less reliable than in other markets.

Forward Prices

Looking at the forward market, prices are determined by seasonal expectations of supply and demand rather than on the current spot price and storage costs. Seasonal expectations of supply and demand are generally the same every year. Consequently, prices in the forward market tend to mirror consumer demand—both are high in the winter and fall dramatically in the spring of every year (Figure 2.1.8).

Forward prices follow a very regular pattern. Compared to other markets where forward prices are determined by interest rates and storage costs, this is a very different relationship.

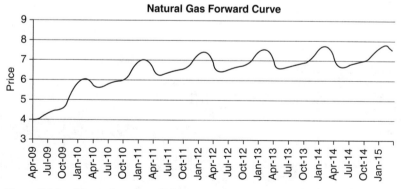

Figure 2.1.8. Natural gas forward prices are highly cyclical, without the smooth upward slope in prices of storable commodities

Price Certainty

The price of natural gas becomes less certain close to delivery rather than further away, unlike most other markets. This is because short-term disruptions to natural gas supplies have a big effect on prices. However, unless prices change for a lasting fundamental reason, large price movements in the spot market do not have a large effect on future prices. Forward prices tend to revert to prices based on typical consumer demand and expected supplies. This can be seen in the graph in Figure 2.1.9. Prices are more volatile in the spot price than in the forward markets.

Spot Prices

Spot prices do not show the same seasonality as future prices. While forward prices have a regular, seasonal trend, spot prices are all over the place. This is because they are based on short-term supply and demand issues. Looking at spot prices, they are very different from the highly predictable prices in the forward market (Figure 2.1.10).

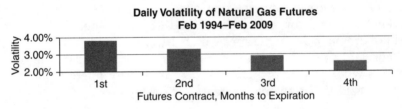

Figure 2.1.9. Natural gas prices become more volatile as the time for delivery approaches

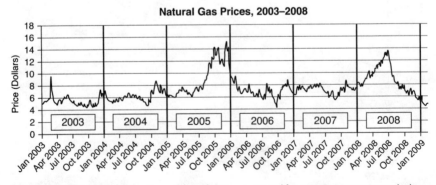

Figure 2.1.10. Historical prices of first future contract (the next contract to expire)

Part of the reason for this difference is the complexity of storing or transporting natural gas on short notice. Natural gas in one location can't just be exchanged for natural gas in a different location—it has to be physically moved there. If there isn't enough time to arrange the transportation, there is no longer any linkage between the source and destination locations. Natural gas that needs to be delivered at a specific time has a similar issue. Natural gas requires specialized facilities to store it. If someone doesn't have access to a storage facility—and most market participants do not—they can't buy the commodity early for delivery at a later date. The typical natural gas customer is forced to buy natural gas either in the forward market or on the spot market on the day the gas will be used. They can't buy a supply of gas when it is cheap on the spot market and store it until it is needed.

There are two major effects as a result. First, spot volatility is much higher than forward volatility. This effect was illustrated in the discussion of future prices. Second, the spot correlation between two different locations works differently than forward correlations. In the forward market, when it is still possible to arrange gas to be moved from one location to another, most natural gas prices are highly correlated. If they weren't very similar, it would be possible to shift gas between locations for an easy profit. The only constraints to this trade would be the cost of transporting and storing the natural gas.

In the spot market, none of that is possible. Just as more supply is prevented from coming in, demand is prevented from leaving. There is no way for consumers to shift demand from one area to another easily. For example, it isn't possible for most homeowners to move to another state for a week if the prices are better there.

Prices, Supply, and Demand

When very long time frames are considered, the assumption that natural gas prices are a function of supply and demand is misleading. For exploration and development purposes, the supply of natural gas depends on its price. Higher natural gas prices make the extraction of natural gas from difficult-to-reach reserves more economical. It also makes exploration a better investment. In other words, in the long run supply depends on prices and demand rather than the other way around.

As a result, predictions about future prices are mostly a function of expected demand for natural gas. Exploration companies maintain predictions on what it will cost to deliver that supply, and factor in a set profit. Higher demand leads to higher prices, and those higher prices make it economical to open up new supplies of natural gas.

Demand and Weather

On a national basis, the single largest factor affecting demand for natural gas is temperature. During the winter, natural gas is used for heating. In the summer, natural gas is used to fuel electrical generators that are used to supply electricity for air-conditioning. The demand for natural gas is lowest in the spring and fall and peaks in the coldest winter months. A graph showing natural gas consumption is shown below in Figure 2.1.11.

Predicting the demand for natural gas is very much an exercise in predicting warm and cold weather. There is a linear relationship between cold temperatures and an increased consumption of natural gas. The relationship between prices and temperatures can be seen in the chart.

Users of Natural Gas

The three largest users of natural gas are industrial clients, residential clients, and power plants. Of the three, the use of natural gas in power plants to produce electricity has risen the most quickly. Most of the power plants built since 1990 depend on natural-gas-fired generators.

- **Industrial.** Natural gas in commonly used as a source of heat by industrial clients. It ignites quickly, and turning off a natural gas furnace doesn't waste any fuel. A natural gas furnace goes out as soon as the supply of fuel is stopped. In comparison, a coal furnace will continue to burn until the coal in the furnace is fully used. If it's necessary to start and restart a coal furnace multiple times, a lot of fuel can be wasted. Manufacturing of metal or glass, cooking, dehumidification, and waste incineration are all examples of industrial uses of natural gas.

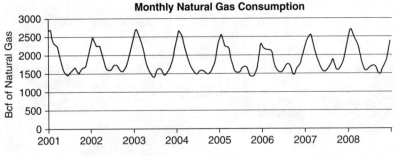

Figure 2.1.11.   Monthly natural gas consumption measured in billions of cubic feet

- **Residential.** About half the homes in North America use natural gas for heating. The largest residential use of natural gas is home heating (primarily in the winter). There are a variety of other residential uses, since it is common for natural-gas-fueled homes to have several natural gas appliances. Kitchen ranges, hot water heaters, clothes dryers, and outdoor grills are all commonly found.
- **Electrical Generation.** Power plants are the fastest growing users of natural gas since natural-gas-powered plants produce less greenhouse gas emissions than coal or oil-based plants. Some natural gas power plants operate year round, others are more seasonal. The seasonal plants usually turn off in the winter, when the price of natural gas is usually at its peak.

The Burner Tip

End users of natural gas are often called the *burner tip*. At one time gas appliances were fitted with special dispersing heads to make natural gas suitable for lighting, cooking, and heating; hence the nickname. Most modern appliances no longer use burner tips, but the name has stuck for any location where natural gas is ignited to create a flame.

Common Terms

All-in Price.   The price of natural gas at a specific location. The all-in price is equal to the price at the benchmark location plus the basis price.

Basis Price.   The difference in price between a specific location and the price at the benchmark location. In the United States, this is the difference between the price at a specific location and the Henry Hub. Basis costs are a function of transportation costs and storage capability between two areas.

Dry Natural Gas.   Natural gas that is almost pure methane.

Wet Natural Gas.   Natural gas that contains substantial amounts of hydrocarbons other than methane, or natural gas that contains substantial impurities.

Citygate.   The location at which the municipal distribution system takes possession of natural gas for distribution to retail customers.

Hub.   An interconnection between two or more natural gas pipelines.

Western Gas Markets

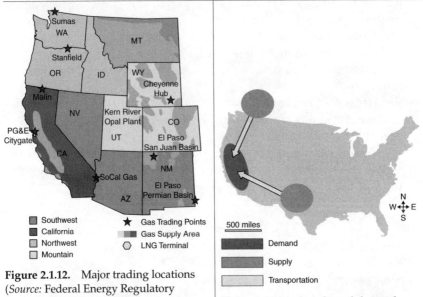

Figure 2.1.12. Major trading locations (*Source:* Federal Energy Regulatory Commission [March 2009])

Figure 2.1.13. Supply and demand

- Electrical generators throughout this entire region depend on natural gas as a primary fuel. The summers are very hot, and natural gas is especially in demand then to provide electricity for air-conditioning. The major competing power source is hydroelectric power from the Pacific Northwest. As a result, precipitation and snowmelt can have a large effect on regional natural gas prices during peak demand periods. Most of the region has mild winters.

- In the western United States, the geography is dominated by the Rocky Mountains. The West Coast (Washington, Oregon, California) and parts of Arizona are heavily populated. However, most of the region has a sparse population. California is the biggest user of natural gas, and trading commonly revolves around imports to the California market. These imports come from Canada and the Desert Southwest.

- Storage capacity is extremely limited. This can lead to sharp price movements during periods of peak demand.

- Western basis prices are not highly correlated with NYMEX futures (Henry Hub) since the region does not directly import natural gas from the Gulf Coast, where Henry Hub is located.

- A substantial amount of gas is produced at the eastern edge of the Rocky Mountains in Wyoming, Utah, and Colorado. However, most of this gas flows to the Midwest rather than to the population centers on the West Coast.

Midwestern Gas Markets

Figure 2.1.14.   Major trading locations (*Source. Federal Energy Regulatory Commission* [March 2009])

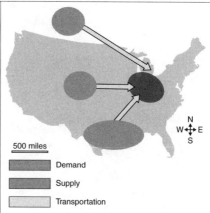

Figure 2.1.15.   Supply and demand

- The Midwest is a major consuming region during winter months. Cold winters characterize the entire Midwest region and there is a strong seasonal demand for natural gas in the winter to provide residential heating.

- This region does not use natural gas as a primary fuel for electrical power plants. Coal is the primary fuel for power in the Midwest. There is comparatively little demand for natural gas in the summer months.

- Numerous storage facilities and extensive local distribution networks are located in the region. Many of these areas have government mandated obligations to meet residential demand during winter months. For example, to ensure that consumers have access to fuel, governments might force gas in storage facilities to be delivered to residential customers rather than saving it for a commercial use.

- Large pipelines connect the Midwest to all of the major supply basins in North America. Canada and the Rocky Mountains supply the bulk of the Midwest's natural gas requirements. However, some gas also comes from the Gulf Coast region when it is available.

- Basis prices in the Midwest are somewhat correlated with NYMEX futures (Henry Hub). The region imports gas from the Gulf Coast, but also has access to other gas supplies.

Eastern Gas Region

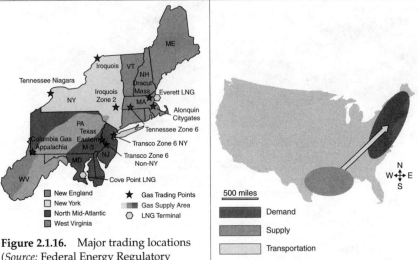

Figure 2.1.16. Major trading locations
(*Source:* Federal Energy Regulatory
Commission [March 2009])

Figure 2.1.17. Supply and demand

- On the East Coast, natural gas is used extensively for both residential heating and electrical generation. As a result, there is a year-round demand for natural gas in this region.

- There is a limited amount of storage available in the region. Combined with the high seasonal demand for both heating and electricity in the winter, basis prices (prices relative to the supply regions) are often the highest in country.

- LNG (liquefied natural gas) terminals are being built to import gas from other countries and provide additional storage.

- The East Coast is a heavy importer of natural gas from the Gulf Coast region. As a result, basis prices are highly correlated with NYMEX futures (Henry Hub).

Texas and Gulf Coast Region

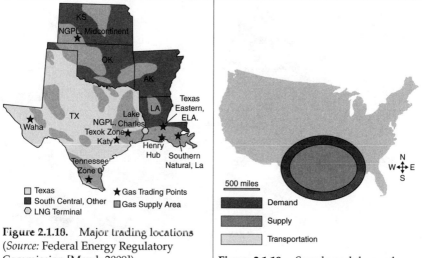

Figure 2.1.18. Major trading locations (*Source:* Federal Energy Regulatory Commission [March 2009])

Figure 2.1.19. Supply and demand

- The Texas/Gulf Coast region is a net exporter of natural gas. It is the most important natural gas producing region in North America. Most of the exports flow to the East Coast and the industrialized Midwest.

- Abundant local supplies have made the region heavily dependent upon natural gas as a fuel for electricity generation.

- The region has mild winters, and there is a limited seasonal demand for natural gas during winter months for heating.

- There is a substantial amount of storage in the region. This helps processing plants located in the Gulf Coast region balance their production with consumer demand from other parts of the country.

- The basis prices in the region are highly correlated to NYMEX future prices. The settlement location for NYMEX futures, Henry Hub, is located in western Louisiana.

Southeast Region

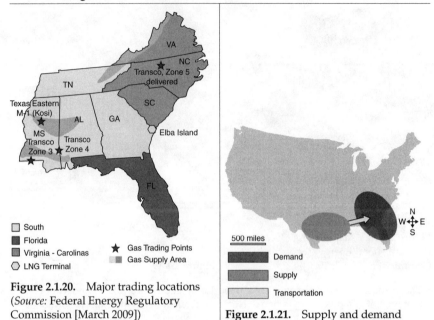

Figure 2.1.20. Major trading locations (*Source:* Federal Energy Regulatory Commission [March 2009])

Figure 2.1.21. Supply and demand

- Natural gas is primarily used to provide electricity in the southeastern United States. The demand for electricity peaks during summer months as the hot summers create a high demand for air-conditioning.

- Mild winters limit the need for seasonal residential heating.

- The Southeast region has very limited or no storage capacity.

- LNG (liquefied natural gas) terminals are being constructed to supply additional natural gas and provide storage facilities. There is a major LNG terminal at Elba Island.

2.2

ELECTRICITY

 30-Second Summary

Purpose

This chapter introduces electricity trading.

Summary

The electrical trading market is unique among trading markets because its final product is a steady supply of electricity. Electricity can't be easily stored. It must be continually generated and transmitted to customers. This makes it substantially different from commodities where it is possible to follow a buy and hold strategy. Understanding the physical constraints of power generation is essential to understanding the electricity trading market.

Key Topics

- Electricity pricing and trading
- Causes of electrical demand
- Generation
- Heat rates and spark spreads
- Transmission and distribution
- The major regional power markets

The generation and transmission of electricity is one of the primary reasons for the existence of an energy market. Electricity is used to power a large variety of modern devices and conveniences; industrial equipment, computers, and air conditioners are just a few examples. Electricity is so common that it is hard to imagine life without it. Unfortunately, electricity can't be stored and it's very expensive to transmit over long distances. Consequently, there is no unified national electricity market—it's a collection of small regional markets with their own unique characteristics and regulations. In each market, supply and demand must constantly be matched, resulting in highly volatile prices.

Each regional market is coordinated by its own *Transmission Service Operator* (TSO). Some TSOs are government-sponsored monopolies, and others are *Independent Service Operators* (ISOs) or *Regional Transmission Organizations* (RTOs). Both ISOs and RTOs maintain the power grid in areas where the government-sponsored monopoly has been disbanded. ISOs are limited to doing service in a single state and are exempt from federal jurisdiction. RTOs do business across several states and fall under federal jurisdiction. Many RTOs began in a single state as ISOs and became RTOs when they expanded across state boundaries. Commonly, these RTOs still keep ISO as part of their name. A map showing the major deregulated markets can be seen in Figure 2.2.1.

A *deregulated market* is a service area where an RTO/ISO, rather than a government-sponsored monopoly, coordinates generation and transmission. In these areas, anyone can own a power plant and connect it to the transmission grid to sell power. All of the participants in a deregulated market are guaranteed equal access to transmission lines, and economic innovation is encouraged. As a general rule, deregulated markets use economic incentives to effect changes, while regulated markets use legislative mandates. Most energy trading occurs in deregulated markets.

The most important characteristics of a deregulated market are daily power auctions, or *nondiscriminatory auctions*, which set the price of power for a transmission grid. Power producers submit the price at which they are willing to supply power, and are activated in order from the lowest to highest bid. These are called "non-discriminatory auctions" because all winning bidders get paid the same price regardless of their bids. The price of power for every producer and every wholesale consumer is set to a single price called the *clearing price*, or alternately, the *wholesale price*. Smaller customers pay a slightly higher price for their power—the *retail price* for power.

In deregulated markets, power plants are activated in order of their bids (lowest to highest) until the consumer demand is completely met. The last power plant activated sets the clearing price of power for the entire transmission area. Some common terminology in these auctions describes the importance of the last activated power provider. The cost of bringing the last unit of electricity into the market is called the *marginal price* of power, and the most recently activated plant is the *marginal producer*. Therefore, in deregulated markets, the clearing price is set by the marginal price of power.

Usually there are two types of auctions coordinated by RTO/ISOs. A *day-ahead* auction sets the price of power for the following day in one-hour increments. This auction is commonly completed in the early afternoon on the day before delivery. This allows power producers time to arrange fuel and operating schedules for the delivery day.

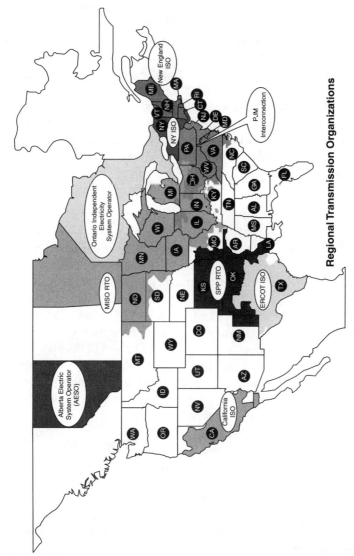

Figure 2.2.1. Map of RTO/ISO operators
(*Source:* Federal Energy Regulatory Commission [March 2009])

The actual demand for power isn't known when the day-ahead auction occurs. Instead, this auction is based on a prediction of the next day's required load.

The second auction is a *real-time* auction, which is run continuously throughout the actual delivery day. This auction balances the actual demand against the predictions made the previous day. It is typically bid in five-minute increments. If a power plant is not chosen to operate in the day-ahead auction, it can still participate in the real-time auction. However, the real-time auctions require power plants to turn on and off quickly, and not every plant has this capability.

Only power plants participate in the daily auctions. However, the auction mechanism is important to every market participant since it determines the price of power in each region. An expanded discussion of this topic can be found in Chapter 4.2, "The Generation Stack."

ELECTRICAL TRADING MARKETS

The *forward power market* is where the bulk of speculative trading occurs. This market is open to anyone with sufficient money to meet trading requirements. The forward market depends on the prices set by the daily auctions, but they are very different markets. The daily auctions are open only to power providers with the ability to generate power and place it on the transmission grid. In contrast, the forward market is much more accessible. The forward market doesn't require any ability to generate power at all—it is possible to trade both *physical contracts* (requiring delivery of power) and *financial contracts* (which settle in cash). To distinguish the two markets, the daily power auctions are sometimes called the *spot power market*.

The forward markets trade large blocks of power at a limited number of locations around the country. This is a critical difference between the daily auctions and the forward markets. It is possible to buy spot power in arbitrarily small sizes for immediate use anywhere in the country. However, it is only possible to trade it in monthly blocks at about 20 locations. The most important of these locations are shown on the map in Figure 2.2.2. The forward markets limit the number of trading locations so a sufficient number of buyers and sellers are forced to be active in each contract.

Trading power in large units at a limited number of locations makes it easier to standardize contracts and find trading partners. This is a necessary compromise for a liquid trading market. However, it also presents a major problem: the tradable locations represent extended geographic areas. These locations may not reflect the exact price of

Major Hubs for Electricity Trading in the United States

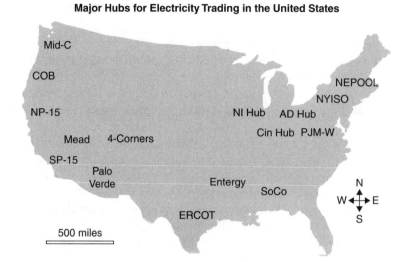

Figure 2.2.2.   Major hubs for trading electrical power

power everywhere in the surrounding area. Getting an exact price at a specific location commonly requires additional trades that may or may not be possible. As a result, power is often traded in two pieces—standardized forward trades made at major hubs to get the desired regional exposure approximately correct, and then smaller fine-tuning trades to lock in an exact price.

Transmission Realities and Daily Power Auctions

In the daily auction market, the assumption that all power providers are equally able to deliver power isn't always true. In periods of heavy demand, power lines can become overloaded and may require electricity to be routed around the congestion. The primary way of rerouting power is to activate power plants closer to the areas of high demand. Because low cost generators are normally activated first, turning on a generator closer to the demand means that a high cost plant is being activated *out-of-merit order*. If that price was allowed to set the clearing price of power for the whole grid, there would be a jump in everyone's costs for the sake of a small minority of customers. In most deregulated power grids, rather than having the entire grid pay the higher price, it is paid only by the affected parties. Because this price only occurs for a single location, this is known as a *Locational Marginal Price* (LMP).

Aligning power prices with the actual cost of delivering power was one of the major reasons energy markets deregulated. The alternative to deregulated markets—having prices legislated by local governments—actually interferes with matching prices to costs. If prices are always going to match costs, there is no need for legislation—the market is deregulated. Legislation involves adding loopholes and exceptions to a general rule. Under the *Standard Market Design* (SMD) recommended by the FERC, the costs of line congestion are paid by the affected parties rather than being shared across every user of a power grid.[1] Congestion costs aren't just paid by consumers, power producers pay them too. There is a charge for routing power into a high load area over congested power lines, and a credit for producing power that bypasses the congestion. Most of the United States is moving toward this model of allocating costs.

Another part of the Standard Market Design is a penalty for remote generation. Historically, generators were paid for the quantity of power that was placed on the grid at their generation site. But if a generator was a long distance from the demand, *line losses* on the intervening transmission could substantially decrease the amount of power actually delivered to customers. Under an LMP methodology, power producers only get paid for deliverable power—not on the gross power placed onto a power grid.

These two changes have had a huge effect on the business of selling power. In addition to fuel costs and efficiency, *location* has become a major factor determining the profitability of a power plant. The power grids have become much more reliable. There is an economic disincentive to build power plants that can't actually deliver power to customers, and an incentive to put up power lines that relieve congestion.

Implementing the FERC's Standard Market Design (SMD) requires assigning different prices to different locations on a power grid. In most regions, this price (the Locational Marginal Price) consists of three parts: a *clearing price*, a *congestion charge*, and a *line loss charge*. The clearing price for power is the same everywhere on a power grid, but the congestion and line loss charges are specific to each location.

Under the SMD, there are several types of locations for which prices are calculated: *nodes*, *zones*, and *hubs*.

Node prices correspond directly to the price of power at a specific piece of physical hardware. Commonly this is an interface, called an "electrical bus," where power enters or leaves the transmission grid. Generators get paid the nodal price of the electrical bus where they deliver power into the transmission grid.

---

[1] The Federal Energy Regulatory Commission (FERC) is the government agency that oversees the power grids in the United States.

Zone prices are the average of all nodal prices within a limited geographical area. Usually, electrical buyers pay the zone price for the power they receive. Zone prices are used for customers, since they require less detailed metering equipment.

Hub prices are an average of selected nodal prices across several zones. The hub price serves as the benchmark price for a power grid. Hub prices are used extensively in the forward market for trading. In most ISO/RTO regions, the clearing price for power and the hub price are synonymous.

Closely linked to the concept of Locational Marginal Prices is a financial instrument called a *Financial Transmission Right* (FTR). These instruments help customers manage the price risk of having purchased or sold power at a major hub and then being forced to pay a different price when they deliver or receive power at a specific node. FTRs are tradable contracts made between two parties. These parties take opposite sides of an obligation to pay or receive the difference in price between two nodes. If there is no congestion, the price at the two nodes will be the same. However, if there is congestion, one party will need to pay the other. This payment can go either way—either party can end up paying or receiving cash. Sometimes that isn't what is desired, so these contracts can be structured as options. FTR options allow one party to pay an upfront fee (a premium) to avoid paying on congestion charges. Essentially, buying an FTR option is like buying insurance against higher prices due to congestion.

Electrical Demand

Because of the way power auctions work—where power plants are activated until the expected demand is fully met—predicting customer demand for power before it occurs is a critical part of power trading. The actual demand for power changes constantly. Every time a light is turned on or a computer is turned off, the load on the power grid changes. Since electricity can't be stored, this changing demand must constantly be matched against supply. There is a huge infrastructure (including the day-ahead and real-time auctions) built to balance the supply of electricity against this consumer demand. However, these auctions can't just be reactive—they need to ensure there are enough power plants active or on standby to meet upcoming demands for power. Building excess capacity into a system is one way to approach this problem, but keeping too many plants on standby costs a lot of money. Making accurate estimates of the future load on the power grid is a key factor in ensuring affordable power.

Load forecasting is also important for power plant operators. Power plants often need several weeks to line up fuel supplies for extended periods of activity. They need to know when to schedule maintenance, and when it makes sense to run continuously versus stopping and restarting. In a competitive market, accurately predicting consumer demand is essential to a power plant's profitability.

Fortunately, the demand for power is fairly predictable. It varies by the season, day of week, and time of day in a cyclic manner. In each region, each part of the year has a typical demand profile that is relatively consistent under a wide variety of circumstances. However, the load profile for every part of the country is different.

During cold weather, where daily high temperatures are below 60° F, there are two distinct periods of peak demand. The first occurs in the morning when people wake up for work. Homes and offices need to be heated around 6 A.M. The second occurs in the evening when people arrive home from work. This relationship is illustrated in Figure 2.2.3, which shows the typical demand for electricity in cold weather. The lines indicate the percent of daily power used each hour. The dashed line indicates the coldest days, and the solid line indicates the warmest. Notice that the shape is pretty much the same despite the large difference in temperatures.

While having a different profile than cold weather, the demand for power in hot weather is also fairly consistent. On hot days, demand builds up all day, peaking in the mid-afternoon when air-conditioning is working most heavily (Figure 2.2.4). This peak is most pronounced

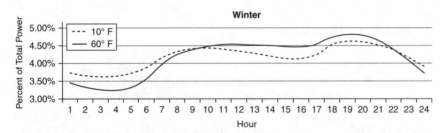

Figure 2.2.3. Shape of electrical load in winter, daily high temperature

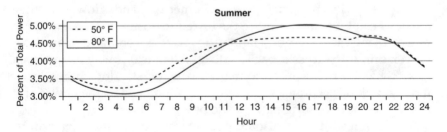

Figure 2.2.4. Shape of electrical load in summer, daily low temperature

on the hottest days (the solid line on the chart), but much less pronounced during more comfortable temperatures (the dashed line).

Seasonality, Weather, and Power Demand

The relationship between temperature and demand doesn't just affect when power is used during the day—it also has a major effect on the total amount of power being used. Substantially more power is required in the summer and winter months than in the more temperate spring and fall months (Figure 2.2.5).

The distinctive peaks in the summer and winter have given a name to periods of lower demand: the fall and spring are called the *shoulder* months. Even during shoulder months there is a *baseline* level of power required every day. Most industries keep fairly standard working hours that don't change substantially throughout the year. As a result, the biggest variable demand for electricity comes from heating or cooling requirements. There is a clear correlation between temperature and electrical demand, or *load*. Since different parts of the country have different climates, there is a substantial variation in average seasonal load between regions.

The relationship between temperature and electrical demand can be seen in Figure 2.2.6. Temperature is located on the left axis of the graph. As temperatures become uncomfortable (moving above or below 70° F), the demand for power increases (shown on the bottom axis). The points on the right side of the graph are when the peak demand occurred within the mid-Atlantic region in the years 2004–2006. These peaks correspond to the warmest and coldest days.

The cyclical nature of electrical power affects how it is traded. Power is normally traded for an entire month based on the time of day. Forward contracts are commonly broken up into day and night power

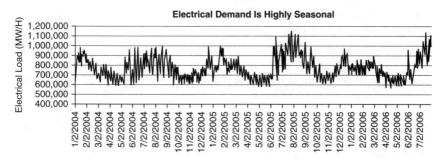

Figure 2.2.5.   Seasonal demand for electrical power in Mid-Atlantic Region
(*Source:* Load data is based on data from PJM-ISO for the PJM-East Zone [approximately the Baltimore/Philadelphia area] for 2004–2006)

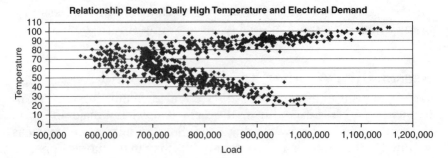

Figure 2.2.6. Daily high temperatures plotted against consumer demand in the Mid-Atlantic region
(*Source:* Load data provided by the PJM-ISO for the PJM-East Zone [approximately the Baltimore/Philadelphia area] for 2004–2006)

by month. For example, it is possible to find trading contracts for August daytime power with delivery at Cinergy Hub, or January nighttime power for delivery in Southern California. However, there isn't a single commodity called "electricity" that is consistent throughout the year. Instead, there are hundreds of separately traded electricity products that differ based on location, month or season, and time of day.

Daytime hours (usually 7 A.M. until 11 P.M.) are called *peak* hours. Nighttime hours are called *off-peak* hours. Every region of the country uses slightly different definitions for their power products. As a result, power products are commonly described in shorthand. This abbreviation is *weekdays by hours*. For example, 7×24 refers to power 7 days a week, 24 hours a day. *Peak* power is 5×16 or 7×16 (depending whether weekend days are included). If weekends aren't included in peak power, there will be a separate 2×16 product. *Nighttime off-peak* hours are typically 7×8—they start at 11 P.M. the day before and run until 7 A.M.

Finally, technology has a big effect on electrical demand. For example, air-conditioning changed the entire dynamic of the power market. Many of the economic studies made in the late 1960s and in the 1970s regarding energy efficiency are now incorrect because of the increased popularity of air-conditioning. With the advent of air-conditioning, the demand for summer power went from being fairly low to extremely high. Predictions on typical demand have to keep up with these changes.

GENERATION

There are lots of ways to produce electrical power. Most power plants use a similar technology—generators driven by superheated steam.

Fossil fuel plants can burn oil, natural gas, or coal to produce this steam. All of these fossil fuels produce *greenhouse gases* like carbon dioxide (CO_2) when they are burned. The amount of pollution depends on the efficiency of the power plant. More efficient plants use less fuel, thereby producing less pollution, per megawatt of generated power. Of all fossil fuels, coal-fired generation is the most polluting: it produces two to three times the pollution of the other fuels.

Nuclear generators use nuclear fission to turn water into steam. Nuclear fuel provides a lot of electricity per weight—a pound of highly enriched uranium is approximately equal to a million gallons of gasoline. But like fossil fuels, enriched uranium is subject to severe shortages and presents environmental problems. It is also difficult to store safely once discarded.

Hydroelectricity is a relatively common form of power generation. Unlike fossil fuel plants and nuclear generators, instead of using steam, hydroelectric dams use flowing water to drive a turbine directly. In most cases, dams are built across a river, trapping the water on one side to form a lake. Water is allowed to flow through holes in the dam into the river, which is usually located several hundred feet below the lake level. As water flows through the dam, the falling water spins a water-based turbine to generate electricity. Depending on the amount of water flowing in the river and the capacity of the lake, it may not be possible to turn off the flow of water without flooding nearby communities.

For energy trading, the most influential power plants are fossil fuel plants, which are *marginal* producers of power in most areas. As such, in any market that sets the *clearing price* of electricity to the *marginal price* of power, fossil fuel plants have a disproportionate impact on the price of electricity. Perhaps the most common description of a fossil fuel power plant relates to its efficiency in converting fuel into electricity. This efficiency is called a *heat rate,* and it is typically expressed as a ratio of heat input to work output (Btu/KWh or MMBtu/MWh). A lower heat rate indicates a more efficient power plant.

Generators

Electricity is usually generated by manipulating the relationship between magnetic fields and electricity, which are two parts of the same force (electromagnetism). Spinning a wire in a magnetic field creates a current in the wire. Magnetic fields generate electrical currents, and vice versa.

The easiest way to generate electricity is to rotate a coiled wire inside a pair of magnets, as depicted in Figure 2.2.7. As the wire spins,

A Simple Electrical Generator

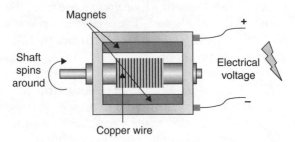

Magnets

Shaft
spins
around

Electrical
voltage

+

−

Copper wire

Figure 2.2.7.   Example of a simple electrical generator

it will start to build up a magnetic charge that can be removed in the form of electricity. By continuing to spin the coiled wire, a steady supply of electricity can be removed through a circuit. This force works both ways—electric generators and electric motors use identical technology. Applying a voltage to the positive and negative terminals of a generator will cause the shaft containing the wires to spin.

When wires connect a voltage source to an electrical load, it is called a *circuit*. The definition of an electrical circuit is any closed loop of wire than contains a voltage source—often a generator or a battery—and a load (an electrical device of some kind). A load is anything that uses electricity—a common example is a lightbulb, but any device powered by electricity can be described by the term. In circuit diagrams, these terms are often abbreviated. Voltage is commonly abbreviated v, current abbreviated i, and resistance (load) abbreviated R.

Voltage is a measure of the potential energy in an electromagnetic field. When a wire connects two points with different voltages, electrons will start flowing through the wire. They will move from the low voltage area to the high voltage area, eventually causing the voltage to equalize.[2] In the case of a battery, when the voltage equalizes, the battery is dead and needs to be replaced or recharged.

However, if the voltage is being continually created through a generator, the current will continue to flow indefinitely. The speed at which the current flows through the wire depends on the voltage and load. The more work the electrons need to do on their way through the wire, the slower they travel. This is a very important relationship, because if the current moves too fast, the wire will heat up and possibly melt.

---

[2] Since electrons are negatively charged particles, they move in the opposite direction of a positive current.

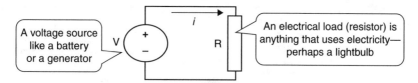

Figure 2.2.8. An electrical circuit is a closed wire containing a voltage source (v) and a load (R)

The relationship between voltage, current, and resistance can be described by the formula $v = iR$ (Ohm's law). Voltage equals the current multiplied by the resistance. Figure 2.2.8 is a simple circuit diagram showing each of the fundamental pieces of a circuit.

The key concept is that voltage, current, and load on a system are all interrelated. This is true of the simplest circuit and the largest power grid. If the current on any transmission wire gets too fast, it will start to heat up the wire. When it gets hot enough, the wire will melt. The only way to prevent transmission wires from melting is to match the level of production (the voltage) and the demand for electrical power (the load). Since a power grid can't directly control the amount of power that consumers are using, it needs to alter the amount of power being produced. There has to be a proper balance between generation and demand. Generating too little power will cause *brownouts*, and generating too much power will melt the transmission lines and cause a *blackout*.

Steam Turbine Plants

About 80 percent of the world's power is generated through the use of steam turbines. Steam-turbine-based power plants vary widely in efficiency and complexity. Simpler turbines are less efficient, but are cheaper to build and have lower operating costs. More complex turbines are more efficient, but they are also more expensive to maintain.

Regardless of complexity, all steam turbines operate in a similar manner (Figure 2.2.9). Superheated steam is created by heating water in a *boiler*. When the water turns into steam, it expands, moving past a turbine (which is essentially a big fan), causing the turbine to spin. The turbine is attached to a generator, causing it to spin as well. Spinning the generator causes electrical power to be generated. After moving past the turbine, the steam enters a cool metal chamber (the *condenser*). As the steam touches the cool sides of the condenser, it turns back into water and is then sent back into the boiler to begin the process again. The faster the steam turbine spins, the more electrical power is produced.

A steam turbine is essentially an electrical fan operating in reverse. Instead of an electrical motor spinning a fan, a steam turbine operates

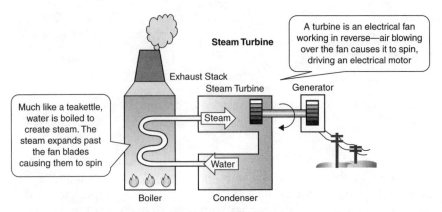

Figure 2.2.9. Simple diagram of a steam turbine

by having air spin the fan, as can be seen in the diagram. This drives the "motor" in reverse and produces electricity. From an engineering perspective, the key issue is how to push the fan blades—to spin the turbine. In a steam turbine, this problem is solved by using steam coming out of a boiler. The boiler acts like a teakettle—when water starts to boil, steam exits the boiler at high speed, spinning the turbine along the way.

It takes less energy to boil already hot water than it takes to boil cold water. If the condenser cools the steam to a point just slightly below its boiling point, it is still very hot. When this hot water reenters the boiler, only a small amount of additional heat will be required to convert it back into steam. The most fuel-consuming part of operating a steam turbine is heating the system when it starts up. After the water is heated up, keeping the steam turbine continually operating is a very efficient way to produce more electricity. As a result, it is often worthwhile for power plant operators to keep their plant operational, and take a loss in low demand periods, in order to avoid the costs associated with a cold start.

Cogeneration

To condense the gas back into a liquid, it is necessary to cool it down slightly. The area where this cooling occurs is called the *condenser*. Fairly commonly, the condenser is a large metal container submerged in cold water. As the steam from the turbine touches the cold sides of the condenser, it cools down and condenses into a liquid. At the same time, the cold water outside the condenser heats up. If this goes on long enough, the water outside the container will eventually become hot. Most of the time, this hot water is discarded—it is allowed to flow into a local river or evaporates in a cooling tower. However, if this hot water is used for some purpose, the useful output of a plant is now increased—the plant will produce both electricity and hot water. This is the definition of a *cogeneration* plant.

Cogeneration doesn't work for all power plants. The first problem is that there is often no need for superheated hot water in an area. Selling superheated water requires a buyer that wants to purchase it. A second problem is that even if someone wants to use the hot water, the water needs to be transported from the power plant to the location where it will be used. In most cases, this requires the purchaser to build a facility adjacent to the power plant or to build a pipeline connecting the two. Third, cogeneration places increased operational restrictions on the power plant. If an industrial facility needs superheated water to operate, it will want a stable supply. For the power plant, this is bad. A power plant won't want to be obligated to produce hot water in periods where it is unprofitable to produce power.

The benefit of cogeneration is that it provides an additional income source for power plants. It doesn't make the electrical generation part of the plant any more efficient, but since it provides more income for the same fuel use, it can be thought of as lowering the cost of fuel. When cogeneration is a result of using waste heat produced from a condenser, it is called *topping cycle cogeneration*. It is also possible to reduce fuel costs by eliminating or reducing the need for a boiler. If heat from an industrial process provides heat to the boiler, the fuel necessary to run the plant can be reduced or eliminated. This type of cogeneration is called *bottoming cycle cogeneration*.

Gas Turbine

The other major technology for producing power, the *gas turbine* (Figure 2.2.10), skips the step of producing steam by creating

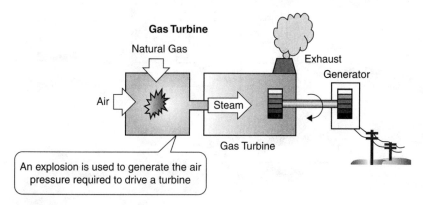

Figure 2.2.10.   Simple gas turbine

superheated gas directly through combustion. A mixture of natural gas and air is ignited in an explosive reaction that sends superheated gas past a turbine. This is very similar to the operation of a jet engine. The linkage between the spinning turbine and electrical generator works the same way as a steam turbine.

Since the waste gas can't be reused in a gas turbine, it is less efficient than a steam turbine. However, gas turbines are much simpler to build and maintain. Also, there is no lengthy process required to heat up the water into steam, so gas turbines can start producing power at peak efficiency as soon as they are turned on. As a result, gas turbines are commonly used for power plants that need to turn on quickly or to adjust their power output regularly.

Combined Cycle Plants

In the same way that a bottoming cycle cogeneration plant uses heat from an industrial process in its boiler, a steam turbine can use the exhaust heat of a gas turbine. The primary waste product of a gas turbine is superheated gas. This gas is extremely hot, but since it isn't expanding anymore, it can't be used to power a second gas turbine. However, it is perfect for heating water to produce steam. A *combined cycle* power plant is a gas turbine whose exhaust gases power a steam turbine (Figure 2.2.11). Combined cycle plants are more complicated than

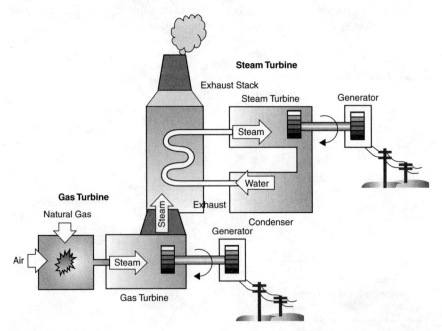

Figure 2.2.11.   Combined cycle power plant combines gas and steam turbines

either gas or steam turbine plants, but they are also more efficient since there is less wasted heat.

The steam turbine portion of a combined cycle plant operates like a normal steam turbine, and its waste product—hot water—can be re-used as well. When used to cogenerate heat, a natural gas combined cycle plant is a highly efficient power plant that produces a minimal amount of pollution for each megawatt of power.

Heat Rates

The efficiency at which a plant converts fuel into electricity is called its *heat rate*. This quantity is usually expressed in terms of British thermal units (Btu) per kilowatt hour (KWh), or millions of British thermal units (MMBtu) per megawatt hour (MWh). Lower heat rates imply a more efficient power plant since less fuel is required to produce the same amount of electricity.

$$\text{Heat Rate} = \frac{\text{Quantity of Fuel used}}{\text{Quantity of Power produced}}$$

The heat rate of a plant is an easy way of determining when a power plant can operate profitably. For example, if a natural-gas-fired power plant has a heat rate of 8.5 MMBtu/MWh, it can sell power profitably when the price of power is 8.5 times the price of natural gas. Since this comparison is so common, the ratio of power to fuel prices has its own terminology. That ratio is called the *market implied heat rate* and is also in units of MMBtu/MWh.

$$\text{Market Implied Heat Rate} = \frac{\text{Power Price}}{\text{Fuel Price}}$$

As a rule of thumb, natural gas power plants commonly have heat rates between 7 and 10 MMBtu/MWh. Power plants closer to the 7 MMBtu/MWh level are extremely efficient. The ones close to 10 MMBtu/MWh are less efficient models. Sometimes, heat rates are expressed in Btu/KWh units. It is possible to convert between MMBtu/MWh units and Btu/KWh units by multiplying by 1,000. In these units, typical natural gas plants have heat rates between 7,000 and 10,000 Btu/KWh.

Spark Spreads

The heat rate of a power plant provides a way to estimate profitability. This estimate, called a *spark spread*, is the theoretical profit that a

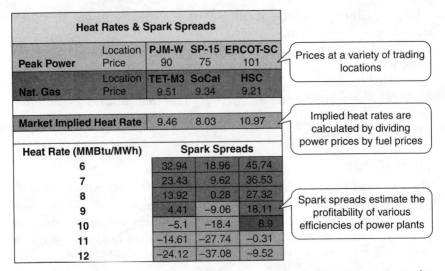

Heat Rates & Spark Spreads			
Peak Power Location Price	PJM-W 90	SP-15 75	ERCOT-SC 101
Nat. Gas Location Price	TET-M3 9.51	SoCal 9.34	HSC 9.21

Prices at a variety of trading locations

Market Implied Heat Rate	9.46	8.03	10.97

Implied heat rates are calculated by dividing power prices by fuel prices

Heat Rate (MMBtu/MWh)	Spark Spreads		
6	32.94	18.96	45.74
7	23.43	9.62	36.53
8	13.92	0.28	27.32
9	4.41	−9.06	18.11
10	−5.1	−18.4	8.9
11	−14.61	−27.74	−0.31
12	−24.12	−37.08	−9.52

Spark spreads estimate the profitability of various efficiencies of power plants

Figure 2.2.12. Heat rates and spark spreads are used by traders to approximate the behavior of electricity generators

natural gas generator can make from buying fuel and selling power at current market prices. This profit estimate does not include any charges for operating costs.

$$\text{Spark Spread} = \text{Price of Electricity} - (\text{Price of Gas} \times \text{Heat Rate})$$

When multiple spark spreads are discussed, it is necessary to specify the heat rate and pricing location. Figure 2.2.12 is an example display that a trader might use to examine spark spreads and heat rates. The "market implied heat rate" in the figure indicates which power plant efficiencies are currently profitable in each region, while the bottom of the chart estimates the gross profitability of power plants in each region by heat rates.

If products other than natural gas are examined, different terms are used to describe the profitability spread. *Dark spread* refers to coal-based generation plants. When emissions credits are included in the profitability estimates, the name of the spread typically has the word *clean* or *green* in the front (as in a *clean spark spread*).

TRANSMISSION AND DISTRIBUTION

Once power is generated, it needs to be brought to the customer. A higher voltage makes it easier to transfer power over long distances, but it is also more dangerous. As part of the generation process, power plants use several different types of power lines—high voltage lines are used for long distance transmission and lower voltage lines for residential distribution. *Transformers* and *substations* step the voltage up or down between different types of power lines. *Transmission* refers to the bulk transfer of power from the power plant to a substation via high voltage lines. *Distribution* refers to the transfer of power from a substation to various consumers using much lower voltage lines.

Power plants, transmission lines, and substations form the *power grid*: a set of interconnecting power lines that provide multiple ways to route power between any two locations. The redundancy of a power grid is crucial for reliability. It prevents any single line from overloading. This helps prevent blackouts due to a single point of failure. Most power lines are overhead lines—they are attached to tall poles suspended safely above ground level. In urban areas, electrical power lines are sometimes buried. Buried power lines are less reliable and harder to maintain than overhead lines. Burying power lines is uncommon in suburban and rural areas.

The choice of voltage and location for power lines is a trade-off between safety, reliability, and efficiency. As part of the transmission process, power is wasted—it's converted into heat that must be dissipated on the power line. This waste is proportional to the current: the higher the current on a line, the greater the losses become. This waste can be reduced by using higher voltages (effectively reducing the current). However, higher voltage lines are more dangerous than lower voltage ones and can't be used in many areas.

Power is almost always transmitted over three power lines. The power on all three lines oscillates, but the sine curves are offset from one another. When power on the three lines is combined, the net current and voltage equal zero. This is a very important property for transmitting power. In a circuit, the net current at every point needs to be zero. Current can't just disappear. It has to be canceled, move somewhere else, or turn into something else, like heat. In most circuits this is achieved by having the same amount of current enter and leave every point.

Using three-phase power means that electricity doesn't need to flow in a circle around the entire power grid. Instead, it can be run into a dead end and canceled out. This addresses the problem of ensuring that every point in a circuit has zero net current. If power had to flow out of each location, a single break (like a light switch turning off) would shut down the entire power grid. Three-phase power allows a transmission grid to avoid being a chain of serial circuits like Christmas tree lights that don't work if any one of the bulbs is burned out.

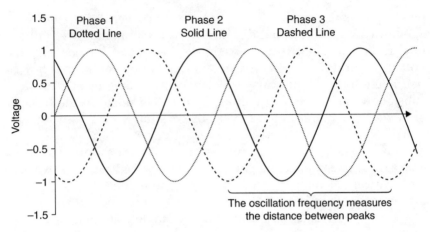

Figure 2.2.13. Alternating current power is usually transmitted as three waves that can cancel one another out

In a three-phase power system, power on all three lines oscillates with the same frequency, but the starting points of the waves are different, as can be seen in Figure 2.2.13.

Because it is necessary for three-phase power to cancel, it is crucial that all of the voltages in an AC network have the same oscillation frequency. Keeping the power grid operating requires every power plant to synchronize the oscillation frequency on each of its power lines with the outputs from other power plants. If two power plants are producing power with different frequencies or starting points, the line voltages will interfere with one another—sometimes canceling, sometimes adding, but never doing anything useful. If the current isn't canceled out at every point, it doesn't just stand still. It will move somewhere else (causing short circuits or shocks) or turn into heat (melting power lines and causing fires). This will wreak havoc on a power grid. Synchronizing power plants is a major responsibility for each Transmission Service Organization (TSO) and a major obstacle between integrating adjoining power grids.

Almost all transmission lines use a three-phase system for transmitting power. Looking at transmission towers, this means that most will contain a multiple of three wires. Since smaller wires help reduce the electromagnetic fields around power lines, it is fairly common for six power lines to transmit power (two groups of three lines). When multiple small wires are used to transmit three-phase power, this is called *bundling*. It helps prevent the air around power lines from picking up an electrical charge (called *ionization* or *corona*) that sometimes affects very large transmission wires.

Regional Markets

There are three major integrated power grids in the United States (Figure 2.2.14): the *Eastern Interconnect* (east of Rocky Mountains), the *Western Interconnect* (west of the Rocky Mountains), and *ERCOT* (Texas). Inside each interconnection, all of the transmission lines are synchronized. This allows power to be transported across long distances within those interconnections. However, differences in population, industry, and weather still make electrical prices a regional phenomenon. Because of this, long distance transmission of power (called *wheeling*) between fundamentally different markets is the source of a large number of trading opportunities. Wheeling power can be expensive since there are large losses when power is transmitted over long distances. Wheeling is economically profitable if power can be obtained cheaply enough and sent to a high price region.

Texas Interconnect

The Texas Interconnect is the smallest interconnection in the United States and is located entirely within the state of Texas. Unlike the other interconnects, which cover wide geographic areas, the power in this

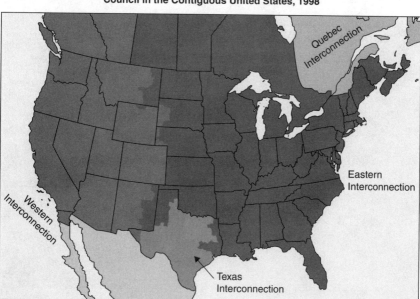

Figure 2.2.14.   Map of major power interconnections in North America (*Source:* Energy Information Agency [October 2000])

area is coordinated by a single ISO, the Electric Reliability Council of Texas (ERCOT). There are a number of DC power lines connecting the Texas power grid to the Eastern Interconnect and the Mexican power grids. However, those lines have limited capacity.

Western Interconnect

There are seven major trading locations in the western United States (Figure 2.2.15). The Rocky Mountains dominate the regional geography of the area. The Western Interconnect is a long line of regional grids stretching from the Pacific Northwest into the Desert Southwest, with California in the middle. Much of the trading in the Western Interconnect revolves around the flow of power into or out of the highly populated areas of California. The Pacific Northwest (MIDC) and

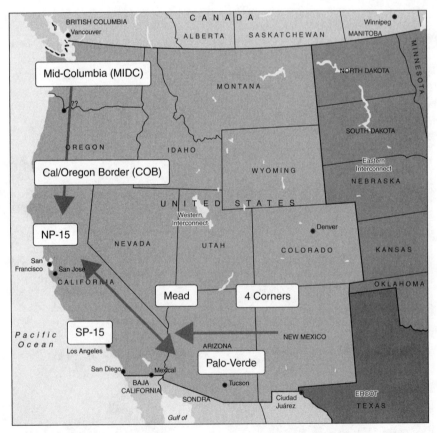

Figure 2.2.15. Western Interconnect. During periods of peak demand, power flows toward California

Colorado River (Mead) near Las Vegas are major sources of hydroelectric power.

The amount of available hydroelectric power and the weather differences between regions determine how power moves around the Western Interconnect. Hydroelectric power supplies about 70 percent of the power supply in Washington and Oregon. Because it is so prevalent, small changes in water flow can result in substantial changes to regional power supplies. In the spring, when the snow melts, more power is produced in the Pacific Northwest than can be used locally, and it needs to be transmitted to an area of higher demand (usually Northern California).

California has an extremely dense population. In the summer, it often imports power from both the Pacific Northwest and the Desert Southwest to meet peak demand. However, in the fall, when temperatures in California are mild but temperatures in Las Vegas and Phoenix are still extremely hot, power can be exported from California into the desert areas. This direction of flow can change at any time based on the relative temperatures of the two regions.

Since the marginal producers of power in California are usually natural-gas-fired plants, a steady supply of natural gas is required. The southern part of the region receives natural gas from the Rocky Mountains and West Texas. The northern part receives natural gas from western Canada. When the price of fuel in the two areas diverges, regional power prices can also be affected.

Eastern Interconnect
Unlike the Western Interconnect, the eastern half of the United States is less dominated by geography. It is a combination of RTO/ISOs and regulated entities forming an interconnected grid that looks like a spiderweb (Figure 2.2.16). The two most important RTO/ISOs lay in the industrialized north: PJM (originally named the Pennsylvania, New Jersey, and Maryland Interconnection) and MISO (Midwest ISO). The two most liquid trading locations in the Eastern Interconnect are Cinergy Hub (abbreviated MISO-Cin Hub) and PJM Western Hub (PJM-W).

A variety of fuels and different regional weather patterns provide many trading opportunities in the Eastern Interconnect. Some of the most important trades are between regions using coal-fired plants and those using natural-gas-fired plants. Other trades are weather related. The southern part of the Eastern Interconnect has an extended summer and mild winters. The northern part has cold winters and a shorter summer air-conditioning season.

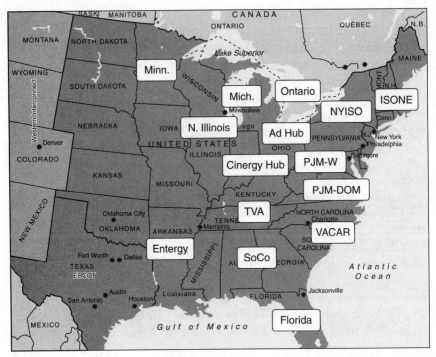

Figure 2.2.16. The Eastern Interconnect is the largest and most integrated power grid in North America

California (CAISO)

California is a heavily populated state that is divided into two major zones, NP-15 and SP-15 (Figure 2.2.17). Most of the year, the daily temperatures are moderate to warm. However, the dense population and hot summers can cause spikes in the electrical loads due to a demand for air-conditioning.

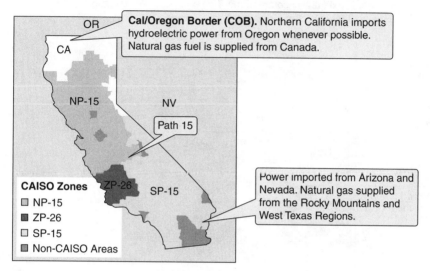

Figure 2.2.17.   California electricity market
(*Source:* Federal Energy Regulatory Commission [March 2009])

The major transmission lines are called "paths." One of these transmission lines, Path 15, bisects the state into two approximately equal parts and has given its name to the two major zones, NP-15 and SP-15.

NP-15 (North Path 15) covers the northern part of the state (San Francisco Bay area) north of Path 15. When rainfall or melting snow allows, this region imports low cost hydroelectricity from the Columbia River Basin in Oregon. For the remainder of the year, natural gas plants set the price of power in NP-15. The plants are supplied primarily from western Canada.

SP-15 (South Path 15) is the pricing zone for most of Southern California. It is south of Path 15. This zone is a major importer of power from Arizona (natural gas and solar power) and Nevada (hydropower from the Colorado River). Natural-gas-fired plants in the south are fed from supplies in the Rocky Mountain and West Texas regions.

ZP-26 is a large, but less important, pricing zone that has a relatively low population and excess generation capacity. It connects to both the NP-15 and SP-15 zones.

Desert Southwest

The Desert Southwest has moderate winter temperatures and prolonged hot summers. Much of the year, the area has a surplus of generation capacity and is a major exporter of power to Southern California (Figure 2.2.18). Natural gas is the most common marginal fuel due to the abundant natural gas reserves, but coal and hydropower are relatively common too. This area also receives a great deal of sunlight, making it an attractive location for solar power.

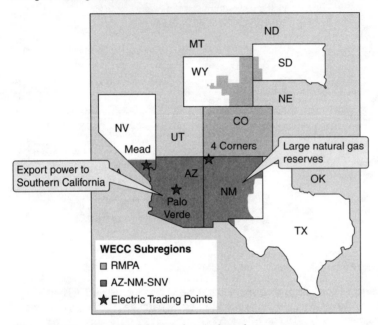

Figure 2.2.18.   Desert Southwest electrical market
(*Source:* Federal Energy Regulatory Commission [March 2009])

There are three major hubs for electricity trading in the area: Mead, Palo Verde, and Four Corners. Major power generation facilities are located near each hub.

Mead is located on the outskirts of Las Vegas. Lake Mead is the artificial lake formed when the Hoover Dam was built on the Colorado River. The Hoover Dam is a major source of hydroelectric power and the primary delivery point for power in southern Nevada.

Palo Verde is located at a major nuclear power plant and switching yard about 45 miles west of Phoenix, Arizona. Many high power lines to California are located at this switching yard.

Four Corners is located in northwestern New Mexico at the interconnection of several major transmission lines.

Pacific Northwest

In most years, the Pacific Northwest sells surplus power into California and the Southwest (Figure 2.2.19). About two-thirds of all the electricity in the Pacific Northwest region comes from hydroelectric production. As a result, the quantity of surplus power depends heavily on precipitation. Water flow in this region directly affects the price of power in California.

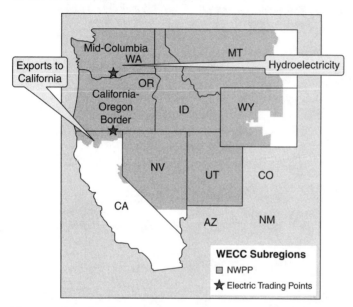

Figure 2.2.19.   Pacific Northwest power markets
(*Source:* Federal Energy Regulatory Commission [March 2009])

Melting snow from the Cascade Mountain range, which runs through central Washington and Oregon, is a major source of river water. To the west of the mountains are several major population centers: Seattle, Washington, and Portland, Oregon. The climate in these regions is fairly temperate all year. To the east of the mountains is the start of the northern plains states. This area is characterized by cold winters and hot summers.

Mid Columbia (MIDC) is a delivery hub for a number of hydroelectric plants on the Columbia River.

Cal-Oregon Border (COB) is a major switching station in southern Oregon, adjacent to the California border, that interconnects several major transmission lines.

Mid-Atlantic (PJM ISO)

The Mid-Atlantic region contains many large population centers, like Washington D.C., Baltimore, and Philadelphia, on the eastern seaboard. This area formed one of the first independent power grids, the PJM ISO, named after its constituent states: Pennsylvania, New Jersey, and Maryland. PJM has since expanded to include West Virginia, Delaware, large parts of Ohio, parts on northern Illinois, and Virginia. It is one of the largest and most liquid electricity markets. Within PJM there are a number of active trading hubs. Several of the most important are shown on the map in Figure 2.2.20.

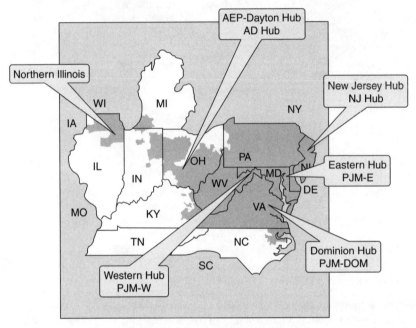

Figure 2.2.20. PJM service area and major trading hubs
(*Source:* Federal Energy Regulatory Commission [March 2009])

Geographically, the PJM service area is very diverse. Large reserves of coal native to Pennsylvania and West Virginia serve as the marginal fuel for western part of the PJM service area. Power on the East Coast and Virginia is commonly determined by gas-fired power plants. The climate in the northern half of the region ranges from cold winters to hot summers. The climate in the southern half of the region is warmer— mild winters and extended hot summers.

A large number of power plants in the less populated areas of the PJM service area export power into the more populated regions. As a result, the power lines between these areas are often congested.

Midwest (MISO)

The Midwest ISO coordinates power for the north-central United States (Figure 2.2.21). The eastern part of the MISO region is heavily industrialized, while the western section is more rural. There are several major trading locations in the region. Of these, Cinergy Hub is the most influential.

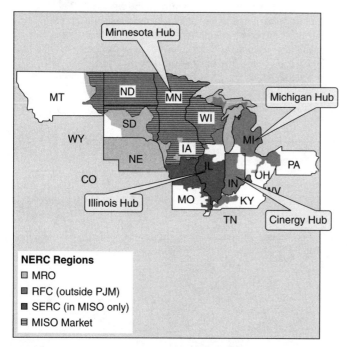

Figure 2.2.21. Map of MISO service area and major trading hubs (*Source:* Federal Energy Regulatory Commission [March 2009])

From a climate perspective, the middle of the United States has cold winters and hot summers. The cold weather usually starts in December, but can arrive in early November and usually lasts through April. The summer months—July and August—are hot and humid, but the weather cools off quickly in September.

Many of the power plants in the region, including a large number of marginal producers, are coal powered. As a result, coal prices often determine the price of power in the Midwest even in high demand periods. This is a unique feature of the area. In most of the United States, the price of power is set by natural-gas-fired plants. Power is often wheeled from the Midwest to adjacent regions when the price of natural gas spikes upward.

Because of the cool *shoulder months* (the spring and fall) in the Midwest, power is often wheeled to southern states where hot weather is more common. Some hydroelectric power is available from the Great Lakes and Tennessee Valley areas. Depending on the time of year, power might be imported from either of these two regions.

New York (NYISO)

The New York power grid is self-contained in the state of New York (Figure 2.2.22). The southeastern part of this region contains one the most heavily concentrated areas of demand for electricity in the country: New York City and Long Island. The region is characterized by the flow of low cost power from the northern and western sections of the state into the high demand regions surrounding New York City.

Most of the New York metropolitan area is located on islands. As a result, there is limited ability to transfer power to those areas from other parts of the region, and a high reliance on inefficient generators during periods of peak demand. This has made the New York City area one of the most expensive power markets in the country. In order to assure reliable service, power plants in the New York metropolitan area are subject to much stricter rules and regulatory requirements than are common in other regions.

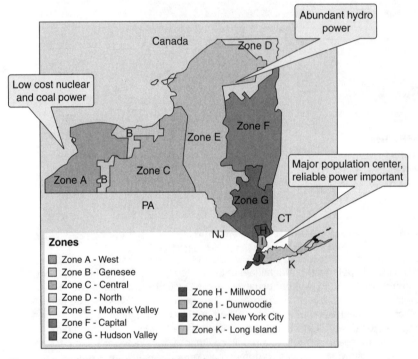

Figure 2.2.22.   New York electrical market
(*Source:* Federal Energy Regulatory Commission [March 2009])

New England (ISO-NE)

There is only a single trading hub in the New England region. The prices at this hub are based on selected nodes around the Boston area (Figure 2.2.23).

New England has to import fuel for almost all of its power generation requirements. The marginal fuel for the region is natural gas. The bulk of this supply comes from the U.S. Gulf Coast and eastern Canada. There are efforts to augment this supply by constructing liquefied natural gas terminals in Massachusetts.

Most of the population in New England is in the southern part of the region: Connecticut and the area around the city of Boston, Massachusetts. In contrast, the northern part of the region is relatively unpopulated.

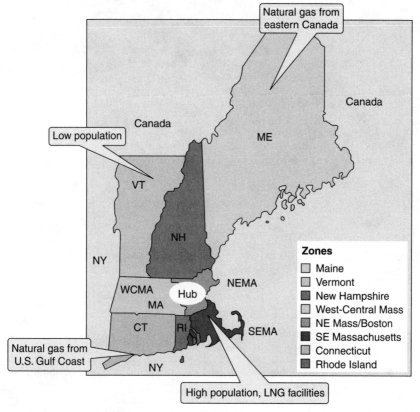

Figure 2.2.23.   New England power markets
(*Source:* Federal Energy Regulatory Commission [March 2009])

Southeast and Gulf Coast

Unlike regions with independent power grids, power in the Southern states is provided by integrated power companies (Figure 2.2.24). Each of these companies is linked to nearby grids and power can be traded between them. However, because these are still regulated markets, there is little opportunity to trade power within the service area of any of these companies.

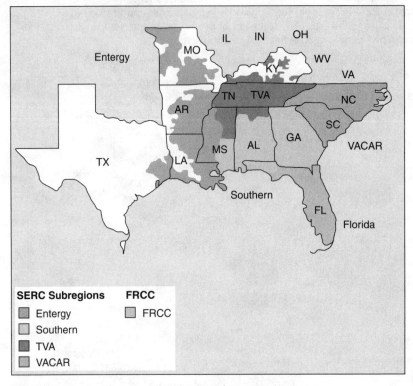

Figure 2.2.24.   Southeastern electricity markets
(*Source:* Federal Energy Regulatory Commission [March 2009])

The Gulf Coast region is characterized by mild winters and prolonged hot summers. Long-lasting heat waves can start affecting the area in the early spring and may last until late October. Consequently, seasonal demand is quite different from the northern states—demand is low most of the winter and peaks for an extended time in the summer.

From a precipitation perspective, the southeastern United States has a tropical climate. There is a wet season running from November to May, and a dry season running from June to October. There is substantial hydroelectrical generation in the Tennessee Valley area that is affected by this rainfall. During periods of high rainfall, the Tennessee Valley can export power to other parts of the Southeast, the Midwest, or the East Coast.

Coal and natural gas are both marginal fuels for the area. There are ready supplies of both fuels locally—the Gulf Coast is a major source of natural gas, and the Appalachian Mountains contain abundant coal deposits.

Texas (ERCOT)

ERCOT is the ISO that provides power to Texas.[3] ERCOT is dived into five primary regions (Figure 2.2.25). Most of the region's population is located in the northeastern part of the state. ERCOT North contains the greater Dallas/Fort Worth area, and ERCOT Houston contains the Houston metro area.

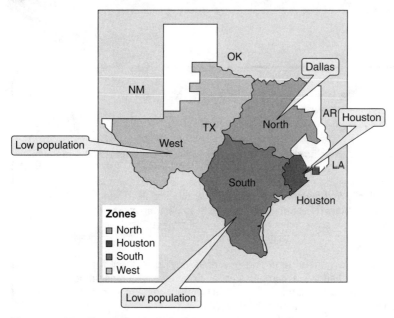

Figure 2.2.25.   Texas electrical market
(*Source:* Federal Energy Regulatory Commission [March 2009])

Due to abundant local supplies, the marginal fuel for the area is usually natural gas. The climate is characterized by mild winters and prolonged hot summers. Currently, most of the generation is located in the North and Houston zones—close to the greatest areas of consumer demand. However, substantial solar and wind-based generation is being built in the western part of the state. This might change the dynamics of the market—requiring power to be transmitted from the western zone into the more populated zones.

---

[3] ERCOT stands for the Electric Reliability Council of Texas.

2.3

OIL

 30-Second Summary

Purpose

This chapter explains the market for trading crude oil and refined petroleum products.

Crude oil is the most traded commodity in the world. Even though producing electricity and household heating is only tangentially related to petroleum products, the impact of petroleum trading is so pervasive, every energy trader needs to have a solid understanding of the oil market.

Summary

Petroleum is a general term that describes any liquid fossil fuel. Crude oil, gasoline, and heating oil can all be called petroleum. The most important petroleum commodity is crude oil. Crude oil is unrefined petroleum that has been removed from the ground prior to being processed. There is a global market for crude oil and a large infrastructure to transport and process it. As a result, the price of crude oil is approximately the same everywhere in the world.

There are smaller, regional markets for refined petroleum products like gasoline and heating oil. For a variety of reasons, including safety and the stability of local governments, refineries are usually located in industrialized countries near the market for their refined products. Refined petroleum products are usually not transported long distance after refining. As a result, the price of refined petroleum products is regional in nature and local areas have their own supply and demand.

Like natural gas and coal, petroleum is an important fuel for electrical generation and home heating. However, the global impact of oil trading exceeds its value to the energy market. Energy (heating and electrical generation) is a secondary market for oil. The primary market for oil is as a transportation fuel and raw material for the plastics industry. Still, energy traders need to have a reasonable understanding of the petroleum market because of its global influence.

Key Topics

- Crude oil is the single most traded product in the world, measured by both volume and value.
- Almost all international trading is for crude oil rather than refined products
- There are regional markets for refined petroleum products, like gasoline. The prices for these products vary substantially throughout the world, and each region's prices are set by local supply and demand considerations.

Oil, or *petroleum*, is a liquid fossil fuel formed when decaying plant life becomes trapped in a layer of porous rock.[1] After millions of years, heat and pressure convert decaying plant life into hydrocarbons. Some of these hydrocarbons are gases, others are solids, and still others are liquids. Petroleum is the generic name for any hydrocarbon that is liquid under normal temperature and pressure conditions. Like other fossil fuels, the mixture of hydrocarbons in petroleum can vary widely. When petroleum is first extracted from the ground, it is called *crude oil*.

It can be dangerous to burn crude oil directly since the lighter portions of it can form explosive vapors and the heavier portions may not flow easily or ignite smoothly. As a result, crude oil is usually separated into components that are more uniform in composition. This separation is done in a refinery through the process of *distillation*. After crude oil is distilled, there are specific names for each liquid produced (gasoline, heating oil, etc). The term "petroleum" refers to crude oil and all of the products refined from it.

The liquid properties and high energy density of petroleum make it a popular fuel for vehicles. Compared to hydrocarbon gases like methane or propane, petroleum contains a lot of energy per unit of volume. For example, a tank of a hydrocarbon gas, like propane, will only fuel a backyard grill for a couple of hours. However, the same volume of gasoline will be sufficient to drive a car for several hundred miles. Additionally, compared to solid hydrocarbons like coal, liquids are much easier to move around inside an engine.

Crude oil is the single most traded commodity in the world. As a result, the global importance of oil is far greater than its impact on the energy industry. Because of the global high profile of crude oil trading, the oil industry is subject to a very high level of international scrutiny. It is often viewed as a benchmark for the energy sector, and can have a disproportionate impact on electricity and heating costs.

Petroleum

"Petroleum" is a catchall term that can describe any hydrocarbon fuel that is a liquid at room temperature. Petroleum can mean crude oil, gasoline, heating oil, or jet fuel.

---

[1] Literally, petroleum means "rock oil" in Latin. It comes from the words *petra*, meaning rock, and *oleum*, meaning oil. Petroleum, coal, and natural gas are all hydrocarbon fossil fuels. They differ in that petroleum is liquid at room temperature, coal a solid, and natural gas is a gas.

Crude Oil Market Participants

The trading of crude oil is dominated by the relationship between the suppliers and consumers. The largest importers of crude oil are the industrialized nations of North America, Europe, and the Asia-Pacific region. The major net exporters are less developed countries in the Middle East and South America. Transportation and storage costs are the primary determinant of where supplies originate and where they end up. All things being equal, oil is transported to the nearest market first. If that market has enough supply, the next closest market is chosen.

International politics and environmental regulations also affect the flow of petroleum. Sometimes, countries will refuse to buy or sell oil to one another. For example, in 1973, OPEC countries refused to sell oil to Western Europe, America, and Japan because of their support for Israel.[2] Another example of oil not going to the nearest market is due to environmental regulations. The United States requires that gasoline and diesel contain very low quantities of sulfur, which is a major pollutant and source of acid rain. Compared to countries that don't have those restrictions, low sulfur crude oil is more valuable to the United States than to other countries, and it is worth shipping long distance to get to that market.

There are four major types of participants in the petroleum market: producers, refiners, marketers, and consumers.

- **Producers.** Oil is produced around the world. About half the world's supply of crude oil is located in the Middle East. Since the region has a relatively low population and a low demand for oil, it is the single largest exporting region. There are many other oil producing regions worldwide. Several industrialized countries, like the United States, are major oil producers. However, industrialized countries tend to be net importers of oil due their high domestic demand.
- **Refiners.** Crude oil is converted into finished products like gasoline at refineries. These facilities are most commonly located near the consumer markets. The net profit of a refiner is proportional to the region's *crack spread*—the profit from buying a barrel of oil, splitting it into its components, and selling the components. Refiners typically try to eliminate their exposure to petroleum prices.

---

[2] Organization of Petroleum Exporting Countries. A major crude oil cartel consisting of the governments of 12 countries: Algeria, Angola, Ecuador, Iran, Iraq, Kuwait, Libya, Nigeria, Qatar, Saudi Arabia, the United Arab Emirates, and Venezuela.

- **Marketers.** Many companies specialize in trading, buying, and reselling petroleum products. These organizations can be anything from a hedge fund to a gas station operator. Typically, marketers will try to buy finished products and resell the same products at higher prices.
- **Consumers.** The end users of petroleum products, consumers run the range from industrial manufacturers to private individuals filling up their cars with gasoline.

Common Units

Barrel (bbl). In the United States, petroleum of all types is traded by volume. A barrel contains 42 U.S. gallons (in the United States) or approximately 159 liters (metric units).

Tonnes (t). In Europe, oil is typically traded by weight. A tone (or metric ton) is a unit of mass equal to 1,000 kilograms, or approximately 2,204.6 U.S. pounds.

Conversion Between Barrel and Tonne. A rough approximation is that there are 7.5 barrels in one tonne of crude oil. However, because the composition of crude oil can vary substantially, each type of crude oil will have its own conversion ratio. These can range from approximately 7.2 barrels per tonne (for Persian Gulf crude) to about 7.5 barrels per tonne (for premium light crude like WTI or Brent).

Descriptions of Crude Oil

Crude oils are typically described by their *density* and *sulfur content*.

Density is usually measured by API (American Petroleum Institute) gravity. Low density, or *light*, crude oils have a higher proportion of light hydrocarbons that can be recovered through simple distillation. In contrast, *heavy* crude oils contain a larger portion of low value products that require additional downstream processing to be valuable. The density of crude oil is fairly apparent by visual inspection—light crude oil will flow freely, while heavier crude oil will be much more viscous.

High **sulfur content** is highly undesirable for crude oil. Sulfur is a major pollutant and can only be removed through expensive processing. *Sweet* crude oil contains has a low sulfur content, while *sour* crude oil contains a much greater amount of sulfur.

Exploration and Drilling

Oil, like other fossil fuels, is formed when decaying organic material is trapped underground. Commonly, liquid and gas hydrocarbons

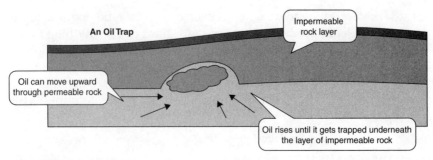

Figure 2.3.1.   Diagram of an oil trap

are found in the same area. Both liquid and gas hydrocarbons (petroleum and natural gas) are lighter than rock and will naturally migrate upward unless that movement is prevented by a layer of impermeable rock. This combination of an impermeable layer of rock overtop a permeable layer of rock is called a *trap* (Figure 2.3.1). Oil exploration involves looking for traps in areas likely to contain oil or gas.

The most common way to search for oil traps is to use *seismology* which is the study of how energy waves—like sound waves or earthquakes—pass through the earth's surface. Different types of rock transmit energy at different speeds. Engineers can determine the type of rock layers in an area by creating sound waves and sending them into the earth. Some of the sound will echo back toward the engineers. The timing of how quickly the sound returns, and its strength, will be a good indication of the type of rock layers and their relative depths. However, seismology is not an exact science. Even if seismologists know that a liquid is underneath a trap, they might still need to dig a well to determine the exact nature of the liquid.

Common Terms

Associated Gas.   Natural Gas produced from the same well as oil.

Permeable.   A measure of how easily liquid and gas pass through rock. In practical terms, this depends on the amount of connections between the pores (open spaces) within a rock. A porous rock may be impermeable if none of the pores are connected.

Porosity.   The ratio of empty space to the total volume of a rock. A highly porous rock has a lot of open space.

Trap.   An impermeable layer of rock located above a porous, permeable layer of rock.

Refining

Refined petroleum products are created by separating crude oil into various components. This process starts with *simple distillation,* where crude oil is separated into fractions by boiling it at progressively higher temperatures. Since each component of crude oil will boil at slightly different temperatures, slowly increasing the temperature of crude oil will cause products to progressively boil off. These gases are then trapped and cooled to bring them back into liquid form.

After the initial separation of products, many refiners continue to process the heavier fractions to increase their value. In general, lighter petroleum products, like gasoline and jet fuel, are more valuable than the heavier products, like asphalt. By splitting the heavier products (cracking them) into simpler products, their value is increased. This postdistillation processing (called *downstream processing*) also removes sulfur from the oil and is used to increase the octane of gasoline. Downstream processing can substantially alter the output of a refinery. For example, where simple distillation might produce 20 percent of its output as gasoline, downstream processing can increase that percentage to around 50 percent. Because the lightest, least dense, petroleum products are the most valuable, this downstream processing typically converts a 42 gallon barrel of crude oil into approximately 45 gallons of finished products.

It is impossible to produce just one distilled product, like gasoline, without producing the others. The process of converting crude oil into gasoline involves creating every refined petroleum product at the same time. Thus, if a refinery increases its output in response to higher gasoline prices, it runs the risk of glutting the market with its other refined products. The typical mix of refined products in a barrel of crude oil is shown in Figure 2.3.2.

Approximate Mix of Products Made from 42 U.S. Gallon Barrel of Crude Oil

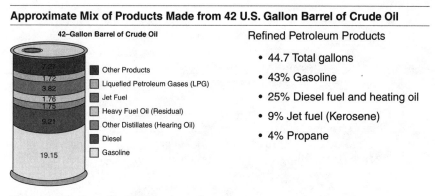

Refined Petroleum Products

- 44.7 Total gallons
- 43% Gasoline
- 25% Diesel fuel and heating oil
- 9% Jet fuel (Kerosene)
- 4% Propane

Figure 2.3.2. Barrel breakdown by gallons
(*Source:* Energy Information Agency [October 2008])

An even simpler approximation is that a barrel of crude oil contains a half barrel of gasoline and a quarter barrel of diesel fuel. However, the actual products from a barrel of crude oil can vary substantially. Every barrel of crude oil contains a different mix of raw materials. Crude oil that converts into a high proportion of lighter products through simple distillation is called a *premium crude*. Premium crude oils are more expensive than lower quality crude oil. Other common terms for crude oil describe its viscosity and sulfur content. *Light sweet crude oil* pours easily and contains relatively low sulfur. *Heavy sour crude* has a thick, syrupy consistency and contains high levels of sulfur.

The process of distillation links the prices of refined petroleum products to crude oil prices. If the price of crude oil rises, all of the refined products will become more expensive. However, there is a different type of link between the prices of the refined products. If a gasoline shortage forces refiners to increase their gasoline production, the market will become flooded with other petroleum products. As a result, there is often a negative correlation between the prices of the refined products. The relationship between crude oil and distilled products is known as the *crack spread*.

Is There a Shortage of Refineries in the World?

There haven't been any new refineries built in the United States since 1976, and it's unlikely that any will be built in the future. Even in an environment that is highly profitable for refinery owners, refineries are a long-term asset. They are extremely expensive to construct and it might take a new refinery 15 or 20 years to pay back its construction costs. Building a new refinery is an investment in a very long-term asset. They have to be built in expectation of market conditions 20 years in the future.

Unfortunately, global oil production is expected to peak around 2010 and start decreasing in subsequent years. The world is running out of crude oil. Even in an environment of rising prices for refined petroleum products like gasoline, new refineries are unlikely to be profitable in the long term. Today's existing refining capacity will probably be sufficient to handle the refining of any crude oil that remains in 20 years. It doesn't make a lot of sense to increase capacity in a market whose size is expected to decline over time.

For similar reasons, the number of offshore drilling rigs is also on a decline. Building a substantial number of new drilling rigs would be a substantial investment that would take years for a profitable return. Given shrinking drilling opportunities and the continued volatility of oil prices—there were oil price crashes in the 1970s and 1980s—no one is willing to fund new drilling rigs in response to a short-term spike in prices.

Fractional Distillation

Crude oil is refined (separated into its component pieces) by fractional distillation. It is placed into a large vertical container, called a *distillation tower*, and heated. The lightest elements, with the lowest boiling points, rise to the top, while the heavier fractions settle at the bottom. By selectively siphoning off the lighter fractions, crude oil is separated into pieces. A simplified picture of a refinery is shown in Figure 2.3.3.

After crude oil is separated into its components by distillation, many of the heavier liquids are further processed by subjecting them to high temperatures and pressures. This process, called *cracking*, breaks the heavier liquids into lower density liquids.

Comparing Crude Oil to Refined Petroleum

While there is active trading in both crude oil and refined petroleum products like gasoline, the two markets are very different.

Crude oil has a global market. It is transported around the world and is approximately the same product and price wherever it is traded. For example, if the price of oil is higher in New York than Paris, tanker ships will be diverted from France and start heading to New York. The refineries in the northeastern United States and northern Europe can each accept crude oil intended for the other location.

In comparison, refined petroleum products, like gasoline, are typically regional markets. Prices and product formulations vary

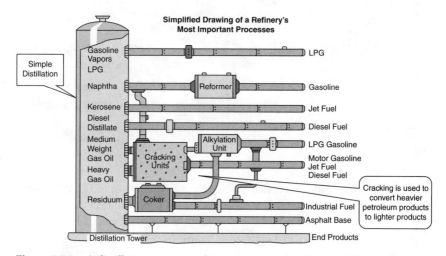

Figure 2.3.3.   A distillation tower used to separate crude oil into salable products (*Source:* Energy Information Agency [October 2008])

substantially between regions. Historically, it has been considered very risky to locate refineries outside the industrialized countries. As a result, finished products are refined close to their final destination. There is a limited international infrastructure for transporting finished petroleum products in bulk. There is some international trade in these products, but the volume of trading is much lower than for crude oil. Local environmental regulations further fragment the market for refined products. For example, gasoline used in North America is required to use a different formulation than gasoline used in Europe. This is true even on a national level. Gasoline in California often uses a different formulation than gasoline in New York.

Gasoline

Gasoline is the primary fuel used to power automobiles and light trucks around the world. In 2007 it accounted for 44 percent of all petroleum consumption. The demand for gasoline increases during periods of good weather. Demand starts to rise during the spring and peaks in the late summer.

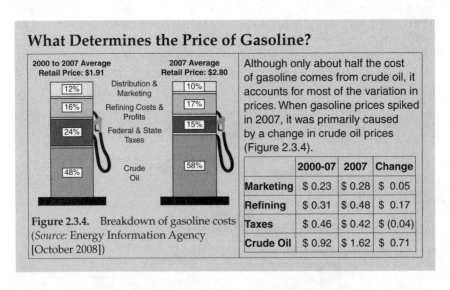

What Determines the Price of Gasoline?

2000 to 2007 Average Retail Price: $1.91

12%	Distribution & Marketing
16%	Refining Costs & Profits
24%	Federal & State Taxes
48%	Crude Oil

2007 Average Retail Price: $2.80

10%	
17%	
15%	
58%	

Although only about half the cost of gasoline comes from crude oil, it accounts for most of the variation in prices. When gasoline prices spiked in 2007, it was primarily caused by a change in crude oil prices (Figure 2.3.4).

	2000-07	2007	Change
Marketing	$ 0.23	$ 0.28	$ 0.05
Refining	$ 0.31	$ 0.48	$ 0.17
Taxes	$ 0.46	$ 0.42	$ (0.04)
Crude Oil	$ 0.92	$ 1.62	$ 0.71

Figure 2.3.4.   Breakdown of gasoline costs (*Source:* Energy Information Agency [October 2008])

The primary method for distributing gasoline is through pipelines, which transfer gasoline from refineries to terminals near consuming areas. At the local terminals, gasoline is mixed with additives, like ethanol, to meet local government regulations. Then the gasoline is transported by tanker truck to local gas stations, where it is sold to consumers. In the United States, gasoline is differentiated by its *octane* level and *formulation*. Along with local taxes, these factors account for most of the regional variation of prices. Other factors influencing the retail price of gasoline can include transportation costs and the marketing plan of the individual gas station owners.

Octane is a measure of how much gasoline resists ignition. When gasoline resists ignition, less power is delivered to the power train of the car. Instead, it will be wasted as heat. Octane is not a measure of the energy in a tank of gasoline. For example, ethanol has a higher octane than gasoline (it is easier to ignite), but contains less energy. Adding ethanol to gasoline increases the octane of gasoline, but still decreases the total miles per gallon of the car using that gasoline.

The *formulation* of fuel refers to the various additives that are required or prohibited. For example, a state might mandate that all gasoline sold between March and October contain 10 percent ethanol. Sometimes additives are prohibited. Lead was once used as an antiknock agent in gasoline in the United States. (Antiknock agents are used to increase the octane rating of gasoline.) But the lead pollution from automobile exhaust became a major health hazard and its use was later banned. Sulfur is another example of a regulated pollutant.

Gasoline prices fluctuate throughout the year based on crude oil prices, consumer demand, and formulation. As a general rule, gas prices tend to increase rapidly in the early months of the year, spring and then summer, as shown in Figure 2.3.5. Prices stabilize in the later summer and decline in the coldest winter months. Gasoline prices tend to be very volatile because there is there is a limited amount of supply that can be generated from refineries, and consumers can't substitute other fuels for gasoline.

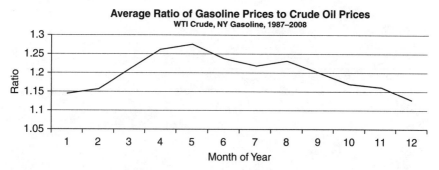

Figure 2.3.5. Gasoline prices, shown as a percentage of crude oil prices, typically spike in late spring and early summer, then decline in the winter

Octane Ratings

Higher octane ratings mean that engines can operate more efficiently. In this case, "efficiently" means that less heat is wasted when fuel is ignited to produce power. Engines have to be optimized for a specific octane level of fuel—using higher octane fuel does not automatically make an engine more efficient. Under normal combustion, fuel is pumped into an engine cylinder and ignited. The expanding gas that results from igniting the fuel will push the cylinder outward to drive a crankshaft. This provides the mechanical power in a car (Figure 2.3.6).

Normal Operation	Knocking
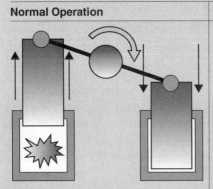	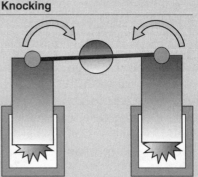
Figure 2.3.6. Normal piston operation	**Figure 2.3.7.** Gasoline ignition not synchronized
Igniting fuel pushes up one cylinder, turning a crankshaft, and depressing a paired cylinder. The cylinders alternate to provide smooth supply of power to the pivot point (the crankshaft).	If the ignitions are precisely controlled, the cylinders won't alternate properly. Depending on the severity of the mistiming, the engine won't work as efficiently and may be damaged.

In an engine, there are multiple cylinders that all need to work in concert with one another. The fuel in each cylinder will ideally ignite in a process that drives the piston outward in smooth motion. When the pistons on the other side of the engine ignite, the original piston will move back to its starting position. If the fuel in all of the linked cylinders does not ignite at the same time, a number of problems can occur (Figure 2.3.7). If one piston is still expanding when it should be falling, it will decrease the power being created by the engine.

Higher octane fuel ignites in a more predictable manner. There is less uncertainty about the timing of its ignition. There have been a number of fuel additives used over the years to prevent the problem of unpredictable fuel ignition. For a long time lead was the most popular choice; currently, high octane fuels like ethanol are used. Some common terms for the problem of cylinder mistiming are "knocking," "pinging," or "pinking."

Heating Oil and Diesel Fuel

Heating oil and diesel fuel are variations of the same product, a distillate of petroleum called *No. 2 Fuel Oil*. Of the two, diesel fuel typically has stricter requirements for a minimum pentane rating (similar to octane ratings on gasoline) and lower sulfur content. Otherwise, both chemically and in the financial markets, the two products are nearly identical and used interchangeably.

About 80 percent of No. 2 Fuel Oil is used as diesel fuel. The remainder is used for residential and commercial heating. Nearly all large trucks, buses, trains, farm equipment, and large boats in the United States use diesel engines. The majority of diesel fuel is used for on-highway vehicles like semitrucks and tractor trailers.

There is a small international trading market for diesel fuel. Almost all of the diesel fuel used in the United States is produced domestically, with the surplus shipped to other countries. Like most petroleum products, it is much more common for the raw materials (crude oil) to be traded internationally than the finished product.

When used as heating oil, the largest use for No.2 Fuel Oil is for residential heating during winter months. In the United States, almost all of the houses that use oil heat are in the Northeast. As a result, heating oil prices are strongly influenced by winter temperatures in Mid-Atlantic and New England areas. Prices are lowest in summer months and spike during the winter (Figure 2.3.8). Households often try to reduce oil costs by filling up their storage tanks during summer months when prices are low. However, since most households lack sufficient storage capacity to go an entire winter without refilling their supply, there is continued demand for heating oil throughout winter months. Most households will need to refill their heating oil four or five times a winter.

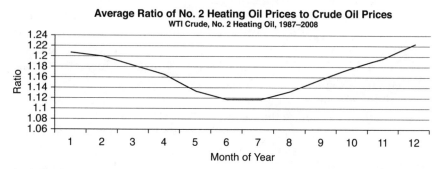

Figure 2.3.8.   Diesel and heating oil prices are lowest during the summer months and increase in the winter
(*Source:* Prices from EIA)

Crack Spreads

Cracking refers to the process of separating out and transforming the components of crude oil into commercially saleable products. A *crack spread* is the difference between the price of finished petroleum products and the price of crude oil. Since most refined petroleum products are not exported internationally, crack spreads will vary substantially throughout the world. Each region will have its own crack spread set by the supply and demand considerations of its local market for finished petroleum products.

The crack spread is the wholesale price of refined petroleum products less the cost of raw materials. It is approximately equal to the gross profit that a refiner will earn by converting crude oil into refined petroleum products. If the spreads between finished products and crude oil are too narrow to produce a refining profit, refiners will cut back on production until the price of the finished products rise.

A typical trade in a crack spread would be to "buy" a future crack spread that is too small for refiners to make a profit, and benefit when refiners cut back on production and prices rise. Buying a crack spread means the trader benefits from a rise in finished petroleum products and a fall in crude oil prices. Because the price in all of these products tends to move up and down together, a crack spread has limited exposure to the price of crude oil. Another variation of a petroleum spread trade might allow traders to speculate on the relationship between gasoline and heating oil.

Each region has a typical grade of crude oil used as a benchmark. In North America, West Texas Intermediate crude (WTI crude) is most common. In Europe, Brent crude is used. For a crack trader, the different types of crude oil don't just mean the prices vary slightly. Different crude oils vary in composition. Premium crude oils, like West Texas Intermediate crude or Nigerian Bonny Light, will produce a higher percentage of the lightest gasolinelike products through distillation compared to less desirable crude oils. As a result, refiners have to optimize the mix of crude oil entering the refinery to produce the most profitable mix of refined products desired in their region. The chart in Figure 2.3.9 shows the typical mix of products produced by simple distillation of several crude oils.

Refiners are natural traders of crack spreads, which are a primary tool for refiners to hedge their output. There is a substantial price risk between the time refiners buy crude oil and when they can sell their finished products. In most cases, they attempt to lock in their profits by agreeing to a sales price of their most important products ahead of time. They do this by trading financial contracts in crude oil, gasoline, and diesel/heating oil. Crack spreads also allow major users of

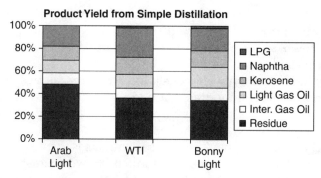

Figure 2.3.9. Typical mix produced by distillation
(*Source: International Crude Oil Market Handbook,* EIA)

refined products to lock in spreads without taking on a large exposure to crude oil prices.

Since the major oil products are all widely traded on exchanges, almost anyone can make crack trades. There is a very active market in crack trades. The most common spread trades are based on crude oil, gasoline (RBOB), and diesel fuel (heating oil). The ratio between these three products defines the crack trade. Usually this ratio is abbreviated X:Y:Z, where X is the number of crude oil contracts, Y is the number of gasoline contracts, and Z is the number of diesel fuel contracts. The most common ratio is a 3:2:1 relationship, but 2:1:1 and 5:3:2 ratios are also fairly common.

Refiners are naturally *long the crack spread*—they benefit when refined products appreciate in price relative to crude oil. Refiners can eliminate this exposure by *selling a crack spread* (alternately, going short the crack spread). This means the trader will benefit when the price of crude oil rises or the price of refined products decline.

Exchange Traded Spreads

Sometimes crack spreads are their own financial instrument. It is possible to enter into a crack spread by trading futures in each of the underlying petroleum commodities. Every time traders make a futures trade on an exchange, they are required to post margin to ensure that they have enough money to meet their financial responsibilities. The amount of margin required is directly proportional to the risk of the trade. Entering into a crack spread by trading individual commodities can result in a substantial amount of capital being locked up in margin accounts. However, the combination of trades in a crack trade is much less risky than holding an outright position in any of the underlying commodities. As a result, less money is required up front to trade the spread as a single unit.

Exchanges commonly offer crack spread trading alongside markets for the underlying commodities. As a result, it is fairly common to talk about a "crack spread" as its own traded instrument. Moreover, it is often possible to buy "crack spread options" and "crack spread futures" on an exchange. The behavior of these contracts is identical to creating a crack spread through individual products. However, margin requirements are lower and all of the futures are traded simultaneously.

Ethanol

Ethanol is an alternative to petroleum fuels that can be produced by fermenting and distilling almost any crop that contains starch. It is a clear colorless liquid chemically identical to the alcohol found in intoxicating beverages. Ethanol intended as fuel is *denatured* to make it unsuitable for drinking because alcohol intended for human consumption is subject to a lot of government regulations. Ethanol is fairly easy to manufacture from common crops like corn or sugarcane. It is a renewable fuel source that produces fewer greenhouse emissions than fossil fuel.

On the downside, since fertilizer and farm equipment both require petroleum fuel and produce a lot of pollution, it is unclear if ethanol production actually reduces either petroleum demand or pollution. Ethanol also does not have the same energy density as gasoline. Because of this, the transportation of ethanol is relatively more expensive than that of gasoline. Ethanol is also highly corrosive and absorbs water. As a result, engines and gasoline pipelines have to be specifically built or modified to handle ethanol.

Another drawback of ethanol is that it produces higher amounts of some types of ground-level pollution than gasoline. For example, ethanol produces twice the ozone of a similar gasoline engine. Another criticism is that it raises food prices, since ethanol is produced from crops that would otherwise be used as food. Given the limited amount of cropland in the world, using crops to produce ethanol means less food is available for a growing population.

Compared to gasoline, ethanol is an inferior fuel. Its popularity is a result of the expectation that the world will be running out of easily obtainable petroleum in the near future. Ethanol can be produced today in larger amounts than other alternative fuels, and much of the existing infrastructure for gasoline can be retrofitted to accept ethanol.

Starch is converted to ethanol through the process of *fermentation*. This is essentially the same process used to produce most alcoholic drinks. First, the raw materials are *milled* by grinding them into a fine powder called *meal*. Then, liquid is added to the meal to produce a slurry that is heated. Heating helps the meal dissolve into a liquid solution and kills any bacteria that might be present. Then the mixture is cooled and enzymes are added to turn the starch into simpler sugars. After that, yeast is added into the mix. This yeast converts the sugars into alcohol and carbon dioxide. Finally, the alcohol is separated from any solids or liquids that may have formed during the fermentation process by distillation.

The Corn Crush and Related Trades

Because the raw materials for ethanol are food crops that must be grown every year, there can be substantial differences between the price of ethanol and its raw materials. Government regulations specify that ethanol be mixed into gasoline at a fixed ratio. Unless ethanol is more expensive than gasoline, its price is determined by the value of the displaced gasoline. In comparison, the raw materials used to produce ethanol are affected by weather, crop conditions, and competing demands for corn as a food crop.

Just like a crack spread, it is possible to speculate on the relationship between ethanol and raw material prices. For example, if ethanol is highly expensive and corn is cheap, distillers can start buying up corn for conversion into ethanol. This will result in higher food prices and lower ethanol prices.

In the United States, the most common raw material for ethanol is corn, which represents about two-thirds the cost of producing a gallon of ethanol. The major by-products of the conversion are distillers dried grains and carbon dioxide pollution. Although distillers dried grains have potential to be used as a feed crop for livestock or as the raw materials for biodiesel, they are currently extremely cheap and not a major source of profit for an ethanol distiller. Since it takes about a bushel of corn to produce 2.6 gallons of ethanol, the spread between these two prices is often called a crush spread.

$$\text{Corn Crush Spread} = \text{Cost of Ethanol}\left(\frac{\$}{\text{gallon}}\right) \times \frac{2.6 \text{ gallons}}{\text{bushel}} - \text{Cost of Corn}\left(\frac{\$}{\text{bushel}}\right)$$

Ethanol can be created from a variety of raw materials (corn, sugarcane, and petroleum are all relatively common). Most traded contracts will accept any variety of ethanol as long as it meets delivery grade requirements. In the future, it might be necessary to first calculate the cheapest-to-delivery raw material prior to entering into a crush trade. Alternatively, the crush spread calculation might change if a market for distillers grains develops.

Biodiesel

Like ethanol, biodiesel is an alternative fuel that is receiving a lot of research attention.

Biodiesel is an alternative fuel for diesel engines created by removing glycerin from vegetable oils. Although biodiesel does not contain any petroleum, most diesel engines can use biodiesel without modification. Commonly, biodiesel is blended with petroleum diesel and the mixture is denoted Bxx where xx represents the percentage of biodiesel in the blend. For example, B20 is 20 percent biodiesel.

There are some substantial advantages to using biodiesel. It is biodegradable, renewable, and generally produces lower emissions than standard diesel fuel. It is also nontoxic, and since it has a higher flashpoint than conventional diesel, it is safer to transport and store.

On the downside, engines fueled by biodiesel have about a 10 percent reduction in fuel economy and power compared to burning diesel fuel. Biodiesel also emits more nitrogen oxides than standard diesel. However, the biggest limitation of biodiesel is its cost. Currently, it can only be produced in limited amounts and is substantially more expensive than regular diesel fuel.

Common Terms

Brent Crude.   Brent crude is a light, sweet crude oil that serves as an international pricing benchmark. It is a premium crude oil from the North Sea.

WTI Crude.   West Texas Intermediate oil is a premium crude oil that provides a high proportion of valuable light petroleum products through simple distillation. It is a light, sweet crude oil and the most common benchmark for U.S. crude oil prices.

Feedstock.   Crude oil of any type that enters a refinery is called feedstock.

RBOB Gasoline.   Reformulated Blendstock for Oxygen Blending is a grade of gasoline suitable for mixing with ethanol or other gasoline additives. RBOB is gasoline before it has been mixed with additives.

Fuel Oils.   Fuel oils are the liquid fuels heavier than gasoline. Typically, they are classified into six categories, with the lower-numbered oils flowing more easily than the higher numbers. The two most common categories are No. 2 Fuel Oil (diesel) and heavy oil (No. 4 to No. 6 Fuel Oil).

Kerosene (No. 1 Fuel Oil).   Kerosene is the lightest grade of fuel oil. In a distillation stack, it falls between gasoline and diesel fuel. It is uncommon to see kerosene traded in the futures market.

Heating Oil (No. 2 Fuel Oil).   Heating Oil is essentially diesel fuel. It is the second largest fraction of a barrel of crude oil after gasoline. Most types of crude oil will produce about half as much heating oil as gasoline when refined.

Heavy Oil (No. 4/5/6 Fuel Oil).   Heavy oil, also known as Bunker fuel, is a term for the heaviest fuel oils. Typically, these fuels must be heated to turn them into liquids before they can be used. This is a delicate process, and as a result these fuels are only commonly used aboard large ships or in power plants. Because of its limited uses, heavy oil is typically cheaper than gasoline or diesel fuel.

2.4

COAL

 30-Second Summary

Purpose
This chapter introduces coal trading.

Summary
Coal is a solid hydrocarbon fuel that is readily available throughout the world. It is easy to store and relatively inexpensive to produce relative to the amount of electrical power it can generate. In many ways it is the perfect fuel. Unfortunately, it is a major source of carbon (CO_2) and sulfur (SO_2) emissions. The pollution that results from burning coal has made it unpopular among consumers.

Coal is the least expensive way to generate electricity. However, it has the drawback of being the most polluting fossil fuel. The competing desires for cheap electricity and less pollution are at odds with one another. Global efforts to reduce carbon emissions have typically deadlocked on the issue of coal-powered generation. Most countries want to use coal-fired power plants for cost reasons, and would like other countries to stop using them because of pollution concerns. Coal is approximately one-fifth the cost of other fuels. As bad as pollution is, having electrical bills 5 or 10 times higher is not a viable option for the economic health of most countries.

Because the price of coal is generally low, transportation makes up a much higher percentage of delivery cost than other fossil fuels. As a result, most coal is used within a couple hundred miles of where it is mined. By far the biggest application for coal is electrical generation. Electrical power plants and coal mining companies are often located close together. As a result, there are relatively few people buying or selling coal on the open market. Coal is not a heavily traded financial product.

Key Topics
- Coal is closely linked with electrical power generation. It is the most popular fuel for the generation of electricity, and 90 percent of coal production is used to generate electric power.
- Coal-fired electrical generators are a major source of pollution. Coal produces more pollution than any other type of fossil fuel, and this has made coal politically unpopular.

(Continued)

- In the financial markets, coal is much less important than other fossil fuels. It is primarily used to provide energy for electric power generation. However, coal is usually cheap enough that it doesn't actually determine the price of power. Financially, coal is more closely linked to market-based initiatives to limit global climate change than to electric power prices.
- Coal-based power plants have a large economy of scale. Big centralized coal-fired plants are cheaper to operate than small plants. The current nature of the power grid—centralized generation and extensive transmission lines—is in large part due to this economy of scale.

Coal is a major fuel used to generate electricity. About half the electrical power in North America is generated from coal plants. While there are a number of industrial uses for coal, like making steel or providing raw materials for plastics, these applications are much smaller markets for coal than electric power generation. Over 90 percent of the coal used in North America is used for generating electricity. Globally, coal generation accounts for about over half of the world's electric generation capacity. However, despite the dependence of electric generation on coal, coal has less of an effect on the price of electricity than natural gas because it is much cheaper.[1] As a solid fuel, coal has different operating constraints than either oil or natural gas. For example, it is much harder to use a solid fuel in an engine. Something has to physically move the coal into the fire box—it isn't like gasoline, which can use a suction pump. Coal fires are also harder to start up and shut down than oil or natural gas fires. Natural gas or oil engines can be turned off by cutting the fuel supply. This isn't the case with coal—any coal currently being burned will continue to burn for a while even after the engine is shut down.

One reason coal is much cheaper than either petroleum or natural gas is because its potential uses are more limited. It is easier to make an internal combustion engine that runs off a liquid than a solid. Another reason is that coal mining is generally less complicated than either oil or natural gas drilling. Many coal mining problems can be addressed by application of additional brute force. For example, if more coal is

---

[1] Chapter 4.2 describes how the price of electricity is determined. In deregulated markets, the most expensive power producer that is currently activated determines the cost of power across a power grid. Power producers are activated from lowest to highest cost, depending on consumer demand. Since coal plants are some of the lowest cost power producers, coal rarely determines the price of electrical power.

needed, either new technology or longer working hours can be used to address the problem.

The major drawback of coal is the amount of pollution created when it is burned. Coal is the single largest source of air pollution in the world. Some of this is due to the fact that it is so commonly used, but another part of the problem is that megawatt for megawatt, coal produces more pollution than either oil or natural gas. As a result, the coal markets are closely associated with market-based approaches to limiting global climate change.

On a physical level, "coal" is a term that can describe almost any solid hydrocarbon. Its actual composition—everything from the heat energy it contains to the amount of pollution it releases when it is burned—varies substantially. In general, coal is a black or brownish black sedimentary rock that is removed from the ground by mining. Various types of coal are classified by the amount of heat energy they can produce, as well as the amount of pollutants they contain.

Compared to other fossil fuels, coal is fairly easy to store and transport. It can be stacked into a pile, and it won't evaporate or leak out of the bottom of a rail car. The most common method of transporting coal is by train. It is also fairly common for coal to be transported on barges and trucks. Since coal is typically traveling from mines to power plants, there isn't a large consumer distribution system.

Even though coal transportation isn't particularly difficult, it can be expensive. Since coal is cheap, even moderate transportation costs can make up a substantial portion of its retail cost. As a result, it is common for coal-fired power plants to be located near coal mines. In other cases, unique technologies are built to transport coal cheaply. For example, coal pipelines can be built to link power plants to a continuous supply of coal from a distant mining location. To pass it through the pipeline, the coal might be crushed and mixed with water to form a slurry or compressed to form a solid log.

There is a limited international market for coal. The primary reason is that coal power plants are generally built close to an abundant local supply. Because transportation costs account for a substantial percentage of its final price, imported coal is usually much more expensive than local coal. As a result, it is usually uneconomical to transport coal over long distances.

Partially as a result of this, coal prices are much less volatile than the prices of other fossil fuels. The major consumers of coal are power plants that operate continuously throughout the year. They sign long-term supply contracts with nearby coal mines. It is fairly straightforward for power plants to stockpile supplies, and difficult for them to

Coal Pipelines

Although coal is a relatively cheap fuel, it is fairly heavy. The cost of transporting it can make up a substantial portion of its final cost. As a result, having access to a cost effective transport network is an important factor in determining the economics of a coal-based power plant. Perhaps the easiest solution is to locate the power plants close to a mining region. However, that may be impossible due to the need to transmit power to some service area.

If there is a very long distance between the source and destination, coal pipelines can be an attractive alternative to railcars or barges. There are two main technologies used to transport coal through pipelines. Slurry pipelines crush the coal into small pieces and mix the pieces in a liquid solution. Alternately, the coal can be compressed into logs that are suspended in water.

There are a number of serious environmental considerations with coal pipelines. One problem is that they use a tremendous amount of water. Coal slurry pipelines use a 1:1 ratio of coal to water and make the water very difficult to clean after it is used. Since a large coal-fired power plant might burn 1,000 tons of coal a day, the amount of water involved can be significant over the course of a year. This is particularly true if the pipeline is located in a region with limited water supplies. For example, the 273-mile coal slurry pipeline supplying the Mojave Generating Station in Laughlin, Nevada, was using a billion gallons of water a year prior to being shut down by complaints from local Indian tribes.

To address the concerns of water usage, new pipeline technologies are being researched. For instance, compressing the coal into a log allows three or four tons of coal to be transported for each ton of water used. These pipelines also leave the water cleaner than slurry pipelines.

A second problem with pipeline transportation is that the coal needs to be dried out prior to being used. The most effective way to dry the coal is to burn some of it. However, that has the side effect of further increasing carbon emissions and raising transportation costs.

resell unused coal because there are few counterparties interested in coal trading. Power plants spend a lot of time optimizing their transportation from their local suppliers to minimize that aspect of their costs. Consequently, it is difficult for them to switch over to a different supplier on short notice.

The major influences on the price of coal are the price of other fossil fuels and environmental legislation. Prolonged periods of high oil and natural gas prices can make coal relatively more attractive for generating electricity. When prices for other fuels rise, coal power plants become comparatively more economical. This ultimately leads to an increased use of coal and higher coal prices. However, even when it goes up in price, coal generally stays much less expensive than oil and natural gas.

Market-based approaches to reducing carbon emissions and pollution also have a major effect on the price of coal. Because coal is heavily used and very polluting, it is the primary target of these regulations. These approaches seek to make it less economically viable to use coal as a primary fuel. Coal is heavily used as a fuel for producing electricity because it is cheaper than the alternatives. So, to reduce coal usage, most environmental initiatives operate by making coal-based generation more expensive.

Types of Coal

Because the chemical makeup of coal can vary substantially, it is usually classified based on how much carbon it contains and how much heat energy it can produce. The four main types of coal used for fuel are *lignite*, *sub-bituminous*, *bituminous*, and *anthracite*. Other varieties of coal exist, but they are generally not used as fuel. For example, graphite and diamonds are almost 100 percent carbon, and technically can be considered coal, but are neither easily ignited nor efficient to use as a fuel.

There is a trade-off between ease of ignition and the energy content of coal. Low quality fuel is easy to ignite, but does not contain as much energy as higher quality coal. Higher quality coals are harder to ignite, but contain substantially more energy. Extremely high quality coal, like graphite or diamonds, potentially contain a tremendous amount of heat energy. However, extremely high quality coal is nearly impossible to ignite under normal circumstances. Coal also varies by the type of pollution it contains.

- **Lignite.** Also called *brown coal*—or more colloquially, *burnable earth*—lignite contains the lowest energy content of any other fuel coal. It contains about 30 percent carbon, and has a high moisture content. As a result, it is often soft and crumbly. Its low energy density means that it is inefficient to transport over long distance, so it is almost never traded internationally. Unless stored carefully, it is subject to spontaneous combustion. The only commercial use of lignite is for power generation by nearby power plants. Compared to black coal, lignite contains an especially high proportion of pollutants, and its use is a politically charged topic. The only reason to use lignite is to provide a low cost source of electricity.

- **Sub-Bituminous.** The properties of sub-bituminous coal fall between lignite and bituminous coal. Sub-bituminous coal has higher carbon content than lignite—about 40 percent—and contains more heat energy. Typically it also contains less moisture than lignite. As a result, it is slightly more efficient to transport over long distances, but there is still a relatively small international trade in this grade of coal. A little less than half the coal produced in North America is sub-bituminous, which is used almost exclusively as a fuel for electrical power generation.
- **Bituminous.** This is coal that has been subjected to high temperature and pressures. It is about 70 percent carbon. The most abundant type of coal found in North America, it contains between two to three times the heat energy of lignite. There is an active international trade in bituminous coal, and it is used for both power generation and as a source for industrial raw materials. Bituminous coal is usually black, but it can also be dark brown. It commonly has visible striations of bright and dark material. About half the coal used in North America is bituminous.
- **Anthracite.** The highest grade of fuel coal, anthracite contains about 95 percent carbon and typically has a hard glossy black surface. Anthracite ignites with difficulty, but produces a steady flame once lit. It has low moisture content, produces relatively little pollution, and contains approximately the same heat energy as bituminous coal. But anthracite coal is much less common than bituminous coal, and its high price makes it uneconomical to use in power plants.

Sulfur Content

The second primary classification of coal is by its sulfur content. When sulfur is burned, the sulfur oxides that are released into the atmosphere combine with water to form sulfuric acid. Along with carbonic acid and nitric acid, sulfuric acid is one of the main components of acid rain. However, the danger from sulfuric acid is not limited to rain. Almost any liquid runoff from a coal mining facility or coal burning power plant will be somewhat acidic. Over time this tends to kill nearby plants and wildlife. Power plants that use high sulfur coals generally have more acidic runoff than ones that use low sulfur coal.

Sulfur oxide emissions are an example of a localized pollution problem. When sulfuric acid is present in small quantities, it is not harmful to plant or animal life. However, when it is allowed to build up over time, it can reach a critical mass where species start dying off.

As a result, the areas directly surrounding coal mining and coal power plants, downwind of the plants, or downstream from plants, are at the highest risk. Farther away, the magnitude of the problem becomes less severe. Acid rain isn't dangerous in small concentrations.

When coal contains sulfur, the sulfur usually comes in one of two forms. Most commonly, sulfur is found combined with iron to form pyrite crystals that are scattered throughout a coal vein. Pyrite is a yellow crystal sometimes called "Fool's Gold." Alternately, sulfur can also be found chemically combined with the carbon in coal, called *organic sulfur*. Pyrite can be removed prior to burning the coal, but organic carbon requires installation of scrubbers on the exhaust stacks of power plants.

Pyrite is heavier than coal, and most of it can be removed by crushing the coal and submerging the combination of coal and pyrite in water. Coal will float to the top of the water, and the pyrite will sink. This process is called *coal washing*. This is a relatively simple process. However, it can have a high cost since the coal needs to be dehydrated prior to being burned. In some cases, there may only be a nominal incremental cost to washing the coal: for example, if the coal is already being crushed and transported in a slurry pipeline.

Removing organic sulfur from coal is substantially more complicated. It requires installing scrubbers on the exhaust stacks of coal-fired power plants. This process is known as *flue gas desulfurization*, commonly abbreviated FGD. A coal scrubber uses lime or limestone to remove sulfur dioxide emissions. Lime is a base that combines with acid to form a neutral product. The lime is mixed with water to form a mist that is sprayed across the top of the smokestack. When sulfur oxide gas rises out of a smokestack, it combines with the mist to form a solid by-product called *gypsum*. Lime scrubbers can remove between 90 and 97 percent of the sulfur being emitted from a power plant.

Gypsum scrubbers can be very expensive to install and maintain. Since a solid by-product is being formed, it is necessary to build ledges or shelves inside a smokestack to catch the falling residue. It is also necessary to clean out the residue on a regular basis. Generally, this means the power plant needs to go offline throughout the year for maintenance.

Coal and the Power Grid

In addition to pollution, coal power plants play an important role in another major problem facing the energy markets—the reliability of the transmission grid. Coal power plants benefit from economies of scale.

The bigger the plant, the less fuel is required to produce the same amount of electricity. However, large centralized power plants require elaborate long distance transmission systems. Coal-fired generators are not the only power plants that benefit from a substantial economy of scale (nuclear power has a similar issue), but historically they have been the primary power plants used in the electrical industry.

When electric power was first being introduced, the two major advocates were Thomas Edison and George Westinghouse. Thomas Edison advocated using direct current (DC) power to transfer electricity from the generator to the consumer. The major problem with Edison's DC power was that the voltage on the power lines dropped as it traveled farther away from the generator. There is no efficient way to step voltage up or down in a DC transmission system. This means that small local generators would need to be built close to the end users.

In contrast, George Westinghouse advocated using an alternating current (AC) system invented by Nikola Tesla. With the Westinghouse system, transformers could be used to step up or step down the voltage multiple times. This enabled a single large power plant to supply power to a wide area. It also enabled a single power plant to support different types of customers. For example, high voltage power could be supplied to industrial sites, and lower voltage power supplied to residential consumers. The greater efficiency of large generation plants tipped the scale toward AC power. As a result, AC power has become a universal standard for electricity transmission.

For most of the following century, behemoth power plants were built a long way from consumers. Extensive transmission networks had to be constructed to transmit power from these outlying generation plants to get that power to customers. Unfortunately, there is a trade-off between the cost of generating power and the cost of transmitting it. North America is now experiencing problems with the complexity of its transmission grid.

When transmission systems are simple, they are relatively inexpensive and reliable. However, when they get complicated, they get progressively more expensive and less reliable. In the first 50 years after electricity was introduced, electrical generation faced a different set of problems than it does today. Historically, electrical power was used primarily for lighting, and urban population density was lower. As a result, transmission systems were relatively simple. Over time, as more electrical appliances were introduced and the population increased, the transmission systems became more complicated. This has made the transmission grid more expensive and less reliable.

Coal Mining

There are two main methods of mining coal: surface mining and underground mining. Both types create environmental problems. Of the two, surface mining is simpler and requires fewer miners. However, the highest quality coal is usually located deep underground.

- **Surface Mining.** Also called *strip mining*, surface mining is the easiest way to mine coal when the coal deposits are located close to the surface. The first step in the process is to remove the topsoil and rock on top of the coal. The ground cover and topsoil can usually be removed through fairly standard earth-moving equipment like bulldozers. The rock layer is more difficult to remove. It must first be cracked through the use of explosives, and then shoveled out or excavated. In general, strip mining uses equipment that is fairly similar to standard excavation equipment, built on an unbelievably large scale. The primary economic factors affecting surface mining are the amount of coal available and the amount of earth that needs to be removed.

  In most cases, after an area is strip-mined, it is contoured. Then the topsoil is replaced and the area replanted with ground cover. Historically, strip mining gained a bad reputation for blighting the environment. This is much less of a concern currently, when mining companies are required to restore the land that was used for mining. Surface mining is common in the midwestern and western United States.
- **Underground Mining.** When the coal is too far underground to be removed by surface mining, tunnels will need to be dug into the ground. Miners will create a series of underground rooms to work in. Modern mining makes use of continuous mining machines that move up and down large faces of coal (approximately 50 feet in length). Although underground mining is now a highly mechanized process, it remains fairly dangerous. Because material is being physically removed from the ground, coal mines constantly face the danger of a collapse. Whether a mine collapses purposefully (to prevent a problem later) or accidentally, the land on top of it will be destroyed and need to be restored. In the United States, most underground mining occurs in the Appalachian Mountain range east of the Mississippi River.

Coal Trading

Coal can be traded on both exchanges and in the OTC marketplace. Because of the close relationship between coal mining companies and electrical power generators, the coal market works a bit different than other energy markets.

The only type of coal available for trading by individual investors is high grade coal that it might be worthwhile transporting over a long distance. It isn't possible to speculate on the relationship between different grades of coal. Most of the time, low grade coal is never transported far—it is always used near where it is mined. Additionally, there isn't an active financial market to trade the location of coal. Unlike natural gas, where transportation trades are common, there are limited opportunities to make coal transportation trades. In general, no one wants to transport coal over long distances, so there isn't a lot of trading.

Another limitation on coal trading is the weak relationship between electricity prices and coal prices. The primary use for coal is in generating electricity. However, except in limited cases, the prices of electricity and coal are not correlated. Electric power prices are usually determined by the most expensive fuel in a region rather than the cheapest. The only traders that can actually benefit from the spread between coal and electricity prices are the investors that own coal-fired power plants.

Historically, coal prices are much less volatile than other energy commodities on a price per energy basis. Being relatively easy to store, coal does not have a strong seasonal price trend. The chart in Figure 2.4.1 shows the relative price of coal, heating oil, and natural gas on a MMBtu/dollar scale.

Location of Coal Deposits

Worldwide coal reserves are concentrated in the Northern Hemisphere. In particular, the United States and Siberia have vast coal deposits. As

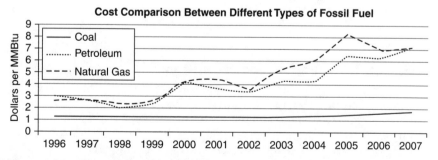

Figure 2.4.1.   Comparison of fossil fuel prices
(*Source:* Raw data provided by EIA)

Common Terms

Coal prices have their own pricing terminology. There is a distinction between the price that an individual investor will pay for coal (on an exchange) and the price a large consumer of coal pays.

Spot Price. The *spot price* and *forward prices* are typically set by exchange-based trading. The spot price is the price of a cash transaction at the futures delivery point.

Captive Price. This is the price for coal when it is transferred between two branches of the same company or between two affiliated companies. Because of the close relationship between coal mining and electric power production, it is not unusual for coal mining companies and coal-fired electric generation companies to be affiliated. It is impossible for an unaffiliated person to get coal at this price.

Open Market Price. The price of coal sold on the open market. It is the prevailing prices for coal traded between large unaffiliated producers and consumers of coal.

Delivered Price. The actual cost paid by a consumer of coal after transportation costs are included.

can be seen in Figure 2.4.2, there is a relative lack of coal in Western Europe, South America, and Africa.

Compared to other energy commodities, the global market for coal is relatively small. About 80 percent of the coal produced worldwide is used close to where it is mined. The cost of transporting coal as a percentage of its total cost effectively divides coal trading into two regions: an Atlantic market and a Pacific market. In the Atlantic, coal is imported into the UK, Germany, and Spain. In the Pacific market, coal is imported into Japan, Korea, and parts of China. About two-thirds of the international coal trading occurs in the Pacific.

Energy Independence vs. Pollution

For many large countries, energy independence and pollution are conflicting goals of an energy policy. The United States, China, and India have abundant coal reserves but limited amounts of petroleum and natural gas. Even though coal remains a highly polluting fuel, its low cost and local availability make it an extremely attractive fuel from the standpoint of cost and political stability.

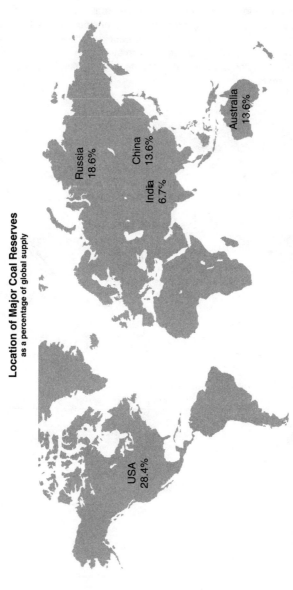

Figure 2.4.2. Locations of various fossil fuel resources around the world (*Source:* Data based on EIA International Energy Annual 2006)

Coal Producing Areas

Appalachian Mountains

The Appalachian Mountains are a major source of high quality coal and produce about a third of North America's total output. These mountains are located on the eastern part of the United States (Figure 2.4.3). The region is characterized by large underground mines that produce high quality bituminous coal and anthracite. West Virginia and Pennsylvania are the largest coal producing states in the region and have a long history of coal mining. Unlike western strip mines, which are open to the sky, mines in this region are dug deep into the Appalachian Mountains, forming extensive cave complexes.

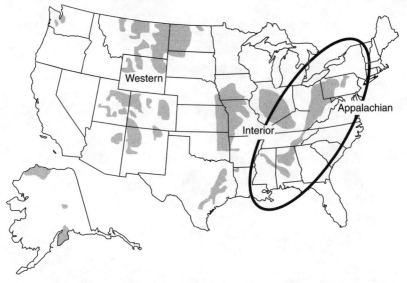

Figure 2.4.3.   U.S. coal reserves/Appalachian Mountains
(*Source:* Energy Information Agency [October 2006])

Western Region

The West is the single largest coal producing region in the United States. This region, centered on the state of Wyoming (Figure 2.4.4), is characterized by extremely large surface mines. Very thick bands of coal, sometimes 40 or 50 feet deep, lie close to the surface. These mines produce low sulfur, low ash sub-bituminous coal that is used to provide fuel for power plants throughout the central United States. Some of the largest surface mines in the world are located in this area. The Western Region accounts for about half the coal produced in the United States.

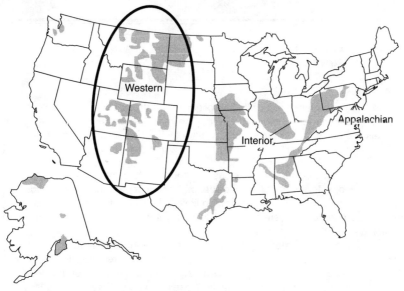

Figure 2.4.4. U.S. coal reserves/Western Region
(*Source:* Energy Information Agency [October 2006])

2.5

EMISSIONS MARKETS

 30-Second Summary

Purpose

Government initiatives to reduce the risk of global climate change have had a profound impact on the energy market. This section introduces the emissions trading markets that governments are using to achieve their environmental goals.

Summary

Motivated by signs of global climate change, countries have begun taking steps to reduce global levels of carbon dioxide, sulfur dioxide, and nitrogen dioxide emissions. The two most popular ways to limit pollution are through *taxes* and through *cap-and-trade* systems. Of the two, only the cap-and-trade system is a trading market.

A cap-and-trade system sets a limit on the amount of a substance that can be produced. Everyone producing that substance is required to have a license for production. This has the advantage of ensuring a cap on pollution levels. When licenses are freely tradable, those with an ability to shift to a less polluting technology can do so and make a profit by selling their licenses. By reducing the amount of licenses over time, a free market encourages the most economical changes to be made first. The two main problems facing cap-and-trade systems are how to distribute licenses and how to enforce compliance.

The emissions markets are also closely linked to the use of coal to generate electricity. Although it produces more pollution, coal can produce electricity for a fraction of the cost of any alternative fuel. To a large extent, the goal of the emissions market is to make it possible to continue to use coal as a major source of electricity and reduce carbon emissions through other means.

Key Topics

- Attempts to reduce pollution, particularly nontoxic greenhouse gases, are controversial because they increase energy prices.
- Market-based approaches to reducing emissions are popular since they allow the free market to minimize the cost of reducing emissions. It is believed these systems will have a greater chance of being fully adopted because they keep costs to a minimum.
- The most common type of emissions market is a cap-and-trade system. In this type of system, a limited number of pollution credits are issued. Anyone that pollutes is required to turn in a pollution credit.

The possibility of global climate change, sometimes called global warming, has forced most countries to adopt policies that limit the creation of greenhouse gases and other pollutants. This is complicated by the fact that reducing these emissions makes electricity more expensive. Coal is the lowest cost and most polluting fuel. Completely eliminating coal from the generation stack will cause a large increase in the price of electricity. The goal of the emissions markets is to keep that cost to a manageable level. It is crucial that consumer prices be prevented from jumping to 5 or 10 times today's prices. A price jump of that magnitude would almost certainly send the economy spiraling into a depression and eliminate the possibility of future reforms.

Having someone else pay the cost of more expensive electricity is not a feasible solution. It is the primary reason that international discussions on reducing greenhouse emissions have deadlocked. Ignoring the flowery political speech, the ultimate issue is that reducing carbon emissions will be very expensive. Neither consumers in industrialized countries or developing countries, can afford to pay electric and heating costs that are 10 times higher than their current bills.

Emissions markets offer the promise of finding the lowest cost way to lower greenhouse gas emissions. They provide a reasonable approach to what would otherwise be an intractable problem. In a practical sense, affordable power is synonymous with coal power. Coal is easy to mine and there are plentiful reserves in the United States, the former Soviet Union, China, and India. Coal has such a price advantage over alternative fuels that it is hard to develop a scenario where coal power isn't being used to keep power prices affordable.

Why Is Global Warming Dangerous?

The primary concern about greenhouse gases is that climate change will destroy the arable land needed to provide food for a growing world population. Crops require a balance of sunlight and rain, and almost any disruption in that balance is harmful. If a regional climate changes, the local plant and animal life in that region will probably die out. Even if the climate in some other region changes so it can support those organisms, there is no easy way to move the inhabitants from one area to the other.

History

Global climate change became a hot topic around 1990. Scientific concerns over global warming spawned a series of international discussions on greenhouse gas emissions hosted by the United Nations.

The goal of these international discussions was to create a set of bind-ing international treaties that limited emissions of greenhouse gases to 1990 levels. The UN coordinated many of the discussions, since it is ineffective for a single country to cut emissions if other countries don't slow down their output at the same time. Ultimately, these discussions were derailed by disagreements over who had the responsibility for paying the cost for reducing greenhouse emissions.

For example, Europe has a high proportion of relatively efficient power plants. The European Union advocated taxing countries with highly polluting power plants and paying the proceeds to countries with efficient power plants.

Another plan was put forward by Russia and the other states of the former Soviet Union. Russia advocated capping emissions rights at the historical level of 1990, but by the time of these discussions took place in the mid-1990s, Russia had suffered an economic collapse following the dissolution of the Soviet Union. Its emissions during the mid-1990s were 30 percent below its emissions in 1990—leaving it plenty of spare capacity to resell to other countries.

The role of developing nations in reducing carbon emissions is also problematic. China and India are the first and fourth largest emitters of carbon dioxide in the world. Moreover, both countries are rapidly building coal-based power plants and increasing the pollution they produce. However, with their vast populations, these countries ad-vocate allocating emissions targets per capita. This would allow both countries to continue to build highly polluting coal power plants while still maintaining surplus emissions rights to sell to other countries.

On the other side of the argument were the industrialized coun-tries. The United States, the European Union, Russia, and Japan agreed to cut emissions to 5 percent below 1990 levels. However, these cuts—which would involve a substantial expenditure of cash—would still be insufficient to halt global climate change if developing countries con-tinued to build highly polluting coal-based power plants. Ultimately, the UN committee was unable to reach an international compromise. Even so, a lot of countries have voluntarily agreed to follow most of the United Nations' suggestions. However, because of the lack of a global compromise solution, carbon emission schemes have been im-plemented unevenly around the world.

Reducing Carbon Emissions

There are two popular mechanisms for encouraging the development of environmentally friendly emission technologies: taxes and trad-ing. The first approach, a *carbon tax*, would have to be paid whenever

The Kyoto Protocol

In 1997 the Kyoto Protocol became the first global agreement to limit the production of greenhouse gases. The core of the Kyoto agreement is the creation of a *cap-and-trade* system that imposes both international and national limits for greenhouse gas emissions. It was approved, in principal, by almost every country in the world. However, the agreement in principal did not turn into a binding agreement.

Determining the right level for the national allocations for emissions rights became a highly political process. The core disagreement is whether the United States should be forced to replace its coal-based power plants to allow the rest of the world to construct their own coal-based generation. On one side is arguments that carbon limits should be set per person, on the other is the argument that the world shouldn't be constructing highly polluting technologies regardless of the current carbon output per person of each region. Ultimately, the disagreement is over who pays for more expensive power.

The two countries that produce the most pollution are China and the United States. China is rapidly building coal-based power plants and will soon overtake the United States as the largest carbon producer in the world. With its large population, China would benefit if carbon limits were set per person. Population-based caps would allow it to continue its rapid construction of highly polluting coal-based power plants. The United States did not feel that it should be responsible for removing less polluting power plants so China could replace that carbon output with even more polluting plants.

The issue comes down to who pays a higher cost for power.

carbon dioxide, or other greenhouse gas, is produced. The second approach is a trading scheme that caps the amount of emissions and requires possession of a freely tradable permit that is consumed whenever pollution is created. In practice, the two policies often coexist and are not mutually exclusive.

Carbon taxes are a price-based approach that makes more polluting technologies less attractive. Taxes are a highly effective way of making highly polluting technology more expensive and cleaner technology less expensive. This is achieved by taking money received in taxes and using it to subsidize the cost of less polluting technology. Within a single country, taxes are relatively simple to implement. Most countries already have a mechanism in place to apply taxes to many activities.

In a *cap-and-trade* system, the total amount of emissions is fixed (capped), and the right to create pollution becomes a tradable commodity. This allows companies to make their own economic decisions about how to lower their individual costs. Because the only transactions are generally exchanges of goods (cash for permits) between private companies, trading can easily cross country borders and span multiple currencies. Trading provides the best way to minimize everyone's cost of complying with environmental goals.

Cap and trade adds a variable surcharge to energy costs that fluctuates based on supply and demand. In comparison, a carbon tax adds a fixed cost. Another difference is that in a cap-and-trade system the government is usually revenue neutral—it doesn't make a profit from the emissions system. Taxation usually involves a direct cash payment to a government. Any taxation system involving multiple governments is substantially complicated by the need to determine which government receives revenue.

Public Goods and Common Land

Emissions are hardly the first time that humanity has had to deal with the problem of sharing a cost among a large group of people. Humanity has been dealing with this type of problem for hundreds of years, and economists have developed their own terminology to discuss this issue.

"Public goods" is a term used by political economists to describe something that benefits everyone regardless of who pays the cost. National defense is the classic example—it is impossible to defend the borders of a country without protecting everyone in the country. As long as the costs are paid by someone, everyone gets the same benefit. The term applied to people who take benefits without contributing any money is "free riders."

One way to look at the reduction of greenhouse emissions is as a public good. There will be a cost associated with the change, but once it is made, everyone will benefit. Typically, these types of problems have been addressed by taxes—everyone is required to pay something to the public coffers. The major problem with this approach is that much of the world doesn't make heavy use of electricity nor does it have money to pay the costs of lowering emissions.

Another way to look at the problem of emissions is to think of carbon emissions rights as a limited commodity. There are a limited number of emissions rights, and when used, an emissions right gives the owner the right to low cost electricity. Political economists refer to this subset of public goods problems as *Common Lands* problems. The name comes from shared lands often found in England, Scotland, and Wales prior to the seventeenth century. When thought about this way, the emission problem becomes more of a problem of distributing low-cost electricity permits.

Emissions Trading Markets

The emissions trading markets, of which there are a number world-wide, are all based on cap-and-trade systems. The rationale behind trading emissions rights is that it doesn't matter where cuts are made—as long as emissions are reduced, everyone is better off. This allows the trading market to dynamically reallocate savings in response to changing interest rates, foreign exchange rates, and to employ similar economic stimuli.

Cap-and-trade systems create property (emissions rights) where no property previously existed. These rights are a license to pollute, or alternately, the right to use affordable (coal) power. There is no way of allocating these rights that makes everyone happy. Ultimately, someone—perhaps lots of people—will have to pay a higher cost for their power.

In theory, cap-and-trade systems have a couple of advantages over taxes to reduce carbon emissions. By capping the maximum amount of carbon emissions, the total amount of pollution is well known. Cap-and-trade systems also give businesses maximum flexibility in determining how to meet government requirements. These producers can either install more environmentally friendly technology or buy emissions credits. Because it can be done globally, there is no danger of companies relocating factories from high tax to low tax regions.

Another advantage to cap-and-trade systems is that they are broadly applicable across countries and different types of greenhouse gases. Because no government needs to be involved as an intermediary, cross-border transactions are relatively straightforward. For example, a trading market would allow cuts to be paid for in one country using one currency, and the benefits received in another country with a separate currency. Additionally, unlike a taxation system that would need to be constantly adjusted by a legislature, a trading system can adjust itself to changing economic situations.

Distributing Rights

Because no one naturally owns emissions rights, there is the problem of determining who is allowed to produce carbon emissions. Often this problem boils down to which people have access to the low cost electricity provided by coal-fired power plants. The tempting solution is to say that everyone pays the same amount for power, which is at odds with the concept of the trading market. The primary benefit of the trading market is to find the greenhouse gas emissions that can be eliminated most easily and to compensate those people for cutting their emissions.

Another complication is that consumers need to be protected during the whole process. The largest source of greenhouse emissions is power generation. Governments can't allow power generators to go out of business. When a power plant goes bankrupt, the government can't allow the municipality served by that plant to go without power. The government would need to step in and assume the obligations of the power plant operator. In the end, it is the residential consumer who would be left paying the high cost of complying with environmental regulations.

Emissions Credits

There are two ways to get emissions rights in most cap-and-trade systems. The first is to receive the right from the administrator of the cap-and-trade system. Usually these rights are allocated or auctioned off. The other way is to create something that offsets carbon emissions in some manner. This might be through creating a carbon sink (like planting a forest), capturing carbon dioxide emissions and storing them underground (carbon sequestration), or by creating a nonpolluting source of electricity (building a hydroelectric plant or solar power installation).

The ability to creatively reduce carbon dioxide is a key advantage of a cap-and-trade system. Essentially, this allows countries to keep using coal power until alternative sources of power can be developed. In many cases carbon capture doesn't have to be done close to home either. Particularly under cap-and-trade systems conforming to the Kyoto Protocol, it is possible to offset carbon emissions anywhere around the world. This ensures that the lowest cost alternative can be found.

Carbon Sequestration

Carbon dioxide is a necessary by-product of almost all combustion. The process of forming carbon dioxide is what creates heat when fuel is burned. Long chains of carbon are completely broken up, forming single carbon molecules that combined with oxygen. As a result, as long as we use hydrocarbon fuels, it is impossible to stop the creation of carbon dioxide.

It is possible to capture CO_2 exiting fossil fuel power plants. This CO_2 then needs to be stored somewhere, like a depleted natural gas well or water reservoir. This is called *carbon sequestration*. Carbon storage facilities are very similar to natural gas storage facilities except that they store carbon dioxide instead of methane.

Another way of reducing carbon emissions is to use plants or bacteria. Plants use carbon dioxide to form wood, bark, and leaves. However, plants usually require the use of fossil fuels for fertilization and harvesting. Bacteria can also be used to absorb carbon dioxide. The advantage of using bacteria is that a very dense colony of bacteria can be located in a small area and it doesn't require a lot of petroleum products to maintain.

Limitations to Cap-and-Trade Systems

In practice, while cap-and-trade markets sound good, they face several implementation problems. Tracking all carbon dioxide emissions is impossible, and even if it were possible, it would be far too complicated to trade. For example, animals naturally produce carbon dioxide when they breathe. They produce even more than normal when they exercise. It isn't possible to have a cap-and-trade system that applies to something like jogging. As a result, emissions trading markets must pick and choose the carbon dioxide sources they want to restrict. Most carbon trading is focused on reducing carbon dioxide resulting from the combustion of fossil fuels.

However, emissions credits can be created from almost any source. This means that cap-and-trade systems run the risk of funny accounting when emissions credits are granted for offsetting carbon emissions. If a region is capping power plant emissions but not car emissions, for instance, it might seem to make sense to shut down a local commuter railroad that is powered from the local power plant to encourage more driving. After all, this would reduce the "emissions" at the power plant. However, in reality, since cars are also a major source of pollution, this would actually increase the amount of carbon emissions in the area.

A related limitation on carbon trading is that it can force companies into making investments in carbon mitigation systems that would normally be considered poor ideas. For example, if a power producer wants to protect its customers, it needs to minimize the risk that speculators corner the market on emissions rights. The primary way to eliminate this risk is to be able to create emissions credits on demand. Essentially, companies that utilize carbon credits need to ensure that they have a way to "manufacture" carbon credits in the event of a spike in prices.

The chance of speculators trying to corner the market is high—it is just about the only way for speculators to make a profit trading emissions credits. However, since emissions credits can be manufactured by carbon offsets, the easiest way to get protection against speculators is to keep a couple of carbon offset ideas on the side. The economic value of these ideas might be really bad—it just has to be better than being held hostage by speculators.

Carbon Taxes

Although they commonly coexist, *carbon taxes* are generally considered the primary alternative to cap-and-trade systems. Taxation adds a surcharge to energy costs and relies on high costs to incentivize adoption of new technologies. Most countries have implemented domestic energy taxes. However, an international tax remains unlikely because of concerns over who gets the money. As a general rule, countries favor tax schemes that levy taxes on other countries and benefit themselves.

Compared to a cap-and-trade system, there are some big advantages to taxes. They can be applied universally to a wide variety of things and require minimal administration. For example, adding a surcharge to the price of gasoline is much easier than checking if someone owns enough gas credits to be allowed to purchase gasoline. Taxes are simple. Taxes can also be used to promote domestic carbon reductions. This is accomplished through reinvesting tax money into local projects. With carbon trading, cash is commonly transferred away from local consumers to a carbon sink in some other jurisdiction. With taxes, the money can stay in the local economy.

On a domestic level, the biggest problem with taxation is that energy consumers are a captive audience. Energy companies pass along taxes directly to consumers. As a result, the only group that is being financially affected by the taxes is consumers. The power companies, who have the ability to adopt less polluting technology, don't have a lot of motivation to improve their technology under a taxation system.

Trading Carbon Emissions

It is possible for carbon emission trading to achieve its goal of reducing global climate change without ever becoming a major financial market. Speculators don't have a clear role in the emissions market. In most markets, having a large number of people willing to transact, limits volatility and keeps transaction costs low. However, in the emissions markets, it seems likely that speculation will increase volatility and raise consumer costs.

Over time, the general economic thought is that a rising population and demand for power will force the price of emission rights upward. However, no one—particularly the government—benefits from higher carbon emissions prices. The only downside to low prices is that companies might not have any incentive to invest in environmentally conscious technology. As long as environmental targets are met, governments prefer low prices. Governments also have some excellent tools to stabilize prices—they can both issue new rights and determine how easy it is to create carbon credits through offsetting.

If carbon prices are too high, the cost gets paid by consumers (voters) and the economy. Governments have a civic obligation to keep their local power grids operating and their economy moving forward. As a result, along with a great ability to manipulate emissions market prices, governments have an incentive to keep emissions prices at the right level. Governments want prices high enough to spur changes but low enough so the economy and their citizens are not negatively affected. Governments don't want speculators cornering the emissions markets and making a windfall profit at the expense of consumers.

Carbon Equivalents and Other Pollutants

Although this chapter has concentrated on carbon dioxide trading, there are other emissions markets. These markets are substantially similar to the carbon market and share much of the terminology and trading limitations. The biggest difference is that most types of pollution only affect a limited area. As a result, most emissions markets are regional (covering a couple of countries) rather than global in nature.

- **Carbon Equivalents.** There are a number of greenhouse gases other than carbon dioxide. Methane, nitrous oxide, and ozone are examples of other greenhouse gases. These are usually converted into "carbon dioxide equivalents" and traded as part of the carbon market.
- **SOX.** Sulfur oxide is a source of acid rain. Acid rain is a regional problem commonly addressed through emissions markets. These markets are separate from the carbon emission markets and typically organized by region.
- **NOX.** Nitrogen oxide markets are closely associated with the sulfur markets. Like sulfur oxides, nitrogen oxide emissions are associated with acid rain.

3.1

POLLUTION

30-Second Summary

Purpose

This is an introduction to pollution caused by the combustion of fossil fuels.

Summary

There are a number of different types of pollution. The first general category of pollution is caused when *impurities* or *small particles* trapped in the fuel are released into the air when the fuel is burned. The second type of pollution is an intrinsic part of combustion—the creation of *greenhouse gases*. In fact, greenhouse gases don't present a health hazard and are generally safe. However, when large quantities of greenhouse gases are released into the atmosphere, they have the potential to change the world's climate.

Key Topics
- Some types of pollution can be prevented by using fuel that contains fewer impurities.
- Other types of pollution, like carbon dioxide, are an unavoidable part of combustion.

The burning of fossil fuels (combustion) produces a variety of unwanted by-products that are collectively termed "pollution." Some types of pollution are poisonous to humans, while other types have the potential to harm the world around us. Combustion is an *oxidation* process. Carbon-based fuels are combined with oxygen to produce heat. Some types of pollution result from the release of particles trapped inside the fuel as it burns. Other types of pollution are a result of the chemical reaction that produces heat.

Pollutants that cause an immediate health risk are generally caused by impurities trapped within fuel. These include *heavy metals*, like mercury and lead. Even small quantities of these toxic particulates pose an immediate health hazard. Other trapped particles, like supersmall grains of sand called *fly ash,* are dangerous without being poisonous. The small size of fly ash means it is easy to breathe into the lungs, causing strokes and chronic breathing problems.

Other impurities, like sulfur and nitrogen, are not directly poisonous but can cause secondary chemical reactions sometime after combustion. These substances form *acid rain* when in the presence of water. Sulfur is commonly found trapped within coal deposits. Nitrogen is present in the atmosphere and combines with atmospheric oxygen under temperatures necessary for combustion.

In addition, every fossil fuel produces some unavoidable by-products. The combustion of any hydrocarbon fuel (which covers almost all fuels) produces water (chemical formula H_2O) and carbon dioxide (chemical formula CO_2). It is the creation of these products that produces energy. It is not possible to create energy without producing these by-products. Neither by-product poses an immediate health threat—these are the same by-products caused by breathing and vigorous exercise.

There is no single approach that works equally well for every type of pollution. For example, the carbon dioxide emissions from any single power plant aren't particularly important. Carbon dioxide is a non-toxic gas that makes up a large portion of the atmosphere around us. Plants rely on carbon dioxide to grow. However, the aggregate carbon emissions from every power plant can be significant enough to affect the earth's climate. Greenhouse gases are a global problem.

Acid rain is another type of pollution that becomes important in aggregate. A little bit of acid raid isn't dangerous. Water is commonly slightly acidic. However, while water evaporates, most acids do not. Given enough time, sufficient acid can accumulate in a single area to present a health threat to wildlife and plants. Acid rain is generally a regional problem. It declines in intensity the farther it is from its source. When combined with the output from several plants, the cumulative sum of the acid rain might be extremely harmful.

Combustion Pollution

The first three types of pollution (carbon dioxide, nitrogen oxides, and sulfur oxides) are by-products of *combustion.* Also called *burning,* combustion is an oxidation process where some type of chemical bond (which will vary by the product being burned) is broken and replaced with an oxygen bond. Replacing almost any type of chemical bond with an oxygen bond is an exothermic reaction that releases heat. For example, when coal is burned, carbon-carbon bonds are broken and

Major Types of Pollution

- **Carbon Dioxide.** Chemical formula CO_2, carbon dioxide is one of the principle by-products of combustion. It is impossible to burn any plant-based fuels without producing CO_2. It is a nontoxic, odorless gas that naturally exists in the atmosphere. Large amounts of CO_2 can increase the strength of the greenhouse effect.
- **Carbon Monoxide.** Chemical formula CO, carbon monoxide is a product of incomplete combustion (a fire where there was insufficient oxygen to create CO_2). Carbon monoxide is a poisonous gas. When breathed in by a human, it will bind tightly to hemoglobin and prevent normal breathing. In the presence of nitrogen oxides or sulfur oxides, it will form acid rain.
- **Nitrogen Oxides.** Most commonly nitrogen dioxide, NO_2, but can be any combination of nitrogen and oxygen. These compounds are commonly abbreviated NOX (sounds like the word "knocks"). Nitrogen oxides are one of the major causes of acid rain.
- **Sulfur Oxides.** Most commonly sulfur dioxide, SO_2, but can be any combination of sulfur and oxygen. These compounds are commonly abbreviated SOX (sounds like the word "socks"). Sulfur oxides are one of the major components of acid rain.
- **Heavy Metals.** Mercury, lead, and plutonium are all highly toxic metals that accumulate in living organisms. When these metals build up in the body, they don't decay, so getting rid of them is difficult. These metals are often trapped in fossil fuels and released in the combustion process.
- **Fly Ash/Soot.** General terms for inert particulate matter trapped in fossil fuels. Commonly, these are supersmall grains of sand or coal that were not completely burned. When suspended in the air, it is easy for these particles to get caught inside someone's lungs. This will create breathing problems and can lead to lung damage and diseases like *silicosis*.

replaced with carbon-oxygen bonds. The source of the fire's heat is the breaking and the creation of chemical bonds. Carbon dioxide is an unavoidable part of combustion.

Different fuels will have different types of bonds that can be broken to provide energy. For example, the primary component of natural gas, methane, has the chemical formula CH_4. There are four carbon-hydrogen bonds that can be broken to create energy. When methane combines with oxygen (Figure 3.1.1), it will produce a chemical reaction that creates heat, carbon dioxide, and water (Figure 3.1.2).

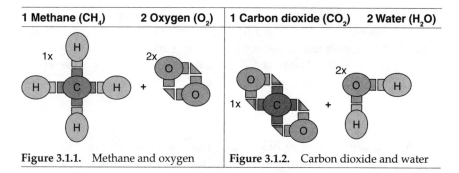

1 Methane (CH$_4$)　　2 Oxygen (O$_2$)	1 Carbon dioxide (CO$_2$)　　2 Water (H$_2$O)

Figure 3.1.1. Methane and oxygen　　**Figure 3.1.2.** Carbon dioxide and water

When methane is burned, the carbon-hydrogen bonds are broken, and the carbon and hydrogen combine with oxygen to produce heat. To be combustible, a substance needs some bonds that can be replaced with oxygen bonds. For example, it is impossible to burn water in oxygen. The chemical formula for water is H$_2$O—there are two hydrogen oxygen bonds in a water molecule. There is no net energy gain that results from breaking one hydrogen-oxygen bond to create another. Therefore, water is not combustible in oxygen regardless of its temperature.

Most types of combustion require some heat, like a spark, to get started. For methane to combust, something must provide the energy to break the first carbon-hydrogen bond and the first oxygen-oxygen bonds so the methane and oxygen can combine. Upon combining, heat will be produced. If that heat is sufficient to cause additional chemical bonds to break, the reaction will be self-sustaining, until there is nothing left to burn.

Carbon Oxides

The most common by-products of burning hydrocarbon fuels are carbon oxides (either carbon dioxide or carbon monoxide) and hydrogen oxides (primarily water). Since water is not considered a pollutant, the primary concern is the production of carbon oxides. Carbon dioxide is a colorless, odorless, nontoxic gas that wouldn't be considered a pollutant except for concerns over its effect on the global climate. In contrast, carbon monoxide is highly toxic. It is formed when there is an insufficient amount of oxygen available for complete combustion. Power plants try to completely eliminate carbon monoxide emissions.

However, it is impossible to eliminate carbon dioxide creation. Any type of carbon-based fuel will produce carbon dioxide when burned. The relative quantities of carbon dioxide and water produced by combustion vary by fuel. Methane has the highest proportion of hydrogen to carbon (a four-to-one ratio). Longer chain hydrocarbons, like coal, will contain more carbon. As a result, compared to burning methane, coal will produce a much higher portion of carbon dioxide relative to the amount of water produced. Restrictions on carbon dioxide emissions are commonly seen as a global issue.

Nitrogen Oxides

Nitrogen is a colorless, odorless gas that makes up 78 percent of the earth's atmosphere. Sufficiently high temperatures will force atmospheric nitrogen to combine with oxygen. Since most combustion uses air to provide oxygen, nitrogen will also be present. It is possible for either nitrogen oxide (NO) or nitrogen dioxide (NO_2) to form. This has led to the generic term NOX to refer to any nitrogen oxide. In sunlight, nitrogen oxides will often break apart and cause ozone to form (O_3). Ozone is a major source of smog and can cause shortness of breath, chest pain, asthma, and coughing attacks. It is also a source of acid rain. NOX pollution is generally a localized problem addressed on a regional level.

Sulfur Oxides

Fossil fuels often contain sulfur distributed throughout the fuel. When this sulfur is burned, it creates sulfur dioxide (SO_2). The generic abbreviation for a sulfur oxide is SOX. In the presence of a catalyst, like nitrogen dioxide (NO_2), sulfur dioxide converts into sulfuric acid, a major component of acid rain. A little bit of acid rain generally isn't dangerous, but it can build up over time. When enough acidity builds up, the plants and animals exposed to the acid will die. Like NOX emissions, SOX emissions are usually addressed on a regional level.

Particulate Pollution

Heavy Metals

Coal burning power plants are one of the main sources of atmospheric heavy metal pollution. For coal-fired power plants, the most dangerous of these pollutants is mercury. In many regions coal-fired power plants can account for 90 percent of the mercury released into the atmosphere. Mercury is a powerful neurotoxin that has been associated with a host of medical problems ranging from autism and sensory impairments to death. While the magnitude of the public health risk due to mercury emissions can vary dramatically between regions, it is such a powerful toxin that cap-and-trade solutions are impractical. Unlike greenhouse emissions and acid rain restrictions, any level of mercury emissions is dangerous. Lead and cadmium are examples of other heavy metals that can be released through combustion.

Fly Ash/Soot

A large number of small particles can be released by combustion or formed as a result of SOX and NOX emissions. These particles are a major cause of breathing problems and can lead to heart attacks and strokes. Some of these particles are so small they can easily be breathed into the lungs and enter blood vessels. Once in the body, they can cause substantial damage to the body's respiratory system. Children, people with asthma, and the elderly are the most at risk. Particulate pollution also reduces visibility and is a major cause of urban haze.

CO_2 Emissions and Fuel Type

Longer chain hydrocarbons that are primarily carbon-carbon bonds, like coal, produce more CO_2 emissions than natural gas because they contain more carbon. At two extremes, comparing natural gas (methane, see Figure 3.1.3) and graphite (pure carbon, see Figure 3.1.4) the difference in chemical structure is obvious.

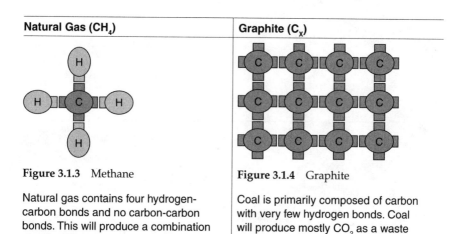

Natural Gas (CH_4)	Graphite (C_x)
Figure 3.1.3 Methane	**Figure 3.1.4** Graphite
Natural gas contains four hydrogen-carbon bonds and no carbon-carbon bonds. This will produce a combination of H_2O and CO_2 when burned.	Coal is primarily composed of carbon with very few hydrogen bonds. Coal will produce mostly CO_2 as a waste product.

Toxic Pollution

After it is produced, there are only a couple of options for dealing with toxic chemicals. The first option is to combine the toxin with something that makes the substance nontoxic. Another approach is to dilute the toxic substance until it is no longer a major health risk. A third approach is to concentrate the toxin into something that is extremely deadly and then try to store it. If it can be done, the first approach is always the best approach. For example, sulfur dioxide (an acid) can be combined with lime (a base) to produce a harmless substance (gypsum). At that point, even if placed in a landfill, the toxic substance isn't a major health risk.

If it isn't possible to make the pollution safe, it's necessary to choose between two bad alternatives. For example, nuclear waste can't be made nonradioactive. Diluting a toxic substance means spreading out—basically polluting everything a little bit. The alternative, which isn't a lot better, is to concentrate the toxin and attempt to store it somewhere it can't escape. A leak of a concentrated toxin is usually catastrophic.

3.2

GASES, LIQUIDS, AND SOLIDS

 30-Second Summary

Purpose
This section introduces the science behind physical state changes and gives examples on how energy trading is affected by chemistry and physics.

Summary
Some materials transition between solid, liquid, and gas phases when heated. This is called a *phase change,* and it is a reversible process. Other materials undergo a chemical reaction when heated. A chemical reaction, like cooking or being burnt, is not reversible. The energy industry uses the ability of substances to shift between solid, liquid, and gas phases for a variety of jobs.

One important task that is made possible by phase shifts is the separation of specific gases and liquids out of mixtures. Refining of petroleum products and distillation of ethanol are both examples of separation processes based on this science.

Another important physical property of materials is that if you compress a gas, it gets hot. If you want to compress it enough to make it into a liquid, you need to cool it substantially. If you don't keep it cool, it will start to expand again. The ability to shift substances between liquid and gas forms and compress gas is the key to air-conditioning and refrigeration systems.

Finally, gas pipelines are affected by phase shifts. The temperature in pipelines isn't constant, so engineers have to design pipelines to handle both gases and liquid condensation.

Key Topics
- Every substance has a unique melting and boiling point that can be used to separate out mixed substances. The primary method of separating substances is called distillation. This process requires a tremendous amount of energy due to the heating and cooling required.
- Refrigeration and cooling systems are based on the ability to transfer materials between gas and liquid phases. Like distillation, cooling requires a lot of energy.
- Gases are much more complicated than either liquids or solids. They have to be contained or else they will evaporate. In addition, the pressure, volume, and temperature of a gas are all interrelated, and this makes certain operations much more difficult.

PHYSICAL PROPERTIES

All substances have two major types of properties: *chemical* and *physical*. The chemical properties of a substance determine how it combines with other substances. For example, combustion is a chemical reaction between a fuel and oxygen. Physical properties involve changes in substances that don't represent a chemical change in a substance. In general, physical changes are reversible.

The physical state of a substance, called its *phase*, describes whether it is a gas, liquid, or solid. This state has a big effect on energy trading. The physical phase of fuel determines how it must be transported and what type of engine has to be built to burn that fuel. Controlled state changes, like the ones that occur in distillation or air-conditioning systems, are the key to many processes in the energy markets. Uncontrolled state changes, like condensation, can be very destructive.

The reason that state changes are important is that solids, liquids, and gases each have different physical properties. Solids and liquids generally stay put—you can place either in a cup and they won't immediately disappear. This isn't the case with gas—anytime a gas isn't contained, it immediately dissipates. Also, when gas is compressed, it gets hot and will radiate heat into the environment. When gas is allowed to expand, it cools down and will absorb heat. For example, gas will need to be cooled substantially if you try to compress it enough to turn it into a liquid. Even then, if liquefied gas isn't kept cool and prevented from absorbing heat, it will start to expand again.

States of Matter and Separation

Energy products typically need to be purified prior to being used. This usually means separating out one piece of a raw material from everything else. Examples of separation processes are removing gasoline from crude oil or removing ethanol from an ethanol/water mixture.

There are three primary states of matter under normal conditions: solid, liquid, and gas.[1] As the temperature of a solid material is increased, it does one of two things. Usually, it will transition sequentially from a solid to a liquid to a gas, or it will undergo a chemical transformation. Exactly what happens will depend on the substance being heated. A common

---

[1] Under nonstandard conditions, there are a number of other states of matter that are not included in this discussion. These can run from Bose-Einstein condensates, which exist in the center of black holes, to plastic crystals like glass, to superheated ionized gases called "plasma." While these states are all important under some conditions, they are all much less common than the primary three phases.

example of physical state transformation is ice being melted to form water, and then further heated to turn into steam. An example of a chemical reaction is cooking a piece of meat. A state change can be reversed (water can be frozen to form ice), but a chemical reaction is generally a one-way transition (once one's dinner is burnt, cooling it down won't help).

The ability to transition certain substances between liquid, solid, and gas states plays an important role in energy trading. There are discrete temperatures at which a substance will transition from one phase to another. The two most important temperatures are the *boiling point* (where liquid/gas transitions occur) and the *melting point* (where solid/liquid transitions occur). By heating or cooling a mixture of certain substances, it is possible to separate them by carefully controlling the temperature. Each substance has a unique boiling and melting point that isn't shared with other substances. Because it is unique, when a mixture is slowly heated, substances will melt off or vaporize one at a time.

In practice, it is fairly common for most mixtures to undergo both chemical reactions and physical state changes in response to changes in temperature. It is also possible under some conditions for substances to convert directly from solids into gases.

Solid
In a solid state of matter, the molecules of a substance are closely packed and hold fixed positions relative to one another. As a result, the volume of a solid is constant unless altered through application of sufficient physical force. Application of sufficient physical force to deform a solid substance will result in a permanent deformation.

Liquid
A liquid is a fluid where molecules are loosely arranged. It is characterized by a distinct boundary at its edges that will hold molecules into the main mass of the substance. This surface tension is not sufficiently strong to prevent liquids from freely deforming in shape, but will hold the bulk of the liquid in place. Liquids conform to the shape of the container in which they are stored, but are not permanently deformed. When a liquid is moved to a new container, it will change to conform to that shape. The volume of a liquid is determined by its temperature and pressure.

Gas
In a gas, molecules are almost completely independent. As a result, gases are much less concentrated and have a much lower density than

either liquids or solids. Like a liquid, the volume of gas is determined by temperature and pressure. It is relatively easy to heat or cool gas by compressing it or allowing it to expand.

Distillation

Distillation is the process of heating a liquid mixture until it starts to boil and then capturing and cooling the resulting gas. It is a common method of separating liquids and identifying unknown hydrocarbon liquids. Distillation is a physical process that does not rely on chemical reactions. Instead, it takes advantage of each substance having a unique boiling point.

There are two major pieces in distillation units: a *boiler* and a *condenser*. The boiler is a container used to heat up the mixture to the boiling point of one of the liquids. At the proper temperature (the desired boiling point), one (and only one) of the liquids will turn into a gas and into the tubing to exit the boiler. At that point that gas (now a purified substance) is cooled in the condenser to be turned back into a liquid (Figure 3.2.1).

When a liquid reaches its boiling point, it will stay at that temperature until it is fully converted into a new state of matter. For example, if water is boiled, as long as the water vapor can escape, the liquid will stay at a constant temperature. Continuing to heat boiling water won't make the water hotter; it will just cause a faster liquid-to-gas conversion. Distillation is important because this is the primary method for separating a mixture of fuels into pure products.

Physics of Gas

Another place that science affects trading is in the natural gas markets. Unlike solids or liquids, which have relatively constant volumes, the volume occupied by a gas can change dramatically in response to outside conditions. These changes in volume affect both the pressure and temperature of gas. This can be very important since temperature could cause the fuel to change between gas and liquid states, spark a chemical reaction, or separate from some substance with which it is mixed.

Unless constrained, gases will expand to fill whatever is containing them. Gas spreads from areas of high pressure into areas of low pressure and will continue to move until the pressure is equalized. The primary way of moving gases is to create a pressure difference between two areas. Both a straw and a gas pipeline work by this phenomenon.

Distillation Requires a Lot of Energy for Heating and Cooling!

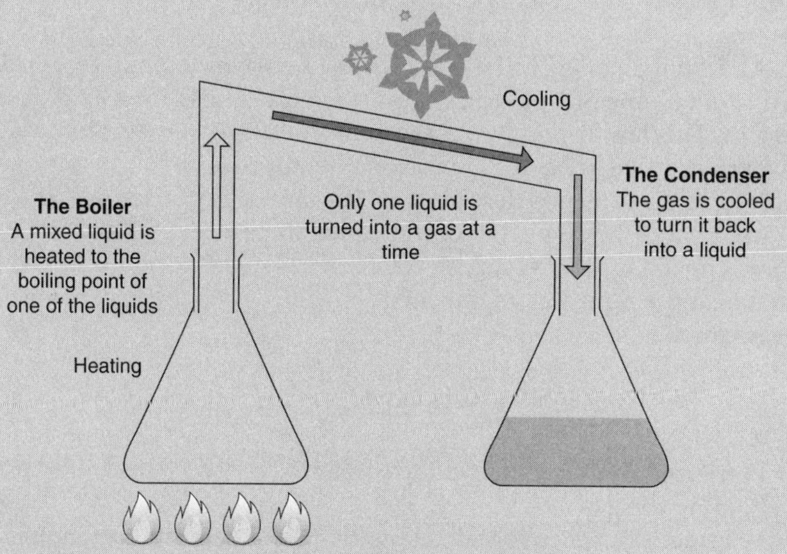

Cooling

The Boiler
A mixed liquid is
heated to the
boiling point of
one of the liquids

Only one liquid is
turned into a gas at a
time

The Condenser
The gas is cooled
to turn it back
into a liquid

Heating

Figure 3.2.1. A simple distillation unit

The major drawback of distillation is the energy requirements. Consider how many cars are on your street. Each one of those cars has a 15 or 20 gallon tank of gasoline. Try to estimate how much fuel is required by the cars on a single street, and the energy required to bring that much liquid to a boil. Then consider the number of cars worldwide and the amount of fuel those cars require. The amount of fuel required would be immense. And, every bit of that fuel went through a distillation process. Every drop of gasoline and ethanol in use had to be heated up to its boiling point and then cooled down again.

For example, it is possible to create a vacuum by sucking on one side of a straw. Gas will move into and through the straw to balance out the pressure. The higher the difference in pressure, the faster the gas will move through the straw.

Things get more complicated when temperature is introduced into the equation. The temperature, pressure, and volume of a gas are all interrelated. It is impossible to change one quantity without affecting the other quantities. Compressing a gas will raise its temperature, and allowing it to disperse will lower its temperature. Fuels like methane are rarely pure methane. There will be a large number of trace gases also in the mix. Temperature changes can be especially important if the temperature of the gas cools below the boiling point of some gas in the mixture. If that happens, liquids will start to accumulate in a pipeline.

At a layman's level, the relationship between temperature, pressure, and volume of a gas can be approximately described by the *Ideal Gas Law*. This law applies to gases where collisions between molecules are perfectly elastic, and is a reasonable approximation of the most important relationships described in the chapter. For example, if temperature rises (the right side of the equation gets bigger) and volume is held constant, the pressure needs to increase (because the law is an equality, if the right side of the equation gets larger, the left side needs to get larger too).

$$\text{Ideal Gas Law: } PV = nRT$$

P = Pressure. The force that the gas exerts on the wall of the vessel holding the gas.

V = Volume. The space contained by the vessel holding the gas.

n = quantity of gas (measured in moles). The quantity of gas will be proportional to its energy content (usually measured in MMBtus).

R = Universal gas constant. A constant value introduced to convert between different types of units.

T = Temperature. The temperature of the gas.

Common Relationships

- When gas in a contained area gets hotter, its pressure increases.
- When gas in a contained area gets cooler, its pressure goes down.
- If pressure is held constant, a pipeline or storage container will hold more cold gas than warm gas.

Gas Moving Through a Pipeline

Gas is often moved through pipelines through the use of compressors (Figure 3.2.2). These compressors operate like a fan—they create a vacuum on one side and a high pressure area on the other. Since compressors affect the pressure of the gas, they will also affect its temperature. A pipeline is a long chain of compressors linked by pipes, and it provides perfect conditions for corrosion.

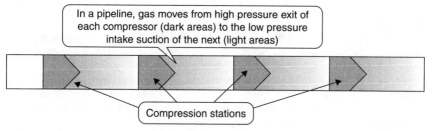

In a pipeline, gas moves from high pressure exit of each compressor (dark areas) to the low pressure intake suction of the next (light areas)

Compression stations

Figure 3.2.2.   Gas in a pipeline is moved by the use of compressors

Low to High Pressure	High to Low Pressure
Cool, Low Pressure Warm, High Pressure 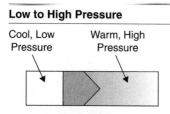	Warm, High Pressure Cool, Low Pressure 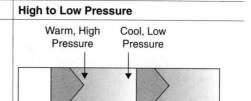

Figure 3.2.3. Compressing a gas changes its temperature

Figure 3.2.4. Gas moves from high to low pressure

When a gas moves between pipe segments, it passes through a compressor unit that alters the pressure of the gas. As a result of the pressure change, the temperature of the gas will increase (Figure 3.2.3), and if any part of the gas is chemically reactive, corrosion becomes more likely.

Within a specific segment of a pipe (the space between two compressors), gas will migrate from the high pressure output area of one compressor to the low pressure intake area of the next (Figure 3.2.4). As a result of the pressure change, the gas will cool as it moves through the pipe and might cause some of the gas to condense into a liquid. Unless it is removed (remember, these pipes need to be airtight!), a substantial amount of liquid might eventually build up in the pipe.

How Does an Air Conditioner Work?

Air-conditioning and refrigeration have revolutionized modern culture—but they are incredible energy hogs. Cooling systems depend upon physical state changes to move heat between different locations. The key to any cooling system, whether it is a household air conditioner or an industrial natural gas liquefaction facility, is finding a chemical that can easily transition between liquid and gas phases. This chemical (the working fluid) is turned into a gas to cool it down (so it can absorb heat from something), and then compressed (to heat it up), so it can radiate the heat somewhere else.

As pressure increases, the temperature of a gas increases. When pressure drops, the temperature of a gas will decrease. The core of an air conditioner is a mechanical device that compresses the fluid before it goes outside (to raise its temperature), and decreases the pressure of fluid when it comes inside (to lower its temperature).

There are three main parts to a cooling unit: a *compressor,* a *condenser,* and an *evaporator.* The compressor and condenser are typically located outside, and the evaporator inside. The working fluid circulates between these three units (Figure 3.2.5).

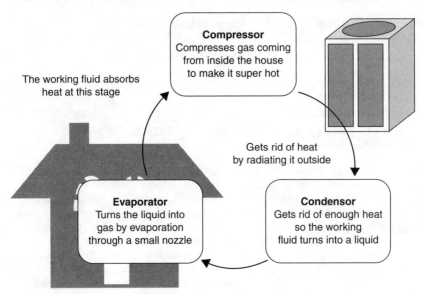

Figure 3.2.5   The air-conditioning cycle

Stage 1: Compressor

When gas leaves the interior of the house, it is pulled into a *compressor.* The compressor takes the warm gas from inside the house and compresses it to make it into a very hot gas. Compressing the working fluid increases its temperature substantially. When the superhot fluid is exposed to outside air, it will cool down by radiating heat into the environment.

Stage 2: Condenser

The mechanism that actually radiates heat into the environment is called the *condenser*. The condenser is a set of metal fins that radiate heat into the outside environment. Typically, a fan forces outside air over the fins, cooling the working fluid. When the working fluid cools down enough, it turns into a liquid and is sent inside the house.

Stage 3: Evaporator

The liquid that is sent inside is still fairly warm—it's at least as warm as the outside air temperature. It will need to be further cooled if it is to absorb heat from inside the building. To do this, the working liquid is forced through a narrow hole into a low pressure container called an evaporator. Liquids boil more easily at low pressures. As the liquid converts into a low pressure gas, it absorbs heat. The working liquid, now a cold gas, is then free to absorb heat from the interior environment. After warming up, the working liquid is sucked into the compressor to start the cycle again.

3.3

STATISTICS

 **30-Second
Summary**

Purpose

This chapter is an introduction to some of the mathematical vocabulary used by traders to communicate numeric results between one another. A substantial amount of trading vocabulary comes from the mathematical discipline of statistics: the branch of mathematics focused on organizing, analyzing, and summarizing data.

Summary

Statistics is a tool traders use to describe things to other traders. Traders spend a lot of time analyzing prices, and it is necessary to convey those results unambiguously to other people. Statistical terms like *volatility* and *correlation* have a specific meaning that isn't open to personal interpretation. Every trader needs to understand those terms.

Volatility is used by traders to describe the risk of holding an asset. The definition of volatility is the standard deviation of continuously compounded returns. It measures the likely dispersion of prices between two periods of time. A highly volatile asset is one that commonly experiences large price changes. The term "volatility" does not describe the investment merit of a trade.

Correlation is used by traders to describe how closely two things are related. When two assets are highly correlated, their prices tend to move together. There may or may not be a causal relationship between the two assets. Correlation can result from either random chance or a shared cause for behavior.

Key Topics

- Volatility is heavily used by traders as a measure for risk.
- Risk/reward relationships (*Sharpe* or *Information Ratios*) are commonly used to compare the merits of multiple investments.
- Correlation is used to describe how closely two price series are related. This is a key variable in many option pricing models used in the energy world.

There are three main goals of statistical analysis: *summarizing* time-series data, determining the *confidence* that the summary is accurate, and *identifying relationships* between phenomena. It is important to understand the difference between statistics, facts, and wishful thinking. Statistics aren't facts. At best they are a simplified description of something that may or may not be true. As a result, statistics come with an *error bound*—a description of how likely the statistic is to be a fact.

Too much data is incomprehensible. To understand data it is often necessary to organize it and determine whether it is important or unimportant. Sometimes this is called *data reduction,* in other cases it is called *summarizing* the data. In either case, it is common for some data to be eliminated so that something important can be seen in the remaining data.

Data reduction is not perfect. It is as easy to eliminate important data and to summarize the unimportant data as vice versa. By judiciously removing parts of the data, it is possible to come to almost any conclusion—all this requires is eliminating the right (or wrong) data. Statistics is not a substitute for understanding what is going on. It is a tool to clearly summarize data for other people—and it is just as easy to summarize bad data as good.[1]

Because it is so easy to come to the wrong conclusion, a second focus in statistics is to attempt to estimate the probability that a conclusion is wrong. Commonly, this involves the estimate of the *margin of error,* or the development of a *confidence interval.* Like summarization, estimating the likelihood of being wrong is not a perfect process. However, making the effort to estimate the reliability of a conclusion is a good habit for traders. It's one of the things that make statistical analysis more reliable than pulling numbers out of a hat.

Finally, statistics are used to precisely describe relationships between things—how much two things are alike or different. For example, a vague description of a relationship might be: "The two prices act alike most of the time." A more precise estimate is: "The two prices are 40 percent correlated." In this case, statistics is used to eliminate ambiguity and vagueness.

---

[1] Numbers don't make wrong data more accurate—a fact that is well known in popular culture—but still confuses people on a daily basis. A famous quote on statistics was written in the autobiography of Mark Twain, where he quotes Benjamin Disraeli as saying, "There are three kinds of lies: lies, damned lies, and statistics."

It is possible to misuse comparisons. Being overly precise with unnecessary data is both confusing and misleading. Even if a correlation exists, it does not imply that a cause/effect relationship also exists. For example, there is a superstition in the stock market that the NFL team that wins the Super Bowl determines whether the market will go up or down in the following year. Historically, the market has risen fairly commonly when an NFC team beats an AFC team. However, that doesn't mean there is a cause/effect relationship between the two events.

Common Terms

Statistics has its own terminology, which is commonly used as shorthand. The most common notation for indicating an average is to place a bar over the top of some name. For example, $\bar{x}$ represents the mean (arithmetic average) of the x distribution. Another convention is for the letter n to represent the number of elements in a distribution.

$\bar{x}$ A bar over a letter indicates the average of a series of numbers. The letter is the name of the series (in this case, the series is named x).

x_n A subscript indicates a member of a series. For example, x_n indicates the nth member of the x series.

n The lowercase letter n is a reserved letter that refers to number. For example, n might represent the number of observations in series x. It is also common for n to receive a subscript. If there are two series (named x and y), n_x would be the number of observations in series x, and n_y would be the number of observations in series y.

$\sum_{i=1}^{10} x_i$ The capital Greek letter sigma represents a sum. In this example, it is a sum of the first 10 elements of the x series. Below the sigma is the starting point of the sum ($i = 1$), and the number above the sigma indicates the ending point of the series. The subscript on the x indicates that the letter i refers to different values of x.

So, if x represents some series of numbers (1, 2, 5, 8, 10, 12, 15, 20), then subscripted values of x refer to the individual components of the series: $x_1 = 1$, $x_2 = 2$, $x_3 = 5 \ldots x_8 = 20$. There are eight elements in this series, so $n_x = 8$. The formula for the average of x is the sum of all values of x (between values 1 to n), divided by the number of samples (n).

$$\bar{x} = \frac{\sum_{i=1}^{n} x_i}{n}$$

In this case, there is only one series, so the n has not been subscripted. Had there been more than one series described, it would be necessary to weigh the disadvantage of an even more confusing notion (subscripting n as n_x) against the need for greater precision.

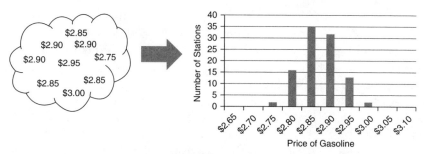

Figure 3.3.1. Organizing samples makes them easier to understand

Sampling

The simplest use of statistics is to organize and describe some type of data. For example, there might be 100 gas stations in the area, each selling gasoline at a different price. However, learning anything useful about those prices will be difficult unless they are organized into some type of summary. An example of a way to summarize data is a *histogram*. This kind of chart organizes data into columns showing the number of samples (gas stations in Figure 3.3.1) that match each column.

Typically, histograms are summarized with a smooth line because that makes it easier to use mathematics to analyze the data. The two types of smooth-line charts most commonly used to summarize statistical data are *frequency distributions* and *cumulative distributions*. Both allow the calculation of the probability that a random draw will be between two points in a distribution. These charts are different ways to look at the same data.

Frequency Distribution	**Cumulative Distribution**
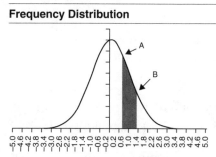	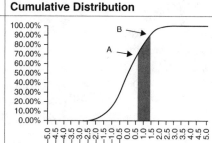
Figure 3.3.2. A frequency distribution	**Figure 3.3.3.** A cumulative distribution
Histograms are often approximated by numerical equations that are easier to manipulate. The equations can be graphed as a curve, where the total area under the curve represents 100 percent of possible values. The shaded area represents the frequency at which values fall between points A and B (Figure 3.3.2).	A cumulative distribution is an alternate way for showing the same data. A graph of this function shows the percentage of samples less than a certain value. The amount of samples between two points can be found by subtracting the value at point A from the value at point B (Figure 3.3.3).

In a *frequency distribution,* the area under the curve represents 100 percent of the possible values. The likelihood is that a random selection will be within a range of values found underneath the curve between those two points. Frequency distributions are basically smoothed out version of histograms.

A *cumulative distribution* function is an alternate way of looking at the same data. For every point on the X axis (gasoline prices in the initial example), it shows the percentage of samples (gas stations) that have prices equal to or lower than that price. The benefit of a cumulative distribution function is that it is possible to find the probability that samples will be within a range found through subtraction. For example, it is possible to find the percentage of gas stations with gas prices between $2.95 and $3.00 by subtraction. The cumulative number of gas stations with prices less than $2.95 can be subtracted from the cumulative number of gas stations with prices less than $3.00. Although they are not quite as intuitive, the cumulative distributions are generally easier to use because of this subtraction property. As a result, most spreadsheet statistical functions use cumulative distributions.

Mean, Median, and Mode

One of the best ways to describe either a frequency distribution or a histogram is by its central tendency. In other words, what values of the distribution can be expected to come up most commonly? The three standard measures of central tendency are *mode, median,* and *mean.*

The mode of a distribution is the value that occurs most frequently. For example, a distribution might contain the numbers 1, 1, 1, 3, 5, 8, and 12. The number 1 comes up three times—more frequently than any other number. Therefore, the number 1 is the mode of the distribution. In practice, mode is not used very often because it is difficult to calculate. It requires searching the entire distribution for the value that comes up most frequently. Another reason mode is not often used is that there can be more than one mode for a distribution. For example, heads and tails are equally likely on a fair coin flip. As a result, both heads and tails are modes.

The median of a distribution is its midpoint. It is the value that separates the highest 50 percent of samples from the bottom 50 percent. For example, in a distribution of seven numbers such as 1, 3, 5, 7, 14, 20, and 25, the middle of the distribution is 7. There are three numbers below 7, and three numbers higher. In the case of an even number of samples, the median is halfway between the two middle numbers. For instance, if a new value of 30 was added to the distribution, the median would become 10.5—the value halfway between 7 and 14. In a practical sense, the big problem with using a median is that it requires

Calculus and Statistics

Calculus examines properties of lines, and this makes it well suited for examining statistical distributions. With calculus, it's easy to find the area under a line (Figure 3.3.4). This process is called *integration*. For example, it is often necessary to find the area underneath a frequency distribution. The area underneath a frequency distribution represents the probability that a sample randomly chosen from the distribution comes from that part of the curve. For example, in the chart in Figure 3.3.4, there is approximately a 22.8 percent chance that a number will be between 0.5 and 1.4. Integration is similar to counting the number of samples in a specific column of a histogram.

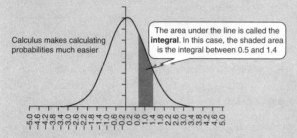

Figure 3.3.4. The area under a curve can be found by calculus

To explain integration, it is easiest to start with a simple example. Using a histogram, it is possible to manually approximate this number of samples between two points (Figure 3.3.5). The height of each bar in a histogram indicates the number of samples in that column. Counting the number of samples in those columns and dividing by the total number of samples provides an estimate of the probability that a sample would come from that area.

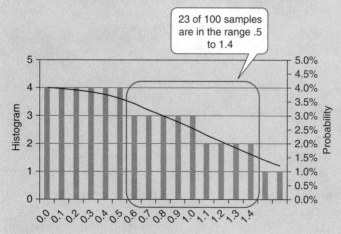

Figure 3.3.5. Comparing a histogram to a frequency distribution

(*Continued*)

Integration of a line works the same way. The only difference is that the height of the line is defined by an equation, and a large number of columns are chosen. The more columns that are used for a histogram, the more precise the estimates become (Figure 3.3.6).

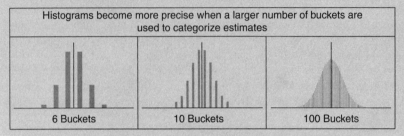

Figure 3.3.6. Examples of the same data set approximated by varying levels of detail

Mathematically, the notation for integration is pretty straightforward. The symbol sigma (Σ) is used to indicate a sum. For example, the probability that a sample chosen randomly from a normally distributed series will be the sum of the columns between .5 and 1.4:

$$\text{Probability} = \sum_{.5}^{1.4} \text{Percentage of Samples}$$

Calculus is a study of what happens when the number of columns approaches infinity. In that case, a similar notion is used. An integral sign (which looks like a stretched out *S*, as seen in the following equation) replaces the sum sign (Σ), but means much the same thing. The table of discrete values (which we called "samples") is replaced by a mathematical function abbreviated $S(x)$. This can be read that the function S depends on the variable x. Finally, the sum will be in relation to the X axis (which we will denote by the symbol dx).

$$\text{Probability} = \int_{.5}^{1.4} S(x)\, dx$$

Even if you don't know how to solve a calculus equation, it is usually possible to find a spreadsheet formula or add-in that will do the math for you. However, you still need to know what function to call and what parameters the function requires.

sorting the sequence. Even on a fast computer, sorting a very large set of samples can take a while.

The mean (arithmetic mean) is the final and most important measure of central tendency. It represents the expected value of a random variable (like the typical gasoline price in one's neighborhood).

The mean is the average value of all the samples. The biggest benefit of the arithmetic mean is that it is very easy to calculate. It can be calculated by adding up each value and dividing by the number of values.

Even though mean, median, and mode all describe a central tendency, these values do not always behave the same way. Some different distributions are shown in the table below. The mean of each series is indicated by a black vertical line. The white and gray shaded pieces show the bottom and top halves of each distribution. Finally, the mode is always located at the peak of the distributions.

Normal Distribution	**Double Distribution**
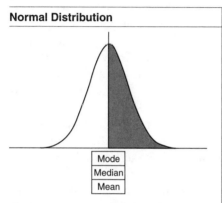	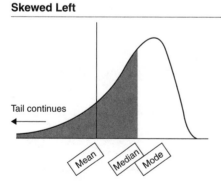
Figure 3.3.7. A normal distribution	**Figure 3.3.8.** A double distribution
The mean, median, and mode are located at the same point in a normal distribution (Figure 3.3.7).	In a double distribution, there are two modes, and the mean and median represent the relatively less common midpoint (Figure 3.3.8).
Skewed Left	**Skewed Right**
	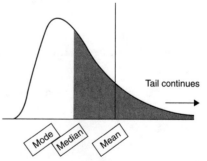
Figure 3.3.9. Negatively skewed distribution	**Figure 3.3.10.** Positively skewed distribution
In a skewed distribution, the mean is heavily affected by outlying values on one side or the other. The median and mode are close together (Figure 3.3.9).	An example of a skewed distribution with the outlying values in the positive direction (Figure 3.3.10).

Variation and Volatility

In most cases, just knowing the average behavior of some data isn't sufficient information. It is also necessary to know how much variation there is in the sample data. For example, it is possible for two sets of data to have the same average behavior and still look very different from one another, as shown in Figure 3.3.11. Even though the distributions in both graphs are shaped like bell curves and have the same central tendency, the curve on the right has a much wider range of values than the series on the left.

For energy trading, variation is often a very important piece of information. For example, the two graphs might represent the expected payoffs from two different investments. Both have an expected payoff of $10 million. However, there is a huge difference between a relatively certain payoff (the graph on the left) and one that has a huge range of outcomes (the one on the right). It's the type of information that an investor—or your boss—will definitely want to know.

In trading, the term "volatility" is used to refer to the *standard deviation* of a series. However, this number is fairly complicated to calculate, so two other measures of dispersion will be examined first: *mean absolute deviation* and *variance.*

The mean absolute deviation is the average distance between a set of sample points and the mean of a distribution. Since distance is always a positive number, this means that the average distance is the average of the absolute difference between each point and the mean of a series divided by the number of samples.

$$\text{Mean Average Deviation} = \frac{\sum \left| x_i - \bar{x} \right|}{n}$$

This would be an excellent measure of variance except for one problem—absolute value is difficult to incorporate into calculus

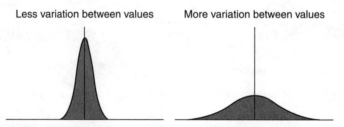

Figure 3.3.11. Distributions with the same average behavior but different variations

equations. Calculus is the key to making statistics problems easier to solve. It's a bit more work to solve an equation the first time through with calculus, but afterward anyone can plug in values to get the correct result. Most people aren't going to actually solve the calculus themselves—they are going to use a prebuilt spreadsheet function or math library that someone else has written. As a result, it will be necessary to use a measure of variance that can be used in those functions.

Fortunately, there is another way to ensure that a number isn't negative—it is possible to multiply a number by itself. This is called taking the square of a number. Applied to variance formula, squaring the distance between the mean and each value will calculate the *mean squared deviation* of a number. This quantity is also called "variance." In mathematical formulas, variance is typically abbreviated σ^2 and called "sigma squared." If this number is calculated for every element in a set of data, the formula for variance will be:

$$\text{Variance (of entire population)} = \sigma^2 = \frac{\sum (x_i - \bar{x})^2}{n}$$

Taking the square root of the variance gives an answer in the same units as the original series. For price series, the units of variance are dollars squared. These units are less understandable than having a result in dollars. Because the square root of variance is the most common measure of deviation, it is usually called the *standard deviation*. It is typically denoted by the lower case Greek letter sigma (σ). In scientific and engineering applications, it is called the *root mean square* or RMS. In financial applications, this value is known as *volatility* of a set of data.

$$\text{Standard deviation} = \sqrt{\text{Variance}} = \sqrt{\frac{\sum (x_i - \bar{x})^2}{n}}$$

Volatility is a key concept in trading. It is commonplace to hear traders discussing market volatility. For example, it's common to overhear someone saying, "The market was volatile today," or "The volatility in the market has doubled in the last month." Although the general intuition is that prices have moved around a lot recently, "volatility" actually refers to the root mean squared deviation of recent returns.

Estimating Variance and Standard Deviation from Sampled Data

In many cases, it is impossible to include every possible value of a distribution in a variance or standard deviation calculation. This causes a problem because estimating the volatility of an entire set of data from a sample consistently *underestimates* the actual volatility and variance. This error can be corrected by modifying the formulas for variance and volatility slightly; dividing by $n - 1$ instead of by n.

$$\text{Variance (of a sample)} = \frac{\sum (x_i - \bar{x})^2}{n-1}$$

$$\text{Standard Deviation (of a sample)} = \sqrt{\frac{\sum (x_i - \bar{x})^2}{n-1}}$$

In most cases this doesn't make much of a difference. For example, if $n = 1,001$, there isn't a lot of difference between dividing a number by 1,000, and dividing that same number by 1,001. However, for a small number of samples, this can be an important correction.

Risk/Reward Measures

When traders analyze trading opportunities, neither the average return nor the volatility of an investment indicates whether it was a good investment without considering the other factor. A more useful measurement of investment performance is *reward-to-risk* measure. In this type of measure, the average return is divided by the standard deviation of returns. Commonly, this is known as a *Sharpe Ratio* or an *Information Ratio*.[2] Both of these ratios work the same way. The average return of the investment (net of some benchmark) is divided by the variability of the return (net of some benchmark).

$$\text{Sharpe Ratio, Information Ratio} = \frac{\text{Average Return}}{\text{Standard Deviation (Returns)}}$$

Higher ratios are considered superior investments to lower ratios.

---

[2] A Sharpe Ratio subtracts out the risk-free rate of return from the average return. An Information Ratio subtracts out some industry benchmark. The distinction is important to investment managers who benchmark their returns against an index. However, for everyone else, the most important thing is to ensure that a consistent measure is used across a business, and either a Sharpe Ratio or an Information Ratio will work equally well.

The Danger in Using Historical Data to Estimate Volatility

In the financial markets, one common way to estimate the volatility of an asset is to use a rolling window of time. For example, a risk manager might estimate the volatility of spot petroleum by examining the prices for the past year or two.

In this calculation, one new value joins the distribution each day and another leaves. If a large outlier leaves the calculation, it is possible for the volatility to fall dramatically overnight. For example, in Figure 3.3.12, on June 11, 1986, there was a 9.21 percent one day jump in the price of crude oil. Using seven days of historical data to estimate volatility, the June 19 calculation includes the large price move. However, the following day, June 20, does not. This causes the June 20, 1986, estimate of volatility to fall dramatically from the day before. The seven-day estimate of volatility fell from 3.5 to 2.1 percent because the largest variation in the data set dropped out of the sample.

To a trader or risk manager, this is pretty important. The value of many financial instruments, like options, is extremely sensitive to volatility estimates. Many of these volatilities are estimated based on historical prices. If that largest outlier leaves the sample set, volatility estimates can drop dramatically even though recent prices haven't changed at all. Of course, the real probability of large price moves is unlikely to have changed substantially. This can make for an awkward conversation to explain why an option portfolio just made or lost millions of dollars in the absence of a major market move.

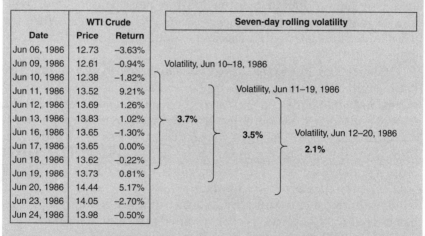

Date	WTI Crude Price	Return
Jun 06, 1986	12.73	−3.63%
Jun 09, 1986	12.61	−0.94%
Jun 10, 1986	12.38	−1.82%
Jun 11, 1986	13.52	9.21%
Jun 12, 1986	13.69	1.26%
Jun 13, 1986	13.83	1.02%
Jun 16, 1986	13.65	−1.30%
Jun 17, 1986	13.65	0.00%
Jun 18, 1986	13.62	−0.22%
Jun 19, 1986	13.73	0.81%
Jun 20, 1986	14.44	5.17%
Jun 23, 1986	14.05	−2.70%
Jun 24, 1986	13.98	−0.50%

Seven-day rolling volatility

Volatility, Jun 10–18, 1986 — 3.7%
Volatility, Jun 11–19, 1986 — 3.5%
Volatility, Jun 12–20, 1986 — 2.1%

Figure 3.3.12. Effect of large samples dropping out of a rolling historical estimate

Like any model, risk/reward ratios have to be used carefully. These measures are not predictions of the future. Typically, these ratios use historical data, and they rely on that data to be representative of actual performance. If market conditions change, or if accounting sleight of hand is being used to smooth out earnings, these measures will fail to work properly. Also, these measures only work right when returns are positive. When returns are negative, higher volatility leads to better (less negative) ratios.

Finally, it is misleading to look at an investment opportunity without considering its effect on the entire portfolio. Unless the returns for different strategies are perfectly correlated, a combination of strategies will always have a lower volatility than any single strategy. For example, consider two strategies. One strategy always makes $1.00 when the price of natural gas rises, and loses $0.98 when the market falls. Another strategy always loses $0.99 when the price of natural gas rises, and makes $1.00 when the market falls. The long strategy (the one that makes money when the market rises) is the better strategy if the market is equally likely to rise and fall. However, the combination of both strategies is far superior to either one alone. A combined strategy makes a risk-free profit!

Correlation

Another part of statistics that is particularly useful for energy traders to understand is *correlation*. When two things are statistically correlated, they have a direct linear relationship. For example, natural gas prices in New York and New Jersey are usually correlated. When the prices in one area are high, prices in the other area are also likely to be high.

Often it is possible to see the relationship between two numbers by plotting two price series on a graph. For example, it might be useful to understand if the price of peak electricity in an area is correlated to the price of natural gas. Even though plotting the data on a graph won't indicate the exact relationship between the two prices, it is a good way to see if there is a relationship. Another way of looking at the data is to use a scatter diagram to compare prices. The two different ways of looking at the data are shown in Figure 3.3.13. The left graph shows daily prices for each commodity, and the right is a scatter graph that matches natural gas prices to peak electricity prices of the same day.

Correlation assumes that there is a linear (straight-line) relationship between two data series. It's fairly obvious from both graphs that the prices of the two assets acted similarly throughout this entire

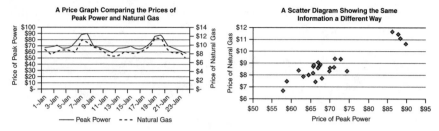

Figure 3.3.13.   Two different ways of looking at related data

period. A straight line can be drawn through the scatter diagram and capture the primary relationship between electricity prices and natural gas prices. However, it would still be helpful to summarize the strength of this relationship in a single number. Ideally, this would work the same way that the average and standard deviation describe a single set of data.

The most common way to measure the relationship between two sets of data is to use the *correlation coefficient*, abbreviated r. The correlation coefficient produces a number between -1 and $+1$ that indicates the strength of the relationship between the two data series. A correlation coefficient equal to $+1$ means that the series behaves identically in all situations. A correlation coefficient of -1 means that prices are inversely proportional to one another (when one price rises, the other price falls). A correlation coefficient of zero indicates no relationship between the two values.

Using the example of correlated prices, a positive correlation indicates that the prices move up and down together. A negative correlation indicates the prices tend to move in the opposite direction—when one rises, the other falls. No correlation means that prices tend to move up and down randomly—sometimes rising together and sometimes rising at opposite times (Figure 3.3.14).

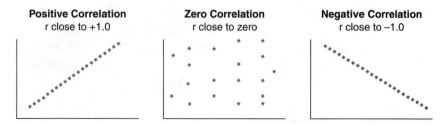

Figure 3.3.14.   Examples of various types of correlation

The calculation of the correlation coefficient, r, is defined by the mathematical formula:

$$r = \frac{\sum (x - \bar{x})(y - \bar{y})}{(n-1)\,\sigma_x\,\sigma_y}$$

Where:

x	The first set of data
$\bar{x}$	The average price of the first data set
σ_x	The standard deviation of the first data set
y	The second set of data
$\bar{y}$	The average price of the second data set
σ_y	The standard deviation of the second data set
n	The number of samples (the first and second data sets need the same number of values)

The key to understanding correlation is examining numbers that are far away from the mean. Prices for each series are multiplied together after having the mean of their respective series subtracted out. If either the x or y value is zero after subtracting the mean value, it will cancel out the other value. Multiplication by zero is always zero. However, multiplying two large numbers produces a very large number. As a result, what matters in a correlation relationship is the behavior of outlying results. As long as the outlying values of x (the values far from the mean) match up to the outlying values of y, the two series will show a strong relationship. Particularly in the case of energy prices that are very volatile, a couple of outlier prices often determine the correlation between two price series.

Correlated Does Not Mean a Good Hedge!

One of the most dangerous traps an energy trader can fall into is to trust statistics without actually looking at the underlying data. For example, because energy prices are cyclical, it is common for all energy prices to be highly correlated. But that doesn't necessarily mean those prices are trending in the same direction. A graphic example of this is shown in Figure 3.3.15—the two series are highly correlated with an $r = 0.5$, but are going in opposite directions!

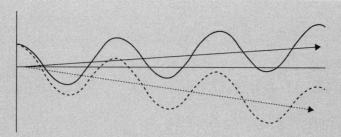

Figure 3.3.15. Correlated series that are trending in opposite directions

A practical example might be a steel producer that is a major user of electricity. The year is 1990, and the steel producer is located in the PJM-East service area halfway between Washington, D.C., and Baltimore. For protection against a rise in electricity prices, the steel producer wants to buy electricity futures. However, exchange-traded futures are not available for PJM-East. The closest futures trading location is PJM-West. This service area is located to the west of Washington, D.C., near the intersection of western Maryland, West Virginia, and Pennsylvania. The steel producer checks that PJM-East and PJM-West prices are highly correlated, finds they are, and buys $500 million of PJM-West power forwards; $20 million of forwards per year for the next 25 years.

Going forward 10 years, the population in the Baltimore-Washington area has boomed. New housing developments and increased commercial activity are straining the power grid. As a result, power prices in PJM-East are soaring. However, the population to the west of Washington, D.C., has not experienced the same population growth. Instead, power prices in PJM-West have declined. The price of power in the two regions has remained highly correlated, since the weather in both areas is nearly identical. Power prices reach their peaks on the same days (hot summer days in August) and are low on the same days. However, the price of power in PJM-East has gone up, while the power in PJM has declined in value.

The steel producer, relying on estimates of correlation, never noticed that the prices were diverging for almost 10 years. Because the prices in the two areas generally moved up and down at the same time, the futures effectively limited the day-to-day volatility. Since correlations remained high, no one thought to actually look at the underlying data. As a result, by the time the problem was identified, the steel producer faced a huge loss on the hedge! His cost for electricity has gone up, and he lost money buying PJM-W forwards, even though these prices were highly correlated.

3.4

FINANCIAL OPTIONS

 30-Second Summary

Purpose

This section provides a nonmathematical introduction to financial options. A mathematical discussion on option pricing is located in the next chapter. Options are important because they are used in a variety of trading strategies, for risk management, and for modeling energy investments.

Summary

An option is a contract between two people. It gives the buyer of the contract the right, but not the obligation, to buy or sell property at some future date at a fixed price. The right to buy is called a *call option.* The right to sell is called a *put option.* Options have an up-front cost, called a *premium,* which is paid when the buyer purchases the option. For the buyer, options have limited downside risk. Buyers will either lose their premium or will make a profit.

Key Topics

- Options are a contract between two individuals where the buyer pays the seller money up front for the possibility of a bigger payoff sometime in the future.
- Options represent a decision where the buyer of the option has the ability to decide whether or not to take some action based on economic reasons.
- Options are like insurance: it is rarely profitable to purchase them purely for speculative reasons. They offer the promise of a big payoff with limited downside. But, if options are fairly priced, most option purchasers will lose money to counterbalance a couple of purchasers making a lot of money.

Option is a financial term that describes a common feature of many contracts. This feature gives one person in the contract the ability to make some kind of decision in the future, usually to buy or sell something at a fixed price. Being able to place a dollar value on the ability to make future decisions is a cornerstone of modern investing. Option contracts work by having one person pay another for the right to take some action in the future. The money paid by the buyer to the seller when the contract is signed is called the *premium*. The decision to take action is an *exercise*. It is usually obvious when an option should be exercised. The difficult decision is determining how much to pay for the option in the first place. For example, if an option buyer purchased the right to buy gasoline in the future for $4.00/gallon, he would only exercise that right when prices were above $4.00. Otherwise, he would be wasting his money. The value of the option depends on the probability that prices are above $4.00.

Options are important because it is possible to represent many types of investment decisions this way. For example, a combination oil well and refinery might be able to produce gasoline at $4.00/gallon. Owning this installation would give the owner the option to "buy" gasoline at $4.00/gallon for immediate resale. By comparing the cost of building and operating the installation to the economic value of the option, it is possible to determine whether this would be a good investment.

Financial option contracts, as opposed to approximations of physical investments, are an all-or-nothing investment. It is possible to buy a million dollars worth of options and lose everything. This is like buying insurance. Most often, the purchaser will pay a premium and have the contract expire worthless. Occasionally, the contract will pay off big when an unusual event occurs. Even though the size of the downside is small (losing the premium) compared to the potential upside (a huge profit), the odds of making a profit are stacked against the buyer. Similar to buying insurance, buying options is generally unprofitable. It only makes sense as part of a broader strategy. The option seller is taking on a risk from the buyer and needs to be compensated for taking that risk.

Two common applications for options are risk management and modeling energy investments. In the energy market, there are a lot of physical decisions that need to be made on a daily basis. Do I turn my power plant on and convert my fuel into electricity? Do I lock in a fuel supply for the winter now or should wait a little longer? Should I invest in building a new power line between Oregon and Northern California? Option theory provides a way to quantify those decisions.

From a transaction standpoint, option trading requires both a buyer and a seller. The seller takes on the possibility of a big loss in exchange for money up front. The buyer pays a *premium* to the seller for that service. If the option pays off, the seller will need to find the cash to pay the buyer. With options, money is not magically created; it is simply transferred between the two parties. The option buyer is described as being *long the option* or being *long volatility* (since rare events will mean a big profit). The option seller is described as being *short the option* or being *short volatility* (since rare events will mean a big loss).

The amount of money that needs to be transferred between the buyer and seller is determined by the *payoff* of the option. Every option is assigned an *exercise* or *strike price*. This is the fixed price at which trading can occur in the future. For example, a call option involves the right to buy an asset at a fixed price. The owner of a call option benefits when an asset price rises above the strike price. This allows the owner to buy at a lower price than is otherwise available. The owner can also make an immediate profit by reselling the asset at the current price.

$$\text{Call Payoff} = \text{Asset Price} - \text{Strike Price}$$

if the Asset Price > Strike Price at expiration.

A put option works similarly. It gives the owner of the option the right to sell an asset at a fixed price. If the market price is greater than the fixed price, a put option is worthless. No one will willingly sell at a lower price than necessary. However, if the fixed price is higher than the market price, the put buyer makes a profit by selling at a higher price.

$$\text{Put Payoff} = \text{Strike Price} - \text{Asset Price}$$

if the Strike Price > Asset Price at expiration.

Derivatives

In the energy market, the term "derivative" is interchangeable with the term "option."

Derivative is a catchall that refers to any financial instrument that derives its value from something else. That something else is always called the *underlying*. Anything other than a spot transaction—for example, a forward, future, swap, or option trade—is technically an example of a derivative. However, in practice, the term "derivative" usually means an option trade. Similarly, a *complex derivative* is an instrument that has an option trade embedded into it. Swaps, futures, and forward trades are typically referred to by their more specific names.

Particularly in the energy world, the dictionary definition of "derivative" is a meaningless distinction. There isn't an active trading market for most spot commodities. The spot market is where small consumers purchase energy. Unless it is possible to buy and resell that spot commodity, there might be a transaction market without having a trading market. As a result, in the energy markets, where almost all trades are lined up in advance, the standard contracts are forwards and futures. Energy derivatives usually refer to contracts that are based on futures or forwards.

In other trading markets, like the stock and bond markets, the term "derivative" has some additional meaning as a way to separate the primary focus of the market (trading stocks and bonds) from the secondary focus of those markets (trading futures, swaps, or options on the primary commodity).

Intrinsic and Extrinsic Value

Options contracts exist for a period of time. During that time, the value of the option will change regularly. The *intrinsic value* is the money that could be obtained by exercising the option immediately—forgoing the chance at more money. The option is said to be "in the money" if its intrinsic value is positive, and "out of the money" if its intrinsic value is zero or negative. The *extrinsic value* of an option is the value of the option that comes from holding on to it longer.

For example, consider a $1 lottery ticket that pays the winner $1 million and gives the owner an ability to flip a coin for more money. If the ticket holder wins the coin toss after winning the first million, he gets another $2 million. However, if he loses, he gives up the initial $1 million. After winning the first million, the lottery ticket is no longer riskless. The owner has the option of taking a million dollars and walking away. The owner of the ticket no longer has a dollar at stake. He has a million dollars at stake! The higher the intrinsic value of the option, the more risk is involved.

Continuing this example, a savvy trader might realize that a 50/50 chance of making $3 million compared to losing $1 million is a profitable investment. If losing a million dollars wasn't a hardship (maybe a multibillionaire was playing the game), it would make good economic sense to take the coin toss every time it was offered. The extrinsic value of the option is the value of not exercising the option. In this case, the extrinsic value would be $500,000—a 50 percent chance of making $3 million while only having $1 million at risk.

Calculating Extrinsic Value

The coin flip in the example is really a 50/50 chance of making $3 million or going home with zero money. The coin flip represents a 50 percent chance of winning $3 million, giving the lottery ticket an expected value of $1.5 million. Since exercising the option immediately would give $1 million risk free, the value of taking the extra coin flip (the extrinsic value) is the value of the entire lottery ticket ($1.5 million) less the intrinsic value ($1 million).

Not wanting to risk losing a million dollars, and being a savvy trader, the owner of the winning lottery ticket might decide to sell the lottery ticket instead of exercising his option to take the risk-free million dollars. For example, the owner of the lottery ticket might decide to offer it for sale for $1.4 million. After all, a 50/50 chance at $3 million for $1.4 million is still a profitable investment. In this way the owner of the option could get most of the benefit from the coin flip without actually exposing himself to the risk of losing the million dollars.

The initial cost of the lottery ticket determines whether playing the lottery was a good or bad investment. For example, a free ticket would be a great investment. However, high up-front costs transform options, and lottery tickets, into poor investments. The potential for a big payoff at low risk does not make a good investment by itself. If the up-front costs are too high, both lottery tickets and options become risk-free ways to lose money!

Early Exercise

With some options, it is possible to exercise the option early. This will lock in some of the profits (the intrinsic value) but give up any possibility of any additional profits (the extrinsic value). Rather than giving up the additional profits, it is usually more profitable to sell the option. As a general rule, options are never exercised early. If the option buyer wants out of the position, the option will be sold rather than liquidated.

There are exceptions to this general rule but they are fairly rare. Sometimes, owning the underlying gives a benefit that isn't accrued to the option owner. For example, a stock might pay a dividend that will reduce the value of the stock and make a call option less valuable. The owner of the stock will receive the dividend to offset the loss in stock price, but the option owner will not. If the dividend is large, it may be worthwhile to exercise the option and give up the extrinsic value of the option.

In energy trading, options are typically written on futures or forward contracts rather than directly on the underlying commodity. This is because an actual transfer of a commodity takes time to set up ahead of time. For example, an option to buy electricity will almost always be an option to buy a forward contract rather than physical electricity. This eliminates the complication of being forced to deliver a commodity on short notice. It isn't possible to buy a call option on October off-peak power (cheap power) and exercise it early to get daytime power in August (expensive power). If the call option is exercised early, the buyer would get an October off-peak forward contract. This tends to eliminate the value of exercising energy options prior to their expiration date.

Basing options on forward and future contracts reduces the benefit from early exercise. An option that can be exercised at any time is called an "American" option. An option that can only be exercised at expiration of the option is called a "European" option. In most cases, whether an option is an American or European option isn't a big deal. It is almost always more profitable to resell the option rather than to exercise it early.

Typical Payoff from Trading Options

If options are priced fairly, with both buyers and sellers breaking even over the long run, a strategy of buying options loses money most of the time. This is because buying an option will occasionally return a big profit. To counterbalance that big profit, there needs to be a series of small, frequent losses. Selling options will have exactly the opposite payoff. It will return steady small profits, and occasionally have a large loss.

Some profit and loss graphs demonstrating these typical payoffs can be seen in the the table that follows.

Typical Payoff from Buying Options	Typical Payoff from Selling Options
A strategy of buying options will frequently lose small amounts of money, and occasionally make a large profit. A graph of the profit will often show slow losses and occasional large profits (Figure 3.4.1).	Selling options will provide steady, consistent profits with an occasional large loss. The profit line will slowly increase with the occasional drop in prices (Figure 3.4.2).
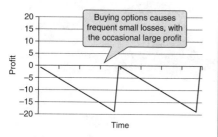	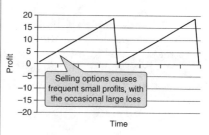
Figure 3.4.1. Profit over time from buying options	**Figure 3.4.2.** Profit over time from selling options

Bid/Ask Spreads

Options, like other financial products, typically have a bid/ask spread. The price at which market makers sell to buyers—the *ask price*—is higher than the price where they are willing to buy options—the *bid price*. Relative to the size of the premium, most options have a very wide spread between their bid and ask prices. Somewhere between the two prices will be the fair price for the option.

The bid/ask spread is generally proportional to the amount of trading done in a particular option contract. If buyers and sellers can easily be matched up, allowing the market maker to make a low risk profit, spreads will be very tight. However, if the market maker won't be able to get out of the trade easily, and thinks that he might need to hold on to the option until expiration, there will be a very large spread. For example, for an illiquid option with a "value" of $6, it might not be uncommon to see a $2 bid price and a $10 ask price. Wide bid/ask spreads generally make speculating with options a losing proposition.

Becoming an option market maker isn't particularly hard—it mostly requires enough capital to cover losses. The downside of being an option market maker is that they are always trading against informed investors.

Volatility

Volatility is the tendency of the market to see a large price move. Market volatility goes in cycles—sometimes the financial markets are quiet and very little is going on, and other times prices can change rapidly. Because of the way options pay out, option buyers and sellers are very exposed to the market volatility cycle. For an option buyer, options offer unlimited benefits if the prices move in one direction, and limited losses if the prices move the other way.

- An option buyer who is *long volatility* benefits when large price movements become more likely.
- An option *seller* who is *short volatility* will benefit in a quiet market or if prices stay exactly where they started. The premium is the only profit made by the option writer. An option writer won't make any more money if the option finishes very far out of the money rather than just out of the money. However, the option writer has a great deal to move if prices move in the wrong direction.

Why Traders Use Options

Most commonly, traders buy options as insurance. Although options may not make good speculative investments, they are a very cost effective way to buy insurance. Having an open market ensures competitive pricing. Nothing forces traders to transact at other people's bid and ask prices. All traders—assuming they have assets to meet their obligations—can sell options too.

In some cases, options can be a good way to get into trades that would otherwise be too risky. A good rule of thumb is that no single decision should ever be so risky that it risks shutting down the trading desk. If a trading desk is close to its risk limit, and strongly believes in a trade, options can be a good way to take on more exposure without taking on a large risk.

Another reason that options are important is their use in investing. Many investment decisions can be modeled as financial options. For example, building a power plant gives the operator the "option" of burning fuel to produce electricity. The power plant operator will probably make the decision to produce electricity whenever it is profitable. This is the same way that financial options work. As a result, options provide a good way to analyze any investment that involves a decision.

A Zero Sum Game!

One of the reasons options are often unprofitable to trade is that they are a zero sum game. The only way to make money trading options is for someone else to lose money. Options involve a direct payment from one market participant to another. As a result, an option trader has to be smarter, or luckier, than the people with whom he is trading. Trading tends to be a Darwinian business: traders that lose money consistently get pushed out of their jobs, leaving only smart, lucky people still in the business of trading.

Other markets do not behave the same way. For example, in the stock market, everyone can make money at the same time. Some of this effect is because companies become more valuable as the economy expands. There is a natural tendency for the fundamental value of stocks to appreciate over time. But even more than that, stock trading is not a zero sum game because of how profits on trading are calculated.

The price of everyone's stock is set by the last traded price. Every share of a particular stock is priced at the same level. If any owner of a stock sells at a price higher than the previous sale, everyone makes money. For example, if there are a million shares of a stock, and one person sells the stock at a price $10 higher than the previous trade, $10 million of wealth is created. Each of those million shares has gone up in value by $10. No one had to lose money on that sale either—the seller got out of his position at a higher price, the buyer exchanged cash for stock, and the other owners all saw a profit without being required to do anything.

Of course, when the stock market crashes, everyone can lose money at the same time too. The different investment styles don't mean that one market is better than another, but it is a very different dynamic.

Payoff Diagrams

Traders often represent the risks of an option position with payoff diagrams. These diagrams show the final profitability of the option with respect to the price of the underlying instrument.

For example, an option might give the buyer the right to buy a natural gas futures contract for $100. At expiration, if the futures contract is worth more than $100, the option buyer will exercise the option. Even if he doesn't plan to personally use the contract, he can purchase the futures contract and resell it at a profit. If the futures contract is worth $300, buying at $100 and reselling at $300 gives a payoff of $200. However, if the futures price at expiration is $50, the option is worthless. There is no good reason for the option buyer to pay $100 when the same product can be obtained for $50.

The payoff of a forward contract looks like a straight line (Figure 3.4.3). The value of the future contract varies directly with the price of the underlying product. For example, if a trader agrees contract to buy 100 MMBtus of natural gas at $8, he loses money when prices are below $8, and makes money when prices are above $8.

Options are agreements that allow the buyer to make a transaction at a specific price in the future but don't require the option buyer to make a transaction. If a call option expires with the price of the underlying product above the strike price, the option is valuable. Otherwise, the call buyer will choose not to exercise the option. As a result, the payoff for an option looks like half the payoff of a forward (Figure 3.4.4). When the price of the underlying product is above the strike price, the option is profitable ("in the money"). When it is below the strike price, the option expires worthless ("out of the money").

The payoff of an option is further complicated by the fact that options aren't free—it costs money to buy an option. This shifts the payoff for the option. When an option expires out of the money, the seller makes a profit. When an option expires in the money, the gross profit

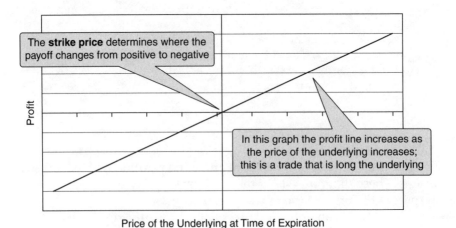

Price of the Underlying at Time of Expiration

Figure 3.4.3.   The payoff of a forward contract

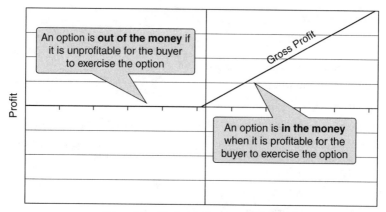

Figure 3.4.4.   The payoff of a call option

has to exceed the cost of purchasing the option before the buyer makes a net profit. For example, if a trader purchases an option to buy something at \$100, and the option costs \$20, the buyer will only make a net profit when the price of the underlying product is above \$120. The *break-even* price is the strike price plus the premium.

In the graph in Figure 3.4.5, the solid line shows the final payoff of the option as a function of the price of the underlying at expiration. The net profit is a combination of the final payoff and the premium that the option buyer needed to pay to buy the option initially.

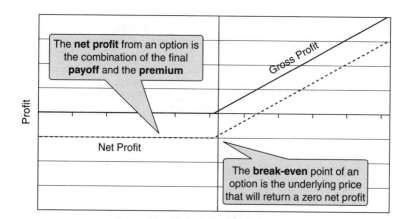

Figure 3.4.5.   Payoff of a call option net of the strike price

Forwards

Like options, forwards are agreements to buy or sell something at a prearranged price in the future. Unlike options, forwards are binding agreements—both sides have committed themselves to a transaction at a future date.

The buyer of a forward will:

- Pay no money when the trade is entered.
- Agree to purchase the underlying at the strike price on the expiration date.
- Benefit if the price of the asset rises. The buyer of a forward has a long position in the asset since she benefits by buying at a price lower than the prevailing market price.

The seller of a forward will:

- Pay no money when the trade is entered.
- Agree to sell the underlying at the strike price on the expiration date.
- Benefit if the price of the asset falls. The seller of a forward has a short position in the asset since she benefits by selling at a price higher than the prevailing market price.

Long a Forward	**Short a Forward**
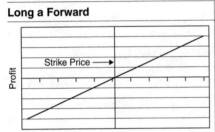	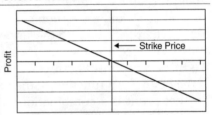
Price of the Underlying at Time of Expiration	Price of the Underlying at Time of Expiration
Figure 3.4.6. Payoff of a long forward	**Figure 3.4.7.** Payoff of a short forward
The purchaser of a forward contract enters a binding contract to purchase the underlying at a fixed price. The higher the price rises, the better this deal becomes, because the purchase is at a fixed price (Figure 3.4.6).	The writer of a forward contract agrees to sell the underlying to the contract purchaser at a specific price (the strike price). A forward seller will profit when the price of the underlying falls, since he is selling at a high price relative to the spot price (Figure 3.4.7).

Call Options

A call option is a contract between two parties that gives the option buyer the right, but not the obligation, to purchase some product (the underlying) at a specific price (the strike price) for some length of time (ending at the expiration date).

The buyer of a call will:

- Pay a nonrefundable premium to the writer of the option when entering the trade.

- Have the right to purchase the underlying at the strike price when the option is exercised.

- Benefit if the price of the underlying rises. (The buyer has a long position in the underlying.)

The seller (writer) of a call will:

- Receive a premium for writing the call, paid by the option buyer at the time of the trade.

- Be required to sell the buyer of the option the underlying at the strike price if the option is exercised.

- Benefit if the price of the underlying falls. (The seller has a short position in the underlying.)

Long a Call	Short a Call
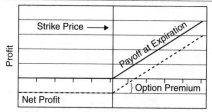	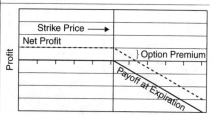
Price of the Underlying at Time of Expiration	Price of the Underlying at Time of Expiration
Figure 3.4.8. Payoff of a long call	**Figure 3.4.9.** Payoff of a short call
The owner of a call profits when the price of the underlying rises. The owner of the call benefits by being able to buy at a fixed price and sell high (Figure 3.4.8).	The writer of a call profits when the price of the underlying stays constant or falls. The writer of a call benefits if the option is not exercised (Figure 3.4.9).

Put Options

A put option is a contract between two parties that gives the option buyer the right, but not the obligation, to sell some product (the underlying) at a specific price (the strike price) for some length of time (ending at the expiration date).

The buyer of a put will:

- Pay a nonrefundable premium to the writer of the option when entering the trade.
- Have the right to sell the underlying to the seller at the strike price when the option is exercised.
- Benefit if the price of the underlying falls. (The buyer has a short position in the underlying.)

The seller (writer) of a put will:

- Receive a premium for writing the call, paid by the option buyer at the time of the trade.
- Be required to buy the underlying from the option buyer at the strike price if the option is exercised.
- Benefit if the price of the underlying rises. (The seller has a long position in the underlying.)

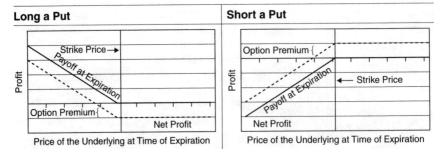

Long a Put	Short a Put

Figure 3.4.10. Payoff of a long put

Figure 3.4.11. Payoff of a short put

The owner of a put option benefits when the price of the underlying falls. The owner benefits by being able to buy cheaply and sell at a fixed price (Figure 3.4.10).

The seller of a put option profits when the price of the underlying stays constant or rises. The seller of the put benefits when the option is not exercised (Figure 3.4.11).

Put/Call Parity

It is possible to combine the payoffs from multiple option transactions. This is the basis of many types of option trades. The most important combination of payoffs is the combination of put and call options to form forwards (Figure 3.4.12). The ability to combine calls and puts to form a forward forces a link between these two products. For example, if a trader simultaneously buys a call and sells a put, he can replicate the payoff from owning a forward.

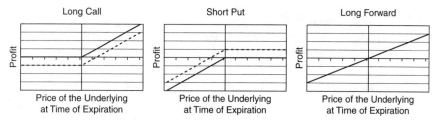

Figure 3.4.12. A synthetic forward can be created by combining a long call and a short put

The price of the call and put have to be identical (within the limits of a bid ask spread, at any rate). Otherwise it would be possible to reverse engineer an option payoff and make an arbitrage profit. This would be done by buying one type of option and synthetically creating an identical payoff to liquidate the position. Replicating the payoff from an option by using other options is called a *synthetic option*. An example of creating a long put from a short forward and a long call is shown in Figure 3.4.13.

Key Facts: Put/Call Parity and Synthetic Options

The ability to synthetically create calls and puts has several major implications:

- Combined properly, puts and calls can be used interchangeably in a trading portfolio.
- The premium for puts and calls of the same underlying, strike, and expiration has to be identical.
- The implied volatility (a quantity explained in the next chapter) of puts and calls based on the same underlying, strike price, and expiration date has to be identical.

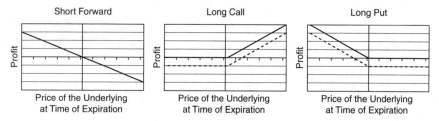

Figure 3.4.13. A synthetic long put can be created by combining a short forward and a long call

Trading Example: Long Option Straddle

A Category 5 hurricane is barreling into the Gulf of Mexico and has the potential to knock out oil production for several months. Oil prices have been creeping upward for the past week in anticipation that prices could spike.

1. **The Opportunity.** If the hurricane knocks out a large number of oil wells, oil prices will skyrocket even higher. However, if the hurricane misses the oil wells, prices can be expected to fall substantially.

2. **The Intuition.** Oil prices seem unlikely to stay at their current level—they are likely to either rise or fall dramatically. A combination of option trades can be used to benefit from a sharp move in prices.

3. **The Strategy.** The trader wants to be long volatility—he wants to benefit from a price move in either direction—and that means buying options. To benefit from a price move in either direction, the trader will buy both a call and a put option at the same strike price. The combined payoff diagram looks like a V as seen on Figure 3.4.14.

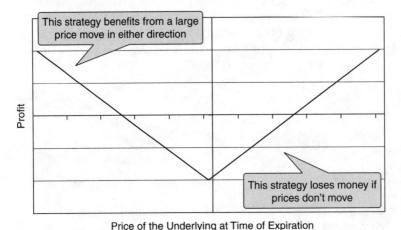

Price of the Underlying at Time of Expiration

Figure 3.4.14.   Payoff of a long option straddle

4. **The Risks.** The option buyer is paying a large premium in anticipation of a large price move in one direction or another. If prices don't actually move, the option buyer will lose money.

Common Terms

American Option.   *American* applied to an option means an option that can be exercised at any time.

Asian Option.   An *Asian* option is an *average price option*. At expiration, the value of an Asian option depends on an average of the underlying's price over some period of time. Typically, Asian options cannot be exercised early. For example, an Asian option might pay the difference between a strike price and the average cost of peak power over a month.

At the Money.   An option where the strike price of the option equals the current price of the underlying.

Derivative.   In its most general form, a derivative is any financial contract whose value is derived from the price of something else. In practice, a derivative usually refers to an option.

European Option.   The term "European" applied to an option means that the option can only be exercised at the expiration. A European option cannot be exercised early.

Extrinsic Value.   The time value of the option. This can be found by subtracting the intrinsic value of the option from the current price of the option.

In the Money.   An option with a positive intrinsic value. An option that would be profitable to exercise immediately.

Intrinsic Value.   The amount of money the option buyer would receive if the option was immediately exercised.

Out of the Money.   An option with zero intrinsic value. Alternately, an option that is worthless if exercised at the current time.

Premium.   The money paid by the purchaser of an option to the seller of an option.

Strike Price.   The exercise price of an option contract. Alternately, the price where the call buyer can purchase the underlying asset or the put buyer can sell the underlying asset.

Synthetic Option.   The process of duplicating the payoff of an option by using a combination of other options and forwards.

Underlying.   An asset that is used to determine the price of a derivative. It is possible for the underlying to be a derivative of some type (like a forward or a future), and for options to have more than one underlying (spread options).

3.5

OPTION PRICING

30-Second Summary

Purpose
This chapter introduces the mathematics behind option pricing.

Summary
Options theory has simultaneously revolutionized the financial markets and caused a huge number of financial collapses. The mathematics behind option pricing can be very complicated. However, the basic principles are straight-forward. Options give the ability to buy or sell an asset, called the *underlying asset*, at a fixed price. Options prices are calculated by developing a plan to replicate the payoff of the option by continuously buying and selling small amounts of the underlying asset.

Mathematical models are used to calculate how the price of the underlying asset is likely to move in the future. Then, additional models determine how much of the underlying asset needs to be bought or sold to replicate the option payoff. This isn't a perfect process. Real life is more complicated than any model. As a result, option models are not a substitute for understanding what is actually going on. Option modelers face a constant temptation to create a "perfect model" that will never break down. However, this isn't an achievable goal. All models have flaws and need to be watched. The more people that watch and understand models, the faster problems can be found and fixed.

Assumptions can change over time, but option models seldom experience a catastrophic failure overnight. Usually, problems in an option model start to show up years before there is an economic impact. It's up to the people using the model to identify when things aren't working and make sure problems are fixed quickly. If a model gets too complex, it becomes harder to identify problems before substantial losses occur. As a result, simple models, even when they have flaws, are usually preferred over complex models.

Modern option trading sprung out of research by Fischer Black, Myron Scholes, and Robert Merton in the late 1960s and early 1970s. Their research combined earlier ideas of dynamic hedging, price diffusion, and put/call parity into a continuous time framework. This allowed the creation of an easy-to-use option pricing formula, the Black-Scholes formula, which opened up option trading

(Continued)

to the masses. The Black-Scholes formula and related work on continuous time finance revolutionized the financial markets and won a Nobel prize for the researchers.[1]

The concept behind option pricing is counterintuitive to many. Options are priced by replicating their payout through continuously trading the underlying product. By and large, the approach that was first developed by the 1970s, *dynamic hedging*, still works well today. The general concept of dynamic hedging was that it is possible to duplicate the payoff of a stock option by constantly trading the stock and a risk-free investment (usually a government bond). This concept has been carried into the energy market.

Options are closely associated with volatility. Since there is an asymmetric payout for holding an option, a large price move that has a 50/50 chance of going up or down helps the buyer of the option more than the seller. The potential losses of the buyer are limited, but the potential profit is not. An option buyer benefits from large price moves, and an option seller benefits from price stability.

Key Topics

- Option pricing can be used to solve problems that can't be solved in other ways.
- All option models involve assumptions about how underlying prices move. Attention needs to be paid to these assumptions to ensure that they are reasonable.
- A good option model has to balance an ability to be understood against more realistic assumptions of how prices actually behave.

Options act like insurance contracts in many ways. However, they are priced very differently. Insurance pricing is based on statistical tables of future probabilities. These probabilities typically don't change quickly, and insurance writers can spend years spotting changes in trends. Option writing, in contrast, is based on the behavior of an underlying contract whose behavior can, and often will, change dramatically over short periods of time. Using statistical probabilities based on historical observations to price options is a sure-fire way to lose money.

Historical prices are not accurate predictions of the future. Even the most skilled financial professionals cannot accurately predict

---

[1] Myron Scholes and Robert Merton won the Nobel prize in 1997. Fischer Black had died in 1995, but the Swedish Academy strongly indicated that he would have been a co-winner had he still been alive. While these gentlemen were not the only contributors to option pricing theory, their work opened up the options markets to general investors.

the future of the financial markets with any degree of certainty. The option pricing revolution began when traders began working on strategies to replicate option payoffs through frequent trades in the underlying product. This process, called *dynamic hedging*, required modeling the behavior of asset prices. Option models are based on assumptions about asset prices. A standard set of assumptions defines commonly traded, "vanilla," options. When the standard assumptions work reasonably well to describe the behavior of the underlying prices, option valuation is easy. It is possible to plug numbers into a well-known option pricing formula like the Black-Scholes formula. In other cases, the standard assumptions don't work so well, and then it is necessary to use a more complicated approach to calculating option prices.

Options that use nonstandard assumptions about prices are commonly called "exotic" options. Knowing when to use an exotic option model requires understanding what is going on in real life. Option formulas basically say that "I can be used if X, Y, and Z are true." It is up to the user of an option model to determine if X, Y, and Z are true in their specific case. If not, some other formula needs to be found. A substantial amount of academic literature describes nonstandard option models.

Option writing is the limiting factor in the option market. There is no shortage of option buyers in the market looking for a deal—after all, there is no downside to owning an option other than the cost. The difficulty comes from finding someone to take on the risk of selling options. The goal of option pricing, and the definition of a fair option price, is a price that fully compensates an option seller for the risk he is taking on.

History of Option Pricing

Commodity options have been traded in European financial markets for several thousand years. However, it wasn't until that start of the twentieth century that a pair of insights started to revolutionize option trading and financial analysis.

The first major breakthrough in the mathematics of option pricing occurred in 1900 when Louis Bachelier published a book, *Théorie de la spéculation*, as part of his doctoral thesis. His book discussed the use of Brownian motion to evaluate the movement of stocks. Brownian motion is a diffusion process where a moving particle (or price) diverges from its starting point in a *random walk*. This provided the theoretical framework for modeling price movements even when the exact probabilities of future prices couldn't be predicted.

Arbitrage Free Pricing

Arbitrage means to make a risk-free profit by simultaneously buying one security and selling another. A common assumption in option pricing is that arbitrage opportunities do not exist. Or, if they do exist, alert traders will quickly take advantage of the opportunity and force prices back into an arbitrage-free situation.

Arbitrage free pricing refers to the concept that if two assets are worth the same amount of money throughout their life and at expiration, then their prices should be identical at all times too. Otherwise, it would be possible to buy one asset, sell the other, and make a risk-free profit. Although traders are always free to transact at any price they choose, they usually try to make a profit. As long as someone takes advantage of easy profit opportunities, there isn't a real difference between the *strong form* of the assumption that no arbitrage ever exists, and the *weak form* of the assumption that arbitrage opportunities don't last very long.

The second breakthrough occurred with the realization that the value of an option can be described as a percentage of the price of the underlying. For example, if a call option has a strike price of zero, it has to be worth exactly the same price as the underlying. It doesn't matter what the future probability of prices looks like—the option will always be in the money. As a result, the option premium has to be equal to the price of the underlying or else it would be possible to arbitrage the option and the underlying. On the other extreme, if the strike price for that option is so high that it would never be met, the option premium has to be zero. Since the option will never be exercised, it is worthless!

Delta hedging is the term that describes how the value of an option changes relative to changes in the price of the underlying. If the value of a call option with a zero strike price is exactly equal to the price of the underlying, it is said to have a *hedge ratio* of 1.0—the payoff of one option can be exactly duplicated by holding one unit of the underlying. A higher strike price means the option is less valuable. If the strike price is so high that the option will never be executed, the hedge ratio is equal to zero. The option is worthless, and the payoff of the option can be duplicated by holding nothing (a hedge ratio of zero).

Most of option pricing takes place between these two extremes, where hedge ratio is greater than zero and less than one. For example, an option that has a strike price close to today's forward price might have a hedge ratio of 0.5. The term "Delta" is used synonymously with hedge ratio.

Common Terms

Arbitrage.   The simultaneous buying and selling of two different assets to make a risk-free profit. In option pricing, the value of an option is determined by the cost of replicating the option with other assets. The process of setting the value of an option equal to the value of the replicating assets is called "arbitrage free pricing."

Brownian Motion (Wiener Process).   A mathematical process developed simultaneously in two unrelated branches of science to describe random motion. It is either named for the botanist Robert Brown or the physicist Norbert Wiener. This process describes the boundaries of a random walk taken with very small steps.

Martingale.   A special type of random number sequence (aka *stochastic process*) where the best estimate of the future is the current value. For example, flipping coins is a martingale process. Assuming a fair coin flip, the best estimate of the number of heads that will come up at the end of a process is the current number. Flipping a coin is a 50/50 chance: heads are no more likely than tails to come up in the future. If a coin has been flipped 50 times and heads has come up 30 times (tails 20 times), the most likely outcome after 100 flips is that there will still be 10 more heads than tails.

Random Walk.   In finance, a random walk usually refers to a one-dimensional process where prices spread out from a starting point as a function of a single variable (time). The binomial tree model used in this chapter is an example of a one-dimensional random walk. Advanced option models sometimes use more complicated random walks based on two or three dimensions.

Stochastic Process.   A term that can mean either a sequence of random numbers or a process for generating random numbers. The words "sequence of random numbers" can generally replace the term "stochastic process" in any sentence. Stochastic process is a general term since there are many different types of random number sequences. For example, flipping a coin and rolling a pair of dice are two examples of stochastic processes (they are two ways of creating a sequence of random numbers).

Replicating Portfolios

Modern option theory involves replicating the payoff of an option by holding some amount of the underlying security. Adopting this fundamental approach shifted how the financial market approached options. It became less necessary to accurately predict future prices. From the point of view of an option seller, this is a big deal. Option sellers don't have the ability to pick and choose what they trade. They have to be willing to trade whatever product the buyer is looking to purchase. Consistently predicting the future is a nearly impossible task if you have to predict the price of every asset at every time horizon.

There are two steps to most option pricing models. The first is predicting statistical distribution of likely movements in the underlying price. The second step is determining how to replicate the option under those probability conditions.

Models of Future Prices

It is often easier to predict a distribution of future prices than a direction. For example, a probabilistic description of prices might be that 60 percent of the time tomorrow's prices will be within 20 cents of today's price, 20 percent of the time the price will move between 20 and 70 cents, and that 20 percent of the time the price will move to more than 70 cents. This type of estimate is much more likely to be accurate than directional estimates like "the price of oil will rise tomorrow."

Most models start with the assumption that today's price is the best consensus estimate of tomorrow's price. A risk-free profit argument is the most common justification for this assumption. For example, if the price of a natural gas future were priced at $10 today and a trader knew that it would be $20 tomorrow, he could buy the contract today and resell it tomorrow. At that point, the contract could be sold for a risk-free profit.

This assumption that today's price is the best estimate of tomorrow's price leads to the conclusion that the returns (percent changes to the current price) are distributed around today's price. In the energy market, this is a reasonable assumption to make about future and forward contracts. For example, if the price for natural gas delivered in August is currently $10, tomorrow's price for the same natural gas contract won't change dramatically. This isn't the case for physical energy commodities, which have cyclical prices that change on a daily basis due to predictable factors like weather and consumer demand.

A second common assumption is that volatility of returns will stay constant over the life of the option: that the magnitude of returns will be the same a week from now as it will be tomorrow. Combining these two assumptions makes it relatively easy to construct a model of likely future underlying prices. The simplest model of future prices is a *binomial tree* (Figure 3.5.1). A binomial tree assumes that the underlying prices can rise or fall a certain percent every day. That percent stays constant over the life of the option. Prices start at today's price and slowly diverge from it over time.

Example of a Binomial Tree

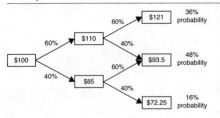

In this example, prices have a 60 percent chance of rising 10 percent, and a 40 percent chance of falling 15 percent. The average future price can be found by multiplying each price by the probability of occurrence. It is $100 in all future periods. Interest rates are zero in this example.

Figure 3.5.1.   A binomial tree

In a binomial tree model, the price of the underlying changes over time. In the first period, the example starts at $100, and will go to either $110 or $85 in the next period. Although downside moves may be bigger than upside moves, there is a higher probability that prices will rise. As a result, the average expected price in second and third period is still $100.

In mathematical literature, mathematical models are usually described by variables (Figure 3.5.2). For example, the probability that the price rises might be denoted by p, and the probability that prices will fall denoted as $(1 - p)$. The amount prices raise might be abbreviated u, and the amount they fall might be abbreviated as v. The price of the underlying is S_x, with the subscript indicating it's a price at a specific period. Also, the first period will usually be Period 0, the second Period 1, and so on.[2]

Example of a Binomial Tree (with More General Notation)

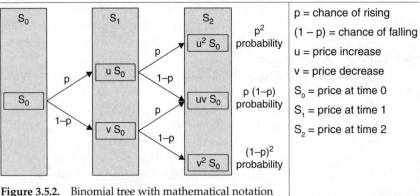

p = chance of rising
$(1 - p)$ = chance of falling
u = price increase
v = price decrease
S_0 = price at time 0
S_1 = price at time 1
S_2 = price at time 2

Figure 3.5.2.   Binomial tree with mathematical notation

---

[2] Prices must either rise or fall in this model. The probability of prices rising plus the probability of prices falling must equal 100 percent. As a result, the probability that prices fall is equal to the probability that prices don't rise. If the probability that prices rise is p, the probability that prices don't rise is $100\% - p$. ($1.0 - p$ in decimal form).

Lognormal vs. Normal Price Distributions

Standard pricing models assume that returns, rather than prices, are normally distributed. In other words, that if one were to graph all of the possible returns for an underlying, the returns would form a normal distribution (a bell curve, Figure 3.5.3). Mathematically, when returns are normally distributed, the logarithm of prices is normally distributed (Figure 3.5.4). As a result, prices are said to have a lognormal distribution.

There is one big advantage in assuming that returns rather than prices are normally distributed. With normally distributed returns, prices will never become negative. This is because the price movements will get smaller as the price gets closer to zero. Assuming that returns are normally distributed implies that prices can hit zero but go no lower. However, there is no upper limit to their price movement. This comes closer to describing the behavior of many asset prices than a normal distribution.

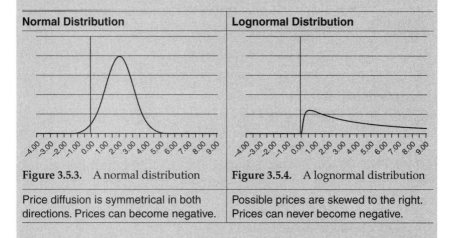

Normal Distribution	Lognormal Distribution
Figure 3.5.3. A normal distribution	**Figure 3.5.4.** A lognormal distribution
Price diffusion is symmetrical in both directions. Prices can become negative.	Possible prices are skewed to the right. Prices can never become negative.

Returns also provide an easy way to compare price movements across different assets. For example, it is easier to compare natural gas to electricity returns rather than prices. The downside of returns is that they become undefined if the starting price ever hits zero, or if prices become negative. This isn't always a safe assumption in energy trading because electricity prices can become negative. However, this is usually the least of the problems with these distributions.

The Fat Tail Problem

A major problem with the lognormal approximation of prices is that price changes are not determined by statistical predictions. Large price moves in both directions are much more common than statistical models

(Continued)

predict. For example, a statistical model would predict that the chance of a stock price hitting zero is astronomically small. However, there are dozens of examples a year where stock prices hit zero because companies go bankrupt.

Stocks get taken over and go bankrupt, hurricanes destroy things, and power lines fall down. These events can have huge effects on prices, and their impact may or may not be predictable with statistical models. As a result, out-of-the-money options—the options whose values are most affected by major price moves—are typically priced with a higher volatility than at-the-money options. The likelihood that large price moves will occur more frequently than predicted is called a *fat tail* problem by traders.

Another problem with option pricing is the assumption that trading the underlying will always be possible. This can be a very dangerous assumption, since trades require both a buyer and a seller. In the energy market, it is sometimes impossible to find someone willing to trade at the same location where you want to trade. The term *jump diffusion* describes periods when prices change dramatically without being tradable at an intermediate level.

Interest Rate Models

A model of interest rates can be calculated using the same binomial framework that was used for prices. With constant interest rates, this graph isn't terribly interesting, but will be used later on to figure out correct value for the option premium (Figure 3.5.5). In this example, with a 5 percent interest rate between periods, a dollar at Time$_t$ is always worth 1.05 at Time$_{t+1}$.

Example of a Binomial Tree for Interest Rates

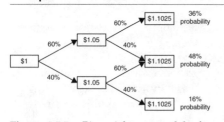

This interest rate graph has the same probabilities as the price graph, but since it is a risk-free interest rate, the price always rises.

Figure 3.5.5. Binomial tree model of interest rates

Arbitrage Free Pricing

The key insight to option pricing is that it is possible to combine underlying and bond prices to replicate an option payout if there is a way to compare their payoffs under likely future conditions. It isn't necessary to predict actual future prices. It is sufficient to predict a likely distribution of possibilities like a binomial tree model (Figure 3.5.6). Then, the underlying prices and risk-free return can be compared to the payoff of a call option in the same circumstances (Figure 3.5.7). The combination of underlying and interest rate payoffs will be used to replicate the payoff of the option.

Replicating the Payoff of a Call Option with a Stock and Risk-Free Investment

A combination of these assets will be used to replicate the payoff of the option to the right.

Underlying Prices

```
            60%    $110
$100
            40%    $85
```

Interest Rates

```
            60%    $1.05
$1
            40%    $1.05
```

Figure 3.5.6.   A one-period binomial model of prices and interest rates

An option with a strike price of $100 that expires at the second time period would have the following payoff:

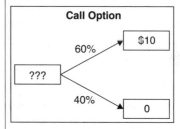

Call Option

```
            60%    $10
???
            40%    0
```

Figure 3.5.7.   The payoff of an option is known, but not its price at the current time

If the underlying price expires at $110, then option is worth $10. If the underlying price is $85, the option will expire worthless.

The temptation is to say the value of the option is $6, because it has a 60 percent chance of paying $10. However, the option seller is taking on more risk than the option buyer. If the prediction of prices is wrong, the option seller has more money at stake. As a result, a $6 price benefits the buyer more than the seller. The chance for the option seller to take a huge loss doesn't really show up on two-period binomial models.

Predicting future prices is both subjective and inaccurate. Option sellers need to have some assurance that they are being fairly compensated for the risk they are taking on. This is done by calculating the cost of eliminating the risk of writing the option contract. The risk can be removed by replicating the option with other instruments. Most commonly, these instruments are the underlying security and a risk-free investment like a government bond.

The general structure of the trade would be to purchase some quantity of underlying and risk-free investment at the starting period and use those profits to offset losses from the option, as can be seen in the following table. The underlying and risk-free investment positions will be liquidated at the expiration of the option. There are two unknowns (the quantity of the underlying and the quantity of the risk free investment) and two equations (the payoff of the option in positive and negative cases). The goal is to buy a certain quantity of the underlying and risk-free investment at Time zero that will duplicate the option payoff at Time 1.

Setting Up the Arbitrage Relationship

These two equations are used to show some combination of the stock and risk-free investment duplicating the payoff of the call option under each of the two scenarios.	The purpose of this work is to find if some quantity of underlying and risk-free investment can be used to duplicate the payoff of the option.
$110 A + $1.05 B = 10 (positive scenario) $85 A + $1.05 B = 0 (negative scenario)	A = units of underlying B = units of the risk-free investment
	We want to find values for A and B that meet the constraint that the combination of investments matches the payoff of the option.

To solve this equation, it will be necessary to eliminate one of the variables. This can be done by combining the two equations. The easiest variable to eliminate is B (the units of risk-free investment) since its payoff is the same in every ending scenario. Eliminating B can be done by subtracting the second equation from the first. This gives the result noted in the table that follows.

Solving for the Quantity of Underlying

$25A = 10	Calculated by subtracting the negative scenario equation from the positive scenario equation.
A = 2/5 or 0.4	Dividing both sides by $25.

Plugging this value for A into either equation will allow us to finish solving the problem by calculating a value for B.

Solving for the Quantity of the Risk-Free Investment	
$85 (2/5) + $1.05 B = 0	Although either scenario can be chosen to solve for B, the negative scenario is chosen here.
$34 + $1.05 B = 0	Simplifying. $85 × (2/3) = $34
$1.05 B = –$34	Simplifying. Subtracting $34 from both sides
B = –$34/$1.05	Simplifying. Dividing $1.05 from both sides
B = –$32.38	Simplifying. $35/$1.05 = $32.38

The value of the option is the cost of entering the trades at the initial period. This can be done by calculating the price of purchasing the right amount of the underlying and risk-free investment at the starting point. For example, if one unit of underlying cost $100, it would cost $40 to purchase .4 units of underlying. Combining the two numbers ($40 – $32.88) gives a $7.22 cost as the fair value of the option.

Extending Arbitrage Pricing over Longer Periods

It isn't necessary to stop an option calculation after just one period. It's much more common to have options valued over a large number of periods. First, a pricing tree for the underlying needs to be created for multiple periods. Then, option prices need to be calculated for the period closest to the expiration date of the option. Once those values are known, it is possible to walk backward until the price of the option on the current day is found.

Multiple period models work by calculating option prices from the expiration date backward. The calculation for earlier periods is calculated by duplicating the option value of previously calculated periods, as graphically shown in Figure 3.5.8.

The period size can be chosen arbitrarily small. For example, a binary tree might choose a day between pricing periods. However, it

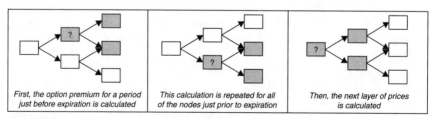

| First, the option premium for a period just before expiration is calculated | This calculation is repeated for all of the nodes just prior to expiration | Then, the next layer of prices is calculated |

Figure 3.5.8. Multiple periods can be handled by calculating the final periods first and working backward

could just as easily try to replicate option prices on the basis of an hour or a minute. The practical intuition behind smaller time periods is that trading could be done more often than once a day.

Benefit of Using a Lot of Periods

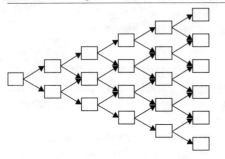

As the number of periods in an option valuation increases, a more realistic distribution of future prices can be obtained. A two-period model with only two ending conditions isn't a comprehensive estimate of the future. However, as the number of estimates increase, a binary tree becomes a more reasonable estimate of likely prices (Figure 3.5.9).

Figure 3.5.9. Binomial trees can get extremely large

Black-Scholes Formula and Continuous Time Finance

If taken to its logical conclusion, the ultimate extension of a binomial tree will have infinitely small time periods. At that point it's no longer possible to algebraically solve the equations. It is necessary to use calculus. In some ways this is a very helpful step because it allows for the creation of a formula for valuing options rather than an iterative procedure. Instead of having to iterate through each node on a binary tree, it is possible to create an equation that can be solved by plugging numbers into a formula. When this approach, known as the Black-Scholes formula, was first developed, it was a particularly innovative piece of work. It provided an easy way to calculate the price of European-style stock options and won a Nobel prize for its creators: Fisher Black, Myron Scholes, and Robert Merton.

The Black-Scholes formula is a closed form solution. That means it has a unique answer that can be found by plugging in parameters to the equation. The formula is a function of five variables: underlying price, strike price, volatility, risk-free interest rate, and time to expiration. With these five numbers, anyone could calculate the price of an option. This opened up option trading to the general investor.

The Black-Scholes formula can be used to value most commonly traded options. However, to come up with a single equation, several assumptions about prices are made by this formula. These assumptions

Open and Closed Form Solutions

The Black-Scholes formula is so commonly used because it is a closed form solution. It is a formula that takes five variables and returns an answer. It isn't necessary to understand how the formula works to get an answer—the user of the formula just needs to supply the parameters.

Closed Form Solution

A formula where a couple of variables can be substituted into the equation to find the correct answer. After it has been developed, using a closed form solution is a very fast way to calculate an option price. The downside of closed form solutions is that they are highly complicated. Quite often, insight into what is actually going on gets lost in the complexity of the mathematics.

Open Form Solution

A formula that must be iteratively solved by a computer. Finding an option with a binomial tree is an example of an iterative solution. The number of steps to solve an open form solution depends on the number of periods in the model. Eventually, the option model will converge on the correct answer as more periods are chosen. The calculation of open form solutions can be very time intensive.

The advantage of open form solutions is that they are simpler to describe and depend on fewer assumptions than closed form solutions. Compared to a closed form solution, using an open form solution is much less a leap of faith. Although, looking at open form solutions requires some understanding of mathematics, it's a level most people can obtain at the high school or undergraduate level. In comparison, the mathematics behind closed form solutions can be difficult to understand even by professionals with Ph.D.'s in advanced mathematics.

are generally reasonable for most of the options in the energy market, which are based upon futures or forwards rather than the underlying commodity. The assumptions:

1. The price of the underlying follows a random process where the best estimate of future prices is the current price (a martingale process).
2. It is possible to buy and sell the underlying without paying large transaction costs or taxes.

3. There is continuous trading in the underlying. The price never jumps without transactions being possible at an intermediary point.
4. It is possible to borrow and lend at the same risk-free interest rate, and that the interest rate remains constant over the life of the option.
5. There is no benefit or penalty from holding the underlying—it doesn't pay dividends or cost money to store.
6. There are no arbitrage opportunities, since any such opportunities are so short-lived that it is difficult to take advantage of them.

The Black-Scholes formula will be inaccurate or wrong if any of the above assumptions are not met. The next chapter, "Spread Options," gives an example of valuing an option using different assumptions. Not every option can be approximated by the Black-Scholes assumptions. However, if the underlying is described by those assumptions, the Black-Scholes formula makes it straightforward to calculate the value of an option. Options that use different assumptions will need to be priced differently (usually using a variant of the binary tree approach that was introduced initially).

More About the Black-Scholes Formula

The Black-Scholes formula is normally shown as two separate formulas, one to calculate the price of a call option, the other to calculate the value of a put option:

$$\text{Call Premium} = SN(d_1) - Ke^{-rT} N(d_2)$$

$$\text{Put Premium} = Ke^{-rT} N(-d_1) - SN(-d_2)$$

Variables in the Black-Scholes Formula

S	Current price of the underlying. The Black-Scholes formula was originally developed for call options, so S is still often used for the price of the underlying.
K	Strike price of the option
T	Time remaining until expiration
r	Risk-free return (needs to use the same time scale as T)
σ	Volatility of the underlying price

Probability Functions for the Black-Scholes Formula

$$d_1 = \frac{\ln\left(\frac{S}{K}\right) + \left(\frac{r+\sigma^2}{2}\right)T}{\sigma\sqrt{T}}$$

d_1 is a measure of the distance between the strike and the current price normalized by the volatility of the underlying.

$$d_2 = d_1 - \sigma\sqrt{T}$$

d_2 is a similar measure to d_1. The most common formula for d_2 is simplification of the actual relationship:

$$d_2 = \frac{\ln\left(\frac{S}{K}\right) + \left(\frac{r-\sigma^2}{2}\right)T}{\sigma\sqrt{T}}$$

$$N(x) = \frac{1}{\sqrt{2\pi}} \int_{-\infty}^{x} e^{\frac{-x^2}{2}} dz$$

$N(x)$ is the cumulative distribution function of a standard normal distribution. It is the probability that the standard normal distribution will be less than the parameter x.

Implied Volatility

A major advantage of arbitrage free pricing is that most of the parameters necessary to calculate the price of an option can be observed. Interest rates, underlying prices, expiration dates, and strike prices can either be observed or estimated without too much effort. The only parameter that can't be directly observed is the volatility of the underlying prices.

Because it can't be observed, volatility plays a critical role in option models. All of the other factors in the model are based on publicly available prices. That means all corrections to the model can be thought of as adjustments to volatility. For example, the assumption that prices are lognormally distributed isn't completely accurate. The options most affected by the lognormal assumptions being inaccurate are those with high or low strike prices, or options with very long maturities. To account for that greater risk, these options can be priced with different volatility assumptions than those used for at-the-money options.

If the volatility for out-of-the-money options is increased, graphing implied volatility against strike prices will show a *volatility smile*, as in Figure 3.5.10. This can be observed in the market by calculating the volatility that is implied by reported option trades. *Implied volatility* is the value calculated by backing out the volatility from the Black-Scholes equation. This is done by finding the latest market price for an option, plugging in the observable parameters, and then choosing implied volatilities until the right price is obtained.

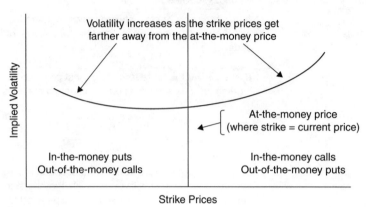

Figure 3.5.10.   The volatility smile

Greeks

Finally, because option prices depend on a number of factors, traders often want to know what happens to option prices when those factors change. For example, a trader might want to know what would happen to the value of her crude oil options if the price of the crude oil falls substantially. Some of the most common factors have acquired specific names. These factors are typically represented by Greek letters. Collectively, these factors are called *Greeks*. The most common Greeks are listed here:

- **Delta.** The change in option value for a $1 change in the value of the underlying. Also called the *hedge ratio* since this is the amount of the underlying needed to duplicate the option payout. Mathematically, this is the first derivative of the option value relative to price. Delta is the best indicator of how much money the option will make or lose during a trading day.
- **Gamma.** The change in Delta for a $1 change in the underlying. Mathematically, this is the second derivative of value of the option relative to price. Gamma is important because it indicates whether the portfolio can suddenly have its Delta change. Gamma is one of the most important risk measures when looking at a combination of options.
- **Vega.** The change in the option value given a 1 percent change in volatility. Mathematically, this is the first derivative of the option price relative to volatility. Vega is important because it indicates the sensitivity of the option price to a quantity that can't be directly observed. If an option has a high Vega, correctly estimating the volatility becomes extremely important.

- **Theta.** The decrease in option value over a one-day period. Options are worth less money close to expiration than when they are far from expiration. That is because a long dated option (one with a long time to expiration) has more time to become valuable to the buyer. The asymmetrical payoff of an option means that a long time to expiration, much like volatility, works in favor of the option buyer.
- **Rho.** The change in option price given a 1 percent change in interest rates. Although not too important for a single option, this becomes important for companies that hold a lot of option exposures.

Monte Carlo Pricing

The mathematics behind option pricing can become exceptionally complicated. Sometimes things get so complicated that professional mathematicians can't make headway into the solution. In these cases it is often possible to use large-scale computer simulations to approximate the right answer.

Monte Carlo simulations use statistical sampling techniques to estimate answers to an equation when it is difficult or impossible to compute an exact result. In many ways, using a Monte Carlo simulation is like taking a multiple choice examination in school. Even if it is impossible to solve a problem, it might still be possible to plug in each answer to see which one works.

Historically, these methods were first popularized when electronic computers were first developed in the late 1940s and the 1950s. The general concept is that computer time is relatively cheap, and that in many cases it is faster to use brute force to come up with an answer than to actually solve the problem mathematically. The development of the hydrogen bomb is a famous example of an early application of Monte Carlo simulations. The physics for the project were extremely complicated, and the physicists needed a way to understand the results of their formulas more quickly.

Another example of a Monte Carlo simulation might find the solution to: "What percentage of the time is it possible to win a game of solitaire with a standard 52-card deck?" It's impossible to win every game of solitaire. However, finding the exact percentage of winnable games is a very difficult problem. However, if it were possible to play enough games, it might be possible to use statistical sampling to estimate the answer to the problem. This approach doesn't require a lot of mathematical knowledge, just a really fast computer playing a lot of games of solitaire over and over.

3.6

SPREAD OPTIONS

 30-Second Summary

Purpose

This section illustrates some of the problems that complicate option pricing in the real world. The previous section described how relatively simple, well-behaved options are priced, and this expands that discussion by adding various complications. Although this section focuses on spread options, similar issues commonly complicate other types of exotic options.

Coming up with an actual pricing methodology is beyond the scope of this discussion. It is expected that most readers will either buy off-the-shelf software to value spread options or will have the expertise to build out their own numerical approach in-house.

Summary

The *spread option* is a specific type of option especially common in the energy market. Spread options are used to price a large variety of physical energy deals. With these options, the owner of the option benefits when the difference between two prices is above a certain level. This is like a normal option except with two asset prices.

Spread options cannot be priced with standard option pricing formulas. They require more complicated mathematics. Developing these formulas is a substantial task by itself. Even then, valuing spread options requires having the appropriate prices, volatility estimates, and correlations. That data is often unavailable and might need to be approximated or guesstimated. People with access to the right data have a huge advantage trading spread options.

Key Topics

- Spread options don't conform to the same assumptions used to price vanilla options. This means that all of the option pricing formulas need to be redesigned for assumptions that are reasonable.
- There is seldom a clean way to value a spread option. All spread option models are complicated. As a result, these models are even more likely than standard option models to break down.

Spread options are an exotic type of option used to model many energy investments. These options are common whenever a trader has the ability to convert one asset into another. For example, a refinery can convert crude oil into gasoline and diesel. A power plant can convert natural gas into electricity. An electrical power line can convert power in one location to power in another location. Most of the time, these conversions don't have to be made, so the trader has the "option" of making the conversion when it is profitable.

The profitability of converting one asset into another depends upon the spread between two prices relative to the cost of conversion: the price here versus the price there, compared to transportation costs; the price now versus the price later, compared to storage costs; and the price of fuel versus the price of electricity, compared to generation costs. This adds another asset price to the standard option model. Spread options depend on a spread between two prices rather than the single price found in vanilla option models.

A spread option can be constructed to look like a standard option in a couple of ways. One way is to set the "price" of the option equal to the spread between the two assets:

Call Payoff = (Asset Price1 − Asset Price2) − Strike Price

Another way is to lump the second asset price into the "strike price":

Call Payoff = Asset Price1 − (Asset Price2 + Strike Price)

One primary difference between an exotic option, like a spread option, and less complicated options is the assumptions used to model their prices. The Black-Scholes formula makes a lot of assumptions about how underlying prices will behave. When those assumptions are reasonable, the formula allows options to be easily valued. However, when those assumptions are not reasonable, a more complicated approach needs to be taken.

Valuing spread options is substantially more complicated than valuing options on single assets. In the two asset case, the correlation between the two assets is very important. The spread between the prices of two highly correlated assets will behave differently than the spread between two uncorrelated assets. In fact, the correlation between the two assets becomes the single most important factor in the option valuation. There often isn't a good way to estimate this correlation either—historical data may be misleading, and there isn't usually a liquid enough market to determine the correlations being used by other people in the market.

Because of correlation's effect on the price of spread options, and the difficulty in estimating it, correlation requires a lot of scrutiny. Managing the risk of an options portfolio requires building an infrastructure to examine correlations between products. Incorrectly estimating correlation is the single easiest way to mess up an option valuation. This estimate isn't just important when a spread option trade is initiated—it needs to be monitored over the entire life of the trade.

Common Terms

Exotic Option.   Any option that doesn't meet the assumptions of the Black-Scholes model.

Vanilla Option.   A normal, plain option with no special features. Vanilla options can usually be priced using the Black-Scholes formula. For example, an option on an asset whose prices can be modeled by a lognormal distribution.

Pricing Models

There is a fundamental difference between spreads and the prices of individual assets. The most common approximation of asset prices (never dropping below zero, but able to increase much more) doesn't describe a spread very well. Although that assumption works for something like a commodity where prices are almost never zero or negative, it doesn't work for a spread between two prices. Spreads between two prices can be zero or negative fairly often. Other standard measures, like the concept of a percent return, don't work either. It is impossible to calculate a percent return on something that starts at a zero price.

The statistical distribution commonly used to model spreads compared to the distribution commonly used to model single assets is shown in Figure 3.6.1. A normal distribution is generally a better description of a spread than a lognormal distribution, as seen in Figure 3.6.2.

Mean Reverting or Martingale?

A coin flip has a 50/50 chance of coming up heads no matter what has occurred in the past (Figure 3.6.3). Not all distributions work in the

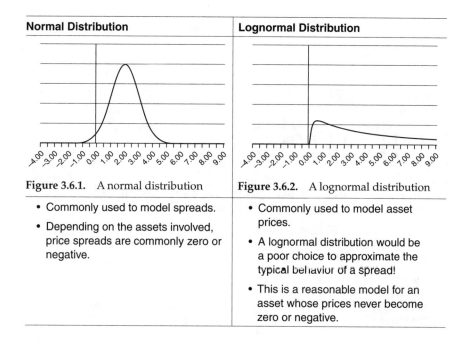

Normal Distribution	Lognormal Distribution
Figure 3.6.1. A normal distribution	**Figure 3.6.2.** A lognormal distribution
• Commonly used to model spreads. • Depending on the assets involved, price spreads are commonly zero or negative.	• Commonly used to model asset prices. • A lognormal distribution would be a poor choice to approximate the typical behavior of a spread! • This is a reasonable model for an asset whose prices never become zero or negative.

same way. Some series have a distinct trend, and others tend to come back to a midpoint the farther they move away from it (Figure 3.6.4).

Spreads might fall into either category. Anytime there is a conversion relationship possible between the two assets, the spread will often oscillate around the cost of conversion. For example, a crack spread relates the price of crude oil to something made out of crude oil (like gasoline). The spread between the prices of crude oil and gasoline are linked by the ability to convert crude oil into gasoline. These prices might be driven apart temporarily by short-term supply and demand issues. However, over the long run competition between refineries is going to bring prices together again.

Using mathematical terminology introduced in the last chapter, it is unsafe to assume that all spreads are martingales.[1] Instead, spreads must be examined to see if they have mean reverting tendencies. Then, the investment has to be examined to see whether it is affected by that behavior.

---

[1] A martingale is a random process consisting of independent periods. Rolling dice or flipping coins are examples of a martingale processes. The likelihood of a specific number or flip coming up is the same, regardless what happened on the previous roll or coin flip. Dice do not have a memory!

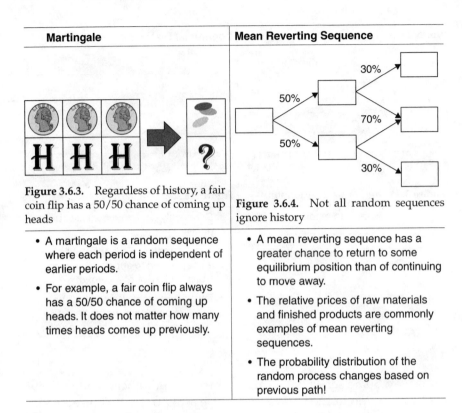

Martingale	Mean Reverting Sequence

Figure 3.6.3. Regardless of history, a fair coin flip has a 50/50 chance of coming up heads

Figure 3.6.4. Not all random sequences ignore history

- A martingale is a random sequence where each period is independent of earlier periods.

- For example, a fair coin flip always has a 50/50 chance of coming up heads. It does not matter how many times heads comes up previously.

- A mean reverting sequence has a greater chance to return to some equilibrium position than of continuing to move away.

- The relative prices of raw materials and finished products are commonly examples of mean reverting sequences.

- The probability distribution of the random process changes based on previous path!

Prices and Correlation Estimates

Another major complication in spread options is determining the actual relationship between two assets by looking at market data. Estimating the correlation between asset prices can be especially difficult in the energy markets. One reason is that prices are often not available. Another reason is that when prices are available, they are often spot prices, which are more volatile (and less correlated) than forward prices.

When two assets are highly correlated, they behave almost like the same asset. As a result, the volatility of the spread between their prices is very low. As correlation decreases, the assets will behave less alike. As a result, extreme events where one asset moves up and the other down in price become much more common. Increasing volatility makes owning any option, including spread options, more profitable. However, correlation works the opposite way. Spread options become more valuable when the correlation drops.

Because future predictions of volatility and correlation are unreliable and have a disproportionately large impact on the value of spread options, risk management has to focus on these items. Misestimated correlation is a common reason for modeling failures. Understanding the relationship of volatility and correlation is one way to catch problems early.

Volatility Increases Dispersion

The dispersion of possible values and the benefit of buying an option, increases with volatility (Figure 3.6.5). Spread options on highly volatile assets are worth more than spread options on nonvolatile assets.

Correlation Reduces Dispersion

Correlation reduces the likelihood that assets move apart (Figure 3.6.6). As a result, spread options between highly correlated assets are worth less than spreads on uncorrelated assets. In the extreme case of two assets being perfectly correlated, there is never a spread between the two prices (or there is a fixed spread).

This is a big deal because dispersion has a direct impact on option profitability. Option buyers benefit from a wide range of possible spreads because an unusual spread will never result in a loss. Option sellers benefit from a tight dispersion of possible spreads since outlying results hurt them—they will never make more than the premium, but their losses are unbounded. If either side estimates the correlation between the assets incorrectly, they will consistently lose money to someone who does a better job estimating correlations.

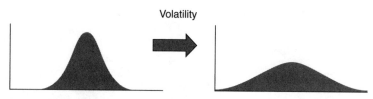

Figure 3.6.5.   Volatility increases dispersion

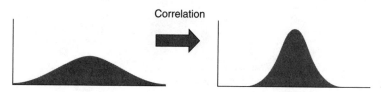

Figure 3.6.6.   Correlation decreases dispersion

Valuation Modeling the Spread

There are two main approaches for valuing the spread. The first approach is to model the spread, and the second is to model the prices of the assets individually. The benefit of modeling the spread is that the option calculation is much easier since it is possible to use a *binary tree* model instead of a *quaternary tree*.

If the spread between the two assets is modeled, it is possible to create a binary tree model to price the option. The binary tree will be based on the possibility that the spread increases or decreases. Typically, the distribution of this spread will be modeled by three factors: the volatility of the first asset, the volatility of the second asset, and the correlation between the first and second assets.

A general diffusion model, like the ones used for Black-Scholes vanilla options, assumes that with enough time there will be a large number of possible values in a spread. However, if the spread is based on correlated assets, the spread will be less wide than it is otherwise. In this regard, the volatility of the assets and the correlation between the two assets pull the distribution in opposite directions (Figure 3.6.7).

A major complication to this approach is that volatility and correlation can be hard to estimate. Because there is no active trading in many areas, energy prices often have to be estimated based on the prices of related commodities traded somewhere else. For example, forward power prices are usually estimated from forward natural gas prices. As a result, comparing the forward prices of power and natural gas will typically overestimate the actual correlation between those assets.

A different problem comes from using spot prices to estimate volatilities and correlation. Short-term disruptions in supply and demand are more important to spot prices than long-term conversion relationships.

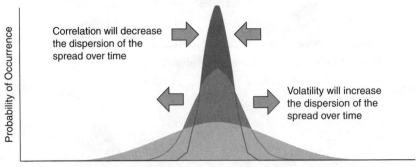

Figure 3.6.7. Modeling the spread requires estimating the volatility and correlation of the assets

This makes the volatility of the spread increase dramatically just before expiration. This problem is further compounded by the fact that there are a limited number of data points for a specific month. August power is a different commodity than July power. If it is necessary to estimate the behavior of August peak power based on historical data, there will only be 21 or 22 samples a year (the number of weekdays during August). And those are unlikely to be independent samples because power prices are strongly influenced by daily high temperatures that tend to persist for several days in a row.

Finally, it is not possible to get futures or spot prices at all locations. There are only a handful of locations where futures are traded. In the rest of the country, only OTC markets are available. It is fairly common for these areas to lack reliable quotes or trades. Pricing surveys will usually guesstimate prices where trading might occur. However, that price may or may not bear any relationship to the price at which trades actually occur in the future. As a result, it is fairly common for prices based on OTC surveys to jump dramatically every so often (when actual trades occur).

More Complicated Approaches to Estimating Prices

The price creation process can be as simple or as complicated as the modeler desires. It is possible for these models to get incredibly complicated. Some of the more common types of pricing models are quaternary trees or three-dimensional surfaces. In a quaternary tree, the price of each of the two assets can go up or down. This gives a total of four endpoints in the tree from each starting point (Figure 3.6.8).

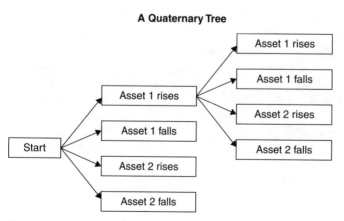

Figure 3.6.8.   A quaternary tree has four possible results every step

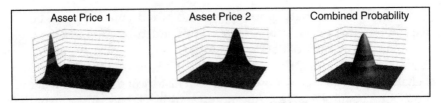

Figure 3.6.9. A combination of two curves will look like a three-dimensional surface

Like a binary tree, which allows prices to go up or down, a quaternary tree can allow more variations of price movements.

Another way to think about joint prices is to make a multidimensional model. For example, it is possible to multiply two bell curves and examine the resulting surface. Mathematically, this is actually relatively easy—it's straightforward to calculate a multiple integration against both the x and y axis. Pictorially, this is shown in Figure 3.6.9—two two-dimensional graphs (just like the bell curve distributions used throughout this chapter) are multiplied together to create a three-dimensional surface.

Ultimately, the real test of these approximations is how well they actually represent the way these prices act in real life. For that, there is no substitute for looking at real prices. The key point to remember is that option models rely on approximation of price behavior in order to value options. These models are often chosen to make the mathematics less complicated. However, models can't capture all of the details of a real-life situation, and testing needs to be done to ensure that modeling assumptions match reality.

Spreads on More Than Two Assets

Although spread options are most commonly based on two assets, there are often spread options on three or more factors. For example, a refinery splits crude oil into a variety of products like gasoline, diesel, and asphalt. It is possible, though complicated, to construct a spread option based on the price of each of the distilled petroleum products minus the price of crude oil. The danger of using that kind of option is increased, since the relationship between assets is more complicated than a two-asset model.

What Does an Actual Spread Look Like?

Modeling spreads is not just a mathematical exercise. Behind the models, options pricing ultimately needs to capture some type of actual behavior. It is often less important to understand the mathematics behind an option model than to understand the approximations of the real world that are being incorporated into a model.

Spread options are a great example of the importance of looking at data. One type of spread is a *spark spread*—the difference between the price of electricity and a fuel like natural gas. It is possible to burn natural gas to produce electricity. This is how power plants make a profit. A power plant essentially has an option to burn fuel and produce electricity.

The operational efficiency of power plants can be approximated by comparing the price of electricity to the price of fuel in the region. For example, in PJM-W during the period January 2000 to June 2002, on average, it took 9.5 MMBtus of natural gas to equal the cost of 1 MWh of electricity.

Looking at the price of natural gas and peak electrical power (Figure 3.6.10), the two prices are obviously correlated. The spread in prices (assuming the typical conversion of 9.5 MMBtus gas per MWh of power), oscillates around zero (Figure 3.6.11). Sometimes the spread is positive, and other times the spread is negative.

Commodity Prices	Spark Spread
During this period, the prices of natural gas and power were generally correlated, although there was one period where the price of power spiked substantially.	The spread between the two prices was close to zero, although the surge in power prices during August 2001 caused a large outlier.
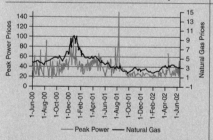	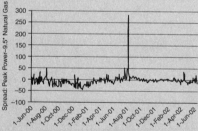
Figure 3.6.10. Peak power and natural gas prices	**Figure 3.6.11.** The spread between power and natural gas prices using a 9.5 MMBtu/MWh heat rate

(Continued)

From a distribution standpoint, although there is a major outlier in prices during August 2001, the spread is clearly distributed around zero. The price of power in August 2001 is much higher than would be predicted by the cost of fuel alone. This isn't especially surprising, since power prices can often spike in the summer. As a result, it is probably a mistake to assume that the outlier is being caused by bad data. Graphing the frequency of each spread price, a normal distribution (shown overlaid in Figure 3.6.12) seems a reasonable approximation of reality except for the huge outlier that the distribution indicates should never occur!

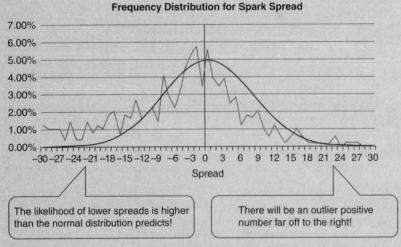

Figure 3.6.12.   Using a normal distribution to model actual prices

Another issue that clouds the predictive ability of this distribution is that the demand for power changes throughout the course of the year. The low demand for power during the spring and fall causes only the most efficient generators to run and keeps the spark spread low. In the winter and summer an increased demand for power allows less efficient power plants to operate and drives up prices. On the hottest days, power prices can spike if the least efficient power plants have to be activated. A more realistic estimate of prices would incorporate a separate distribution for each season.

If more outliers like the August 2001 outlier are expected in the future, the value of owning a power plant is increased. However, if the power grid has taken steps to eliminate similar price spikes, the value of owning a power plant will be reduced. As a result, even if there were a good way to model historical prices, that model may or may not be useful as a prediction of the future.

4.1

Spatial Load Forecasting

    **30-Second
Summary**

Purpose

This chapter introduces the major concepts behind load forecasting, which is a prediction of electrical demand within a specific geographic region for a specific period of time. Load forecasts are important to power traders since the demand for electricity has a huge affect on power prices.

Summary

Spatial load forecasting is the study of *where* and *when* power will be required. As the term "spatial" implies, this is related to a specific region or space; forecasting electrical loads for a limited geographic region. In the short term, load forecasts are used to schedule power plants for operation and maintenance. In the long run, load forecasting is used to evaluate the need for new power lines, power plants, and other infrastructure projects.

Key Topics

- Each load forecast has to be made for a specific area. Each region will have its own idiosyncrasies caused by weather, type of consumers, and geography of the region.
- Each region has a minimum level of demand that must be met at all times. This is called the *base load* of the region.
- Even within the same region, the demand for power will vary day to day. Most of this variation can be explained by calendar effects (like day of week, or hour of day) and weather (primarily temperature).

Power grid operators (RTOs, ISOs, and utility companies) never know exactly how much power that they will need to supply before they need to supply it. Power grids have to estimate consumer demand. This is because consumers don't need to schedule spot electricity purchases. Consumers independently decide how much power they use by turning on and off their appliances. There is no schedule of these decisions ahead of time. The goal of the power grid is to supply the power to consumers where and when they need it. As a result, the power grid operator needs to predict consumer demand ahead of time.

That's where load forecasts come in. In the context of this book, the term "load" is synonymous with *demand for electrical power*. It is an electrical engineering term referring to the power consumed by a circuit or drawn from a power line. In the short term, load forecasting is used to schedule power plants for operation and maintenance. In the long run, it is used to construct new power lines and build new power plants and infrastructure projects.

For power grids, the goal of spatial load forecasting is to estimate both the expected and maximum amount of power that will be used by each portion of the grid. This is necessary so that sufficient power plants can be prepared to meet any contingency. Typically, power grids will have a number of power plants standing ready to turn on at any given time. Power grids need to ensure that these plants can actually deliver electricity to the place it is needed. As a result, it is important to know both the amount of power required and the location where it will be required.

For traders, load forecasts are important because demand has a large effect on prices. Being able to predict prices is a key aspect to trading. The next chapter, "The Generation Stack," discusses how load forecasts can be used to develop estimates of spot power prices.

Expected or Worst Case Scenario?

One of the key considerations for a forecasting model is determining how the model will be used. For example, a utility might want to predict the heaviest load that might be seen on a particular day for a capacity planning project. The utility will need to line up sufficient standby generation in order to supply power to consumers if demand is higher than expected. In contrast, a trader might want to predict the load most likely to occur on a given day as part of a trading strategy.

Although all forecasting models share many similarities, there is no single model perfect for everyone. The only rule in modeling is to think about what is going on and to use some common sense about how to achieve the modeling goal.

Forecasting

The key to short-term load forecasting is developing an understanding for the reasons why people use electricity. Some types of electrical usage are relatively constant. For example, an office might keep a 9 A.M.

to 5 P.M. schedule. The lights might get turned on just before 9 A.M. and turned off just after 5 P.M. This is a calendar type of effect. Every weekday the same pattern will occur. In other cases, demand might vary according to environmental factors. That same office building might keep a constant indoor temperature—using electricity for air-conditioning on hot days and heating on cold days. In that case, electrical demand will be based on temperature.

Not all consumers behave the same way. The central business district of a major city might have a very different electrical demand profile than a residential suburb. For example, in a suburban home, people will wake up, turn on the lights, and get ready for work. Upon leaving for work, they will turn off the lights in their houses and drive to their office, where they turn on the lights. The office building and home have very different power requirements. However, demand for both offices and residences can be modeled by looking at historical behavior.

Location is also a major factor in forecast models. Consumers in central Florida are going to use electricity very differently than the same type of consumer in the Mid-Atlantic coastline. This is because the climate in the two regions is very different. In February, a household in central Florida might have breakfast with the windows open, drinking orange juice, while a household in Philadelphia huddles around a space heater drinking coffee. Some of the most important factors in a load forecast are *type of consumer, location, baseload demand, weather,* and *calendar effects.*

Consumer Type and Location

Load forecasts are made for limited geographical areas. The size of these areas can run from neighborhoods all the way up to multistate regions. The boundaries of a geographic area define what types of consumers are present and the general climate of the region. This is the *spatial* component of spatial load forecasting.

In general, most regions are defined as such because they are connected to the same part of a power grid. It would be helpful if the region contained the same mix of consumers and similar climate throughout, but that is usually a secondary consideration. It's also more helpful if the entire region shares the same calendar for daylight savings changes, holidays, and so on.

Regardless of how a power grid is broken into pieces, each geographic area will contain a specific mix of industrial, commercial, and residential consumers. Commonly these consumers will have a relatively stable energy profile. Exceptionally large consumers of power (like an aluminum manufacturer) might need to arrange for most of their power ahead of time. However, smaller customers will typically be grouped together and treated like a single group for forecasting purposes. The most common division of electrical customers is into residential, commercial, and industrial categories.

Residential consumers are households. Typically, households use most of their energy before or after the working day. As a rough approximation, these customers will use power between 6 A.M. and 9 A.M. in the morning and between 6 P.M. and 11 P.M. in the evening. Some residential consumers will use power all day (leaving the lights on or the air conditioner running). However, most households will reduce electrical usage during the working day. Residences include both apartment buildings and suburban homes.

Commercial customers are offices or retail establishments. Most commonly these businesses operate on a standard schedule and have moderate power demands during the working day. Some commercial uses of electricity are running desktop computers or air-conditioning an office building.

Industrial customers manufacture products. There can be substantial variation among these customers, and they may or may not have a stable demand for electricity throughout the year. Very large industrial customers will typically need to arrange for a steady supply of power from a power provider. This will lower the cost of power for the industrial customer and make the power grid's job much easier.

Base Load Power

One of the most important characteristics of a region is a measurement of the minimum amount of power that has to be supplied at any given time to a power grid. This minimum level is called *base load power*. The demand for base load power determines the number of power plants that have to run full time. Predictably, these are called *base load power plants*.

A good way to get a feeling for the power requirements in a specific region is to take a look at the historical demand. The chart in Figure 4.1.1 shows the historical demand for the PJM-West region between January 2004 and August 2006.

On a quick visual inspection, even though there is a substantial variation in power requirements, the demand in the region never falls below 20,000 megawatts per hour. Doing a little bit of spreadsheet manipulation, it's possible to see the percentage of time that the

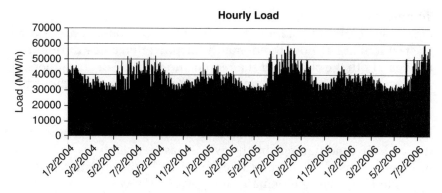

Figure 4.1.1.   Hourly load in the PJM-W region from January 2004 and August 2006

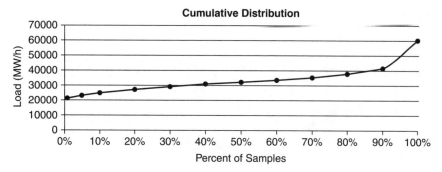

Figure 4.1.2.   Cumulative distribution of loads

regional load was above certain load levels. The load was always above 20,000 MW/h. It was above 30,000 MW/h about half the time. The peak loads on the system were around 60,000 MW/h. This distribution can be seen in Figure 4.1.2.

Ninety percent of the time, the load on the system was less than 40,000 MW/h. As a rough approximation, the region needs about 20,000 MW/h of base load power capacity. To be cost effective, this demand needs to be provided by highly efficient low cost units that can take advantage of the fact that they will be able to work around the clock. The region will need another 20,000 MW/h of capacity to meet most of the variable demand. These power plants will need to be cycled on and off regularly, but a large portion will be in use fairly often. Finally, the region will need another 20,000 MW/h of capacity to meet short-term spikes in demand. These units will operate less than 10 percent of the year, so the primary consideration is that they will be cheap to build, store, and turn on when necessary.

Temperature

Once a general understanding of a power grid is obtained, it's time to start looking at how the demand for power changes throughout the year. Both the climate of the region and the type of consumers in the region affect how the demand for power varies throughout the year.

The temperature of a region has a profound effect on energy demand. One of the most popular uses of energy is to provide heating and air-conditioning. In the winter, as temperatures fall, more electricity is used for heating (Figure 4.1.3). In the summer, just the opposite happens—the demand for power rises when temperatures rise (Figure 4.1.4). The graphs show the relationship between temperature and average hourly load in the PJM-W market.

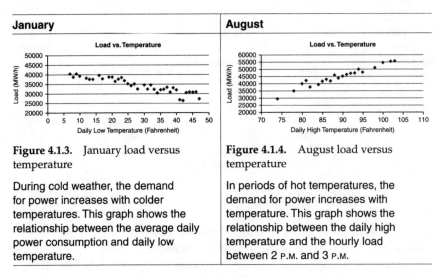

January	August
Figure 4.1.3. January load versus temperature	**Figure 4.1.4.** August load versus temperature
During cold weather, the demand for power increases with colder temperatures. This graph shows the relationship between the average daily power consumption and daily low temperature.	In periods of hot temperatures, the demand for power increases with temperature. This graph shows the relationship between the daily high temperature and the hourly load between 2 P.M. and 3 P.M.

The relationship between demand for electric power and load highlights the importance of short-term temperature forecasts to the electrical power industry. Temperature accounts for a very large portion of the day-to-day variation in the demand for electricity.

Month

Looking at average hourly load by month of the year (Figure 4.1.5), the effect of temperature can clearly be seen. The demand for power is higher in months with either extremely hot or cold weather. PJM-W is located west of Washington, D.C., and has hot summers and cold winters. Peak power demand occurs in the summer and winter months. Power demands are much lower during the spring and fall of each year.

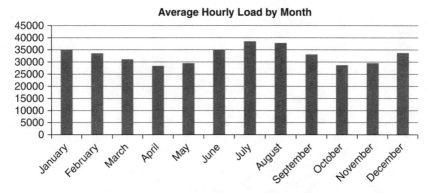

Figure 4.1.5.   Average hourly load by month

Common Terms

To improve the accuracy of temperature-based load predictions, it is common for energy traders to adjust temperatures for humidity and wind chill effects. These are common enough modifications that they have received their own acronyms: *THI* for humidity adjustments and *WCI* for wind chill adjustments.

Temperature Heat Index (THI).   One way to improve a temperature estimate is to include humidity in the calculation. Humidity raises the apparent temperature and makes people feel warmer. Additionally, humidity slows down how quickly a region will cool off overnight. In desert areas where there is little moisture in the air, the overnight temperature falls dramatically from the daytime high. However, in very humid regions, like the Gulf Coast, the overnight temperature falls only slightly—if the daytime high temperature is 95°F, the overnight low temperature might be as high as 90°F.

From a comfort standpoint, there is a huge difference between high and low humidity. Many people don't mind high temperatures in the day as long as it is reasonably comfortable at night when they go to sleep. However, if nighttime temperatures are uncomfortable, a lot more people will use air conditioners. Once people turn an air conditioner on, they will often keep it running during the day so their house doesn't warm up. There is often higher than expected power demand during extremely humid weather because people who normally don't use air conditioners turn them on and leave them operating.

Wind Chill Index (WCI).   Much like humidity increases apparent temperatures, high wind chills can lower the apparent temperature. Anything (like a house) that is exposed to a strong wind will cool off more quickly than it would in stagnant air. When buildings cool off more quickly than usual, more heat is required to maintain them at constant temperatures.

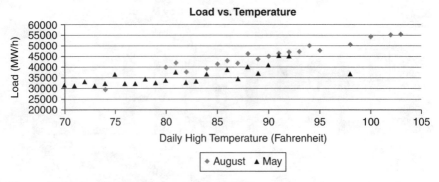

Figure 4.1.6.   Load versus temperature scatter diagram

A next step is to examine how people use power differently in different months. For example, in the Mid-Atlantic region during May, temperatures are fairly pleasant. There may be a couple of hot days, but generally the weather is mild. As a result, even on hot days most people leave their air conditioners off. They wait until a prolonged period of hot weather before turning them on for the summer. However, by August, unrelenting hot weather has convinced many people to run their air conditioners full-time. As a result, for the same daily high temperature, the PJM-W region uses more power in August than it does in May. This can be seen in Figure 4.1.6.

Forecasts

For the United States, the primary source of hourly weather forecasts is the National Oceanic and Atmospheric Administration's (NOAA) National Weather Service (NWS). The NWS produces both short-term hourly forecasts and longer term forecasts. These forecasts can be examined over the Internet at the NWS Web site (forecast.weather.gov).

The NWS produces hourly forecasts of temperature and relative humidity around the country (Figure 4.1.7). The NWS also predicts whether regional temperatures will be above or below average in monthly and quarterly blocks. For example, in the map in Figure 4.1.8, the Desert Southwest was predicted to have a warmer than expected spring in 2009.

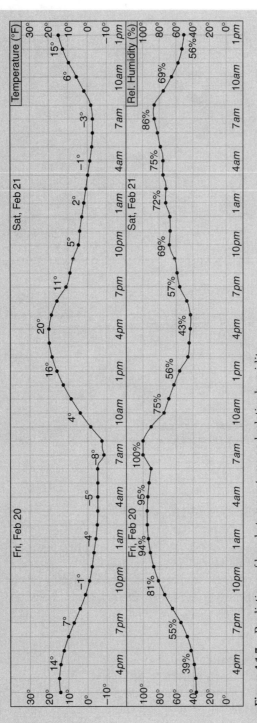

Figure 4.1.7. Predictions of hourly temperatures and relative humidity
(*Source:* National Weather Service [February 2009])

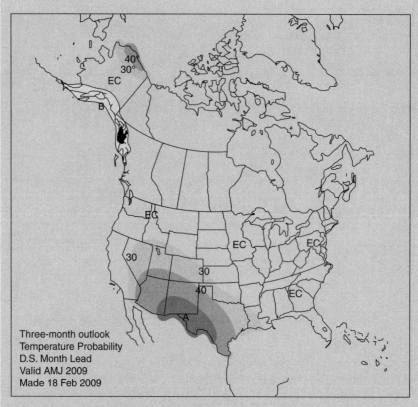

Figure 4.1.8. Long-term temperature forecast
(*Source:* National Weather Service [February 2009])

Weekdays, Weekends, and Holidays

The electrical demand on a specific day also depends on whether the day is a weekday, weekend, or holiday. Not surprisingly, more power is used during the working week than on weekends and holidays. For example, as can be seen in Figure 4.1.9, consumers in the PJM-West area used about 10 percent less power on the weekend.

Hour of Day

Finally, consumers typically use power differently at different times of the day depending on a variety of factors. For example, during the summer, more air-conditioning is required at the hottest part of the day (early afternoon) than early in the morning (Figure 4.1.10). The examples are from the Mid-Atlantic region and might not accurately

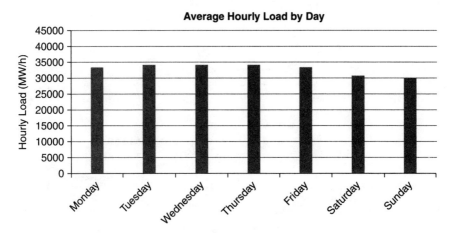

Figure 4.1.9.   Average load by day of week

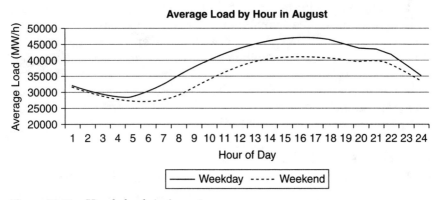

Figure 4.1.10.   Hourly loads in August

represent other parts of the country. Every power grid uses power differently.

In the summer in this region, residential consumers will use more power in the afternoon. Power usage is low overnight and peaks in the middle of the day. Similarly, during cold weather, consumers will typically turn on the heat when they are at home awake, and turn down the thermostat while at work or while sleeping. During the winter, demand can be expected to be highest early in the morning when people wake up, and in the early evening when they arrive home from work.

The August graph shows a comparison of weekday and weekend power requirements. Overnight power usage is pretty constant for both weekdays and weekends. However, substantially less power is used during the hottest part of the day on weekends. There is no need to air-condition the office if no one is there!

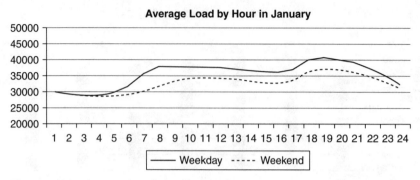

Figure 4.1.11.   Average hourly load in January

The average power use in the winter is different than during hot weather (Figure 4.1.11). During the winter, the Mid-Atlantic region starts using electricity fairly early in the morning (when people start waking up) and spikes again toward the end of the day (when people arrive home from work). Notice how the power use on the weekend differs from the weekday. On the weekend, electricity doesn't start getting used until later in the day—the morning peak is around 10 A.M. rather than the 7 A.M. weekday peak. Perhaps people are sleeping later on the weekend?

Creating a Model

Creating a model from observations is not magic. The best starting point for any model is to look at historical load information (Figure 4.1.12), build some graphs, and look at what is actually going on. The next step is to develop a preliminary model (Figure 4.1.13). In general, a first model should not try to explain too much. After a simple model is completely understood, it can be expanded to account for other types of data.

For example, it might be useful to model the load on the PJM-West region between 2 P.M. and 3 P.M. on August weekdays.

This model starts with two important pieces of information—the "base load" demand for power and effect of temperature on demand. The basic concept behind the model is that power demands rise with temperature. However, demand never drops below the base load requirement. At this point the model isn't complete—but it does capture the most important relationship.

Before doing anything else, it is necessary to see when this model gives a bad estimate of the actual load. This process is called *error analysis*. When a scientist is working on a new theory, the scientist will

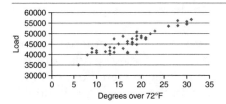

Figure 4.1.12. Load versus temperature

Step 1. Look at the Data
The first step is to look at the data that is being modeled. The left axis shows the hourly load between 2 P.M. and 3 P.M. The bottom axis shows the temperature as degrees above an arbitrarily chosen comfortable temperature of 72°F.

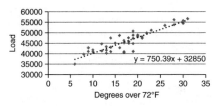

Figure 4.1.13. Approximating actual behavior with a model

Step 2. Create a Linear Model
Since there is a relatively clear relationship, linear regression can be used to create a linear approximation of the observations. Using a spreadsheet, this can be done by adding a trend line to approximate a scatter diagram.

create a hypothesis and then try to disprove it. Modeling works much the same way. A modeler creates an initial model and sees where it doesn't work well. The model can then be modified, hopefully making it more accurate. This process continues until the modeler is comfortable with the model.

Error analysis will compare the model's predictions against actual data. The difference between the actual load observations and the model's predictions is called the *error* of the model. To analyze the error, it will be examined several ways. In this case, three possible reasons for modeling errors will be examined. Initially, this data will be compared to the same data that was used to create the model. This is called an *in-sample* test. Later, the model might be compared to data that wasn't used to create the model. That is called an *out-of-sample* test.

The purpose of error analysis is to explain why the model might not work perfectly all the time. Therefore, it is necessary to think of reasons why it might not work and test them. One possible reason for errors might be that consumers use power differently in late August compared to early August (Figure 4.1.14). For example, we know power is used differently in May than in August. This effect might be visible throughout a month too.

Alternately, the model might be biased against high or low temperatures (Figure 4.1.15). The linear estimate of load has been fit to a large number of samples. It's reasonable to think that some part of that sample is consistently misestimated. For example, the efficiency of air conditioners might go down when it is extremely hot outside. If that's true, air conditioners will both need to do more cooling and require more energy to do that cooling on hot days.

Finally, it's possible that some weekdays behave differently than other weekdays (Figure 4.1.16). For example, if workers tended to leave work a bit early on Friday, that might affect the demand for power on that day. Whether this happens at 2 P.M. in the afternoon is in doubt, but it's something that might be worth checking.

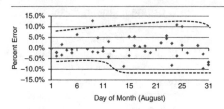

Figure 4.1.14. Check to see if errors are caused by day of month

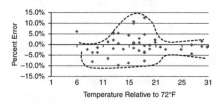

Figure 4.1.15. Check to see if errors are related to temperature

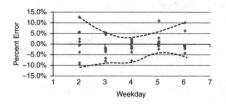

Figure 4.1.16. Check to see if errors are related to day of week

Step 3. Day of Month
The percentage error was graphed relative to the day of the month, and a dashed line shows the location of most of the errors.

The error doesn't seem to be especially biased more toward one part of the month compared to any other part.

Step 4. Temperature
The model is a lot more accurate for high or low temperatures than for moderate temperatures. Most of the model's errors are in the range between 13°F and 20°F above the comfortable temperature. There isn't an obvious solution, but it is something to examine later.

Step 5. Day of the Week
The largest errors are concentrated on Mondays. Although the model isn't perfectly accurate for all the other weekdays, they don't have as wide a distribution of errors as Monday.

4.2

THE GENERATION STACK

 30-Second Summary

Purpose
This chapter discusses how power prices are determined. Although this section is mostly nontechnical, a general knowledge of the electric market is helpful. An introduction to electrical markets can be found in Chapter 2.2, "Electricity."

Summary
In deregulated markets where electricity trading is permitted, prices are set by daily auctions. Each power producer is allowed to submit bids, and the lowest bidders are selected to supply electricity to the power grid. All active providers receive the same price for their power. This price that everyone receives is the price submitted by the highest active bidder.

Key Topics
- The physical capabilities of power plants, particularly the cost of their fuel, determine how they participate in the daily auctions.
- Small changes in the supply or demand of electricity can have a big effect on prices.
- This is a description of a typical deregulated market. Very few markets work exactly in this way since each is governed by local rules and regulations.

In deregulated areas, the coordinating ISO/RTO for the area holds daily auctions to determine the price of power. These are competitive auctions where power plants bid against one another for the right to produce power. The physical capabilities of each generator are a major factor in their bidding strategies. Consequently, the primary way to estimate power prices is to examine power providers ordered by their cost of production. This ordering is called a *generation stack*. For example, if there are four power plants on a power grid with 450 MWh of total capacity, a generation stack ordered from highest cost (on top) to lowest cost (on the bottom) might look like the table in Figure 4.2.1.

Dispatch capacity, often just called *capacity*, indicates how much power each power plant can produce. The *break-even cost* indicates the

Sample Generation Stack		
	Capacity (MWh)	Break-Even Cost
Diesel Peaking	50	150
Natural Gas	100	85
Coal	200	50
Hydroelectric	100	10

Highest Cost

Lowest Cost

Figure 4.2.1.   Sample generation stack

minimum price the power plant can accept for its power and still make a profit. For fuel-dependent power plants, like the natural-gas-fired generator, this cost will be heavily influenced by fuel costs.

   This ordering can help predict the prices produced by the day-ahead and real-time auctions. In most cases, power plants will place bids above their own cost of generation (their break-even cost), and below the costs of the next type of unit in the stack (Figure 4.2.2). As seen in the chart, the coal generator will probably place bids some-where between $50 and $85. The price of power (on the left axis) can be predicted by looking at the predicted consumer demand (on the bot-tom axis). The shaded areas indicate the *marginal* producer and typical prices for each level of demand.

Mechanics of Day-Ahead and Real-Time Auctions

In most regions there are two auctions that determine the *clearing price* of power. The first is a *day-ahead* auction, the second a *real-time* auc-tion. The day-ahead auction uses predictions of the upcoming day's load to schedule power plants the day before power is needed. This auction schedules power producers to be active for an entire hour.

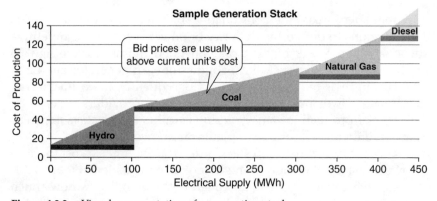

Figure 4.2.2.   Visual representation of a generation stack

If the demand fluctuates throughout the hour, or if the load forecasts are incorrect, an adjustment will be needed to balance production with demand. Adjustments are made in the real-time auction.

In both auctions, generators (also called *Load Serving Entities* or LSEs) participate by submitting offer curves (their generation levels associated with prices they are willing to accept) and their technical constraints (startup costs, minimum up time, etc.). After collecting offers from generators, the ISO selects the winning generators that minimize the cost to the market. For example, a coal power plant with a cost basis of $50 might want 100 MWh of capacity always operating during the period. So, it places its first bid at $0 for its first 100 MWh. Then it will start placing bids for greater amounts of power at progressively higher prices. The last bid (for $83) is placed just under the $85 break-even cost of the next generation unit in the stack (Figure 4.2.3).

When creating a bid, a generator needs to decide whether to attempt to sell all of its power in the day-ahead market or to reserve some capacity to sell into the real-time market. There are potentially greater profits in the real-time market, but the risk of being inactive is also higher. In both cases, bidding strategies are dictated by the physical characteristics of power plants. The most important characteristics are how quickly a power plant can come online and its efficiency at converting fuel into electricity. If a generator is not selected to operate in the day-ahead market, it is still eligible to participate in the real-time market.

Not every generator is capable of participating in the real-time market. The real-time auction requires that generators be capable of quickly starting and have their fuel supplies lined up. Inefficient power providers often have this capability. However, if a low cost provider fails to sell its power in the day-ahead market, technical limitations might prevent it from participating in the real-time market too. Most of the daily generation requirement is auctioned off in the day-ahead market—the real-time auction is used for balancing short-term fluctuations and unexpected demand.

Bid Schedule 200 MWh Coal Plant	
Capacity (MWh)	**Price**
100	$0
101	$51
150	$75
200	$83

Figure 4.2.3.   Example of a bid schedule

Generation costs determine how most power providers participate in the daily auctions. Low cost providers want to lock in profits. They will have already lined up their fuel supplies and are probably hedging their price exposure in anticipation of being activated. If they don't sell power in the day-ahead auction, they may be locked out of the real-time market by operating constraints. In comparison, higher price providers may benefit from waiting until the real-time auction if they can't lock in sufficiently high prices early.

The Dispatch Stack

In deregulated markets, Load Serving Entities are placed into *economic dispatch order* based on the results of the day-ahead and real-time auctions held by each *Transmission System Operator* (TSO). The lowest bidding LSEs are activated first, followed by higher bidders. The order in which power plants are turned on is called the *dispatch stack*. This is a last on, first off ordering similar to a stack of plates (Figure 4.2.4). The unit at the top of the stack (the marginal unit) is the last unit to be activated and the first to be deactivated. The top of the stack is a very important location. The provider on the top of the dispatch stack sets the clearing price of power for a region. This provider is often called the marginal provider.

In most cases the dispatch stack will be ordered similarly to the generation stack. The cheaper a power plant can generate power, the more it has to lose if it doesn't get activated. Once the price of power rises substantially over a provider's cost of production, the power provider will risk losing a large profit if it isn't active. As a result, each

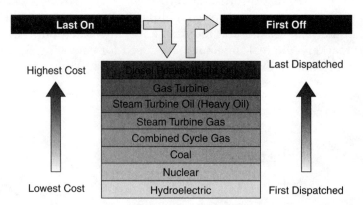

Figure 4.2.4. A generation stack works like a stack of clean plates in a cafeteria: the last unit on is the first one off

power plant will usually actively bid only on a small portion of the generation stack—the part after it becomes profitable, but before it has too much money on the table. After that, they become *price takers*, allowing more aggressive bidders to set the clearing price of power.

Higher cost providers have a different problem—other power plants will know the break-even prices of the providers above them on the stack and bid just under that price. This behavior exists because everyone gets paid the same price for power—there isn't an economic penalty for bidding just under a competitor if someone else sets a higher clearing price.

As a result, power plants with similar capabilities tend to cluster their bids around the same price points. Only a few power plants at any time actively set the price of power. Consequently, the couple of power plants *on the margin* have a disproportionate effect on the price of power. Because similar units cluster their bids, it is usually possible to determine a profile of the marginal producers.

Baseload, Mid-Merit, and Peaking Suppliers

It is common to describe each of the load providers within a generation stack as a *baseload, mid-merit,* or *peaking* unit. These terms broadly describe the behavior of power plants.

Baseload plants are located at the bottom of the generation stack. These power plants are active all year and sell power in the day-ahead auctions. They produce power cheaply, are expensive to shut down, and run continuously even when demand is at its lowest level. Hydro, nuclear, and coal plants all fall into this category. Hydro plants don't have any fuel costs and may not be able to shut down without flooding nearby communities. Nuclear plants require the use of control rods to slow down their nuclear reactions. Without being cooled, a nuclear reaction will keep going at maximum capacity. It costs money to shut down a nuclear reactor. Coal plants are easier to shut down, but can be expensive to restart if allowed to cool down completely. Coal plants are more costly than other baseload producers, but they have a huge cost advantage over other fossil fuel producers. Coal is by far the cheapest of the fossil fuels per Btu of energy. Almost all baseline plants run full-time—they are rarely on the margin, and offer power at low costs in order to avoid going offline.

Peaking generation, the other extreme, provides short-term electricity during periods of peak demand (typically summer afternoons). These generators are at the very top of the generation stack, and the plants need to start up quickly and be cheap to maintain. However, they don't need to be cheap to operate—conserving fuel is an after-thought when power can be sold at sufficiently high prices. Many of these power plants are essentially jet engines. Fuel is pumped in and ignited; there are a minimum of moving parts and a lot of wasted heat energy. Many of these plants only operate a couple hundred hours a year. In order to recover costs, they will charge very high prices. These plants will operate almost exclusively in the real-time auction market except when day-ahead prices are extremely high.

Mid-merit plants are somewhere between the two extremes. In some cases these plants are older, less efficient baseload plants that are no longer cost effective enough to run full-time. In other cases these are highly efficient natural gas plants that are easier to cycle than the baseload generators. These generators are commonly on the margin, and show a lot of variability in their bidding strategies. Base-load generators are always going to bid low—they need to operate full-time. Peaking generators are always going to bid high—they are extremely expensive to operate. Mid-merit generators are going to bid in both day-ahead and real-time markets, and will usually set the price of power.

Active vs. Passive Bidding Strategies

There is a fair amount of gamesmanship in choosing how to bid in power auctions. Generators want to get the highest possible price for their product. However, since there is a single price for power in a region, it isn't important to be the top bidder. As long as a power plant is operating, it is getting the same price as the highest bidder. There is no downside to bidding a zero price if someone else sets the price at a higher level. In contrast, active bidding is risky—power plants that actively try to control the price of electricity run the risk of being inactive and not getting paid.

The basic decision on whether to actively participate in the bidding process, and risk being inactive, often comes down to how much money a power plant stands to lose if it isn't activated. A power plant's profit is the spread between the price of power and the power plant's cost of production. If a power plant has a very low cost of production, it will give up substantially more profit by being inactive than a plant with a higher cost of production.

For example, it might be possible for a power plant to increase the price of power by $1 if it is willing to bid aggressively into the day-ahead market. However, if aggressive bidders stand a 10 percent chance of being inactive, the decision is complicated for providers that are already highly profitable. If the price of power is around $100, it wouldn't be worthwhile for a plant with a cost basis of zero to give up $10 (a 10 percent chance of being inactive and giving up 100 dollars) for a chance to make an extra $0.90 (making an extra dollar 90 percent of the time).

At the other extreme, a power plant with a very expensive cost of production would have a different reaction to the same decision. With a $95 cost of production, a power plant benefits substantially from aggressive bidding. In this case, the power plant would only give up $.50 (giving up a $5 profit, 10 percent of the time) for an extra $0.90 (an extra dollar 90 percent of the time).

Optimal Bidding Strategies

Most generators split their bid into several smaller bids. It is not uncommon for some of these bids to be offered at or below the generator's cost of production. Since most generators are steam turbines that cost money to bring online, unaggressive bids ensure that the generator can avoid unnecessary stoppages. A power plant will often submit bids at higher prices in an attempt to maximize profits. Generally, the placement of the higher bids will depend on who else is bidding at that point.

For example, if a generator can profitably sell power at $50 and the next plant in the generation stack becomes profitable at $60, the first generator is likely to split their bid into two pieces—a piece below $50 to minimize the risk of being completely inactive, and the rest of their bid just under the $60 mark. Generally, this second bid will be as high as possible without tempting the next generator in the stack to undercut that price.

Bidding in this manner requires an in-depth knowledge of all the power plants around a certain point in the generation stack. In most cases this is specialized knowledge learned through trial and error. Power generators usually have a detailed understanding of the generation stack around their own production costs. However, they won't understand other parts of the stack with the same detail. As a result, most power plants only bid aggressively on the portion of the generation stack near their own costs of production.

Because of the need to prevent unnecessary shutdowns and restarts, most optimal bidding strategies do not simply react to prices. Optimal bidding incorporates predictions of likely future decisions into the current decision. In many cases it is worthwhile for a steam turbine to take a loss in some periods to avoid startup costs in a later period. These simulations are often based on a *Game Theory* analysis.

Game Theory

Game Theory is branch of mathematics that is used in economics to analyze behavioral patterns. It focuses on how participants (*players*) make optimal decisions in complex situations (*games*). Since each participant's decisions can affect the other participants, these situations are often competitive; for instance, two people bidding against one another in an auction. There are a number of other common Game Theory terms. The benefit (or loss) that a player receives from playing the game is called *utility*. The goal of every player is to maximize utility. If the utility maximizing decisions converge into a stable pattern, this is called a *Nash Equilibrium*.

Game Theory is often criticized for taking an overly harsh approach to competitive situations. A typical strategy is to look out for oneself at the expense of other players. Intuitively, many people favor cooperative strategies over the very competitive behavior advocated by economists. This is because Game Theory is extremely vulnerable to bad initial assumptions. If a complex situation is incorrectly defined, the *optimal strategy* for that situation can turn out to be a disastrous strategy in "real life."

For example, an economist is out with a potential client on a business trip. He takes the client to a restaurant, and faces a decision at the end of the meal: should he tip the wait staff? The economist and his client received excellent service, but the economist doesn't believe he will return to the same town again. As a result he decides not to tip—he has already gotten his good service, and he decides to save money as well. Unfortunately, his understanding of the game was incorrect. The economist and the wait staff were not the only players. The potential client also witnessed the event. This client might easily conclude that the economist does not value other people's contributions and would be a bad business partner.

Variable Generation

It is common for the generation stack to change. Many power providers can't supply a steady supply of power throughout the day. Solar power is a good example—it depends on sunlight. Sunlight is most abundant during the middle of the day. As a result, the generating capacity of a solar plant will be higher in the afternoon than in the early morning or late evening. The generation stack will change to account for this variable supply. Hydro power, wind generators, and imports and exports from other power grids are all examples of variable supplies of power.

In many cases variable power providers can't turn off their power supplies or guarantee delivery. For example, once power is scheduled to be imported from another power grid, it can't be easily canceled. Solar, wind, and hydro generators also can't shut down on short notice, nor can they guarantee that they will be able to deliver their power. As a result, these power supplies will be price takers—they will bid zero cost for their power and get paid the clearing price set by other market participants.

The production profile for a variable generator can change over time. Sometimes these changes are seasonally predictable, and at other times they are random. It is usually possible to predict the variable supply of electricity a day ahead of time, but longer term predictions become less accurate. Take hydro power, which is very dependent upon seasonal rainfall that can occur anywhere within the space of a month or two. A day ahead of time this water flow on the rivers will be well known. Likewise, solar power plants receive more sunlight in summer months but are also affected by cloudy conditions and precipitation. The most important impact is that even over small periods like a week or two, there can be substantial changes to variable production. The graph in Figure 4.2.5 shows variable generation on two different days in August 2005.

Even small changes to the generation stack can have a major effect on prices because the top of the generation stack is getting displaced. During August 2005, power prices in PJM were around $80. A 4,000 megawatt change in power might change the power prices by $10 or more. This is illustrated in Figure 4.2.6. It shows part of the PJM generation

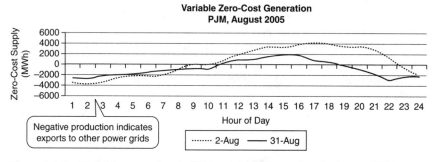

Figure 4.2.5. Variable generation in PJM on two different days in August 2005

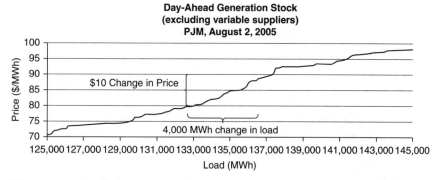

Figure 4.2.6. Small changes in supply can have a big impact on the price of power

stack containing the marginal generators during August 2005 and the effect that an additional 4,000 MWs of power would have on prices.

Variable generation is a major reason why periods in the same day with identical consumer demand can see a wide range of prices. This makes it difficult to back into a generation stack by looking at daily loads and prices published by ISO/RTOs.

Estimating Break-Even Costs Using Heat Rates

No one, except for the ISO/RTO coordinating the daily auctions, knows the exact makeup of the generation stack until the data is released several years later. Auction bids are not made public, nor do load producers publish their break-even costs. To predict power prices it is necessary to look at historical prices and estimate the generation stack from other pieces of information. Of this other information, fuel prices are the most common way to estimate changing power prices.

For fuel-dependent load providers, the cost of fuel and the conversion efficiency of their power plant combine to determine where they become cost effective. Natural gas prices are particularly important in determining the price of power because marginal producers commonly use that fuel. The natural gas/power relationship is so pervasive that it has its own terminology. The ratio of power prices to natural gas prices is called an *implied market heat rate*.

An implied market heat rate is easy to calculate: it is the average price of power divided by the average price of fuel in a specific geographic area. Because fuel needs to be paid for and scheduled for delivery ahead of time, the price of fuel within a particular day is constant. A generation stack can be described by either prices or heat rates, as shown in Figure 4.2.7. The heat rates are calculated by dividing the prices by $12.70 (the price of natural gas on that day).

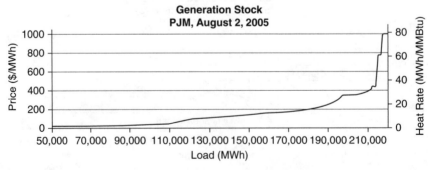

Figure 4.2.7. Prices and heat rates are both ways to describe the generation stack

The prices on the left axis of the generation stack can be divided by the price of natural gas to calculate the heat rate (right axis). On this particular day, August 31, 2005, the price of natural gas was $12.70.

When fuel prices rise, the break-even cost of power providers using that fuel will also rise. As a result, the generation stack for those producers will change. For example, in August 2005 the price of natural gas rose from $8.02 to $12.70. This coincided with a large move in the price of power. A portion of the PJM generation stack at the beginning and end of the month can be seen in Figure 4.2.8. Power prices rose significantly for parts of the generation stack.

The implied market heat rate can identify how much of a change in electricity prices is due to a change in natural gas prices. If implied heat rates don't change, the ratio between power and gas prices remains constant. A constant ratio means that the fuel prices fully account for the change in electricity prices. In August 2005, on the portion of the generation stack where natural gas plants are profitable, there was very little change in market heat rates between the two days. This is illustrated in Figure 4.2.9. The part of the generation stack where natural gas is the marginal fuel is highlighted.

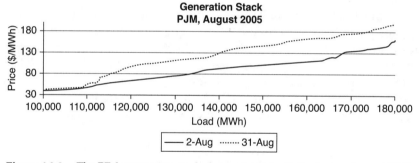

Figure 4.2.8. The PJM generation stack changed substantially during August 2005, which coincided with a spike in natural gas prices

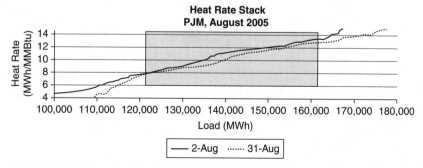

Figure 4.2.9. The natural gas heat rate remained similar between the two days despite the large change in prices

Day-Ahead and Real-Time Auctions

Although there are two separate auctions setting the price of power, the generation stack and the bidding strategies of power producers are nearly identical for both. Most of the generation capacity is locked in during the day-ahead market, with a small amount of balancing required from the real-time market. Although there are fewer participants in the real-time auction, similar bidding dynamics lead to similar generation stacks. A comparison of real-time and day-ahead prices for two days can be seen on Figure 4.2.10. The auction prices are close together most of the time. Occasionally, prices in the real-time market are higher.

The inability of many power plants to react quickly to changes in load is the reason for two auctions. Typically, the day-ahead market activates power plants in half-hour or hour-long increments. The load at the start of the period determines the number of power plants that get activated. However, if demand rises before another set of power plants is activated (either a half hour or hour later), that demand will need to be met by the real-time market. The relationship between changes in hourly demand and the short-term change in prices can be seen in Figure 4.2.11.

In most cases, marginal power suppliers tend to use the same strategy for participating in both auctions. The highly efficient generators at the bottom of the generation stack are the most likely to get locked out of the real-time market. However, except for periods of very low demand, the bottom of the generation stack will be continuously active, and won't be on the margin. As a result, the real-time and day-ahead generation stacks are usually very similar.

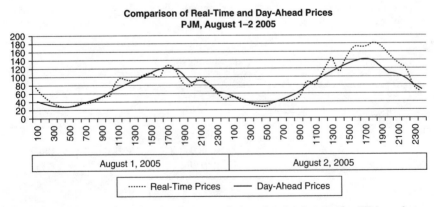

Figure 4.2.10. Comparison of real-time and day-ahead prices in the PJM market, August 1–2, 2005

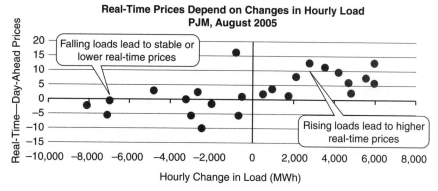

Figure 4.2.11. The real-time market is mostly active when loads are rising

Efficient vs. Economic Dispatch

One of the problems facing economically dispatched markets (markets where generators are activated based on price) is how to deal with pollution. For example, coal-powered plants produce a lot of pollution. However, they are economically competitive because their fuel is extremely cheap in comparison to other fossil fuels. In an economically dispatched market, when environmentally friendly power is brought on line, it usually won't displace the coal generators. Instead, the marginal generators further up the generation stack will be replaced. Most commonly, these will be less polluting combined cycle natural gas plants.

For the same amount of pollution, natural gas produces much more energy than coal. However, due to the higher cost of fuel, natural gas generators will be deactivated before the coal generators. Politically, this creates a problem. When *green power* (environmentally friendly generation) is brought on line, it removes the more expensive fuels like natural gas from the generation stack. Environmental advocates would prefer to see an *efficient dispatch* of power—activating power plants based on minimal SO_2 and CO_2 emissions rather than on an economic basis.

To make efficient dispatch work in a deregulated market, the most common approach is to make coal power more expensive by charging for CO_2 and SO_2 emissions. Making coal production more expensive can raise costs for consumers, but these costs can be refunded by reducing other consumer expenses. Many markets are adopting the use of *emissions credits* for this purpose. Essentially, emissions credits are a tax on highly polluting power plants so that an economic dispatch system also satisfies environmental efficiency requirements.

4.3

TOLLING AGREEMENTS

 30-Second Summary

Purpose

A tolling agreement is a contract to rent a power plant from its owners. These agreements give the renter the ability to convert one physical commodity (fuel) into a different commodity (electricity). This chapter discusses how to determine the economic value of a power plant using options.

Summary

Owning (or renting) a power plant gives a trader the option of converting fuel into power. If power prices are sufficiently high, a power plant can burn fuel to produce electricity at a profit. Otherwise, the trader will usually leave the power plant inactive. This is very similar to the behavior of financial option contracts. As a result, the value of a power plant is often approximated as a portfolio of those contracts.

Key Topics

- Tolling agreements are commonly modeled as a portfolio of option contracts.
- Power plants run for years. Because electricity can't be stored, electricity in one part of the year is a different commodity than electricity at other parts of the year. From a risk management perspective, there are a large number of different underlying products being traded.
- The correlation between fuel and power prices is the single largest factor in determining the value of a tolling agreement.
- Tolling agreements are also commonly modeled by Monte Carlo simulations or as equity investments. However, a full discussion of each technique and its relative merits is beyond the scope of this book.

With deregulation, sweeping changes were made to the ownership of power plants. Power plant operators became responsible for selling power in an open market in addition to maintaining their plants. The safe business of operating a power plant—once thought of as an ultrasecure investment—was now a very risky business. To address this new reality, power plant operators began to specialize. Some focused on maintaining the physical hardware of their plants, and others focused on marketing the power.

The general mechanism for outsourcing trading responsibility is to rent the power plant to a *power marketer*, a company specializing in power trading, through a *tolling agreement*. These agreements can run for any length of time (often 20 or 30 years) and divide the job of running a power plant between the two parties. The owner gets paid a fee to maintain the power plant, while the power marketer makes all of the economic decisions. The marketer is responsible for supplying fuel to the plant and selling the resulting electricity into a competitive market. The power marketer takes on all of the economic risks and earns all the profits above the fixed maintenance fee.

Renting a power plant gives the power marketer the ability to convert fuel into electricity. In a financial sense, this is alchemy—a power plant provides the ability to turn a low cost commodity into a more valuable commodity. Best of all, the conversion doesn't have to be made if it is not profitable. For example, if the spread between electricity prices and fuel prices is unprofitable, the power marketer can turn off the power plant.

This ability to not operate is very similar to the behavior of financial options. The owner of a financial option has a choice of taking an action or doing nothing. As a result, tolling agreements are commonly modeled as a series of financial options. Based on this concept, one way to value a tolling agreement is equal to the cost of replicating a power plant's physical capabilities with financial option contracts. Approximating real behavior with a financial option model for the purposes of valuation is called a *real options* approach to modeling.

Converting Fuel to Electricity

Physically, power plants operate by burning fuel to produce electricity. Some power plants are more efficient at producing electricity than others—they burn less fuel to produce the same amount of electricity. The conversion efficiency of this process is called the plant's heat rate, which we discussed in an earlier chapter. The higher a plant's heat rate, the more electricity it produces for the same amount of fuel.

$$\text{Profit per Unit} = \underbrace{\text{Price}_{\text{Electricity}}}_{\text{Sales Price}} - \underbrace{\text{Heat Rate} \times \text{Price}_{\text{Fuel}}}_{\text{Cost of Goods Sold}}$$

Calculating the profit from this conversion is a standard net profit calculation: a power plant's profit is the sale price of its product minus its cost of materials and operating costs. In most cases, since fuel costs are much larger than other operating costs, the operating costs are ignored and the net profit of a power plant is approximated only by the conversion efficiency of the plant. For a single unit of output, this estimate of net profit is called a spark spread, a concept that was also introduced earlier.

The net profit formula for using a spark spread approximation is shown below. This is a fairly standard net profit formula—the number of units can be multiplied by the per unit profit to calculate the total profit. The terminology in this formula will be used throughout the discussion.

Using standard terminology:

$$\text{Profit} = (\text{Number of Units})\,(\text{Profit per Unit})$$

Using energy terminology:

$$\text{Profit} = \text{Dispatch}\,(\text{Price}_{\text{Electricity}} - \text{Heat Rate} \times \text{Price}_{\text{Fuel}})$$

Dispatch	The dispatch level is the amount of generation capacity currently online. For example, a power plant might be able to produce 100 MW of power an hour operating at full capacity. The typical units are megawatts per hour (MWh).
Price$_{\text{Electricity}}$	The price of electricity. This is usually in units of dollars per megawatt hour: $\frac{\text{Dollars}}{\text{MWh}}$.
Heat Rate	A generator's heat rate determines the efficiency at which fuel is converted into power. This is specific to each power plant and can depend on the dispatch level of the plant, seasonal temperatures, and operating history. The units of this factor will be the heat energy of fuel required to produce one unit of electricity—most commonly, either $\frac{\text{Btu}}{\text{KWh}}$ or $\frac{\text{MMBtu}}{\text{MWh}}$.
Price$_{\text{Fuel}}$	The price of fuel. Fuel prices are either quoted by volume (barrels or millions of cubic feet) or by heat energy (Btus). Prices are quoted in currency per unit, like $\frac{\text{Dollars}}{\text{MMBtu}}$.

Since spark spreads can be negative, the ability of the power plant to turn off means that its profit needs to be approximated by a *spark spread option* rather than a spark spread. A spark spread option is a spark spread whose owner has the option of taking a zero profit, which is similar to a power plant shutting down. When spark spreads are positive, the power plant's total profit is its per-unit profit (the spark spread) multiplied by the total units of electricity the power plant can produce. When the spark spread is negative, the power plant has zero profit.

As a general rule, whenever spark spreads are positive, the owner will take the profit. Any time they are unprofitable, the owner will try to opt for zero payment by shutting down the power plant. Occasionally real life will interfere. For example, the owner might not be able to shut the power plant for regulatory reasons. Alternately, the power plant operator might not want to let the plant cool down too much and would consider it worthwhile to operate at a loss for a couple of hours to avoid the costs associated with restarting a couple of hours later.

Breaking Up the Model

Because the power marketer isn't going to make just one decision on the power plant, a large number of options are required to approximate the physical behavior of a power plant. Most commonly, a power plant will make operating decisions on an hourly, daily, or monthly basis. Typically, a model of a tolling agreement will create an option for each operating decision. Each *leg* of the trade will represent a set of decisions occurring around the same point in time. For example, a tolling agreement might be broken up into monthly pieces where a single on/off decision will be made for the month (Figure 4.3.1).

To value a tolling agreement, it is necessary to split it into pieces. The diagram shows a tolling agreement being broken into monthly pieces. Each piece of the agreement is called a *leg*.

Even though a model of a power plant should be based on how the plant actually operates, there are differences between estimating future decisions and making decisions for the current day. Detailed information, like hourly prices, is not available for future periods. As a result, there is little advantage to using very small time frames if the prices have to be estimated from longer time periods. Choosing longer periods for estimating decisions can simplify a model. Most models have an optimal point of complexity. At that point being more complex doesn't make the model more accurate, it only makes it slower to calculate and harder to test.

The primary factor in choosing an appropriate number of legs is the availability of market data and the physical capabilities of the

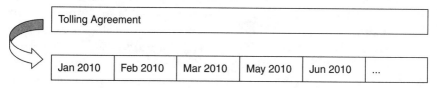

Figure 4.3.1. Tolling agreement

power plant. If the only available prices come from the forward market, which trades monthly contracts, there isn't much benefit in choosing a daily model or hourly model. However, if some type of daily price is available from a simulation, a daily model might be better.

The physical capabilities of the power plant are also important. For example, a gas turbine might benefit from a high frequency model since it can start and stop quickly. However, a steam turbine, which takes a while to get operating at top efficiency, will want to operate for an extended period. In that case, a modeler might use a longer time frame to model a steam turbine.

Underlying Instruments

The description of a *spark spread model* might make it seem like there are only two underlying products: power and fuel. However, this is misleading. Each leg of a tolling agreement requires electricity and fuel prices at the right *time* and *location*. Unless storage is easy, energy products are not the same commodity at different points in the year. For example, August electricity is a fundamentally differently product than May electricity. It is impossible to buy some electricity in May and hold onto it until August.

This has a big effect on risk management—any measure that tries to aggregate risk between multiple legs has to account for fundamentally different underlying exposures. Given the extended length of many tolling agreements, there can be several hundred separate commodities traded over the lifetime of the contract.

Even within a single leg there is often a need for separate underlying instruments. For example, if a tolling agreement is broken in monthly legs that correspond to the forward markets, it has to be based upon the products traded in that local forward market. Commonly traded contracts in the forward market are for peak power (5×16 power), off-peak power (7×8 power), or weekend power (2×16 power). As a result, it is common for each leg of a tolling agreement to depend on a variety of different instruments (Figure 4.3.2). Combined with the time-of-year effect, the different daily products can rapidly add up to a huge number of uncorrelated exposures.

The impact of this on risk management is substantial. Because legs don't share underlying instruments, it is impossible to simply add up the exposures to get a meaningful number. For example, it is wrong to ask, "What's the exposure of this power plant to the price of electricity?" because there is no single price of electricity. It is dangerous to assume that all electricity prices will move together, when prices have historically been uncorrelated.

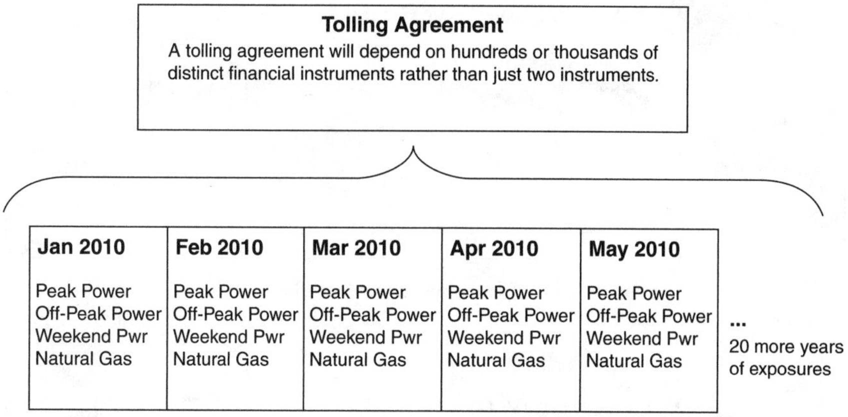

Figure 4.3.2.   Tolling agreements contain a wide variety of electricity and natural gas exposures

Physical Model of a Power Plant

A physical description of the power plant is also required to build a tolling model. For instance, this might be: a natural gas combined cycle power plant with four turbines—two combined cycle steam turbines and two gas turbines.

In this example, the combined cycle turbines are large and efficient. However, they are expensive to maintain and can't respond quickly to changing power requirements. The power plant also has two peaking generators (the gas turbines). These are much smaller and less efficient than the combined cycle turbines. They are used to provide heat for starting up the combined cycle steam turbines, but otherwise operate as separate units. When operating separately, since they are fairly inefficient, the gas turbines are mostly utilized during periods of peak demand.

As an approximation, the combined cycle turbines have two operating modes—normal dispatch or maximum dispatch. Maximum dispatch mode is less efficient at converting fuel into electricity, but produces more power. The operational parameters of this power plant are summarized in Figure 4.3.3. This chart shows the capabilities of each turbine installed in the power plant. Lower heat rates are more efficient and shown in units of MMBtu per MWh.

Both the efficiency of the plant and its total output determine its profitability. The total profitability of a power plant depends on its per-unit profit (the spark spread) and the quantity of electricity that it can produce (the *dispatch rate*). These two factors need to be balanced against one another. Higher levels of production are less efficient— they require more fuel per megawatt of power. As a result, the per-unit profit decreases as more power is produced.

Operating Capabilities of the Power Plant

	Output Dispatch Capability (MWh)	Input Fuel Requirements (MMBtu)	Implied Heat Rate
CC Turbine Max	225	1,800	8
Normal	150	1,125	7.5
CC Turbine Max	225	1,800	8
Normal	150	1,125	7.5
Peaking 1 Max	45	540	12
Peaking 2 Max	45	540	12

Figure 4.3.3. The amount of fuel used multiplied by the heat rate determines a turbine's dispatch capability

Optimal Operating Mode

Running a power plant economically requires an optimization. Sometimes it is more profitable to produce a greater amount of electricity. This happens when the decreased profit per megawatt is overcome by the additional sales. At other times it is more important to be extremely fuel efficient. Lower heat rates indicate a better utilization of fuel per amount of energy produced.

Most power plants are not simply on/off switches. Their value depends upon being able to operate in the most profitable manner. Power plants typically have a variety of modes in which they can operate. Valuing a tolling agreement requires figuring out the best operating mode for each leg.

To simplify the process of determining the best way to operate the power plant, it is common to combine operating decisions for several turbines into an *operating scenario*. For example, it is possible that all of the units will be off, that only the most efficient units are operating, or that all of the units will be operating. Examples of some operating scenarios for the power plant can be seen in Figure 4.3.4. The assumption behind these scenarios is that the less efficient turbines will never be activated before the efficient ones. The scenarios were calculated by summing up the capabilities of generators described in the previous chart.

Power Plant Operating Scenarios

Scenario	Dispatch Capability (MWh)	Input Fuel Requirements (MMBtu)	Implied Heat Rate
All Inactive	0	0	0
Efficient	300	2,250	7.5
CC Max	450	3,600	8
CC Max + Peaking	540	4,680	8.67

Figure 4.3.4. Several combined dispatch scenarios summarized as a combined chart

Operating Scenarios and Day/Night Power

Coming back to a point made earlier, there is often not a single price for power. There are usually several types of power prices that need to be analyzed in conjunction—for example, daytime and nighttime power. These periods will alternate, and it may not be possible to cycle the generator between periods. The value of running the power plant during the day will need to include the cost of running the power plant at night.

Sometimes, turbines will need to operate at night if they are to be active during the day. For example, steam turbines might find it impossible to completely turn off and then restart a short time later. Because of the cost associated with a restart, steam turbines might need to continue operating in a reduced capacity at night.

This creates a problem since prices on nights and weekends are generally much lower than during the day. A power plant might need to take a loss during nighttime hours to be profitable during the day. The value of each scenario needs to group profit and losses together when a single decision determines both values.

The operating scenario chart is expanded below to account for nighttime hours in Figure 4.3.5. The table shows the required linkage between the day and night scenarios. In the CC Max scenario, for example, the combined cycle generators operate at maximum capacity during the day but go to their most efficient operating mode at night to minimize the operating losses. In addition, a new scenario, Peaking Only, was also added. This new scenario address the possibility that especially low nighttime prices make the steam turbines unprofitable to operate at all during the day.

Correlation Between Electricity and Fuel Prices

A second set of problems comes from option pricing considerations. Regardless of which operating scenario is chosen, the value of the power plant will depend on assumptions about the future relationship

Power Plant Operating Scenarios

Scenario	Dispatch Capability (MWh)		Fuel Requirements (MMBtu)		Heat Rate	
	Day	Night	Day	Night	Day	Night
All Inactive	0	0	0	0	0.00	0.00
Efficient	300	300	2,250	2,250	7.50	7.50
CC Max	450	300	3,600	2,250	8.00	7.50
CC Max + Peaking	540	300	4,680	2,250	8.67	7.50
Peaking Only	90	300	1,080	0	12.00	0.00

Figure 4.3.5. Since days and nights aren't separate decisions, they are combined into scenarios

between electricity and fuel prices. Fuel is being burned to convert it into electricity. Wide spreads are good—cheaper fuel and more expensive electricity means higher profits. However, the future of this relationship isn't known at the time of valuation and requires that a number of assumptions be made. For example, because no one is very good at predicting future prices, most models are going to assume each asset follows a *random walk*. However, because power prices are affected by fuel prices, this means that the spark spread is going to depend on the combined behavior of two random (but correlated) walks.

Since the power plant can be turned off to limit exposure, extreme moves in the spread are a good thing. Either the power plant makes a windfall profit or it gets turned off. From a profit perspective, high volatility in the electricity/fuel relationship is good. To a large extent, the value of a tolling agreement depends on the expected correlation between power and fuel prices. Highly correlated power and fuel prices mean less volatility and lower profits. Small changes to the correlation between these prices can have a major impact on the value of a tolling agreement.

Valuation and Volatility

Some of the value of a tolling agreement is known immediately. At a minimum, it is worth its *intrinsic value*—its value if all of the operating decisions were made immediately. This can be done by arranging firm agreements to buy fuel and sell electricity through the forward market. However, there is a second component to an option's value. Uncertainty benefits the owner of an option. The downside risk of owning an option is capped. In the case of a power plant, the power plant can be turned off. A 50/50 chance of making extra money is a great investment when losing doesn't involve spending more money.

The *valuation date* of an option is the day that its value is calculated. The *expiration date* of the option is the day that the power plant actually converts fuel into electricity. Up until the expiration date, it is possible to change the operating decisions for the power plant. After that date, it is no longer possible to change the decision. *Exercising the option* means making a permanent decision on how to operate the power plant. Usually, it is preferable to delay making a final decision for as long as possible.

The payoff of a spark spread option is based on the spread between power and gas prices. Today's prediction of those prices is the *forward spread*. The spread at the time of expiration probably won't be identical to the spread predicted today. However, it is likely to be distributed around the forward spread, as seen in Figure 4.3.6. Mathematically,

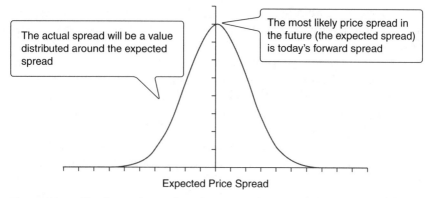

Figure 4.3.6. The forward spread on the current day is a prediction of the spread at a later day

the likely range of spreads is described by a statistical distribution centered on the forward spread.

Some of the possible spreads will be at points where it is profitable to produce electricity. Other spreads will be at points where it is unprofitable to operate the power plant. The efficiency of the power plant (its heat rate) determines which spreads are profitable and which spreads are unprofitable (Figure 4.3.7).

At expiration, the profit per megawatt is calculated by taking the average price of the profitable future spreads. Multiplying the number of megawatts (the dispatch rate) by the average profitable price calculates the expected profit from that scenario.

The width of the distribution is a key factor in determining the profit per megawatt. A spread option is more valuable when the range of possible spreads at expiration is high. The chance for an extremely

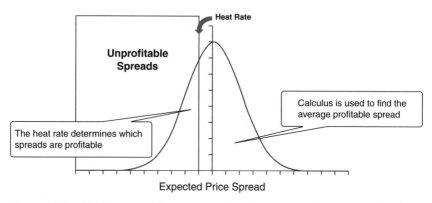

Figure 4.3.7. The heat rate of the power plant determines when it is profitable to operate

positive payoff outweighs an increased chance of losing money. This is due to the asymmetric nature of the payoffs—any loss is worth no worse than zero, but beneficial results are uncapped.

The width of the distribution depends on the time between valuation and expiration and the correlation between power and gas prices. If the price of power and natural gas are highly correlated, the spread at expiration will be very close to the center of the bell curve. For example, if the prices are perfectly correlated, there won't be a bell curve at all because the relationship between prices will never change. Less correlated assets will have a wider distribution of possible spreads (Figure 4.3.8).

All options are highly affected by changes in volatility. In the case of spread options, the volatility of the spread depends on the correlation between power and gas prices. As a result, the value of a tolling agreement is incredibly sensitive to the predicted correlation between fuel and power prices.

Dangers to Using Options

There are dangers to using options to approximate physical behavior—a spread option model can ignore important physical aspects of generation like the time it takes to turn on (*ramp up* or *cycle*) and variable operating costs. For example, a generator might take longer and use more fuel to start operating in the winter than during the summer. Options also assume power plant decisions can be made instantaneously. No matter how quickly a power plant can be cycled, it is going to be slower than instantaneous decisions implied by a spark spread

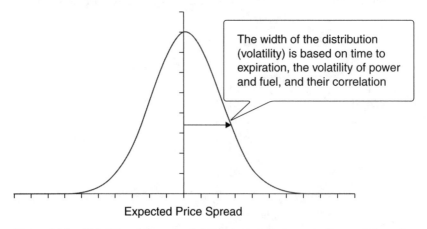

The width of the distribution (volatility) is based on time to expiration, the volatility of power and fuel, and their correlation

Expected Price Spread

Figure 4.3.8. Volatility of the spread depends on time to expiration and the volatility and correlation of the underlying assets

model. Other real life issues—like the effect of local laws regarding grid reliability—can also be difficult to quantify.

Because spark spread option models are less constrained than actual generators, they run the risk of overestimating profitability. This overestimation can be as high as 20 to 30 percent if overoptimistic assumptions aren't caught. These errors can trickle value-at-risk calculations and may not be recognized for years.

Another criticism of spark spread option models is that they are "reactive." They assume that a generator simply turns on or off in response to the current price. In reality, the optimal schedule for a generator must anticipate price changes, perhaps incurring a loss in some periods in order to position the generator to capture higher expected profits later on. Again, there is no one single rule for handling this issue. The relative importance of this problem is different for each generator and how the operating scenarios are selected.

4.4

WHEELING POWER

 30-Second Summary

Purpose

Wheeling is a general term meaning the long distance transmission of electricity. For example, transporting electricity *as if it were on wheels*. Differences in regional prices provide the economic motivation for these trades. Wheeling trades are a good example of how a deregulated market can cost effectively allocate energy resources.

Summary

Wheeling is the act of transporting power from one location to another. Usually wheeling occurs over power lines owned by a third party. Because adjoining regions often set their power prices differently, transmission trades can be very profitable. The driving force behind different prices might be different marginal fuels, weather patterns, or consumption in the two regions.

Wheeling trades must be made in the physical market. When a power line connects two regions, the owner of the power line can buy electricity at one end of a line and transport it to the other end. At least one part of the trade—buying low cost power and transferring it for delivery in another area—has to be made in the physical spot market. This makes wheeling trades different from pure financial transactions. With financial contracts, it is impossible to use a financial contract from one market to meet an obligation in another.

One way to think of a wheeling trade is as an option. After paying an up-front rental cost, the trader has the option of transporting power from one region to another. The trade will be a good investment if the (uncertain) profits from the power line are more valuable than its construction or rental cost. Financially, the rental agreement will be modeled as a series of spread options—one option every time the trader could make the decision to transfer power. To determine if the trade makes sense economically, the value of these options can then be compared to the cost of renting a power line.

Key Topics

- The motivation behind wheeling trades is that adjoining power markets often have different prices caused by differences in marginal fuels, weather patterns, or consumer demands.
- The cost to rent a power line is usually proportional to the cost of building and maintaining the power line, rather than its economic value.

Wheeling is the act of physically transporting electricity from one location to another. Wheeling trades require a physical transfer of electricity over power lines rented from a third party. Because of how electricity markets set their prices, adjoining markets can have very different prices. This is particularly true if the generation stacks of the two areas are different. Most regions set power prices based on the cost of operating their most recently activated generator. There can be a big price difference between regions when one region has most recently activated a natural-gas-fired generator and the other a coal-fired generator.

The purpose of wheeling is to get low cost power into high price areas. There is a trade-off between the long distance transportation of power and local generation. A substantial amount of power can be lost in transmission. Additionally, widespread power grids have many more points of failure than compact power grids. However, sometimes long distance transportation is necessary. Many types of power generators have restrictions on where they can be located. A natural gas cogeneration plant needs to be located adjacent to a large user of the steam. Nuclear power plants are often located far away from the communities they serve. Hydroelectric plants need to be located on a river at a dam. As a result, certain electrical generation choices necessitate the long distance transmission of power.

A map of the United States serves as a chart of average prices in Figure 4.4.1, demonstrating the variability of electrical prices around the country. Compared to low price regions, high price regions like New York and California pay on average twice as much for their power. During peak demand periods, the disparity may be even greater.

In a deregulated power market, trading helps determine when it is economically worthwhile to build transmission lines. These lines

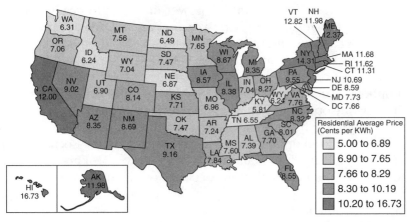

Figure 4.4.1.   Average residential power prices around the United States (*Source:* Energy Information Agency [January 2008])

connect areas of low cost generation to high-priced consuming regions. Private investments—wheeling trades—pay for the construction of power lines, and those investors make profits from their investment. Eventually, as enough transmission capacity between the low cost areas and high price areas is built, prices will converge. In this way, free market trading determines the right level of investment.

Examples of Wheeling Trades

- A power company builds a transmission line to connect the upper Midwest (where coal is the marginal fuel) to the southern United States (where natural gas is the marginal fuel). This trade is a bet on natural gas prices being much more volatile than coal prices.
- A power company examines a wheeling trade to import hydroelectric power from the Niagara Falls region into the New York City metro area. Since there is limited transmission capability between these two regions, this would involve bidding on a scarce resource.
- A cost analysis of whether it is more cost efficient to build a nuclear power plant a long way from a population center or whether it is better to construct smaller natural-gas-fired generators close to population centers.
- Investing in a PV solar installation in New Mexico and building a long distance high voltage DC power line to get the power to the East Coast.

In a physical sense, a wheeling trade involves building a power line to connect two separate areas. Most of the time the cost of the trade is proportional to the cost of building the power line. Once the power line is constructed, its owner has the option of transporting some amount of power (the amount the power line can physically handle) between the two regions. Since power lines are not free to build, there is a strong economic incentive for investors to build power lines that will have the biggest economic impact at the lowest cost.

For valuation purposes, wheeling trades can be modeled as financial options. After paying an up-front cost to build or rent the line, a trader has the option of transporting power over that line. The actual benefit is unknown at the time the power line is rented. The up-front cost is similar to an option *premium*. The variable costs associated with transportation (line losses and any variable expenses) are similar to a *strike price*. The potential profit depends on the price difference between the two regions. When the profit is greater than the transmission costs, it is profitable to transmit power over the transmission line.

From a trading perspective, wheeling deals are interesting because they allow traders to buy an option for the physical construction cost of a power line rather than on the financial value of the option. This is a key aspect of trading physical products. Option premiums can be extremely expensive. If the construction costs are affordable, physical investments provide an alternate way to get the same financial exposures at a much lower cost.

In most cases, the cost to rent a transmission line is proportional to the cost of building and maintaining the power line. If there is only one power line operator in a region, the rental price will probably be subject to government regulations for nondiscriminatory pricing. The logic is that if a lot of people want to rent power lines, there shouldn't be a competitive auction over a limited resource. Instead, the power line operator should be forced to build more power lines and charge back that cost to the investor groups.

Modeling Electrical Flows

Within a power grid, wheeling is closely associated with the problems of line congestion and predicting how power will flow across the grid. Electricity flows across the path of least electrical resistance. That resistance changes throughout the day, depending on how much power each part of the power grid is consuming. Since each transmission line can only carry a limited amount of power, ensuring that the grid can handle imported power is a complicated job.

For example, in a power grid with three points (A, B, and C) it might be necessary to move imported power from location A to meet consumer demand at location B. It would be best if that power moves directly between those two points. However, if the line AB has a lot of load on it, power can also flow from A to C, and then from C to B. The power grid operator cannot control the exact path the electricity follows. He also needs to make sure that too much power isn't transferred over any one line and causes a meltdown. As a result, the power grid operator must ensure there is sufficient transmission capacity available on every power line that might potentially handle the imported load. If that transmission capacity isn't available, power might not be able to reach point B. That means the power grid would need to activate a fast-starting peaking generator close to point B to meet the shortfall.

One of the primary motivations for wheeling trades is to get low cost power into high demand areas. Usually, imported power displaces generation capacity that was already serving the high-demand area. Importing power means decommissioning a local generation unit. However, if the low-cost-imported power can't reach the necessary location, it isn't possible to restart a decommissioned power plant on short notice. The region will have to rely on an even more expensive high-cost peaking unit. A couple of days of using peaking units can eliminate any positive economic benefit from using imported power.

Long Distance AC Transmission

The most common way of transmitting power across long distances is to use overhead high voltage, alternating current electric lines. When power is transmitted across a power line, some of the power gets converted into heat. The amount of energy lost to heat is proportional to the square of the current. The primary way to reduce transmission losses is to decrease the current on a power line.

Voltage and current combine to determine how much power a transmission line carries. To transfer the same amount of power across a line, it is necessary to increase the voltage on the line to reduce the current. *Transformers* can be used to modify the current and voltage of AC power lines. Transformers only work on AC power lines, which is why AC transmission is more common than DC transmission.

Transformers use magnetic induction to alter the current and voltage on a line while keeping the total power constant. The scientific principle behind transformer is that magnetic fields create electrical currents and vice versa. It is possible to use an electrical current to create a magnetic field, and then use that magnetic field to create another electrical current at a different voltage. Transformers are typically composed of two coils of conductive wire wrapped around a shared core. Starting and stopping the current on one wire will induce a current on the other coil.

Transformers

An *iron core* transformer is a simple type of transformer. It consists of an iron frame connected to two electrical wires. The core of the transformer provides a path for magnetic flux. The *primary winding* is the electrical wire connected to an AC power source. The *secondary winding* is the wire connected to the electrical load. The primary winding creates a magnetic flux that induces an electrical current on the secondary winding. The relative voltage on each side of the transformer depends on how many times the wire on that side is wrapped around the core of the transformer (Figures 4.4.2 and 4.4.3).

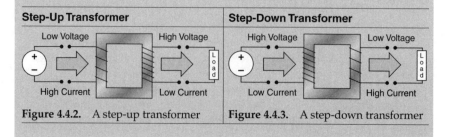

Step-Up Transformer

Low Voltage   High Voltage

High Current   Low Current

Figure 4.4.2. A step-up transformer

Step-Down Transformer

High Voltage   Low Voltage

Low Current   High Current

Figure 4.4.3. A step-down transformer

Long Distance DC Transmission

An alternative to AC power transmission is high voltage direct current (HVDC) power lines. HVDC power lines have been used successfully around the world to transfer power over extremely long distances. Typically, these power lines are lower cost than AC power lines and lose less power in the transmission process. These lines are also commonly used to transfer power between unsynchronized AC power grids or long distances underwater.

On the downside, DC power has to be converted into AC power at the endpoint. No one uses high voltage DC power in a residential setting. It is extremely dangerous, and the voltage can't be stepped up or down using a transformer. A normal DC to AC conversion can result in a 5 to 10 percent loss in power. These conversion losses have to be weighed against reduced transmission losses. As a result, HVDC is usually only used for extremely long distance transmission.

Another disadvantage of a DC transmission is that multiple endpoints are problematic. Whenever any energy is removed from a DC transmission line, the voltage on the entire line will drop. Because DC voltage can't be increased by transformers, a DC power line with more than one endpoint won't have a constant voltage across the line. As a result, it can be very difficult to build an interconnected grid of HVDC power lines. Because of this, HVDC power lines are primarily long distance, point-to-point connections.

For example, if HVDC power lines are built to connect a major solar installation in the Desert Southwest to two points on the East Coast of the United States, as in Figure 4.4.4, it would be very difficult

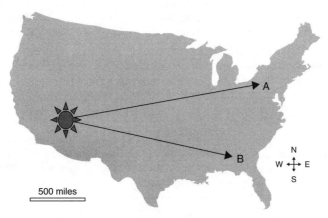

Figure 4.4.4. An example of point-to-point nature of HVDC transmission

to reroute any of that power from one point to another. If the rerouting were to be done on the East Coast, it would be necessary to convert the DC power to AC power and transmit it using the AC transmission grid. It would only be possible to reroute the DC power from the point of origin in the Desert Southwest. However, building direct transmission lines to connect every generation station to every user is an operational nightmare. If there were a couple thousand generation locations, it would be impossible to control the power grid from any centralized location.

Trading Example: Wheeling Trade

A power company examines a wheeling trade to transfer power from the upper Midwest (where coal is the marginal fuel) to the southern United States (where natural gas is the marginal fuel). To a large extent, this trade is a bet on natural gas prices being much more volatile than coal prices.

1. **The Opportunity.** Low ash, low sulfur coal from Wyoming provides the midwestern United States with an abundant supply of low cost fuel for electricity generation. The marginal fuel for the area is coal, and power prices do not see large fluctuations. In the southern United States, most power plants burn natural gas. The price of natural gas is much more volatile than coal. As a result, a transmission line between the Midwest and the southern United States is a way to benefit from the different volatilities.

2. **The Intuition.** Renting a transmission line is like buying an option on natural gas. It will benefit from high volatility. Even if the average cost of power is the same in both regions, the natural-gas-fired areas will see much greater swings in prices and there will be periods where it is profitable to export electricity from the Midwest to the Gulf Coast.

3. **The Strategy.** A large number of trades will need to be made in the spot market to take advantage of the higher volatility. Seasonal trades are possible in the futures market. For example, hot summer weather begins earlier and lasts longer in the southern United States. It is possible to import power from the Midwest during periods when the Midwest is cool and the southern United States is experiencing hot weather.

4. **The Risks.** Renting a power line is a lot like buying an option—the biggest risk is in overpaying for the right to transmit power. Since this transmission line is long volatility, it may be possible to sell natural gas options or lock in seasonal trades using futures. There will be a substantial amount of operational risk due to the necessity of scheduling physical transactions.

5. **Executing the Trade.** A long-term rental agreement is a direct contract between two parties. Additionally, every time the power needs to be transferred, it will be necessary to schedule deliveries, transmission, and sale of the power. This requires a trading desk capable of handling all of the necessary paperwork. There is a high degree of operation risk in this trade.

Spread Trades Compared to Wheeling Trades

The key to a wheeling trade is the ability to transmit power between two regions. If electrical transmission isn't available, it is impossible to buy power in one market and resell it in another. Instead, all purchases must be sold back into the same market where the power was originally purchased.

Location spread trades are a financial speculation on the relative prices between two areas without having transmission available. These trades are often confused with wheeling trades. Spread trades are required to sell back power into the same market where it was originally purchased. As a result, they depend on price movements within a region rather than a difference in prices between two regions. If prices don't move, no profit is made—the power will be bought and sold at the same price.

In many ways, location spread trades are much easier than wheeling trades. With a location spread, it is not necessary to arrange for physical purchases or sales of power. Everything can be done financially and settled in cash. Of course, the primary benefit of the wheeling trade is lost too. With a wheeling trade it is possible to buy power in one location and deliver that power to a different location.

Spread Trades vs. Wheeling Trades

A price spread is the difference in price between two regions. For example, if the price in New York is $100 and the price in California is $120, the New York/California price spread is –$20. Spreads are a way of combining two prices into a single number. Wheeling is an actual transfer of power from one region to another.

Location spread trades are financial trades made in the futures or forward market. They can be done financially with no physical trading capability. The trader takes a long position in one region and a short position in another. Typically, the trades are liquidated before physical delivery is required. Because transmission isn't available, it is impossible to take power from one area and use it to settle an obligation in another area. These trades make money when the actual relationship between two areas turns out to be different than the relationship the market expected at the time of the initial trade.

Wheeling trades involve the physical transmission of power between two regions. These trades require money up front to rent a power line. The trades also require the trader to make physical trades. The benefit of a wheeling trade is that power purchased in one area can be delivered to meet an obligation in another area.

Trading Example: Location Spread Trade

The market is expecting that the snow will melt at its normal time in early April. A trader thinks that this consensus is wrong and that the snow will melt early this year.

1. **The Opportunity.** U.S. government meteorologists predict that warm water temperatures in the Pacific will bring an early warm front to the Pacific Northwest, leading to an early thaw.

2. **The Intuition.** Normally, power prices in the Pacific Northwest reach their low in April when snow in the nearby Cascade mountain range melts. During that time, the rivers in the region swell to capacity, and the local dams need to open fully to avoid major flooding. This causes the hydro plants to run at full capacity 24 hours a day regardless of consumer demand. The hydroelectric plants can't be turned off or their power generation reduced because this would flood nearby communities.

3. **The Strategy.** The trader decides to make this trade as a locational spread between California (NP-15) and Pacific NW prices (MID-C) for March. He wants to benefit from higher California prices (long NP-15 price) and lower MID-C prices (short MID-C) than are being expected by the market.

4. **The Risks.** A major risk in the position is that natural gas prices will decline. Natural gas is the marginal fuel for the California generation stack. As a result, the price of power in the California market is determined by natural gas prices. If those prices drop, the price of electricity in California will also drop. Another risk is the assumption that a spread trade is appropriate here. An early warm front and cheap power from the Columbia River is more likely to cause a decline in California power prices than an increase. The long position in California power doesn't make sense. An outright position in MID-C power might be less risky than this locational spread.

5. **Executing the Trade.** The trader would enter the trade using March futures (buying NP-15 peak power contracts and selling MID-C peak power contracts). When he wanted to get out of the position, he would have to make the opposite trades. Unlike a wheeling deal, these power trades can't be settled by transmission—it is necessary to close out the position by trading.

6. **The Results.** If the futures prices have changed by the time the trade is liquidated, the trader will make money. However, he can't hold on to the position until the physical delivery date. This trade has to be liquidated prior to the expiration of the futures contracts.

4.5

Solar Power

30-Second Summary

Purpose

The section introduces solar power. From an investment perspective, solar power is more expensive than fossil-fuel–based electrical generation. As a result, investments in solar technology are heavily influenced by government programs to encourage renewable energy.

Summary

There are two main types of solar power: *photovoltaic* (PV) power and *thermal solar power*.

Photovoltaic power converts solar power into electricity. It is produced by solar panels exposed to sunlight. The type of equipment and the intensity of the sunlight directly affect the amount of power produced by a solar panel. Correctly estimating the amount of power that will be produced by a solar installation is critical to its successful adoption. If estimates are too conservative, solar power will be deemed uneconomical and bypassed for other technologies. If estimates are too high, there will be a power shortfall and the economic goals of an installation won't be met.

Thermal solar power uses sunlight to produce heat. In many cases this heat can be used to produce electricity by powering steam turbines or to replace electricity that would have been used to produce heat. There are many types of thermal solar installations. They can be anything from small-scale systems to heat outdoor pools to electrical generation facilities. A big advantage of solar power is that heat is relatively easy to store, which allows these facilities to operate around the clock. Although they can only store heat during the day, they can use the stored heat any time.

Solar radiation varies throughout the year—it is affected by weather, the changing location of the sun, and the amount of daylight. The angle of the solar panel, its efficiency in handling direct and diffuse light, and the surrounding environment all affect how much power is collected. To analyze solar installations, historical averages of solar radiation are used. These averages are collected by the regional or national governments and provided for the purpose of estimating solar installations.

(Continued)

Key Topics
- Solar power depends on sunlight. More sunlight equals more power.
- Most commonly, when people talk about solar power they are discussing photovoltaic power (abbreviated PV). This type of solar power uses solar panels to turn sunlight directly into electricity.
- Another type of solar power is thermal solar power, which stores the heat of the sun to do useful work. Heating, air-conditioning, and the generation of electricity can all be driven by thermal solar installations.

Solar power utilizes energy from the sun to produce electricity or heat. Electricity is most commonly produced by exposing large sheets of specialized semiconductors known as "solar panels" to sunlight. In other cases, mirrors are used to concentrate the heat from a large area onto a single point. This allows the concentrated heat to be used for a variety of purposes like creating steam to drive generators and powering air conditioners.

Solar panels produce electricity directly. Sunlight causes electrons to flow out of the semiconductor panels and into wires connected to a circuit. This creates DC power that can be converted into AC power if necessary. When electricity is generated in this way, it is called *photovoltaic power*.

Solar power can also be used to generate heat. This heat can be used to heat homes, warm swimming pools, or generate steam to power an electrical turbine. When solar energy is used to create heat, this is called *thermal solar power*. Both photovoltaic solar power and thermal solar power can be used to generate electricity. However, where photovoltaic power uses solar cells, thermal solar power will use stored heat to drive a steam turbine.

For any type of solar power generation, the amount of sunlight available in an area has a big effect on the efficiency of a solar collector. Dry climates at high altitude located close to the equator are generally the best areas to locate solar power units. The reason for this is that sunlight has to pass through the Earth's atmosphere. The less atmosphere that light has to pass through, the more energy will be available for use in a solar collector.

The amount of particulate matter suspended in the air also has a large effect on how much sunlight hits the ground. Water vapor, clouds, and dust particles all reduce the output of solar power installations. The combined effects of direct sunlight and particulate matter make certain areas more favorable for solar power than others. For example,

Sun Directly Overhead	Sun at an Angle
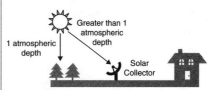	
Figure 4.5.1. One atmospheric depth	**Figure 4.5.2.** Greater than one atmospheric depth
If the sun is straight overhead, it will pass through one atmospheric depth (Figure 4.5.1).	When the sun is directly over some other part of the globe, it will have to travel a longer distance. The long side of a right triangle, the hypotenuse, is longer than the length of either side (Figure 4.5.2).

in the United States, the Desert Southwest is favorably situated to get a lot of solar power. The area around the Great Lakes region receives much less sunlight. Likewise, in Europe, areas around the Mediterranean Sea get a lot of sunlight, while northern Europe receives comparatively little.

Concentrated Solar Power

Finally, it's possible to increase the amount of sunlight that hits a solar panel by collecting it over a large area and focusing it on a specific point. The total effect is a lot like using a magnifying glass on an anthill during the summer. Sunlight from a wide area is redirected to shine on a very small area. There is a trade-off with these systems—sometimes it is better to use a solar collector, in other cases it is easier to use more solar panels. For example, if there is a 10-by-10-foot plot available for a solar collector, it might be better to put in four five-by-five-foot solar panels and fill the entire space with solar panels. Alternately, it might be better to put in a 10-by-10-foot concentrator and use only a single solar panel.

Particularly with concentrating collectors, but to a lesser extent with all solar installations, it is possible to increase the amount of sunlight hitting a solar collector by facing it toward the sun. In the northern hemisphere, this means mounting the unit facing south at a slight upward angle. This can be improved by placing the solar collector on a motorized base that allows it to track the sun as it moves through the sky. Motorized bases increase the amount of energy that is produced. However, they also increase installation and maintenance costs.

The decision on how to configure a solar installation will depend on the efficiency of the solar panel and the maximum energy it can absorb. Solar systems are rated by their efficiency at turning sunlight into useful energy. Most solar collectors can only absorb certain wavelengths of light, and much of the light is reflected or absorbed before it can be used. The percentage of solar energy converted into useful energy is called the *conversion efficiency* of the solar unit. Conversion efficiency is a measure of energy produced to energy absorbed. Both the availability of solar energy and conversion efficiency of the unit contribute to the output of the unit.

Photovoltaic Power

When solar power is discussed, most commonly it refers to *photovoltaic power* (PV). It is called this because of the effect sunlight has on certain semiconductors. Shining electromagnetic energy like sunlight over a semiconductor will knock some of the electrons away from their nuclei. This, called the *photovoltaic effect,* creates an electromagnetic field around the semiconductor. That field can then be converted into electrical current by connecting the two sides of the semiconductor to a circuit. Even though most solar cells are typically reasonably small, they can be connected together into large arrays typically called "solar panels."

The basic component of a solar cell is a semiconductor that absorbs some type of electromagnetic energy to produce electricity. One important property of this semiconductor is its *band gap*. A band gap is the amount of energy required to kick an electron out of its orbit around a semiconductor nuclei. The normal electron orbit is called the *valence band,* and an orbit where an electron is free to move around is called the *conduction band.* When solar energy hits a semiconductor, photons at a lower energy level than the band gap pass through unabsorbed. Photons at an energy level higher than the band gap kick an electron from the valence band into the conduction band. If the energy level of the photon is much higher than the band gap, it will still kick an electron into the conduction gap, but all of the excess energy will be turned into heat.

Once electrons are in the conduction band, they are free to move around. Electrons will move away from negative charges and toward positive charges. To get electrons to move in one direction, it is possible to dope the semiconductor so that one side of it has a positive charge and the other side a negative charge. A *p-type* semiconductor is doped with atoms that are missing electrons to give it a positive charge. An *n-type* semiconductor is doped with atoms that contain excess electrons. A wafer made by sandwiching an n-type and p-type semiconductor will move electrons in a consistent direction. As solar energy hits the

How Solar Concentration Works

It is possible to concentrate sunlight on a specific point. The key to focusing energy is being able to change the direction of the sunlight without changing anything else. By sending a lot of sunlight at a very small area, a very high concentration of energy can be obtained. One common method of concentrating power is to use a parabolic mirror (Figure 4.5.3). This mirror takes sunlight spread out in a large area and reflects it to a precisely calibrated spot.

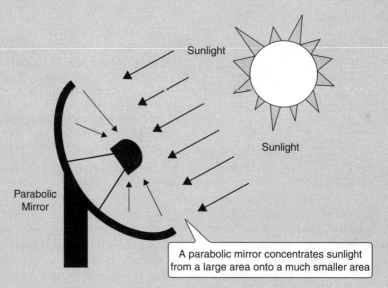

Figure 4.5.3.   A parabolic mirror collects sunlight and redirects it

Sometimes it is a good idea to concentrate power, and sometimes it is not. First of all, a large mirror takes up a lot of space. It also has to be highly calibrated. If the sun changes its location, the focal point of the mirror will change unless the mirror changes its facing too. Moving the mirror requires adding a motor and moving parts to a solar array. That will mean higher maintenance costs. Also, mirrors are fairly vulnerable to damage. If a mirror gets scratched, or covered with dust, its efficiency will drop dramatically.

From an economic perspective, the relative cost of more solar panels has to be compared to the cost of adding mirrors and electric motors to a smaller solar panel. There usually isn't a space savings with a collector, it mostly allows the collection apparatus to be more compact and operate at higher energy or temperature.

n-type semiconductor, an electron is kicked into the conduction band. Once in the conduction band, the electron will move away from the negatively charged side of the semiconductor and move toward the positively charged side. This effect creates an electrical current between the n-type and p-type sides.

How a Solar Cell Operates

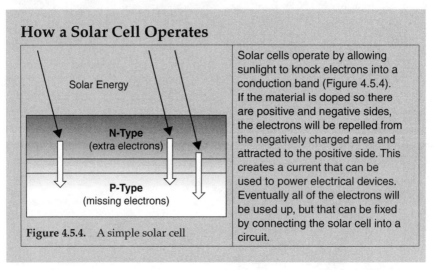

Solar Energy

N-Type
(extra electrons)

P-Type
(missing electrons)

Figure 4.5.4.   A simple solar cell

Solar cells operate by allowing sunlight to knock electrons into a conduction band (Figure 4.5.4). If the material is doped so there are positive and negative sides, the electrons will be repelled from the negatively charged area and attracted to the positive side. This creates a current that can be used to power electrical devices. Eventually all of the electrons will be used up, but that can be fixed by connecting the solar cell into a circuit.

The efficiency of a simple solar cell isn't particularly high because a lot of solar energy is wasted. One way to reduce the amount of wasted energy is to have several layers of semiconductors. The first layer might be a material with a very high band gap, the next one with a lower band gap, and then the final material the lowest band gap. In this way, less energy is lost to heat, and more energy will be turned into electricity.

Thermal Solar Power

The other way to produce solar energy is to create heat. When sunlight hits almost anything, some of that energy will be absorbed by the object and turned into heat. By concentrating that heat, it is possible to achieve very high temperatures. The heat from thermal solar power is usually used to heat up water or another liquid that is stored in an insulated container until it is ready to be used.

For example, a high temperature solar facility might use solar power to raise salt to a temperature of approximately 500°F. At that point, salt melts and turns into a liquid. As a liquid, the salt can be transferred into a heavily insulated container until it is ready to be used. This provides a big advantage over photovoltaic power—although heat can only be produced at certain times of the day, it doesn't have to be used right away. A thermal solar plant can use sunlight during the day to build up a store of superheated liquids, and then use that heat to produce electricity at night.

Of course, it might not be worthwhile to produce electricity with that heat. Heat can be used to drive a variety of other activities that may be more valuable than producing electricity. Air-conditioning, heating, cooking, sterilization, and dehydration systems can all be built using a heat source. The primary way of producing electricity from heat is through a steam turbine, which isn't particularly efficient when it operates at 500°F. Steam turbines get much more efficient when they operate at higher temperatures. For examples, a steam turbine operating at 500°F might only turn 40 percent of its heat energy into electricity; a steam turbine operating at 1,000°F might by 60 percent efficient. As a result, concentrated heat is more valuable—it is better to have a liquid at 1,000°F than to have twice as much liquid at 500°F.

To get high temperatures, the key components of a thermal solar system are the solar power concentrator and the heat storage unit. These components directly impact the cost and complexity of thermal solar systems. The primary way to achieve high temperatures is to focus the energy from a large area onto a small point. Since the sun moves through the day, unless a thermal solar system can readjust its focus, the location where solar energy is being concentrated will also change. As a result, thermal solar systems commonly rely upon some type of tracking system to keep the energy headed to the right spot.

Trading Example: German Solar Power

Although it doesn't receive a lot of sunlight, Germany is a world leader in installed photovoltaic solar power units. This is a simplified example of how a government subsidy can spur installation of solar power.

1. **The Opportunity.** As a general rule, solar power is more expensive that fossil-fuel–based power. To encourage the consumers to use solar power, the German government adopted a policy of feed-in tariffs that paid homeowners higher than retail prices for any electricity they fed into the power grid from residentially installed solar systems. This law was made in conjunction with net-metering policies that allowed households to both draw electricity from the power grid and place it back on. At the end of the month, the above-market cost paid for solar power was split evenly between all customers and added as a surcharge to utility bills.

2. **The Intuition.** This is as easy as a trade gets. Consumers who install solar power onto their houses get a rebate on their electricity. Everyone else pays a higher cost. In this case, the rebate was significant—the power grid paid approximately triple the retail price of power. If power costs $30 per MWh, and you can get paid $90 per MWh placed onto the grid, almost any solar installation is economical.

(*Continued*)

3. **The Strategy.** When homeowners are getting paid triple for any excess capacity they put on the grid, it pays them to install as much excess capacity as possible. Until you produce more energy than you use, solar power is only worth the avoided cost of buying electricity from the grid. However, after that point the value of the electricity triples. The best strategy is to load up each house with as much solar capacity as can fit, and conserve as much power as possible. That maximizes the net amount of power that can head back onto the power grid.

4. **The Risks.** There is an economy of scale involved in this trade—the real payoff is placing energy onto the power grid rather than just mitigating home use. Once a homeowner is a net exporter of electricity during daylight hours, it won't take long for the investment to pay off.

5. **The Results.** Germany, even with its limited sunlight, has the largest installed base of solar power generation in the world. Utility costs went up slightly for anyone who didn't install solar power. However, the increase in power prices was fairly minor, and a large portion of Germany's peak power requirements can be met from solar power.

Trading Example: Solar Panel Resale

Even though it's difficult to invest directly in solar energy, it is possible to buy and resell solar panels.

1. **The Opportunity.** A trader believes the government is about to pass new regulations to encourage solar power installations.

2. **The Intuition.** If the government regulations pass, consumers will start installing more solar panels. The price of solar panels should go up with demand. The intuition is that competition to get solar panels installed quickly will push up prices.

3. **The Strategy.** The trader will enter into a series of long-term purchase agreements to obtain a large quantity of solar panels from several manufacturers. The manufacturers want this business since it allows them to keep their factories operating at peak capacity in between orders. Without long-term contracts, manufacturers either need to ramp their production up and down to meet orders or keep a lot of inventory on hand.

4. **The Risks.** The trader might be left holding a lot of solar panels if the government incentives aren't adopted. Also, even if the regulations pass, solar panels may or may not be easy to resell at a profit. The trader will have to physically transport the panels from the manufacturer to a storage area, store them, and then arrange sales to solar panel installers.

5. **Executing the Trade.** The trader enters into long-term purchase agreements with manufacturers. He also contacts solar panel installers, letting them know that he has solar panels for sale.

6. **The Results.** If all goes well, the trader has entered into a long-term physical commodity business. There are substantial operating risks in this venture, including the danger of holding on to a large inventory. However, being bullish on solar installations, the trader has achieved his goal of becoming long an increased demand for solar installations. He will probably make money if solar power becomes more common, and lose money if interest in solar power fades.

4.6

WIND POWER

 30-Second Summary

Purpose

This section introduces the major concepts of wind-powered electrical generation.

Summary

The wind is a natural source of renewable energy. It has been used for thousands of years as a pollution-free way to power windmills and sailboats. More recently, specialized windmills called *wind turbines* have been built to harness the wind as a source of electric power. These windmills are typically grouped into *wind farms* and located in areas exposed to sustained high winds.

Wind is inherently unpredictable. Fast gusts contain far more energy than slow steady breezes. As a result, the wind supplies irregular bursts of power. Occasionally, wind energy will provide a lot of energy. Power grids that plan on using wind-based electrical generation need to develop some way to minimize that unpredictability.

Key Topics

- The biggest issue of wind power is that it is variable. It is extremely difficult to predict when and how much power will be available. Usually, gaps in supply have to be met by inefficient fossil fuel plants that are easy to cycle into the generation stack.
- Wind units can have very high operating costs. Their high number of moving parts makes them prone to mechanical breakdowns and dependent upon regular lubrication. The amount of lubrication required can raise questions about whether wind power is truly renewable or if it makes an area less dependent upon foreign oil.
- The other large complaints about wind power are danger to migratory flying animals (birds and bats) and aesthetic concerns (where wind farms blot out the horizon).
- In some cases, electricity storage techniques can be used to time-shift the electricity production to a period of higher consumer demand.

Wind power has been used for centuries to provide mechanical energy. Both windmills and sailing ships are examples of early uses for wind power. Since the 1970s *wind turbines* have been harnessing the wind for generating electricity. These turbines use rotating blades pushed by the wind to drive a generator, and operate much like any other electrical turbine. Rotational energy (provided by the wind) spins an electromagnet to produce electricity. A large number of wind turbines located together are called a *wind farm*.

Wind

Wind is produced by an uneven heating of the Earth's surface. The equator receives considerably more sunlight than the poles, and sunlight is unevenly absorbed around the globe. Dark colors absorb more energy than light colors. Combined with the day/night cycles on the Earth, there is a constant steam of expanding and cooling gas moving around the planet. This is a chaotic process where small changes in initial conditions can lead to substantially different atmospheric conditions later on.

There are three basic measures of whether a site is a good candidate for a wind farm. First, wind has to consistently blow across the area. Second, the wind has to blow at high enough speeds to generate a substantial amount of energy. Third, there has to be enough land available to place a major installation. As a general rule, coastlines and flat plains provide the easiest locations to install wind farms. Mountains or uneven terrain are much less attractive locations because of the limited space to place a wind farm and unpredictable wind conditions.

A map of wind energy in different parts of the United States is shown in Figure 4.6.1. This research is conducted by the National Renewable Energy Laboratory (NREL), a U.S. government agency that is the primary source for renewable power data in the United States. Dark colors indicate areas with a lot of potential wind power, and light areas indicate less potential wind power.

Wind Energy

Wind is an inherently streaky type of energy supply. The amount of energy in wind increases with the cube of the wind speed. When the speed of wind doubles, it will contain eight times the energy it did before. This means that very windy days will provide a disproportionately large amount of the wind energy available in an area.

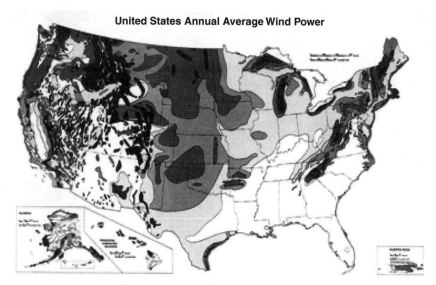

United States Annual Average Wind Power

Class of Wind Power Density

Wind Power Class	10 m (33 ft)		50 m (164 ft)	
	Wind Power Density (W/m 2)	Speed (b) m/s (mph)	Wind Power Density (W/m 2)	Speed (b) m/s (mph)
1	100	4.4 (9.8)	200	5.6 (12.5)
2	150	5.1 (11.5)	300	6.4 (14.3)
3	200	5.6 12.5)	400	7.0 15.7)
4	250	6.0 (13.4)	500	7.5 (16.8)
5	300	6.4 (14.3)	600	8.0 (17.9)
6	400	7.0 (15.7)	800	8.8 (19.7)
7	1000	9.4 (21.1)	2000	11.9 (26.6)

Figure 4.6.1. Average wind power
(*Source:* National Renewable Energy Laboratory [October 1986])

From a trading perspective, the practical implication of this is that it's hard to predict the value of wind energy. The energy will be produced in relatively random spurts that may or may not coincide with a period when people actually want to use power. In addition, because the power production is so intermittent, it will still be necessary to fill in the missing energy with some other type of fuel. If that fuel is nuclear or coal power, those units can't be turned on or off quickly. In that case, even if the wind starts up, it is impossible to shut off those other generators. The excess power will be wasted.

Quickly cycling generators are also poor choices to address the problem of intermittent generation. These units are typically much less efficient than other types of electrical generation. If quickly cycling

Distribution of Wind Speeds	Percent of Total Energy Production
Wind speeds might be approximated by a lognormal distribution. An example is shown below, with the top 25 percent of the distribution shaded in (Figure 4.6.2).	Since the energy in wind is proportional to the cube of the wind speed, relatively rare high wind gusts will provide a disproportionately large amount of energy (Figure 4.6.3). In this example, approximately 75 percent of the total energy produced comes from the samples in the shaded area on the left.

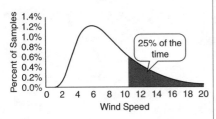

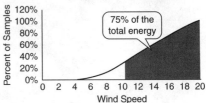

Figure 4.6.2. Typical distribution of wind speeds

Figure 4.6.3. Most wind energy comes from fast wind speeds

generators like gas turbines or diesel peakers are used to cover for intermittent generation, a wind farm is committing a region to the use of highly inefficient, highly polluting fossil fuel generation units. This pretty much eliminates any environmentally friendly aspects of wind power.

Installation and Maintenance

Wind turbines can be expensive to install and maintain due to the constant stress the wind places on their large number of moving parts. When exposed to high winds for prolonged periods, a substantial amount of torque is placed on the frame of the wind turbine. This can cause the superstructure of the turbine to break down and deform over time. This is especially a problem when there are a number of wind turbines in close proximity. When a wind turbine is alone, the air flow around its fan blades is fairly predictable. However, when there are a large number together, the turbulence from the upwind units' blades can cause chaotic air flow over the downwind units. This puts unpredictable stresses on the superstructure of wind turbines and can lead to equipment failure.

This makes it difficult to constrain the size of wind farms. The obvious way around the problem of having units upwind of one another is to spread them out in a long line. Of course, having wind turbines strung out for a 20- or 30- or 100-mile line along a mountain ridge or a coastline is an eyesore. Aesthetically, few people want an unremitting view of industrial machinery as far as the eye can see.

The constant mechanical stress on wind turbines requires regular lubrication and maintenance. This can become very expensive. The gear boxes for wind turbines are typically located near the top of the units several hundred feet in the air. This makes getting maintenance crews to the top of units very dangerous. Typically, these units are not built with elevators and have exterior ladders exposed to high winds. Mechanics are generally chosen for their skills rather than for youth or climbing ability. Climbing 20 stories off the ground while carrying a heavy tool kit in windy conditions is highly challenging. The large amount of oil required for lubrication also raises substantial questions about whether wind power is actually renewable and how much it helps users reduce their dependence upon foreign oil.

Criticisms of Wind Power

The two most common reasons for consumer opposition to wind farms are the danger they present to migratory birds and aesthetic considerations. Wind turbines are often placed on major migration corridors due to the steady sustained winds in those areas. As birds fly past the turbines, they can be hit by the spinning blades and killed. Environmental groups are concerned that if wind power becomes common, the wild bird population will be decimated. Others protest because they consider wind farms ugly and don't want them located nearby.

Financial Modeling of a Wind Farm

Compared to other types of energy, it is difficult to model the behavior of a wind farm. An irregular supply of wind, unpredictable maintenance costs, and irregularly scheduled downtimes combine to raise a lot of questions about the feasibility of wind power generators. Because every area of the country has a different frequency of wind gusts, it's also impossible to develop a generalized valuation model based on option pricing theory. Instead, valuation of a wind farm usually requires a simulation-based approach to get a reasonable expectation of how it might operate.

The task of pricing something like a wind farm gets a lot easier when there is a way to store the energy generated by the wind turbine. Similar to how thermal solar power stores energy in a heat reservoir to time shift solar energy, wind turbines get an immense benefit from being able to time-shift their energy output. A variety of ways of storing electricity are discussed in Chapter 4.8, "Electricity Storage."

4.7

Nuclear Power

 30-Second Summary

Purpose

This section introduces nuclear power.

Summary

Nuclear power plants, like coal-fired power plants, operate by producing super-heated steam to drive electrical turbines. Both coal and nuclear plants benefit by operating at extremely high temperatures. The higher the temperature that these plants can operate at, the more efficient they become. A low temperature plant might return 25 percent of its heat energy as electricity. A larger, hotter plant might return 50 to 60 percent of its heat energy as electricity.

The primary difference between nuclear and coal plants is the way they generate heat. Nuclear power plants generate heat through nuclear fission. Nuclear fission breaks protons and neutrons free from the nucleus of the nuclear fuel. This isn't a combustion process, so no carbon dioxide is produced. However, nuclear power produces a different type of pollution—radioactive waste.

When concentrated, uranium, the fuel used in most nuclear reactors, is highly toxic. The fuel can also be very difficult to obtain. Although there is a lot of uranium in the earth's crust, it is seldom found in large deposits. There are a limited number of areas where sufficient quantities can be found to make its extraction economically feasible. Another worry is that the refining process is often identical to the process needed to make fuel for nuclear weapons. As a result, concerns of nuclear weapon proliferation are closely linked to the construction of nuclear reactors.

Key Topics

- Nuclear power doesn't release CO_2 emissions, but it does cause other environmental problems.
- The primary fuel for nuclear power, uranium, has to be mined and purified before it is used.
- Nuclear fuel is not particularly common. Techniques to refine nuclear fuel are often government secrets.
- Nuclear plants, like coal plants, have an economy of scale. They need to be built large, and no one wants one built in their backyard. As a result, nuclear plants are usually built far from consumer regions. That distance places a lot of strain on the electrical grid.

Nuclear power plants use steam turbines to generate electricity. This technology is identical to the technology used to generate electricity in large coal-fired power plants. Both heat water until it becomes pressurized steam. That steam is used to power a spinning turbine. Because of this, like coal plants, nuclear power plants produce more electricity per unit of fuel when they can operate at high temperatures. Also, they are most efficient when they operate full-time without letting the water cool down overnight.

The primary difference between the two types of power plants is the fuel they consume. Coal power plants produce heat through combustion. Combustion (burning) creates CO_2 and releases any particulate matter trapped in the coal. In contrast, nuclear power plants produce heat through nuclear fission. Nuclear fission involves splitting large atoms (like uranium) into two separate atoms.

Nuclear Fission

Nuclear fission is a natural process that occurs every day. It occurs when the nucleus of an atom splits into smaller particles. Certain elements, like uranium and plutonium, are naturally radioactive. In these elements, the nucleus is unstable enough that it splits spontaneously. This is called *spontaneous fission* or *radioactive decay*. Humans can speed up this process so it happens very quickly rather than over a long period of time. When fission is sped up, it is called *induced fission*.

It is easiest to induce fission in an element that is already breaking down. That is why induced fission utilizes elements that are already radioactive, like uranium and plutonium. When fission occurs, an *alpha particle* consisting of two protons and two neutrons breaks off from the nucleus of an atom. This also causes a pair of electrons to spin off from the nucleus (*beta particles*) and a release of electromagnetic energy (*gamma radiation*).

Almost any atomic nucleus can be broken apart by fission if enough energy is used. However, some atomic nuclei are especially susceptible to fission and require much less energy to break apart than others. These substances are the key to creating a *nuclear chain reaction*. In a chain reaction, the amount of energy released by fission will be sufficient to cause another nearby nucleus to fission as well. If the nearby nuclei are stable, the first fission won't be enough to break another nucleus apart.

The difference between radiation, a nuclear reactor, and a nuclear bomb is the speed of the fission reaction. Nuclear radiation is a slow breakdown of atomic nuclei. There isn't enough energy being released to create a chain reaction. A nuclear reactor involves a faster reaction, where the energy being released from fission triggers additional nuclear reactions at a measured rate. A nuclear bomb explodes every atom in the fuel extremely quickly in a fast chain reaction.

The Nuclear Cycle

The life cycle of nuclear material is typically called the *nuclear cycle*. The first stages in the process are *exploration* and *mining*. These stages remove rocks containing nuclear fuel from the ground and bring them to a processing plant. At the processing plant, uranium is separated from other rocks and *milled* by grinding it up into a powderlike material called *yellowcake*. Uranium is then converted into a gas by combining it with fluoride to form uranium hexafluoride (UF_6). Then, uranium is ready to be enriched. The enrichment process brings fuel to a desired ratio of fissionable material (uranium-235) to nonfissionable uranium (uranium-238). The most common way to separate the uranium is to spin the uranium hexafluoride gas in a centrifuge. The heavier uranium-238 will move to the outside of the centrifuge, allowing the uranium-235 to be collected from the inside.

For a sustained nuclear reaction, there has to be a sufficient quantity of fissionable material in a fuel. Most uranium found in nature is not the right type to sustain a nuclear reaction. *Nuclear enrichment* is the process of getting the right amount of fissionable material into nuclear fuel. One type of uranium—an isotope called uranium-235—is very easy to fission. An atom of U-235 produces more energy when the nucleus splits apart than is required to break the nucleus. Other types of uranium are not as easy to break apart. As a result, getting the right amount of U-235 into nuclear fuel is the key to nuclear fission. A nuclear power plant might want its fuel to contain about 4 percent uranium-235. In comparison, a nuclear weapon might require 90 percent purity or higher.

After it is separated, the uranium is then converted back into a solid form (uranium dioxide, UO_2) in a *fabrication* plant and shaped into its final form. A nuclear power plant will partially control the speed of the nuclear reaction by the shape of the fuel. A nuclear weapon might want the fuel shaped into a ball to maximize the speed of a chain reaction. A nuclear power plant might want fuel shaped into a flat sheet. That way, a lot of the energy will escape from the top and bottom of the sheet. This will reduce the speed of the nuclear chain reaction. The speed of the fission process is fine-tuned by the use of graphite control rods.

Isotopes and Atomic Mass Numbers

Substances that have a different number of neutrons but the same number of protons are said to be *isotopes* of one another. Chemically, they behave identically. However, the stability of their nuclei is because of different atomic weights. In common usage, the term "isotope" refers to an atom with a specific number of neutrons in the nucleus. Isotopes are indicated by a number after the chemical symbol. For example U-238 and U-235 are both isotopes of uranium.

The number after the chemical symbol is the *atomic mass number.* The atomic mass number of an atom is the combined number of protons and neutrons present in the nucleus. These particles weigh about the same, but only protons have an electrical charge.

The *atomic number* of an element is the number of protons in its nucleus. That number is never explicitly stated on a chemical formula. However, it can be looked up on a periodic table. For example, helium is defined as any atom that contains exactly two protons. Therefore, the atomic number for any type of helium is 2. An alpha particle, He-4, will have two protons and two neutrons. The number of neutrons can be found by subtracting the atomic number of the element from the atomic mass number.

These rods can be used to slow down reactions. When they are inserted into the reactor chamber, graphite rods soak up radiation before it triggers fission in another atom.

After the nuclear fuel is used, it must be removed from the reactor. At this point, the fuel, control rods, and water used to cool the reaction and power the steam turbines are all radioactive. Those materials will be undergoing nuclear fission as well. However, this rate will be much slower than the rate at which nuclear reactor was operating. The fuel may be *reprocessed* to remove any remaining uranium-235 that is still unused. After that, it will be necessary to get rid of the wastes.

There are two choices with any toxic waste. The waste can either be diluted and spread out over a wide area or it can be concentrated into something unbelievably toxic. Most areas have regulation to limit release of any toxic substances into the biosphere, so diluting the toxic waste is not a viable solution. As a result, the nuclear waste gets concentrated and placed in a storage facility that is hopefully far away from anywhere it can do any harm.

Thorium Cycle

Uranium-238 isn't the only source of fuel for nuclear reactors. It is also possible to fuel nuclear power plants with uranium-233 derived from an abundant form of thorium. This is more expensive than producing uranium-235 from uranium-238, but it produces less radioactive waste and is more difficult to use in weapons. Thorium is approximately three times as common as uranium-238, and nearly all of the thorium that is mined could be used as a nuclear fuel.

Problems with Nuclear Power

From an engineering standpoint, nuclear power plants present many of the same challenges as coal plants. Both types of plants need to be built on an extremely large scale and placed a long way away from consumers. Adopting nuclear power as a primary power source means making a substantial commitment to a certain type of power grid—one that involves long distance transmission of power. This type of power grid is inherently less reliable than a power grid where generation capacity is located close to consumers.

Compared to coal, nuclear power also doesn't address the problem of importing fuel from other countries. Uranium has to be mined from somewhere. This makes the nuclear power industry just as fuel dependent as any fossil-fuel-fired power plant. For example, North America has some uranium reserves, but these are much less extensive than its vast coal reserves. Other areas, like Europe, have to import nearly all of their nuclear fuel. As a result, nuclear power is not necessarily the best approach for a country to be energy independent.

Another problem is the concern of nuclear weapon proliferation. The enrichment process used to create nuclear fuel is nearly identical to the process used to create nuclear weapons. Ensuring there is a ready supply of nuclear fuel to supply civilian use without making it available for military use is a problem that challenges public policy.

From a pollution standpoint, the good thing about nuclear power is that it doesn't produce CO_2, sulfur dioxide, or nitrogen oxide pollution. However, none of those types of pollution are likely to kill people outright. Fossil fuel pollution might cause climate change, slowly kill off wildlife, and destroy the environment, but it doesn't present the immediate health threat of nuclear waste. Nuclear waste is deadly. Storing nuclear waste is extremely dangerous because even small amounts can be lethal.

4.8

ELECTRICITY STORAGE

 30-Second Summary

Purpose

This chapter looks at techniques that are used to store electricity. None of these technologies are efficient enough to store huge quantities of electricity, but they often make interesting investments.

Summary

Electricity can be stored by converting it into another form of energy, like kinetic energy or heat, and then converted back into electricity. Even though the efficiency of these conversions is usually low, there are cases where it becomes economically worthwhile. For example, anytime electricity can be obtained for very low cost, even inefficient storage systems are economical if they were inexpensive to build. There are a large number of ways to store energy. Some of the examples used in this section discuss pressurized gas, kinetic energy, and gravity. It's equally possible to use chemical energy to store energy in a battery, or to use a capacitor to store voltage directly.

Key Topics

- Storing electricity is not easy, and there is no widespread way of doing it economically.
- Storing electricity usually means converting it into some other type of storable energy and then converting it back to electricity when the time comes to use it.

Better energy storage is the Holy Grail of electrical markets. If it were possible to buy electricity in the spot markets and resell it at a later point, the electrical market would behave a lot differently than it does today. Currently, electricity prices oscillate over time. Prices are often highest sometime during the day and lower at night and on weekends. If energy could be stored, electricity could be bought during lowest demand periods and resold when demand was higher (Figure 4.8.1). Every night, power is cheap. Every day, it is more expensive. Buying

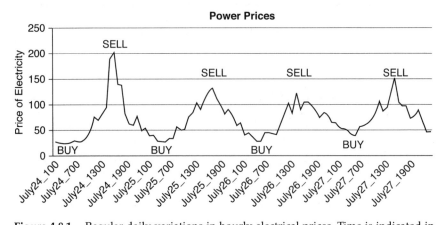

Figure 4.8.1. Regular daily variations in hourly electrical prices. Time is indicated in 24-hour format after the date (e.g., 700 = 7 A.M., 1900 = 7 P.M.).

power during the night and selling it back the next day would be an easy way to make money—if it were possible to store that power.

This sounds like a great idea, but in practice, electrical storage usually is not efficient enough for this type of trading. For example, a storage facility might have 25 percent efficiency, which means that 25 percent of the electricity placed into the facility can be returned after storage. If peak power prices were consistently four times off-peak prices, the system would break even on gross profit—and not even begin to pay the installation and ongoing maintenance costs of the storage system.

However, there are a number of cases where electrical storage does make sense. For example, large nuclear power plants and coal plants don't like to reduce their operations overnight. They are much more efficient when they run at high temperatures around the clock. If they reduce their output at night, they will have to use a substantial amount of fuel to increase the heat of their system in the morning. In those cases, it is more costly for these plants to reduce their output than to give away free power for several hours. For them, electrical power is free—if they don't use it, and they can't sell it, they have to throw it away.

Valuing any electrical storage solution can be fairly complicated. The core of the valuation will depend on how the storage is expected to operate. For example, a system that buys power overnight and then resells it the following day would be a lot different than a storage facility that gets its power for free and plans on holding on to it for several months.

Compressed Air

One way to store electricity is to use it to run an air compressor (Figure 4.8.2), which is run at night or on weekends, when power prices are low, to force air into a storage vessel. Then, when power is required, air is let out of the container (Figure 4.8.3). If the air pressure is high enough, it could be used to run a turbine to produce electricity. It also might be worthwhile to use the compressed air directly—pneumatic air tools are commonly used in a wide variety of industrial jobs. Alternately, since compressed gas is hot and cools rapidly when it expands, it wouldn't be difficult to create an HVAC (heating, ventilation, and air-conditioning) system using compressed air.

Compressed Air: Storing Power	Compressed Air: Retrieving Power
 **Figure 4.8.2.** Storing energy with compressed air	**Figure 4.8.3.** Using compressed air energy
Electricity is used to run a compressor. The compressor is used to load gas into a pressurized container. A small-scale unit might use a pressurized metal container, while a large unit might store air in an underground cavern.	When the compressed air is released from the storage container, it could be used to drive a turbine, power pneumatic tools, or operate an HVAC system.

Flywheels

Another way to store energy is in a flywheel—a mechanical way of storing energy in a fast spinning cylinder (Figure 4.8.4). A flywheel is a big, heavy wheel that spins extremely fast. The wheel is sped up to store energy, and slowed down to pull energy out of the system, as depicted in Figure 4.8.5. The key part of the flywheel design is a way to eliminate friction on the spinning wheel.

One advantage of a flywheel is that they can be relatively compact. Another advantage is that getting energy out of a spinning cylinder is relatively straightforward. The wheel can be connected to an electromagnet to create AC power. Alternately, the flywheel can be connected to a shaft to provide mechanical energy to drive a vehicle.

On the downside, a fast spinning wheel contains a lot of energy. A flywheel can do a lot of damage if an axle breaks. A single flywheel is also going to act like a gyroscope if it is mounted in a vehicle. This will make the vehicle much harder to turn. The gyroscopic effect can be avoided by running two flywheels side by side in opposite directions, but that exposes any shared axle to a lot of torque. However, these problems can all be addressed by engineering solutions.

Flywheel: Storing Power	Flywheel: Retrieving Power
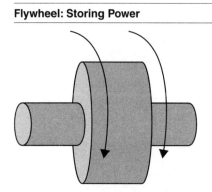	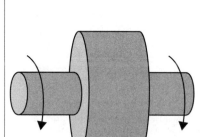
Figure 4.8.4. Storing energy with a flywheel	**Figure 4.8.5.** Using energy stored in a flywheel
A flywheel stores kinetic energy in a rapidly spinning heavy disc. Energy is stored in the disc by increasing its rotational speed.	Power is removed from a flywheel by using the spinning motion of the wheel to drive a turbine or other type of motor.

Pumped Hydro Power

A third way of storing power is to pump water high into an elevated storage facility. The basic concept is that water in an elevated location can drive a hydroelectric turbine. Water stored at the bottom of the facility can be pumped into the elevated reservoir during the storage phase, as shown in Figure 4.8.6, then released to get the power back, as in Figure 4.8.7. This is similar to how a hydroelectric facility operates. Normally, hydro-power plants are powered by water flowing through a river. However, it would be possible to create a closed system that pumps water below a dam back to the top. With sufficiently large reservoirs at the top and bottom of the facility, it is possible to store a large quantity of energy for an extended period.

Pumped Hydro Power: Storing Power	Pumped Hydro Power: Retrieving Power
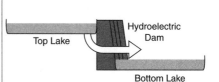	

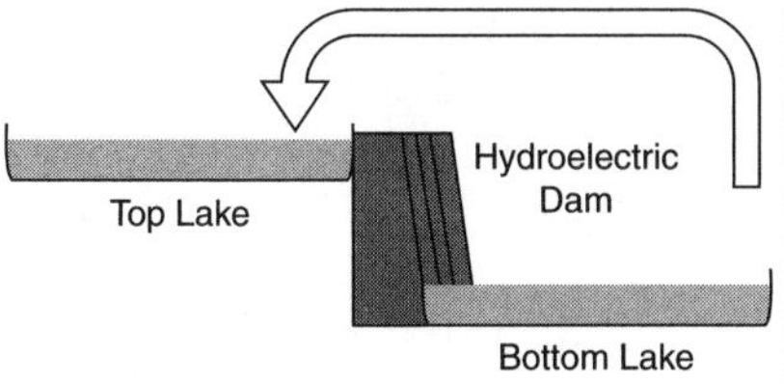

Figure 4.8.6. Storing energy with pumped hydro power

Figure 4.8.7. Retrieving energy from pumped hydro power

To store energy, water is pumped from a lower reservoir into an elevated reservoir.

To retrieve power, the water is allowed to fall into the lower reservoir. Along the way, it spins a turbine to generate electricity.

Trading Example: Compressed Air

The owner of a chemical company needs to keep a large warehouse at a constant temperature. This is one of the major costs of doing business, and he is looking at alternatives to paying peak electric prices.

1. **The Opportunity.** When a chemical company is building a new warehouse, one of the HVAC systems it is considering has the ability to run on compressed air. The air doesn't have to be compressed at run time, it is possible to compress the air overnight. Since the company buys its power wholesale, it can arrange a contract with its power supplier to buy off-peak rather than peak power.

2. **The Intuition.** Because most of the electricity used by the system can be purchased overnight, the price of operating this system is much cheaper than running the compressor during the day.

3. **The Strategy.** If peak power prices rise after the system is installed, it will become a better investment. In a similar manner, the company is obligating itself to buy off-peak power. The cheaper the price of that power, the better the investment becomes. Installing this system is equivalent to a long peak power, short off-peak power spread position. Subsequently arranging to buy off-peak power from a supplier will cancel the off-peak exposure of the unit and leave the owner with just a long exposure to peak power. If peak prices rise, the system will become more valuable. If prices fall, it will have been a less beneficial investment.

4. **The Risks.** This is a piece of physical hardware and not just a financial investment. However, from a financial perspective, installing an energy storage system allows the chemical company to time shift its energy purchases.

Technical Notes

If the owner of the system is going to buy power overnight every night, there is no daily operating decision since the decision will always occur. Because of this, using a real options approach to model the value of this system is probably a bad idea. It might be better to treat this investment as a purchase of futures.

The only real complication to this valuation is that the system might have a 20-year lifetime and power isn't traded further than a couple of years into the future. If traded products were available, valuing this investment would be much easier.

Examining the typical relationship of overnight power to daytime power, the operator notices that overnight power is about 50 percent the price of peak power, but it varies by month (Figure 4.8.8). This seems reasonable: in the winter, power is used at night to provide heating, and in comparison, a smaller percentage of summer energy is used at night. This relationship could be used as a model to estimate peak prices based on marginal fuels, and then to estimate off-peak prices from those estimates.

On first glance, modeling the profit from these trades as a time spread between the prices at two different time periods seems reasonable. However, there is a problem with that approach—electricity prices don't behave like typical asset prices. Most asset prices follow a random walk and slowly diffuse away from their starting point. Spot electricity prices don't work the same way. Future energy spot prices are reasonably

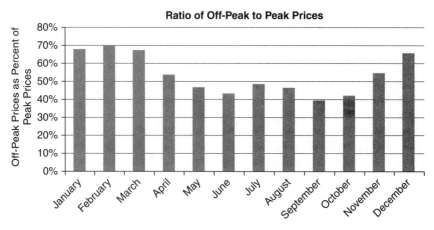

Figure 4.8.8. Off-peak prices are about 70 percent of peak prices in winter and 40 percent of peak prices in the summer

predictable and highly cyclical. As a result, a Monte Carlo simulation approach might make more sense than a real options approach.

Trading Example: Pumped Hydro Power

Polluted coal ponds in upstate New York are located by large hydro-power plants. During the spring snowmelt, these hydro plants run around the clock at maximum capacity. For a period of several weeks the price of power plummets dramatically. By the summer these hydro plants sell power into the high cost New York City market. Using the polluted coal ponds to store the low cost electricity generated during the snowmelt for sale later in the year seems like a possible investment.

1. **The Opportunity.** Pumped hydro-power storage is a way to buy power during the spring and hold it until it can be sold into the high-priced August peak power market. Upstate New York is filled with toxic coal ponds. These are large lakes left over from a time when coal mining was less environmentally friendly. These lakes are conveniently located near mountain ranges, providing easy access to both a supply of water and vertical cliffs that can be used for building dams. The coal mining company is willing to offer this land for free to anyone who will assume full responsibility for the toxic mess that was created.

2. **The Intuition.** Along with the spring/summer trade, there will probably be reasonably frequent opportunities for buying power when it is temporarily cheap and selling it when prices spike. For example, if a heat wave is coming, power prices can be expected to rise with a fairly high degree of certainty. Because most people can't store power, a pumped hydro-power plant is one of the few market participants that might take advantage of this trade.

3. **Strategy.** The general strategy is to identify periods when prices are unusually high or low and either buy or sell power during those periods. Normally this is relatively easy since electricity prices are cyclical. Unless the reservoirs are at capacity, owning a pumped hydro-power plant makes it possible to both buy and sell electricity on short notice.

4. **The Risks.** The cyclical nature of power prices makes buying, storing, and selling, power a low risk investment. However, that nearly guaranteed profit still might not be enough to take on the environmental liability of this investment. Assuming the legal liability for someone else's toxic cleanup is a potential nightmare. Additionally, building a pumped hydro-power plant means building physical property and hiring an operational team to maintain that property. Maintenance costs are probably going to be high because polluted water is often highly corrosive. Overall, this is a complex trade with a lot of liability and operational complexity.

5. **Executing the Trade.** Once the facility is built, this is a physical trade that will involve arranging the purchase and sale of actual power. As a result, there is also a lot of paperwork involved. There will need to be a second team of people that coordinates the purchase and sale of power for this facility every day.

6. **The Results.** Taking on the responsibility for toxic cleanup is a huge risk. That risk alone will be enough to scare off nearly all potential investors. The physical complexity of the job is a second deal killer. Building a dam to pump water up and down a mountain isn't simple under any circumstances. That complexity, combined with the need to run highly acidic water, makes this a complex trade even if there were no liability concerns. Most investors will pass on this investment.

5.1

Natural Gas Transportation

30-Second Summary

Purpose

This chapter examines trading opportunities associated with the use of pipelines to transport natural gas.

Summary

Pipelines are operated by for-profit companies as an economical way to transport large amounts of natural gas over long distances. It is very difficult to transport natural gas without using a pipeline. Moving it by truck or railroad is difficult because of the need to use high pressure metal storage containers. Alternatively, it is possible to freeze natural gas until it becomes a liquid and transport it in an insulated container, though this approach is not practical on a small scale.

Key Topics

- Gas pipelines can't shut down. They must operate continuously. For traders that have access to storage facilities, this can be a source of profits.
- Pipeline operators are private companies that make a profit by guaranteeing delivery of gas. Gas transportation is not cheap, and the financial side of the pipeline business is similar to offering insurance. The various service levels offered by pipelines are often similar to insurance contracts.
- A large portion of natural gas trades involve transferring natural gas from the buyer to the seller. Even in the financial trades, which are settled in cash with no transfer of the commodity, the availability and cost of transportation will determine the settlement price.

Because of cost considerations, natural gas is typically transported by pipeline. Natural gas needs to be kept in airtight containers to prevent it from dispersing. If gas is transported in a container, the weight of the container affects transportation costs. Pipelines eliminate the problem of moving heavy containers, and, as a result, have become the most common method of transporting natural gas.

CHAPTER 5.1   NATURAL GAS TRANSPORTATION

Once they are built, pipelines are cost-effective. They have relatively few moving parts and can operate around the clock. This has effectively eliminated interest in building alternative distribution networks. The downside is that natural gas transportation is generally restricted to areas connected by pipelines. These pipelines form an interconnected network that allows natural gas to flow from production areas to consumption areas. However, when an area is not connected into the pipeline network, it is very difficult to get gas in or out. When natural gas can't be placed onto a pipeline network, it is said to be "stranded."

Natural gas pipelines also have substantial operating constraints. The largest constraint is that they need to operate continuously. Unless there is continuous movement of gas over a pipeline, it won't work. Pipelines must maintain areas of high and low pressure to keep gas moving. If the pressure in the pipeline fully equalizes, gas will stop flowing and it can take a very long time to get moving again.

As their name would suggest, pipelines are long pipes that use compressors to move gas from one end of the pipe to the other. A compressor (like a fan) at the start of the pipe creates a high pressure area, and a compressor at the end of the pipe pulls gas out of the pipeline by suction (a low pressure area). Gas is drawn through the pipe by the pressure differential between the high pressure injection point and the low pressure suction point.

Pipeline Operations

There are many different types of pipelines. Some pipelines connect wells to refineries. Others are transcontinental in nature, moving the gas from producing regions to consuming regions. Still other pipelines are used to deliver gas to consumers. All pipelines work in a similar manner—gas moves along a pipe from an area of high pressure to an area of low pressure. By manipulating the pressure in different areas of the pipe (through compressors) pipeline companies can control the flow of gas through their networks.

It is important that a pipeline maintains the proper ratio of pressures throughout its length. If the pressure at the discharge end of the pipe were to be higher than the pressure at the well head, gas would flow back into the well. In practical terms, this means that if a pipeline is to remain operational, gas must be continually injected at one side and removed at the other. If gas isn't added continuously at the injection point (to create a high pressure zone) and removed at the consumer end (to create a low pressure zone), gas won't flow in the proper direction, and the pipeline won't operate. This is a very important concept: for a pipeline to operate, neither injections nor removals can stop because they are uneconomical. Because of the time required to restart pipelines, it might be necessary to run a pipeline even if no consumers are using gas and there isn't any storage available.

Pipelines and Trading

The trading of natural gas can occur on a number of different levels, as shown in the three figures below—the national, regional, and intraregional.

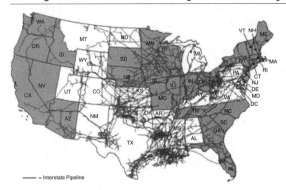

= Interstate Pipeline

Figure 5.1.1. National level of natural gas trades
(*Source:* Energy Information Agency [December 2008])

Nationally
The prices anywhere in an interconnected pipeline network are related to the prices everywhere else on the network. Even though a pipeline network is composed of both consuming regions (shaded gray) and producing regions (white), the ability to transport gas between areas means that prices are correlated most of the time (Figure 5.1.1).

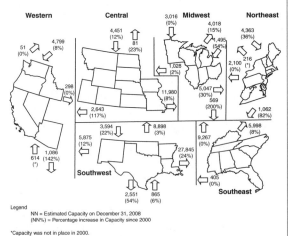

Legend
NN = Estimated Capacity on December 31, 2008
(NN%) = Percentage increase in Capacity since 2000

*Capacity was not in place in 2000.

Figure 5.1.2. Regional level of natural gas trades
(*Source:* Energy Information Agency [December 2008])

Between Regions
Regional supply and demand can have a localized effect on prices. There is a limited amount of transportation capacity between regions (Figure 5.1.2). The amount of capacity relative to consumer demand determines how far regional prices swing away from the national average.

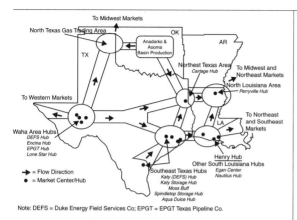

Note: DEFS = Duke Energy Field Services Co; EPGT = EPGT Texas Pipeline Co.

Figure 5.1.3.   Intraregional level of natural gas trades (*Source:* Energy Information Agency [August 2003])

Within a Region

Knowledge of natural gas pipelines is also the key to understanding prices within a region. (Figure 5.1.3). The prices at each hub will depend on the nature of the areas that are connected to the hub by a pipeline. For example, even though hubs in East and West Texas are connected and geographically close, their relative prices are determined by different dynamics of the East and West Coast markets.

Compressor Stations

Compressor stations form the heart of the pipeline network. Similar to how a heart pumps blood throughout a human body, compressor stations push natural gas through the pipeline network. When liquid or gas is compressed, it moves toward a lower pressure area. By controlling the location of high and low pressure areas, compressor stations are used to control the flow of gas through pipelines. The simplest way to think of a compressor is as a household fan. On one side of the fan, gas is being pulled in and a low pressure zone exists. On the other side, air is being pushed out to create a high pressure zone.

One key issue with compression is that it will increase the temperature of the gas being compressed. Cold gas is denser than hot gas. A greater quantity of gas can be transported if the gas is kept cool. As a result, most compressing stations include several cooling stages as part of the compression process. Cooler gas also causes less corrosion. Natural gas is never perfectly pure methane. It almost always contains trace amounts of other gases. Warming and cooling can cause gases to condense into the airtight pipeline where they get trapped. Some of these trace gases are highly corrosive and cause mechanical breakdowns if allowed to accumulate. As a result, compression stations also provide scrubbing systems to remove trace impurities.

A modern compression station will usually contain several compressor units running in parallel. Gas enters the station through a suction header, and then moves through the scrubber system, as shown in Figure 5.1.4. The scrubber system removes particulate matter and most liquids from the gas. Then the gas goes through a series of compression

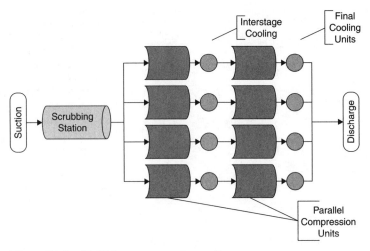

Figure 5.1.4.   Multistage compression unit

and cooling stages before being discharged into the next segment of the pipeline.

Compression stations are located along the entire length of a pipeline. They divide the pipeline into small segments. Gas moves between pipeline segments by traveling from the high pressure discharge point of one station to the low pressure suction point of the next station. Chaining these sections together allows a steady flow of gas through the pipeline. It is very important that all of the stations on a pipeline work together, or else the pipeline will stop operating. Most compressor stations are fully automated, and coordination between stations is handled by a computer at a central location.

On most pipelines, compression stations are located approximately every 50 miles, as shown in the map in Figure 5.1.5.

Transportation Contracts

When arranging transportation on a pipeline, there are two major levels of service: *firm* service and *interruptible* service. Firm service is offered with a guaranteed availability except when prevented by act of force majeure.[1] It is highly reliable but also relatively expensive compared to interruptible service, which is offered on a "best efforts" basis and is relatively cheap. However, the latter can be interrupted (hence the name)

---

[1] Force majeure, French for "greater force," is a common clause in contracts. It frees both parties from liability in cases of wars, natural disasters, and other extraordinary events. Typically these events are outside the control of either party, which would prevent one or both of the parties from fulfilling their obligations under the terms of the contract.

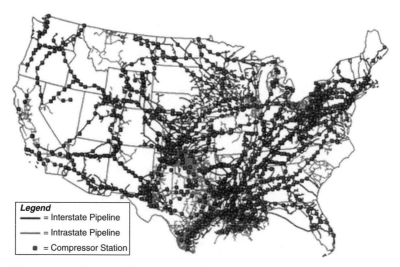

Figure 5.1.5. Inter- and intrastate pipelines and compressor stations (*Source:* Energy Information Agency [December 2008])

for any reason and may not be available at all. There are a number of valid reasons why interruptible service might be disrupted. The most common reason is to balance the flow of gas on a pipeline. Because of the nature of gas, its movement can never be precisely controlled—it always moves from areas of high pressure to low pressure. Even optimizing a relatively simple pipeline can get very complicated.

Four Segment Pipeline

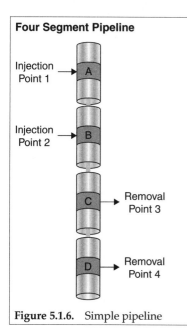

Figure 5.1.6. Simple pipeline

As an example of how complex this balancing can get, let's look at a simple pipeline (Figure 5.1.6). This is a four segment pipeline with two injection points (1 and 2) and two removal points (3 and 4). A shipper has contracted to move gas from Point 2 to Point 3. The pipeline starts with equal pressure in all segments. When gas is injected at Point 2, the pressure in section B will start to rise. This causes gas to flow out of B into the adjoining low pressure areas (gas will flow into *both* sections A and C). The pressure in those sections will then begin to rise.

Gas will also flow between sections C and D. However, the speed of this movement—and even its direction—will depend on the pressure in section D and how quickly gas is sucked out of the pipeline at the withdrawal point (Point 3).

Even in this simple case, gas is being spread all around the pipeline. It would be practically impossible to get all of the gas injected at Point 2, in Figure 5.1.6, out of the pipeline at Point 3. If the pipeline were mostly full of gas, it would be possible to get approximately the same *amount* of gas out of the pipeline as was injected, but it wouldn't be the *same* gas. This has some advantages. For example, if the pipeline were nearly full, and the amount of gas being transported was relatively small, gas could be simultaneously injected and removed from the pipeline. It would take some time for the pipeline to reach equilibrium again, but the so-called "transportation" would occur very quickly.

The rate at which gas flows depends on the pressure difference between areas. High pressure gas moves more quickly than low pressure gas. In the example above, injecting gas into a nearly empty pipeline and injecting gas into a nearly full pipeline give two very different operational results. Starting empty—since the gas will spread out throughout the entire pipeline—it would probably be impossible to fully remove the full quantity of the gas from the pipeline at Removal Point 3.

Pipeline operators have a vested interest in keeping the pipeline as full as possible. While they can't keep it at maximum capacity, since then it would be impossible to inject additional gas, neither can a pipeline be operated at very low pressure.

Firm shippers pay a large premium (a *reservation charge*) in order to guarantee that enough capacity is available at all times for their use. However, the shipper doesn't actually have to put his own gas into the pipeline—perhaps it is a warmer than expected winter and residential demand is much lower than expected. The pipeline operator still needs gas in the pipeline—the pressure in the pipeline can't be allowed to drop too far—so it will offer much lower cost interruptible service to other clients. When the firm shipper wants to make a delivery, the interruptible clients will get shut off.

There are valid business reasons for using either type of contract. It is important that a public service company provide gas heat to residences without interruption. A power plant or industrial facility might also want to guarantee its supply of gas as well. On the other hand, a gas storage facility might opt to use interruptible service for buying gas. A storage facility wants to buy gas cheaply (during periods of low demand) and sell high (during periods of high demand). There is no need to pay a high premium to buy during periods of minimal usage—minimal usage indicates that interruptible service contracts are available.

Transportation Contracts
Between Buyers and Sellers

As opposed to transportation contracts with pipelines, there are three common levels of contracts between buyers and sellers of gas: *swing contracts*, *baseload contracts*, and *firm contracts*. These use similar terminology to the transportation contracts, but mean slightly different things.

Swing contracts are short-term contracts between buyers and sellers utilizing interruptible service. Usually these are only for a couple of days or the balance of a month. If the seller has supply, and the buyer wants it, and there is available transportation, then the trade gets made. If any of those things doesn't happen, there is no obligation on anyone's part.

Baseload contracts are another type of interruptible contract between buyers and sellers. They are generally made with the understanding that both parties will make a "best effort" to meet the terms of the contract every day. They may or may not use firm pipeline transportation, or they might use a combination of firm and interruptible transportation. These contracts are based on trust that each side will hold up its end of the deal.

Firm contracts between buyers and sellers are binding agreements obligating both parties to the transportation—the seller is obligated to deliver, and the buyer is obligated to receive gas. There is legal recourse if either side fails on its side of the agreement. In these cases, the pipeline also needs to be obligated to reserve delivery capacity—these types of contracts will almost always utilize firm transportation contracts.

Trading Example: Pipelines as Insurance Providers

A pipeline offers capacity on its pipeline at two levels of service: *guaranteed service* and *nonguaranteed service*. The pipeline wants to offer as much guaranteed service as possible to earn a higher margin. It is considering whether to buy backup compressors along the pipeline.

1. **The Opportunity.** A pipeline consists of five compressor stations located in a row. Each compressor is active 85 percent of the time and has a scheduled maintenance of one week a year. The pipeline can continue to operate unless adjacent compressing stations are down simultaneously. However, every compressor that is offline causes the pipeline to lose 20 percent of its maximum capacity. A graphic of the pipeline is shown in Figure 5.1.7.

(Continued)

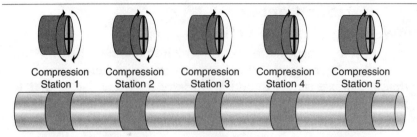

Figure 5.1.7.   Pipeline with five compression stations

A large portion of the pipeline's profit comes from guaranteed contracts. The pipeline offers annual contracts to deliver gas at two levels: firm contracts and interruptible contracts. The pipeline faces a steep penalty for failing to deliver on a firm contract. For each MMBtu of firm transportation that the pipeline successfully delivers, it receives $1. For each undelivered MMBtu of firm transportation, the pipeline must pay $12.50. For each MMBtu of interruptible transportation, the pipeline receives $0.15. If the pipeline fails to deliver the gas, it costs no money.

2. **The Intuition.** The pipeline is losing a lot of money when it fails to deliver on a firm contract. For the past five years it has been unable to operate on 8 percent of the days. It is only able to operate at full capacity 42.5 percent of the time (Figure 5.1.8). The pipeline has offered 60 percent of its capacity in firm contracts. Although it has delivered 91.7 percent of its firm contract successfully, the penalty for nondelivery of the remainder has eaten up all of those profits.

Capacity	Days
0%	8.00%
20%	0.00%
40%	0.30%
60%	8.60%
80%	40.60%
100%	42.50%

Figure 5.1.8.   Capacity/
days operation status

3. **The Strategy.** The pipeline operator plans to increase its profits by improving the reliability of the pipeline. It plans to add a second compressor to each compression station. Even though the second compressor will be idle most of the time, by increasing the reliability of the pipeline, more firm capacity can be sold because there will be a higher certainty of delivery.

4. **The Results.** The pipeline goes from making 15 cents on 40 percent of its capacity, to making $1 on 80 percent of its capacity. The pipeline starts making 100 times the profit it made previously. Even with doubled maintenance costs, this is a tremendous improvement in profitability.

Trading Example: Swing Trades

A chemical processor can produce methanol from either agricultural waste or natural gas. When natural gas is expensive, the manufacturer will use the discarded stalks and leaves of corn plants (*corn stover*). When natural gas is cheap, the manufacturer will use natural gas.

1. **The Opportunity.** One way to think about the natural gas markets is as an auction. The people willing to pay the highest amount for natural gas at that moment win the available supply. Everyone else has to wait for a later time to buy. Around the country, each area has a different amount of supply arriving at any given point, and a different pool of people demanding fuel. The natural gas marketer would like to buy natural gas at a bargain price whenever there is no one else interested in using it.

2. **The Intuition.** The chemical processor would like to buy natural gas when it is cheap. However, the processor finds natural gas uneconomical to use as a feedstock when prices are high. For this type of strategy, it doesn't make sense to reserve firm transportation on a pipeline. If the chemical processor is only going to buy natural gas when prices are low, this coincides with the times when the demand for pipeline transportation is also low.

3. **The Strategy.** The chemical processor agrees to buy natural gas from a natural gas processor using a swing contract. This contract is a nonbinding contract to purchase gas on an as-available basis using nonguaranteed transportation. In other words, to buy gas when no one else wants it.

4. **The Risks.** The chemical processor has little risk in this trade. He is getting a product at low cost when almost no one else is buying natural gas. The chemical processor can then convert that gas into a more valuable product—methanol.

5. **The Results.** Arranging for gas to be purchased with swing contracts and interruptible transportation is the lowest cost way to purchase physical gas. The main downside is that the supply of gas isn't guaranteed, and that during periods of high demand, almost no supply will be available. The chemical processor will have to rely on his other feedstock—corn stover—in those periods.

5.2

Natural Gas Storage

 30-Second Summary

Purpose

This chapter discusses the storage of natural gas and trades related to natural gas storage.

Summary

Because it is a gas, and gases disperse into the atmosphere, it is necessary to store natural gas in a sealed, pressurized location. A huge volume of space is required to contain an economically significant amount of natural gas. For example, to store the natural gas equivalent of the energy contained in a single gallon of gasoline, 900 gallons of natural gas storage are required at standard atmospheric pressure. This space requirement can be reduced by pressurizing the natural gas. However, even highly pressurized natural gas takes up a lot of space and requires a gigantic storage facility. As a result, the most common locations for storing natural gas are naturally occurring underground reservoirs, because of their vast storage capacity.

The owners of storage facilities make a profit by buying gas when it is cheap, storing it, and selling it when it is expensive. The value of a natural gas storage facility is based on the value of buying and holding natural gas. Pipelines need to operate continuously—they can't turn off. As a result, storage facilities play a critical role in purchasing gas when consumer demand is low and supplying gas when consumer demand exceeds the pipeline's capabilities.

Key Topics

- Gas pipelines have minimum operating levels and can't completely shut down. Storage is needed to take in the excess natural gas that can't be immediately used.
- Natural gas storage facilities are usually located underground in large rock formations. The physical capabilities of every facility are different and depend on the geology of each area.
- Many storage facilities are purchased to facilitate a physical trading business rather than as speculative investments. Storage facilities often trade at a premium over their calculated value because storage makes many other types of trading opportunities possible.

Natural gas is constantly moving through pipelines. To avoid wasting gas, it must be used, stored, or sent somewhere else when it arrives. Pipelines can't stop delivering gas. They must send a constant supply of gas from producing regions to consuming regions. Although the rate of flow can be adjusted somewhat, it is important that it never be stopped or interrupted completely.

Because the demand for natural gas is highly cyclical, and pipelines need to operate continuously, it is seldom possible to precisely match the supply of gas coming out of a pipeline with the amount the demand from each consuming region. Storage facilities are necessary to take in surplus during periods of oversupply and deliver gas in shortages. These facilities stockpile gas during periods of low demand (buying cheap) for use in higher demand periods (selling high). Common trading opportunities are nights versus days, weekends versus weekdays, or shoulder months versus peak demand months.

Fortunately, natural gas is chemically stable. It can be safely stored in underground facilities for extended periods. It is nontoxic, so leaks don't hurt the environment, and it has already survived millions of years in storage. While it might evaporate, it isn't going to spoil or poison the environment. Natural gas storage provides a crucial margin of safety for short-term regional fluctuations in demand.

The most common type of storage facilities are *depleted gas reservoirs*. These are underground caverns that once contained natural gas. It is possible to reuse gas reservoirs after they have been depleted by pumping gas back in. Other types of facilities are *salt caverns* and *aquifers*. The main difference between facilities is the cost of construction, the quantity of gas they can store, and how quickly they can inject and remove gas from storage.

It is common for gas to be stored in several storage facilities before it is finally delivered to the customer. The first set of storage facilities is near refineries and major pipeline hubs in the producing regions. A second set of storage facilities is located near consumers at the far end of the pipeline. An example can be seen in Figure 5.2.1.

All storage facilities work in a similar fashion—a large volume suitable for storing natural gas is found and connected to a gas pipeline. To maximize the amount of gas that can be stored in a limited amount of space, the storage facility will usually keep the gas at higher pressure than a pipeline. As a result, gas needs to be compressed to get it into the storage facility. This can be done by applying suction to a pipeline (similar to attaching a vacuum cleaner to it). As long as the suction is stronger than the pressure in the storage area, the gas will flow into the

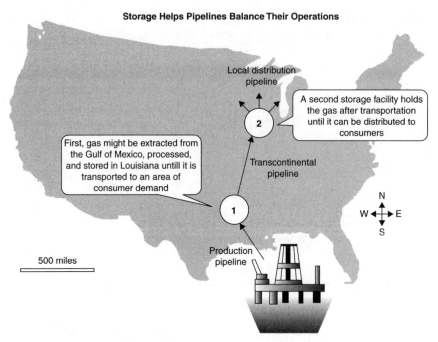

Storage Helps Pipelines Balance Their Operations

Figure 5.2.1.   Storage facilities have a critical role in keeping gas flowing properly

storage area and not back into the pipeline. When the suction is turned off, the connection between the storage facility and pipeline will need to be closed.

The speed at which gas can be inserted or extracted from storage depends on the relative pressure of a storage facility and the pipeline. When the storage facility is nearly full, gas can easily be removed from storage. It is possible to open up the pipeline connection and have the gas flow into the pipeline. However, as the pressure decreases, it takes progressively longer to get the gas out of storage.

As a result, the extractable gas is generally divided into two pieces: *base gas* (or *cushion gas*) and *working gas*. The base gas is used to create sufficient pressure to get the working gas out of the storage facility in a reasonable amount of time. Base gas is rarely removed during normal operation. Operators of a storage facility have to trade off having a large volume of working gas that can only be removed slowly or a smaller volume that can be removed quickly. During periods of peak demand, some of the base gas can be removed from the facility and delivered as working gas. However, over the long run—since removing the gas cushion slows down the speed at which gas can be removed (because removing gas lowers the pressure of the storage facility)—keeping a fixed cushion of gas is required to meet performance targets.

Inserting and Removing Gas from a Storage Facility

Gas normally flows from high pressure areas to low pressure areas. To move gas in reverse, it is necessary to use compression to artificially create a high pressure. This is similar to how a vacuum cleaner operates. A fan spins, creating suction on one side (the intake side) and a high pressure on the other side. If the high pressure is above the storage pressure, gas can be pulled out of a low pressure pipeline and placed into a high pressure storage container. In Figure 5.2.2, on the left of the fan, the fan creates a vacuum. This pulls natural gas out of the pipeline and into the storage facility.

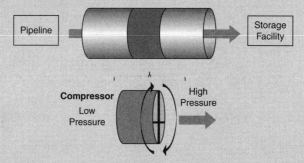

Figure 5.2.2.   A compressor is used to move gas out of a pipeline and into the storage facility

As gas builds up in the storage facility, it will start to push back against the compressor (Figure 5.2.3). To keep the same rate of insertion, more compression will be needed. At some point the maximum safe pressure for the storage facility will be reached and insertions will need to stop.

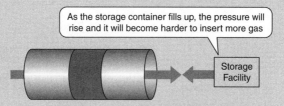

Figure 5.2.3.   More compression is required when the storage facility is nearly full

Removing gas out of the storage facility works in the opposite manner. A compressor is used to create suction to pull gas out of storage and push it into the pipeline. However, there are limits to how quickly this can occur. Once a perfect vacuum is achieved, the high/low pressure differential between storage and pipeline doesn't get any larger. Since the speed of gas movement depends on that differential, the pressure of the storage facility is the limiting factor on the speed of the removal.

This last major physical constraint on a storage facility is its maximum pressure. Higher pressure means that you can store more gas in a given volume and get the gas out more quickly. However, higher pressure can also cause structural problems—more stress on the facility—and a greater possibility of gas escaping into the environment. Since there are a fairly limited number of locations suitable for the storage of natural gas, the pressure constraint is usually a function of what can be found, rather than what is desired.

For a particular area, there is a limited inventory of possible locations suitable for storing natural gas. The cheapest and most reliable storage is *depleted gas reservoirs*. The highest performance facilities are converted *salt caverns*. In areas where neither of those two is available, *aquifers* can be used. Aquifers are permeable layers of underground rock often containing ground water. Methane, the primary component of natural gas, is nontoxic and present in the air we breathe every day. It doesn't pose the health threat that other fuels might create if they start leaking into the environment. From a performance perspective, salt caverns are far superior to the other options since they can stand up to significantly higher pressures.

The map in Figure 5.2.4 shows the locations of all of the underground storage facilities in the continental United States.

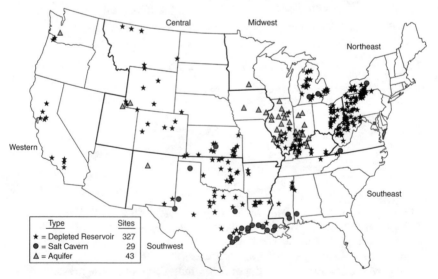

Figure 5.2.4. Map of U.S. underground storage facilities (*Source:* Energy Information Agency [December 2008])

Geology

A storage facility is a large underground area where gas can dissolve, surrounded by an impermeable area that prevents the gas from escaping (Figure 5.2.5). Overall, natural gas storage facilities are similar to other types of pressurized containers and identical to wells where natural gas is found in nature.

Natural gas storage facilities are often located underground. They aren't usually excavated with pressurized metal walls. Instead, they are commonly constructed in areas where naturally existing porous rock is surrounded by a layer of impermeable rock. There are several advantages to reusing existing geological formations. All of this rock makes the facilities fairly sturdy. Equally important is the low cost of reusing existing rock formations. Finding an appropriate existing reservoir is one of the largest jobs in building a new natural gas storage facility.

Natural gas storage shares terminology with natural gas extraction. *Porosity* is a measure of empty space in a rock. Even though many rocks look solid, they often contain microscopic openings where gas can dissolve. These openings are called *pores*. If the pores in a rock are connected together, the rock is said to be *permeable*. Having connected pores allows the gas trapped in the rock to flow in and out of the storage facility quickly. The greater the size of the pores, and the more they are interconnected, the faster the gas can enter or leave the facility.

A storage facility requires a porous, permeable pocket of rock to be surrounded by a layer of impermeable rock. Since gas rises, it is especially important for the layer of rock directly above the storage volume to be impermeable. In every gas storage facility, some gas becomes permanently embedded into the walls. This is called *physically*

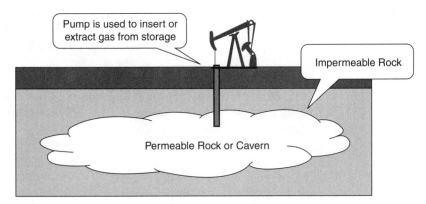

Figure 5.2.5.   Diagram of a natural gas storage facility

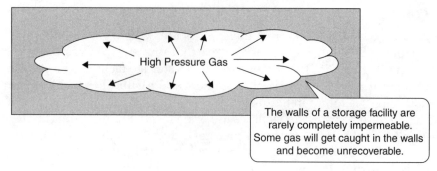

The walls of a storage facility are rarely completely impermeable. Some gas will get caught in the walls and become unrecoverable.

Figure 5.2.6. Physically unrecoverable gas

unrecoverable gas. Even when the facility closes, it is impossible to recover this gas (Figure 5.2.6).

The greater the pressure in the storage volume, the more gas gets pushed into the walls. If enough pressure is added, gas will eventually reach a more permeable area and start to escape from the storage facility. This level is different for each facility. It is determined by the specific geology of the rocks that form the storage facility.

Depleted Gas Reservoirs

Once a natural gas reservoir has been emptied, it can be refilled. This is a very easy way of creating a storage facility. While not all reservoirs are suitable for refilling, if one exists in the right area, is close to pipelines in a consuming region, and has the right geological properties, this can be a very fast, reliable, and cost effective way of getting a storage facility operational.

The physical characteristics of depleted gas reservoirs are usually well known since they already had wells on them. The maximum pressure and geological stability of the area would have been under continuous observation for years. Additionally, since natural gas had been stored in the reservoir for millions of years, there are few concerns about the geological impact of using the facility.

Another advantage of depleted reservoirs is that many still have the equipment that was originally used to remove the gas. Since this equipment can be reused, it allows for substantially lower start-up costs than buying all of the equipment again.

Finally, storage facilities and reservoirs tend to have similar constraints on unrecoverable gas. Because unrecoverable gas can't be removed from a reservoir, it will still exist in the storage volume. As a result, a depleted reservoir won't require additional gas to be injected to form an unrecoverable gas barrier. When natural gas was exceptionally cheap in the early 1980s, pumping in unrecoverable natural gas was not a huge economic concern. However, because natural gas prices have risen substantially, unrecoverable gas is now an important economic consideration.

Overall, depleted gas reservoirs are quick and cost effective to bring into service. Historically, depleted natural gas reservoirs have been the most abundant form of natural gas storage. Given the cost effectiveness of reusing an existing gas reservoir, alternative storage facilities must either provide better functionality or have a location advantage than a depleted gas reservoir. Depleted gas reservoirs need to reserve about 50 percent of their total capacity as a gas "cushion." Salt caverns, which only need to reserve about 33 percent, provide better performance characteristics. Aquifers, which often need to reserve about 80 percent of their capacity, are the least desirable type of storage facility.

Salt Caverns

Underground salt caverns offer excellent properties for natural gas storage. They are more expensive to develop than depleted gas reservoirs, but have much better performance characteristics. These caverns allow very little gas to leak out, have extremely strong walls, and are generally resistant to damage. Essentially, they are high pressure storage vessels. They can operate at higher pressures than the other types of storage facilities, allowing gas to be cycled in and out of the facility more often. This is a huge benefit for customers who require erratic supplies of natural gas.

Storage facilities are constructed by removing salt from deposits and reusing the remaining cavern for gas storage. The best type of salt deposit to use for a storage facility is a "salt dome," which can be several miles across and over a mile high. Typically, salt domes are formed when a marine basin evaporates and is covered with sediment. The salt, being lighter than the surrounding sediment, will tend to move upward, forming a dome.

Salt domes are typically excavated by injecting water into the rock formation and dissolving the salt deposit. This leaves a large empty cavern suitable for storing natural gas. The usual method for doing this is to drill down into the formation and cycle enough clean water through the salt deposit to fully dissolve the softer materials. After all the salt is dissolved, the remaining walls are extremely strong—they are the rock layers that proved impenetrable to the rising salt formation.

In areas where it is not possible to find well-formed domes, it may be possible to form storage facilities out of salt beds. These beds are much shallower, thinner formations, usually a couple hundred feet in height. Because of their wide, thin construction, salt bed caverns are much more prone to collapse than caverns formed from salt domes. Compared to salt domes, salt beds also contain a higher quantity of insoluble rock. This slows down the speed at which gas can flow inside the facility. In general, salt beds tend to be more expensive to excavate and maintain than salt domes.

Because salt caverns store natural gas at high pressure, they require more specialized equipment than other types of storage facilities. Salt caverns are often pressurized to double the level of a standard gas pipeline. As a result, the pipes and fittings used to extract the gas from the facility often need to be much heavier grade than standard pipeline equipment. In addition, since the temperature of gas increases with pressure, gas being discharged from a salt cavern can be extremely hot. All of the pipes, fittings, and valves need to be rated for very high temperature gases, and they should be resistant to the greater corrosion that comes with higher temperatures.

From an economic perspective, salt caverns are much more profitable than the other types of natural gas storage. The ability to insert and remove gas quickly allows salt caverns to benefit from short-term shortages in the natural gas supply. Combined with a fast-starting gas turbine electrical generator, they can provide a good way to benefit from short-term spikes in electricity prices too.

Aquifers

Aquifers are the least desirable and most expensive type of natural gas storage. Aquifer storage facilities are water reservoirs modified to store natural gas. They are only built if they have a large geographical advantage—they are in the right place when nothing else is available. Most of the gas in aquifer storage facilities is unrecoverable. They have the lowest percentage of working gas to total volume of any storage facility, and the slowest injection/withdrawal cycle of any storage type.

Since there is no gas present when a facility is built, a large volume of gas must be placed into a facility. Compared to other storage types, there is also less leeway to remove the gas cushion before impairing the ability of the facility to operate. All existing aquifer facilities were built when natural gas was relatively inexpensive, and it would be difficult to economically make the initial investment in unrecoverable gas today.

The U.S. government has placed restrictions on building new facilities in areas where the water is usable for human consumption or irrigation. This policy, combined with the limited economic viability of aquifers, has made it unlikely that substantial future development in aquifer storage will occur.

Common Terms

Deliverability. The ability to pull gas out of a storage facility for sale. The deliverability of a facility depends on the amount of gas in the facility. When the facility is nearly full, the deliverability will be at its highest.

Cycling. The number of times that a storage facility can be emptied and refilled within a calendar year. For example, many storage facilities are a single cycle facility. It takes so long for them to fill up that they cannot sell gas in both the summer and the winter. If they sold gas in the summer, they wouldn't have enough time to fill up again prior to the winter season.

Gas Storage Capacity. The storage capacity of a facility is typically broken into two pieces: base gas and working gas. Base gas is not normally removed from the facility. The working gas is the gas added and removed during the injection and delivery cycle.

Injection Capacity. The speed at which gas can be placed back into a facility. The more gas in the facility, the longer it takes to inject additional gas. Injection capability is just the opposite of *deliverability*—it is lowest when the facility is nearly full.

Trading Example: Natural Gas Storage

A high performance natural gas storage facility in the New Jersey area has just been constructed. The storage capacity in the facility is being auctioned off to the highest bidder.

1. **The Opportunity.** There is a limited amount of natural gas storage facilities anywhere on the East Coast. Because of this, natural gas prices see more cyclical variations than other parts of the country. Capacity in the storage facility is being sold at auction, so it is necessary to develop an appropriate bid.

2. **The Intuition.** A natural gas storage facility will allow a trader to buy during periods of low demand, hold the gas, and resell it during periods of high demand.

(Continued)

3. **The Strategy.** The valuation of the strategy will examine a number of trades limited by the physical characteristics of the storage facility. The best combination of trades will determine the value of the bid.

- **Seasonal Trade.** The largest amount of gas will be purchased during the spring and fall months, when natural gas is normally inexpensive. It will be resold in the summer and winter, when prices are higher. Many storage facilities can only empty and refill once a year—they can't meet both the summer and winter demand. However, in this case, the facility is a high performance facility that can be emptied and refilled twice in a single year.

- **Weekday/Weekend.** The trader is also considering buying gas on weekends and reselling it during weekdays. This will affect the seasonal trade by slowing down the speed at which gas is injected and removed from the facility. Instead of seven days of insertion or removal of gas, there will only be three net days of insertion or delivery for the seasonal trade. On the two weekend days, gas will be placed into the facility so it can be sold on a weekday.

An optimization of trading will be required to determine which combination of trades is expected to be the most profitable. For example, the operational limits of the facility might make it impossible to do both the weekday/weekend trade and the seasonal trade throughout the year.

4. **The Risks.** Since this is a competitive bidding process, there is a risk of doing the analysis wrong and bidding too high. If that happens, the trader will probably end up winning the auction and overpaying. This is an asymmetric risk, because if the bid was much too low, someone else would always win the auction. Traders use the term the "winner's curse" to describe this possibility.

Another risk of the trade is a change in seasonal dynamics. For example, in the mid-1980s there were very few natural-gas-fired power plants. As a result, there was relatively little demand for natural gas during the summer. Natural gas was almost exclusively used during the winter by homeowners. Twenty-five years of building natural-gas-fired power plants has changed that dynamic. Natural gas is now a major fuel used for electrical generation. As a result, summer natural gas prices have skyrocketed.

5. **Executing the Trade.** Owning a physical storage facility means hiring an operations team to coordinate the physical delivery and sale of natural gas. This is no longer a financial deal—it is a 20-year commitment to keep a staff in place to service this contract. Even if a lot of the trading is arranged ahead of time in the futures market, there will be a substantial amount of daily housekeeping required.

6. **The Results.** One side benefit of owning a storage facility wasn't mentioned yet. In addition to being a potential profit opportunity, a storage facility gives a natural gas trader the ability to deliver and receive natural gas. This might make it possible for the trader to enter into other trading opportunities. For example, the trader might decide to sell other traders insurance that their natural gas deliveries would occur. He would make an up-front premium for the insurance, and if he had to cover deliveries in the event of a shortfall, he wouldn't have to resort to buying the gas on the (probably skyrocketing) spot market.

Natural Gas Storage Reports

The U.S. government agency responsible for producing natural gas statistics is the Energy Information Agency. It publishes a weekly report that indicates the amount of natural gas currently being stored. There are two main parts to this report. The first part is a graph that shows the total amount of natural gas currently in storage relative to the past five years (Figure 5.2.7). The second part is a table indicating the amount of natural gas stored in each region (Figure 5.2.8). A map shows the geographical breakout of the regions (Figure 5.2.9).

Working Gas in Underground Storage Compared to a Five-Year Range

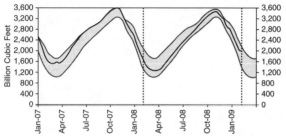

On the chart is a graphical depiction of the current stored gas compared to a historical range. The gray area indicates the maximum and minimum amounts of gas over a five-year range. This chart is useful to give a good indication of whether natural gas supplies are high or low on a historical basis.

Figure 5.2.7. Stored gas compared to five-year range (*Source:* Energy Information Agency [December 2008])

Region	Stocks in Billion Cubic Feet (Bcf)			Historical Comparisons			
	2/13/2009	2/6/2009	Change	Year Age (02/13/08)		5-Year (2004–2009) Average	
				Stocks (Bcf)	% Change	Stocks (Bcf)	% Change
East	947	972	−25	986	−4	1,004	−5.7
West	312	327	−15	216	44.4	243	28.4
Producing	737	721	16	617	19.4	595	23.5
Total	1,996	2,020	−24	1,819	9.7	1,841	8.4

Figure 5.2.8. Stored gas report broken out by region (*Source:* Energy Information Agency [December 2008])

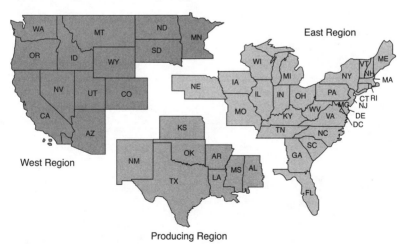

Figure 5.2.9. Map of the regions that correspond with the natural gas storage report (*Source:* Energy Information Agency [December 2008])

Common Terms

Base Gas.   The natural gas that is used to keep the pressure in the storage facility high enough that gas can be removed quickly. Base gas is sometimes called cushion gas.

City Gate.   The connection between a transcontinental pipeline and a local distribution pipeline is called a city gate. This is a special type of hub where gas exits the transcontinental pipeline system. Storage facilities are often located near city gates to hold any excess gas coming out of the pipeline.

Cushion Gas.   See Base Gas.

Flared Gas.   When gas can't be stored or transported, it has to be disposed of by burning. This commonly occurs at production sites and gas processing plants.

Heating Value.   The average number of British Thermal Units (Btus) contained by a specific volume of gas. This has to be determined by testing fuel samples.

Hub.   An interconnection between two or more transcontinental pipelines is called a hub. Hubs often have nearby storage facilities to help keep pipelines operating full time.

Working Gas.   The gas in the storage facility in excess of the base gas. This gas might not be removed at all or it might be removed and replaced several times.

5.3

LIQUEFIED NATURAL GAS

 30-Second Summary

Purpose

This section introduces liquefied natural gas (LNG).

Summary

LNG facilities convert methane from a gas into a liquid that takes up much less volume. Allowing natural gas to take up less volume makes it economical to transport overseas with transport ships. As a result, LNG technology is closely associated with a global market for natural gas. Although there are few trading opportunities specifically related to liquefied natural gas, LNG is having a big effect on the structure of the natural gas market. On a small scale, LNG storage provides an alternative to traditional natural gas storage facilities.

There has been an active LNG trade in the Pacific region for many years. However, the opening up of LNG regasification plants in the North American and European markets has provided a much larger consumer base for LNG producers. This increased customer base allows aggressive investment into better liquefaction technology that, in turn, spurs even more demand. As a result, LNG is rapidly becoming a major factor in natural gas trading after several decades of relative obscurity.

Key Topics

- Liquified natural gas is produced by freezing methane to –260°F.
- Being able to turn methane into a liquid is creating a global market for natural gas (methane) to replace the isolated regional markets that have historically defined the natural gas market.
- As liquefaction and gasification technologies become more energy efficient, LNG becomes more efficient, and more economical too.

Natural gas can be converted into a liquid at standard atmospheric pressures by lowering its temperature to –260°F. This reduces the volume of natural gas to 1/610th of its gaseous volume. Being more compact allows liquid natural gas to be stored or transported when regular storage facilities and pipelines are not available. Although small scale transportation is still not cost effective, cargo ships can transfer enough fuel at a low enough cost that LNG is becoming an economical alternative to domestic production of hard-to-extract natural gas.

The driving force behind liquefied natural gas is the expectation that the United States and European markets will soon require natural gas imports. The United States and Europe consume a large portion of the world's natural gas but have only a small percent of the world's proven natural gas reserves. Sooner or later it will become cheaper for those regions to import natural gas from other parts of the world than to extract gas from domestic reserves. Improved technology and consumer demand tend to reinforce one another. Increasing the number of LNG customers makes it economical to research better LNG technology, which reduces the cost of importing natural gas and in turn spurs more customer interest.

Natural gas producers benefit from being able to transport their natural gas overseas. Historically, the only real markets for LNG were the Asian markets of Japan, South Korea, and Taiwan. Unless natural gas could be shipped to those markets, a natural gas well without a pipeline connecting it to a major consuming region was stranded. The natural gas couldn't be sold. Even if the gas could be liquefied, there were only a few markets that could accept delivery of the liquefied gas. However, opening the North American and European markets to LNG changes that dynamic. Shipments can enter these markets from almost anywhere and feed into their transcontinental pipeline systems.

The LNG market allows natural gas producers to monetize their investment. They can build an LNG liquefaction terminal, and then sign long-term agreements to sell their product overseas. Instead of sitting on a natural gas field that might or might not ever be worth something in the future, producers can build a pipeline to the nearest LNG terminal and ship their product as a liquid into a major consumer market. This gets low cost producers access to the best consumer markets, and it provides them with money to search for new supplies.

There are three main steps in the LNG process: *liquefaction, transportation,* and *regasification.*

- **Liquefaction and Exporting.** Liquefaction plants are located near regions where natural gas is produced. Short-range pipelines transfer the gas from wells to the liquefaction plant. The liquefaction plant cools the natural gas down to –260°F, then loads it into storage containers for transfer to a specially designed tanker ships.

    Bringing natural gas to –260°F is an extremely energy intensive process. A considerable amount of energy is consumed during the liquefaction and subsequent reheating processes. From a climate perspective, the CO_2 emissions resulting from this processing has to be included in the greenhouse gas emissions of LNG as a fuel source.

- **Transportation.** LNG tankers have to be specifically designed to handle extremely cold liquids and keep them insulated. Even then, some of the liquid methane will convert back into a gas. A small percentage of the natural gas will be lost in transportation for this reason. Faster journeys and cryogenic systems to refreeze the boiled-off gas can reduce these losses.
- **Regasification and Importing.** Once LNG is transported, it must be turned back into a gas before it is delivered to customers. This is usually done at a regasification plant. This plant transfers the liquefied natural gas from the tanker ships and stores it in specially designed containers to keep the LNG at low temperature until it is ready to be warmed up. After it is warmed up, it can be placed into a pipeline for delivery to customers.

Concerns

The safety of LNG storage and regasification facilities is the source of major controversy. It is one of the primary reasons for the limited number of LNG terminals worldwide, and a continuing reason why politicians block new facilities. LNG facilities contain a tremendous amount of fuel in a confined space. The concern is that these facilities could cause catastrophic damage in the event of a disaster.

The proponents of LNG claim a strong safety record. Like all natural gas, LNG is primarily composed of methane. Methane is an odorless, nontoxic gas that we breathe every day. It won't poison the environment or kill wildlife in the event of a spill. Unless it is in a contained environment, liquefied natural gas is also not explosive. Although it can burn, it doesn't transition rapidly enough from liquid phase to gas phase to form the overpressure necessary to form an explosion. In the event of a leak, LNG only combusts when it exists at the right ratio of methane to air—like normal natural gas.

Peak Shaving Units

As the technology for liquefying and regasification gets less expensive, LNG becomes an attractive alternative to more traditional methods of storing natural gas. By turning it into a liquid, the amount of storage space required by a storage facility is dramatically reduced. This allows natural gas to be stored in areas that don't have the proper geological formations required for traditional storage facilities. From an investment perspective, these facilities are valued similarly to normal storage facilities.

Trading Example: Peak Shaving Unit

Small scale LNG storage facilities can provide a way to buy natural gas at periods of low demand for use during heavy demand periods.

1. **The Opportunity.** A company owns natural gas peaking generators and is looking to lock in a fuel supply. They are considering investing in a small scale LNG-based storage facility. To reduce the amount of energy consumed by liquefaction and reheating, this facility is partially powered by a thermal solar facility. The solar installation heats rock salt around 600°F, liquefies it, and then stores it in an insulated container so that the sun doesn't have to be shining at the time the gas is warmed up again.

2. **The Intuition.** This is a combination of two technologies: a thermal solar installation and a small scale LNG facility. Both facilities need insulated storage. Liquefying and heating natural gas requires a tremendous amount of energy. However, most of those energy requirements can be met by the thermal solar installation. The size of the solar facility determines how much heating and cooling can be done.

3. **The Strategy.** This facility will operate like any other storage facility. However, instead of being located in an underground rock formation, the natural gas will be stored in insulated containers. Since this does not require a lot of room, it is easier to locate this facility close to an electrical consuming region that often experiences congestion. The combination of being able to buy fuel at low cost, use solar power to handle the ongoing energy requirements, and then resell the electricity at the highest possible price combine to make this an interesting investment.

4. **Valuation.** This valuation incorporates elements of several other types of models. The ability to sell power makes this installation look a lot like a tolling agreement. However, the LNG storage allows a natural gas to be purchased ahead of time and be on hand at the exact time it is most valuable.

6.1

VALUE AT RISK

30-Second Summary

Purpose

This section is an overview of an important part of risk management—how to create a meaningful, high level summary of trading risk without going into a lot of detail.

Summary

The most common measure of financial risk is Value at Risk (VAR). This quantity answers the question, "What is the size of my investment?" or "How much money do I have at risk?" For many financial contracts it is unclear how to describe the size of the financial exposure. For example, it is difficult to compare a $100,000 stock portfolio with a forward agreement to buy 5,000 barrels of oil at $65 in eight months. Some shared factor has to be used to describe these contracts; VAR uses the likely change in the dollar value of the contracts (P&L volatility). This is not a comprehensive measure of risk, so a VAR analysis is typically done in conjunction with more detailed analysis.

Key Topics

- Value at Risk describes the size of an investment.
- Value at Risk is primarily based on mark-to-market accounting and an analysis of P&L volatility.
- By design, a summary report like VAR obscures or ignores individual trades. Even though this measure doesn't describe those risks, they still exist.
- VAR analysis is almost always done in conjunction with more detailed examinations of risk like *stress testing* or a *worst-case-scenario* analysis.
- A large VAR indicates a *larger* investment rather than a good or bad *quality* of investment.

Risk, as a term used in general speech, means a potential for danger. In the financial markets, more specific terms need to be used. *Market risk* refers to the likely size of a profit or loss (P&L) that will occur with a specific probability in some time frame. For example, a trading firm might define risk as the threshold that daily P&L exceeds once a month on average. Although the meanings of "risk" and "financial risk" are similar, they are not the same, and this often causes confusion.

Value at Risk, abbreviated VAR, is a "big picture" summary of the combined risk of an organization.[1] It is a way to describe the size of an investment. For example, someone might describe a stock investment as "I bought $100,000 worth of stock for my retirement account." This works for stocks, but not all investments are so easily described: A forward contract to purchase 1,000 barrels of oil at $75 in six months only requires a small margin payment initially. The payoff of the contract will depend on the difference between the price of oil and $75. The problem comes from the fact that neither the initial margin payment nor the $75,000 face value of the contract can be combined with the $100,000 stock investment to describe the risk of the combined portfolio. Value at Risk provides a way to estimate that "size."

As with using the size of a stock investment, VAR is an important way to answer the question, "How much money is involved?" This is a good starting point for any financial discussion. However, that information alone is not sufficient to determine whether an investment is good or bad. VAR is not a measure of investment quality. Just as a large investment may or may not perform better than a small investment, a large VAR portfolio is neither better nor worse than a portfolio with a small VAR.

The biggest problem with VAR is that people want to use it to describe the possibility of loss. VAR is the wrong tool to use for that analysis. Often, this is couched in terms like "We are only worried about downside risk." The problem is that big losses usually do not occur commonly enough to be predicted through statistics. For instance, if a trader has agreed to sell power to a consumer, the trader is at risk of a spike in prices. It's relatively easy to see how an equipment failure at a baseload power plant during a heat wave could cause a spike in prices. However, unless that specific combination of events has happened previously, neither historical analysis nor statistical modeling are good ways to identify this risk.

The two parts commonly associated with a VAR analysis are *mark-to-market accounting* and an *analysis of profit and loss volatility.* Typically, the term "risk of a portfolio" is synonymous with its P&L volatility. This provides an alternate way to measure the size of an investment. As a result, VAR analysis is commonplace in financial institutions and provides an easy way to examine how mixed investment portfolios change over time. However, because of its limitations, VAR analysis is almost always done in conjunction with other types of analysis.

---

[1] VAR is pronounced "var" and rhymes with "car."

A High Level Summary

The purpose of VAR is to give a simple description of risk. For example, a VAR report might be: "Once a month the trading desk can be expected to make or lose at least $1 million over a one day period." This description is both meaningful and short enough to be conveyed to a large audience. As a single number, it is simple enough to use in daily reports and easy to examine for trends. For example, if the VAR estimate had fallen from $20 million to $1 million in the past week, this would represent a significant decline in the risk (and probably size) of the portfolio.

There are four parts to a VAR description:

1. The *frequency* at which some event will occur. Since there are approximately 20 trading days in a month, the frequency of a *once a month* daily move is one day out of 20. Translating that to percentages, a 1-in-20 chance means an event that occurs 5 percent of the time. More commonly, this is described as a move that exceeds 95 percent of the daily observations.
2. A description of the *time horizon* of the expected move. In this example, the change in P&L is measured over a one-day period. Another possible time horizon might be a weekly change.
3. A description of the *sidedness* of the move. In the example, the P&L can go up or down, so this is a two-sided VAR estimate. If only losses were being examined, it would be a one-sided estimate.
4. A description of the *magnitude* of the move. The magnitude of the expected move in the example was up or down by $1 million.

Because it is so simple, a VAR report does not include a lot of details. For example, it doesn't give any information about what will happen if the price of oil doubles or the stock market crashes. It also doesn't give any information about how bad things could get in the event of a really bad loss. VAR also gives the minimum threshold for a move that can be expected with some frequency. In the example, a daily profit or loss of *at least* $1 million was expected once a month. However, the report did not give a lot of insight into whether the move is likely to be $1 million, $2 million, or $10 million.

Mark-to-Market Accounting

Mark-to-market accounting is the process of using the current *market price* to value assets. The market price is the price that an asset could fetch if it were to be sold into the market that day. In practice, this usually means that prices are based on recently published exchange quotes. In some cases, where published prices aren't available, the portfolio may be marked to a theoretical price called a *mark-to-model* price. Mark-to-market accounting is common in trading organizations because it eliminates many ways to misrepresent the state of a portfolio. It is often forced onto energy portfolios when mark-to-market accounting is used in other parts of a trading firm. However, in energy trading, mark-to-market accounting has some disadvantages that are important to understand in a risk management context.

Before discussing the disadvantages, there is a big advantage to using mark-to-market accounting—it is fairly intuitive for most assets. If an asset is purchased for $100 and the same asset starts selling for $120, under mark-to-market accounting it will show a $20 profit. The alternative, *accrual accounting*, keeps assets marked to their purchase price until they are actually sold. Accrual accounting can be misleading in the cases of long-dated assets because the value of those assets aren't regularly updated. For a book that is actively traded in a liquid market, mark-to-market accounting accurately and clearly represents the economics of the book.

On the downside, mark-to-market accounting assumes there is a liquid, fair market for price discovery. It tends to fail catastrophically when markets can be manipulated or are illiquid. Most of the models discussed in this book—power plants, storage facilities, and almost everything modeled as an option—are not actively traded in a liquid market. The last purchase of an asset may not be at all related to the long-term economics of an existing facility. For instance, a corporate restructuring might transfer a power plant between two companies at low cost.

The unintended consequences of choosing mark-to-market accounting can represent a serious business risk in their own right. For example, many investment funds force a mandatory liquidation when VAR limits are exceeded. In an illiquid market, it may not be possible to sell an expensive asset immediately. If other traders hold the same type of asset, and anyone actually sells for zero, this can wreak havoc in the marketplace. A chain reaction of traders liquidating profitable assets can ensue. A big change in price increases the risk (as measured by VAR) of an asset. Coupled with risk limits that force liquidations, mark-to-market accounting badly exacerbates illiquid market conditions.

Mixing mark-to-market instruments with *accrued* instruments also creates problems. An extreme example might be a power plant that has completely locked in fuel supplies and sold its power for the next 20 years using OTC forwards. The power plant is hedged—there should be limited market risk or cash flows prior to the date of electricity delivery. However, if the power plant receives accrual accounting and the hedges are mark-to-market, large "phantom" profits and losses will make the book look substantially riskier.

How to Manipulate Mark-to-Market Accounting to Manage Earnings!

Mark-to-market accounting is only safe to use in liquid markets where there is enough trading to guarantee rational prices. For illiquid assets, mark-to-model accounting is a much more conservative choice for calculating profits and losses. Not only does mark-to-model accounting eliminate the risk of some other trader liquidating at illogical prices, but it also limits the ability of traders to play accounting games to smooth out earnings.

Consider two traders at rival firms that recently had large losses on their energy trading desks. If those losses are reported to the risk committee of their respective firms, they will be forced to curtail some of their trading and will get smaller performance-based bonuses. So they each agree to buy a small amount of an illiquid asset held by the other at a high price. They don't need to transact with each other at all.

By making a trade at the high price, the other trader will be able to mark a profit of the illiquid asset. The actual size of the trade used to set prices can be very small. If the traders are smart enough to make small trades in a large number of illiquid assets—particularly ones they don't own themselves—this manipulation can be very difficult to catch.

This type of abuse can be eliminated if the trades are marked to a model price instead of a market price. That way, traders have neither the incentive nor the ability to manipulate their reported earnings.

Calculating Value at Risk

Standard definitions of risk are based on the concept that prices can be assigned to assets through mark-to-market accounting, and that those price changes lead to either profits or losses (P&L). Given that assumption, it is possible to define the *risk* of a portfolio as the expected volatility of its profits and losses. In this way, P&L provides a common denominator for almost any type of investment.

VAR summarizes the risk of a portfolio by predicting the size of P&L movements that will occur with a specific frequency. It will use a single number to describe either a distribution or a bunch of distributions added together. For example, since there are approximately 20 trading days in a month, a P&L movement at least as big as the one at the 95 percent frequency can be expected to occur, on average, at least once a month. As a result, a 95 percent level might be chosen to describe the entire distribution. There are three main steps to calculating a VAR number, which are depicted in Figure 6.1.1.

1. Construct a distribution of possible P&L moves (usually by examining what types of moves have happened in the past).
2. Turn all the moves into positive numbers, and sort the P&L into a new distribution.
3. Find the value in the nth percentile of the distribution (the 95th and 99th percentiles are popular choices for VAR).

Not everyone uses the same frequency for VAR. Some people prefer points that are more likely to be accurate and can be checked commonly, while others prefer numbers more representative of a worst case scenario. However, by picking a single point, VAR produces a simpler estimate of risk than having to use an entire distribution of predicted results. VAR gives up accuracy for simplicity. In many cases, different assets can have the same VAR (Figure 6.1.2).

The methodology for calculating the percentile also can vary between firms. Some risk managers prefer to examine only losses, while others prefer to look at the volatility of both profits and losses (Figure 6.1.3). If only losses are examined, the VAR is called a *one-sided VAR*. If both profits and losses are examined, it is called a

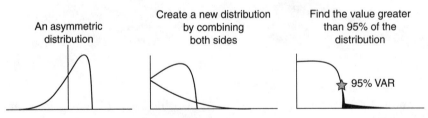

Figure 6.1.1.   Example of how a one-sided VAR is calculated

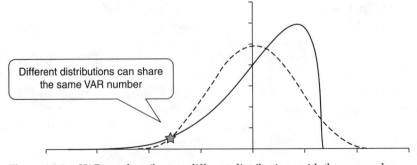

Figure 6.1.2.   VAR can describe two different distributions with the same value

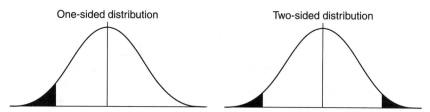

Figure 6.1.3.   In a one-sided distribution, all of the samples come from one side (usually losses); in a two-sided distribution, outlier events are examined from both profits and losses

two-sided VAR. A two-sided VAR will force an asset to have the same VAR whether it is long or short; a one-sided VAR will have different VARs depending on whether an asset is bought or sold. Having a single VAR per asset is useful when combining portfolios—buying and selling the same asset should show zero VAR.

Weaknesses of VAR

Because VAR is a single number, it has some limitations: it abstracts away the fundamental behavior of a portfolio. Typically, P&L is not normally distributed—there isn't an equal chance of making and losing money. Many energy assets—particularly those that can be modeled by options—have asymmetrical payoffs.

For example, a peaking power plant is going to lay idle for most of the year—it will lose money regularly whenever it is inactive. In all but the summer months, small operational charges will accumulate daily. A couple times a year—usually hot summer afternoons—the power plant will have the opportunity to make large windfall profits as it is pressed into duty, as shown in Figure 6.1.4. This is an example of a portfolio that is "long volatility"—a portfolio that benefits from large P&L movements and increasing volatility.

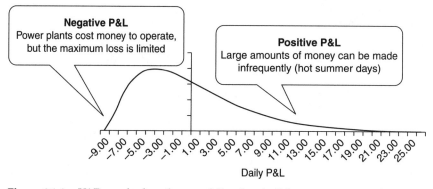

Figure 6.1.4.   VAR poorly describes portfolios that don't have symmetric risks.

Conclusion

VAR is an approximation—being simple means that it gets implemented and examined regularly. However, it is not going to handle all types of portfolios well. Sometimes additional analysis will be required. There are so many possible special cases that no general model will be able to address them all. This doesn't make VAR worthless, just limited. It is useful precisely because it is a simple measure.

Combining VAR Estimates

Combining VAR numbers for a lot of assets can be complicated. The correlation between the portfolios will determine if the risks add or subtract. There are some rules of thumb that can be used as a guideline. First, VAR is always a positive number—risk (volatility) can be zero, but never less than zero. Next, unless two assets are perfectly correlated, their combined VAR will be less risky than the sum of their individual VARs. Finally, a combined VAR will usually never be less than the difference between the individual VARs.

For example, if a portfolio with a $500 VAR is combined with a portfolio with a $100 VAR, the combined VAR will be somewhere between $400 and $600. If the risks offset each other, the VAR will decrease. This will lead to a VAR less than $500. If the risks do not offset, the VAR will be greater than $500.

If one-sided estimates are used, it is possible different VARs will be assigned to the same position depending on whether it is long or short. This is particularly common in options books since they have asymmetric long/short payoffs. This causes a problem when one-sided VAR estimates are used—when long and short option positions are combined, the sum of the VAR won't equal zero. Sometimes there are good reasons to use one-sided distributions. However, operationally it makes consolidating risk calculations less reliable. Keeping VAR as a volatility measure avoids a lot of problems.

6.2

Deltas, Gammas, and Other Greeks

 30-Second Summary

Purpose

This section introduces *sensitivity analysis* and the vocabulary used to indicate sensitivity (various terms with Greek symbols).

Summary

Sensitivity analysis is a way of estimating how much a trading book will go up or down when certain events occur. For example, what happens to P&L if the price of oil goes up by $1, or the spread between New York and Henry Hub natural gas widens by $5? There are five common measures of sensitivity, collectively called the Greeks: Delta, Gamma, Vega, Theta, and Rho.

Key Topics

- Sensitivity analysis is a way to describe the likely profit and loss resulting from various events.
- Most sensitivity is described by Greek letters that come from option pricing formulas.

It is often necessary to describe a portfolio with more precision than is provided by a VAR analysis. Traders often need to answer questions like, "Do I expect to make or lose money if the price of oil continues to rise?" or, "How much money do I expect to make or lose if an unlikely event becomes more likely?" These types of questions can be answered by a sensitivity analysis, which estimates the sensitivity of a trading position to something else. Most commonly, traders want to estimate the profit or loss that will occur if or when some benchmark goes up or down. In other cases they will want to know the how their risk will change if some type of event happens.

Many questions about risk are common enough to have acquired a well-known name, usually a letter in the Greek alphabet. These questions can all be expressed as the sensitivity of one quantity to changes in another. Because they are commonly represented by Greek letters, these factors are collectively called the *Greeks*. A "Greek" is never a stand-alone piece of information like a price. Greeks are always a comparison between two assets (one of which is usually called an *asset* and the other an *underlying*). The value of the asset is sensitive to changes in the underlying.

Here are the five common measures of sensitivity, or Greeks:

1. **Delta.** The P&L, or change in the value of an asset, that occurs when the underlying changes in the price.
2. **Gamma.** The change in an asset's Delta when the underlying changes in price.
3. **Vega.** The P&L that occurs when the volatility of the underlying changes.
4. **Theta.** The P&L that occurs from the passage of some period of time (usually one day).
5. **Rho.** The P&L that occurs when the interest rate changes.

Velocity: Delta

Delta is the most widespread Greek. It relates the change in value of a portfolio (the profit or loss) to the movement in some kind of benchmark. For example, a portfolio of stocks might be related to the movement of the S&P 500 index, or the change in an option's value related to the change in price of its underlying.

Mathematically, Delta is the first derivative of price relative to some underlying. A good way to think about Delta (or any other first derivative) is as a car trip. P&L is similar to distance, and Delta is similar to velocity. The distance traveled by the car, its velocity, and its acceleration are all related. By comparing the distance away from home at different times, it is possible to determine the average speed the car had to travel between observations. The velocity of the car is the first derivative of distance relative to time. For example, if a car traveled 60 miles (a distance) in one hour (a change in the underlying), it had to average 60 miles per hour (velocity). A Delta works the same way and serves the same purpose. It is important to know both how far away you are from your starting point (your profit) and how quickly that profit is changing (velocity or Delta).

Acceleration: Gamma

Gamma, the second Greek, is similar to acceleration. It indicates how quickly the Delta (speed of movement) is changing. This is often more important than Delta. Gamma isn't as directly informative as Delta. However, it indicates a more crucial piece of information—what will happen to a portfolio when the market goes crazy and the underlying

	Driving a Car	**Trading Energy**
Value	**Distance (miles)**	**Price**
	Miles away from home	Value of the asset
First Derivative	**Velocity**	**Delta**
Change in the value per change in some other value	Velocity (speed) is the change in distance per unit of some other value (time). For example, velocity might be measured in miles per hour.	Delta is the change in value relative to a change in the price of the underlying. For example, the option will become more valuable if the stock price goes up in value.
Second Derivative	**Acceleration**	**Gamma**
Change in the First Derivative per change in some other value	Change in velocity per unit time. It is in units of distance per time squared. For example, acceleration might be described as: "The car can accelerate from *zero to 60 in five seconds.*"	Gamma is the amount that the Delta changes per change in the underlying.

changes substantially in price. Gamma indicates the exposure of a portfolio to changes in price—whether a portfolio will get more or less risky when the market really starts to move.

Again using a car example, it's useful to know that a car is going 20 miles an hour on a residential street when it passes a radar gun. That's a very important piece of information. However, it's equally important to know if that car is accelerating rapidly. Even though it might be going 20 mph at the time of the observation, if the car is accelerating fast enough to go from zero to 120 mph in 12 seconds (maybe it's a race car), the driver is still driving in an unsafe manner.

Changes in Volatility: Vega

Vega is the term used to represent the sensitivity of a portfolio to the change in some type of volatility. This is mostly important to a portfolio containing a lot of options. Anyone who is familiar with the Greek alphabet will recognize that Vega isn't actually a Greek letter. It's a star in the constellation Lyra. However, since there aren't any Greek letters that start with V, the term "Vega" was co-opted into the financial alphabet.

Options (and financial assets modeled as options) are often extremely sensitive to volatility. Option pricing is usually based on the concept that prices diffuse outward from a starting point. Small changes in this dispersion pattern will have a big effect on the value of an option. Since there is no downside to holding an option, an increased chance of a windfall profit makes volatility extremely valuable to an option buyer. For an option seller, just the opposite will occur. As a result, an option buyer is often described as long volatility (benefiting if volatility rises). An option seller will be short volatility (benefiting if volatility declines).

The Passage of Time: Theta

Theta is another Greek that is primarily important to portfolios that contain option trades. Certain assets, like options, become less valuable with time. The intrinsic value of an option is the value of the option if it is exercised immediately. The rest of the option value depends on the time remaining before the option expires. If there is a long time before expiration, the option is more valuable than if it is almost at expiration. Theta measures the change in the value of an asset due to the passage of time.

The time value of an option depends on its profitability. For example, if an option is out of the money, a long time horizon will give it more opportunities for it to become valuable. This is very helpful for an option buyer. On the other hand, if an option is already very profitable, the time value of the option is less pronounced. At least for a while, volatility will hurt the option holder almost as much as it helps.

All things being equal, option sellers will make a profit for every day that passes since it becomes less likely that they will be required to pay an even larger amount of money. Option buyers will have the opposite problem. They will *bleed* a small amount of money every day, and will need to make money from the underlying instrument changing in price or by volatility increasing.

Interest Rates: Rho

Rho measures the sensitivity of the value of an asset to interest rates. This is primarily important to financial instruments that are very sensitive to interest rates, like bonds. While this quantity is usually less important for energy products than bonds, energy trading often requires tying up a large amount of capital for an extended period. This means it is necessary to compare the relative return of energy investment to alternate investments (like risk-free government bonds). An investment returning 10 percent annually is worth a lot more when the risk-free rate of return is 2 percent than when the risk-free rate is at 20 percent.

6.3

Model Risk

 30-Second Summary

Purpose

This section introduces the concept of model risk—the risk that a valuation model isn't doing its job properly.

Summary

Energy trading is full of models—risk models, pricing models, and asset valuation models, to name a few. These models are a simplification of real life. Because of this, ensuring that models work correctly is a major component of managing risk. It is fairly common for models to break at some point. When this happens, the problem needs to be identified quickly and solved.

Key Topics

- Bad assumptions, parameter estimates, or market data can lead to financial disaster.
- The primary ways to reduce model risk are setting position limits, taking reserves against potential losses, and reviewing models regularly.

Energy traders commonly encounter *model risk*—the risk that either the methodology or assumptions used to value assets becomes invalid. Poor assumptions and incorrectly designed models cause risk management problems in every financial market. However, the complexity of energy models and their extended lifetimes make these problems especially prominent in the energy markets.

All models are less complicated versions of reality. There is always a risk that something vital is left out of a model, or something unnecessary is incorporated. There is a trade-off between model risk and model complexity. Very simple models may not include enough factors to accurately describe reality. On the other hand, simple models are easy for people to understand. It is possible to address model risk by having a lot of people looking for problems. Complex models include more factors but they are harder to understand. It is often unclear when

357

a complex model stops working, and it is irresponsible to assume that people can verify a model they don't understand.

Bad Assumptions

Making bad assumptions is a major cause of modeling errors. Models are a simplification of real life. They are based on an analysis of typical behavior that may or may not be predictive of the future. Real life has exceptions to almost every rule, and it is not always clear where those exceptions are likely to occur. The most dangerous part of a model is getting basic assumptions about how the market operates wrong. If those are indeed wrong, every conclusion made after that is probably invalid too.

Models and the viability of the model's assumptions change over time. If a model lasts 20 years, a lot of things can change. Investments like power plants, pipelines, and natural gas wells all have an extremely long life span. Even when a pricing model is sufficient at first, there is no guarantee that things won't change. Assumptions made years earlier can be invalidated by regulatory changes, population shifts, and technological changes. Exacerbating this problem is the problem of employee turnover—commonly, the original developers of the models have moved to another job or retired before problems develop.

An example of a reality changing underneath a model is daylight savings time. When the energy savings from shifting the clock an hour was first calculated in the mid-1970s, air conditioners were still relatively uncommon. The 1975 study showed that energy use was cut slightly if the clock was shifted in the summer to have more sunlight in the evening. Thirty years later, Indiana finally switched over to daylight savings. Compared to the period before the switch, adopting daylight savings time caused a noticeable increase in that state's power consumption. The widespread adoption of air-conditioning in the intervening years was thought to be the culprit.

Bad Market Data

A second issue that commonly comes up in energy trading is that many physical trading points aren't very liquid. It is possible to trade at places that don't usually have prices. Of course, the price at the time of trading is known. However, any future prices will depend on other people trading at the same location. If no one trades there regularly, it might be a while before another price exists. As a result, illiquid trading locations often need to be approximated by prices at a nearby liquid benchmark. Sometimes this is a good assumption. At other times the expected relationship between a benchmark and an illiquid location breaks down.

Parameter Estimation Errors

Still another modeling problem concerns the estimation of parameters. For example, a spread option will depend on an estimate of the correlation between two assets. In these cases, the correlation can't be readily determined from an independent source. Historical spot prices will underestimate forward volatility. Forward prices overestimate correlation. As a result, it is fairly common for a couple of model parameters to be chosen (fairly arbitrarily) when a model is created. If any of those parameters turn out to be a poorly chosen, the model might change dramatically.

Steps to Reduce Model Risk

Broadly described, there are two approaches to reducing model risk: testing the model and limiting the loss that will occur if the model breaks.

Testing the Model

It is often easier to watch a model for potential problems than to design a foolproof model. *Observation* is always easier than prevention. Having people pay attention to what is happening to a model means that problems can be found quickly. Most problems start to occur months or years before there is a financial loss, making observation a viable solution to most problems. People who depend on the model need to ensure that problems get reported and examined in a timely manner.

However, it is also possible to catch a lot of potential problems by looking at historical data. *Backtesting* is the process of testing a model against as much historical data as possible. A related concept is *stress testing*, which simulates extreme conditions and unusual combinations of events. This is a way to catch combinations of events that might not have happened historically.

Limiting the Loss

If a model can't be trusted—and no model can be completely trusted—it makes sense to limit the total amount of money lost due to a single problem. This can be done by limiting the total amount of risk that can be taken on by a specific type of trading. This enforced diversification is called a *position limit*. Essentially, it is a mandate that a trading desk not place all of its eggs in the same basket.

A second way of limiting risk is to delay recognizing profits from a valuation model. If a model is hemorrhaging money, a lot of attention will get focused on it. Because of the attention, any modeling problems are likely to be found quickly. A more dangerous situation is a model that shows a steady stream of profits. That model has a much higher probability of being ignored. To limit those problems, it is possible to set aside some of those profits to cover the possibility of future losses. This is called taking a *modeling reserve*.

6.4

COUNTERPARTY CREDIT RISK

 30-Second Summary

Purpose

This section introduces counterparty credit risk.

Summary

A large number of energy trades are contractual agreements made between two trading partners. Both partners depend on the other partner to meet their contractual obligations. *Counterparty credit risk* describes the magnitude and likelihood of danger. This risk is commonly separated into two pieces. The first piece is being able to describe the magnitude of the risk (*credit exposure*), and second is the likelihood of default (*credit quality*).

Key Topics

- Credit exposure is the magnitude of a company's contractual obligations with a trading partner.
- Credit quality is the likelihood that a company will default on its obligations.
- Having credit limits that are too strict will hamper a firm's ability to do business. However, limits that are too loose will expose a trading company to the risk of bankruptcy.

In addition to various types of price and model risks, energy traders are commonly exposed to the danger that their trading partners will be unable to fulfill their obligations. The energy market is full of agreements made directly between two counterparties. Assessing the ability of a trading partner to meet its contractual obligations is crucial to trading energy products.

Credit exposure establishes the magnitude of the risk, and *credit quality* is the likelihood of the risk. Getting this information correct is important. Firms will often have hard limits on how much exposure they can have to a single counterparty. If estimates of loss are too high, business will be hurt because trading has to be curtailed. However, if the estimates are too low, there is risk of catastrophic losses due to a trading partner not fulfilling its obligations.

Credit Exposure

Credit exposure identifies how much money could be lost in the event of a default. At its simplest, calculating credit exposure assumes a complete loss on every contract. This does place an upper bound on the potential loss, but also tends to overestimate its severity. A more accurate estimate includes the possibility of recovering assets through a bankruptcy proceeding or receiving partial payment. For example, certain types of debts (like preferred debt) will have priority over other debts in a bankruptcy proceeding. It is important to understand where the contracts in question fall in the recovery order.

Credit Quality

Credit quality, the other aspect of modeling credit risk, attempts to describe how likely a firm is to default on its payments. This usually needs to be a forward-looking measure since energy contracts commonly last several years. There are a number of ratings agencies that provide credit ratings. These ratings can be augmented by in-house research focusing on a couple of key counterparties. There can be several layers to this analysis—a trading partner's credit risk will depend on the credit quality of its own clients. Also, a company is less likely to default if its large trades have moved in its favor, and more likely to default if trades have moved against it.

A good example of a cascading credit crisis was the bankruptcy of Enron. The single largest energy trader in the world, Enron was almost everyone's largest trading partner. As a result, even companies that didn't trade directly with Enron were exposed to its bankruptcy. When Enron went bankrupt, its assets were frozen. It stopped meeting its financial obligations. As a result, firms that traded with Enron had problems meeting their obligations, and so on. When Enron went bankrupt, the credit quality of many energy trading firms dropped at the same time.

Protecting Against Credit Risk

The most obvious way of avoiding credit risk is to *know your trading partner*. Before trading with someone, most energy trading firms will want to know something about that person or company. For example: What is their line of business? How many assets do they have? What is their business model?

A second way of limiting exposure is to limit the amount of credit that can be extended to a trading partner. Combining payments and receipts is a common way of limiting exposure. In this way, only the net exposure needs to be watched. Another way to limit credit exposure is to have a *credit limit*. A credit limit prevents additional trading when the net exposure to a trading partner gets too large.

A third way to limit credit exposure is to use *collateral*, which is an asset used to guarantee performance of a financial obligation. Typically, collateral is held in trust until the financial obligation is resolved. The collateral remains the property of the person or company guaranteeing performance. It might be in the form of bonds, stocks, or other investments.

If a company doesn't have the assets necessary for collateral and is a fairly high credit risk, it might be required to buy insurance in the form of *credit default swaps* (CDS). There is a trading market specific to credit default swaps where it is possible for a high risk company to pay a low risk company a fee to guarantee the payment of its obligations. This doesn't eliminate credit risk completely, but it does mean a company with a good credit rating is backing the exposure.

Dangers of Limiting Credit Exposure

If credit controls are too strict, it is impossible to conduct an ongoing trading business. A trading firm wants to enter contracts that result in other people owing it money. That is the purpose of its existence. From that regard, it is both impossible and undesirable to completely eliminate credit risk. Companies trade with other companies that want to do business with them. As a result, strict credit limits mean missed trading opportunities and damaged relationships. On the other hand, credit limits are essential to keep yourself out of bankruptcy when a trading partner goes bankrupt or refuses to meet its obligation. Credit limits involve a balancing act between having no limits (and doing lots of business) and having limits (and possibly losing some profit).

AFTERWORD

In the preface to this book, I stated that *there is no substitute for understanding what is actually going on.* This axiom can be applied to almost anything in life. However, as a truism, it is especially applicable to trading, risk management, and energy policy. This is the philosophical core of the book and a key factor to successfully investing in any market.

The reason for this focus is that details are a rich source of trading opportunities. Details are not obstacles to the investment process; rather, they allow traders to pick and choose their investment opportunities. The more complex an issue, the more opportunities exist for trading. Traders don't have to be smarter than everyone else all the time because *they don't have to be invested in the market all the time.* Traders can wait for a good opportunity before investing. Details allow traders to invest only when they have a better than average chance of making money.

However, even when details are perceived as good things, they can still be intimidating. When I first approached the energy market, the sheer number of details made it difficult to understand how the market fit together. In this book, I've tried to subtly introduce two ways of dealing with this problem. I started the book with a high level overview that mapped out where things would go, and then I delved into the details. In each chapter, I typically took the opposite approach— I starting with a couple of specific details, and then I slowly increased their complexity.

Another major theme in this book is the application of quantitative modeling to energy trading. Because there is so much going on in the energy market, the core of quantitative modeling involves eliminating and ignoring some information in favor of concentrating on other information. This is a fairly risky process, and when models fail, it is usually due to bad initial assumptions or bad input data. The only way to prevent these types of errors is to have a large group of people paying attention to details. Obviously, the source of any data and assumptions should be noted in a model. However, the importance of understanding the real world that is being approximated by the model can't be emphasized enough. There is no substitute for having everyone understand what a model is trying to accomplish.

I hope that this book sparks an interest in energy policy and an appreciation for the infrastructure that makes modern life possible. I know it did for me. Starting with the basics of the market and working upward from there made me rethink things that I take for granted. I enjoyed writing this book, and I hope that you enjoyed reading it.

Davis W. Edwards
July 2009

INDEX

Note: page numbers with n indicate a note

A

AC (alternating current), 10–11, 19, 112, 151

Accounting
accrual, 40, 348
mark-to-mark, 35, 39–40
mark-to-market, 66, 346, 347–349
mark-to-model, 348, 349

Accrual accounting, 40, 348

Acid rain, 168

Active budding strategies, generation stack, 264–265

Actual (physical commodity), 64, 77

Actual position, 77

Air conditioner functioning, 182–183

Alpha particle, 307

Alternating current (AC), 10–11, 19, 112, 151

Alternative/renewable energy
geothermal, as alternative energy source, 8–9
hydroelectric power, 8–9, 103, 314–317
nuclear power, 306–310
solar power, 293–300
wind power, 301–305

American options, 204, 215

American Petroleum Institute (API), 129

Analysis in VAR
of earnings volatility, 35
of profit and loss volatility, 346, 349–351

Anthracite, 149

API (American Petroleum Institute), 129

Appalachian Mountains, coal, 157

Appearance of wind farms, 305

Aquifers for natural gas storage, 329, 332, 336–337

Arbitrage, 2, 219, 220

Arbitrage free pricing, 224–227

Arbitrage pricing period extension, 227–228

Asian options, 215

Ask price, 205

Assets
analysis with Greeks, 38–39, 354
liquid/illiquid, 2
more than two assets, spread option, 242
short/long an asset, 5

Associated gas, 130

Assumptions and model risk, 358

At the money, 215

Atomic mass number, 309

Atomic number, 309

Auctions, power
daily, 94, 97–99
day-ahead auctions, 94–95, 260–261, 270–271
electrical trading markets, 7, 94–99
real-time auctions, 95, 260–261, 270–271

Average (*See* Mean)

B

Bachelier, Louis, 218

Backtesting, 359

Band gap, 296

Barrel (bbl), 13, 129

Base gas, 34, 330

Base load power, 248–249

Base load power plants, 248

ABOUT THE AUTHOR

Davis W. Edwards is a managing director at Macquarie Group and is responsible for managing the credit risks of its North American energy investments. Macquarie, Australia's preeminent financial conglomerate, is one of the largest energy trading companies in North America through its subsidiary, Macquarie Cook Energy. Previously, Davis headed the Mathematical Arbitrage Trading Desk at Bear Stearns. With several billion in capital and operated like a private hedge fund, the Mathematical Arbitrage Trading Desk handled Bear Stearns's proprietary investments in the equities, energy, commodities, and option markets.